Years of Nationalism

European History 1815–1890

Leonard W. Cowie
Robert Wolfson

D0263615

Hodder & Stoughton

LONDON SYDNEY AUCKLAND TORONTO

British Library Cataloguing in Publication Data

Cowie, Leonard W.
  Years of nationalism: European history
  1815–1890
  1. Europe—History—19th century
  I. Title II. Wolfson, Robert
  940.2′8   D359

  ISBN 0 7131 7328 9

First published 1985
Seventh impression 1991

Printed in England for the educational publishing division of
Hodder and Stoughton Ltd, Mill Road, Dunton Green,
Sevenoaks, Kent by Clays Ltd, St Ives plc.

Contents

List of Tables

List of Maps

List of Diagrams

Acknowledgements

The authors would like to thank the pupils of Broadoak School and Sandy Upper School for their help with the preparation of the exercises in this book.

The publishers would like to thank the following for permission to include copyright material:

Associated Book Publishers Ltd for L C B Seaman: *From Vienna to Versailles*; Longman Group Limited for D Beales: *The Risorgimento and the Unification of Italy*; Oxford University Press for *Documents in the Political History of the European Continent 1815–1919* selected and edited by G A Kertesz (1968) and used by permission and Denis Mack Smith for his *The Making of Italy*.

We have been unable to trace the current copyright owners of H N Neill: *European Diplomatic History 1815–1914*.

We would also like to thank the following examination boards for permission to include questions:

The Associated Examining Board; Joint Matriculation Board; Oxford and Cambridge Schools Examination Board; Southern Universities' Joint Board; University of Cambridge Local Examinations Syndicate; University of London School Examinations Department; University of Oxford Delegacy of Local Examinations and Welsh Joint Education Committee.

Introduction

(a) General

In this joint work, Leonard Cowie has written the text, and Robert Wolfson has provided the exercises as well as giving valuable help with the text.

The book is written for those in the 16+ age range who are studying this period in detail for the first time and are examination candidates, taking history at the Advanced Level of the General Certificate of Education. It is intended to be both a reading book and a work book, and therefore a variety of exercises, including sets of essay questions from recent Advanced Level examinations, have been included.

These exercises have been designed to develop and improve the analytical skills of young historians. In this way, pupils should both appreciate that the subject is more than just a catalogue of factual knowledge and prepare themselves for the A level examinations. Many of the exercises are deliberately of types that can be adapted to other topics and themes, and we hope that they will encourage teachers to develop their own ideas and exercises.

(b) Essay Titles

At the end of each section, you will find sets of essay titles. These have been taken from the English and Welsh A level papers for the years 1981–83. In this way, it is hoped that students will become familiar with the aspects of topics that are examined; if you study the essay titles *before* reading a chapter, you will find it easier to focus your attention on such aspects. In addition, you should become familiar with the different styles of questioning adopted by particular boards. For example, the London Board's questions are often broken down into several parts, whereas the Oxford and Cambridge Board rarely sets questions of this type. Where questions seek comparison between two topics, or take an overview of a problem examined by two chapters, they have been placed at the latest relevant point. You will find what may seem a large number of questions from the Welsh Board; this is explained by the fact that two syllabuses cover the period 1815–1890. We are extremely grateful to all the examination Boards for their permission to reproduce questions.

(c) Ideas of the Century

The Appendix on 'The Ideas of the Century' is about liberalism, nationalism, socialism, Marxism, Darwinianism, romanticism and religion. It explains the most important concepts which were held at this time and the disagreements which they produced. It is vital that you should understand these. People of this period did not think in the same way as we do today about politics and other aspects of life. Words and phrases which they used did not always mean the same thing as they do today. You should be aware of this difference and appreciate the part that these ideas played in the history of these times.

Page references to this Appendix are made in the chapters of this book. You may wish, however, to study it before you read the book so that you may realize the significance of these subjects when you come across them.

(d) Bibliographies and Documents

Short bibliographies are to be found at the end of each section of the book relating to the topic considered in the section. There are also a number of general works that deal with European history during this period or a part of it.

The following series each contain several volumes on the period:

The New Cambridge Modern History (CUP)

The Rise of Modern Europe (Harper; Hamish Hamilton)

Fontana History of Europe

Fontana Economic History of Europe

Fontana History of European War and Society

These books deal with the whole of the period:

M.S. Anderson, *The Ascendancy of Europe, 1815–1914* (Longman, 1980)

Joel Colton and R.R. Palmer, *A History of the Modern World* (Knopf, 1950)

J.J. Grant and H. Temperley, *History of Europe, 1789–1950* (Longman, 1952)

C. Holbroad, *The Concert of Europe: German and British International Theory, 1815–1914* (Longman, 1970)

S.G. Lee, *Aspects of European History, 1789–1980* (Methuen, 1982)

L.C.B. Seaman, *From Vienna to Versailles* (Methuen, 1965)

D.Thomson, *Europe since Napoleon* (Pelican, 1966)

J. Watson, *Success in European History, 1815–1941* (Murray, 1981)

A. Wood, *Europe 1815–1945* (Longman, 1964)

These books deal with parts of the period:

Alan Sked (ed.), *Europe's Balance of Power, 1815–1848* (Macmillan, 1979)

K.R. Perry, *The Bourgeois Century, 1780–1870* (Macmillan, 1972)

E.J. Hobsbawm, *The Age of Revolution, 1789–1848* (Weidenfeld & Nicolson, 1962)

2

E.J. Hobsbawm, *The Age of Capital, 1848–1875* (Weidenfeld & Nicolson, 1975)

A.J.P. Taylor, *The Struggle for Mastery in Europe, 1848–1918* (OUP, 1954)

T.K. Derry and T.L. Jarman, *The European World, 1870–1961* (Bell and Hyman, 1972)

K. Perry, *Modern European History Made Simple* (Allen, 1976) [from 1871]

A very useful historical atlas is J. Ramsay Muir, *Historical Atlas, Medieval and Modern* (G. Philip, 1968).

A comprehensive collection of documents is G. A. Kertesz, *Documents of the Political History of the European Continent, 1815–1939* (OUP, 1968). Other collections of documents, dealing with different aspects of the period, are published by Longman and Edward Arnold, and there is also the American paperback Anvil Series, edited by L.L. Synder and published by Van Nostrand.

I After the Wars 1815–1830

1 The Vienna Settlement

(a) The Treaties of Paris (1814 and 1815)

'Your sovereigns born on the throne may be beaten twenty times and still go back to their capitals. I, an upstart soldier who rose to power through the camp, cannot do this. My reign will not survive the day when I cease to be strong and feared,' so Napoleon said to Prince Metternich, the Austrian Foreign Minister, at Dresden where the two men met to discuss an agreement between their countries in June 1813.

That month the British forces, who were assisting the Spanish and Portuguese guerrillas, had entirely driven the French out of the Iberian Peninsula, and during the previous winter Napoleon's disastrous invasion of Russia had lost him five-sixths of his army during the retreat from Moscow. Prussia had joined Russia in re-entering the war against France, and Lord Castlereagh, the British Foreign Secretary, had persuaded them both to accept financial help and form the Fourth Coalition.

Metternich wished to take advantage of the situation. He offered Napoleon an alliance with Austria, but expected to receive territory in North Italy in return for his help. Napoleon would not consider this. He was determined to retain the Grand Empire which France had gained as the result of 20 years of military conquest, first by the French revolutionary governments and then by Napoleon himself. The two maps here show how great were the conquests made by France during that period. *Map 1* is of Europe in 1789, the year when the French Revolution broke out. Three years later the revolutionary armies attacked Austria and Prussia, so beginning the Revolutionary War (1792–1802) and the Napoleonic War (1803–1815) which was to bring about the rise and fall of France's empire in Europe.

The conquests were first made by the French Republic. Napoleon became the commander of its armies and then the supreme ruler of the country as Consul for life in 1802 and Emperor in 1804. *Map 2* shows how Europe had been changed by 1812, when Napoleon's power was at its height. Under his control were the French Empire, which he ruled directly, and a number of dependent states which were, in practice, also ruled by him.

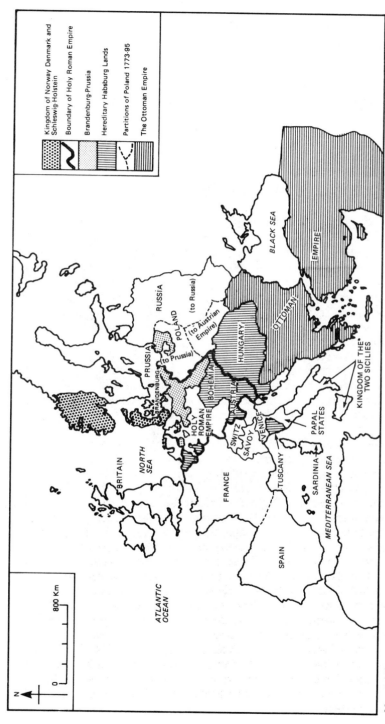

Map 1 Europe in 1789

5

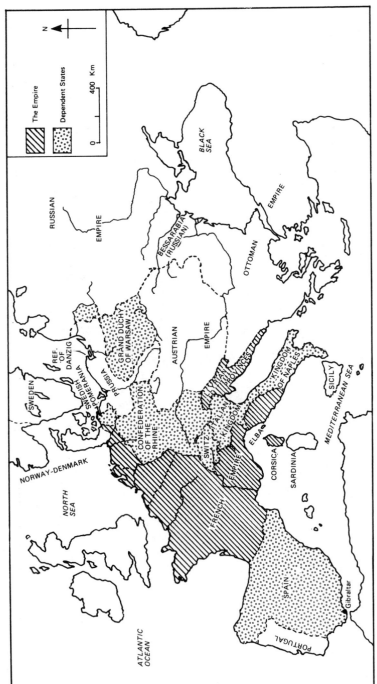

Map 2 **Europe in 1812**

6

The French Empire
The boundaries of France were extended to include:
1. The Austrian Netherlands (Belgium)
2. All German territory west of the Rhine
3. Holland
4. North-West Germany
5. Savoy and Nice
6. Piedmont, Tuscany and all the Papal States west of the Appenines (This Italian territory included the Republic of Genoa and the city of Rome)
7. The Illyrian Provinces west of the Dalmatian coast

Dependent States
1. Helvetic Republic (Switzerland—Napoleon was President)
2. Kingdom of Italy (Napoleon was King)
3. Kingdom of Sicily and Naples (Murat, Napoleon's brother-in-law, was King)
4. Kingdom of Westphalia (Prussia's Rhenish lands—Jerome Bonaparte, Napoleon's brother, was King)
5. Confederation of the Rhine (A union of the other German states except Prussia and Austria—Napoleon was its Protector)
6. Grand Duchy of Warsaw (The Austrian and Prussian parts of Poland—Napoleon's ally, the King of Saxony, was Grand Duke)
7. Kingdom of Spain (Joseph Bonaparte, Napoleon's brother, was made King in 1808)

Table 1. Europe under Napoleon (1812)

Napoleon still possessed most of his territories in the early summer of 1813, and to him they were the sign of his military glory upon which he believed his power and prestige rested. When Metternich told him at Dresden that if he wanted Austria as an ally, the French must withdraw completely from Germany and Italy (so that Austria might be supreme in both these areas), he replied that he found such terms too insulting to consider. He asserted that 'none of the countries joined by constitutional ties with the Empire could be the subject of negotiations;' and he insisted that he would 'never yield an inch of territory.' In Metternich's account of this meeting, which he published long after the event, he said that he told the Emperor, 'Sire, you are lost.'

And, indeed, the exhaustion and depletion of Napoleon's forces meant that he could not be otherwise. Countries, which had suffered at his hands in the past, realized this and were ready to resume the fight to re-establish themselves. Sweden and all the important states in the Confederation of the Rhine, except Saxony, joined Britain, Russia and Prussia in the Fourth Coalition. Metternich, realizing that there was nothing to be gained from an alliance with France, joined too. In October 1813 Napoleon lost the Battle of the Nations at Leipzig and retreated to the Rhine. On the last day of the year, for the first time for 20 years, France was herself invaded, and by the spring of 1814 the whole of the Continental empire founded by Napoleon was threatened by his enemies. Those rulers, whom he had so many times defeated over the years, were now established in their capitals, and his period of rule was approaching its end. While the triumphant allied armies were in occupation of Paris, Napoleon was at Fontainbleau, hoping at this last moment, to save his throne by negotiation. This was thwarted by the summoning in Paris of the Senate of the Empire by Prince Talleyrand, who had served as Foreign Minister under both the Republic and Napoleon, but since 1807 had opposed Napoleon's aggressive policies. He persuaded the Senate to appoint a provisional government, proclaim the deposition of Napoleon and offer the throne to Louis XVIII, a brother of the executed Louis XVI. This was accepted by the allied leaders to whom the restoration of the Bourbons seemed the rightful and probably the most stable arrangement for the government of France. Napoleon had to abdicate, and the allied leaders agreed to banish him to the island of Elba off the Italian coast.

They decided also to make peace immediately with France. Louis XVIII, who had arrived in Paris, accepted the idea that his kingdom should consist of its 'ancient limits,' and the allies defined this as meaning that France should be returned to its frontiers of 1792 with some adjustments, the most important of these being the inclusion under French government of some areas such as Avignon, which had previously belonged to foreign rulers though within the boundaries of France, and the addition of Savoy and Nice to French territory. France regained most of her overseas colonies, but Britain retained Mauritius and the Seychelles, which, before their capture in the 1790s, the French had used effectively as wartime bases for their cruisers to harry British merchantmen. Britain kept also Tobago and St. Lucia, which were well placed for observing French and Spanish designs in the West Indies. There was to be no army of occupation in France nor payment of an indemnity, and the works of art stolen from conquered European cities were not to be returned. These terms were embodied in what came to be known as the First Treaty of Paris, which was signed in May 1814. It was a lenient treaty because the allied leaders did not wish to identify the restored Bourbon monarchy with a harsh settlement and so promote a revival of republicanism or Bonapartism.

This treaty, however, was very short-lived. It was regarded as having been nullified by Napoleon's escape from Elba and his renewal of war against the allies. After his defeat at Waterloo on 18 June 1815 and imprisonment on St. Helena, it was replaced by the Second Treaty of Paris in November 1815. By this France was reduced to her frontiers of 1790 and lost Savoy and Nice to Piedmont as well as the Saar to Prussia. An indemnity was now imposed, and an allied army of occupation was to remain in the frontiers of north-eastern France for five years. The stolen works of art were to be restored to the countries from which they had been taken. Prussia had demanded the cession of Alsace and Lorraine (obtained by France in the later seventeenth century), but Castlereagh and the Russian Tsar resisted this, and the terms of the treaty were still moderate.

(b) The Congress of Vienna

Meanwhile, as had been arranged by an article of the First Treaty of Paris, the European statesmen had assembled at Vienna in November 1814 to draw up a settlement for Europe as a whole which would supplement the peace terms agreed with France. When Napoleon left Elba in February 1815, his first words on landing in France were reported to have been, 'The Congress is dissolved'; but it was not. Its members were anxious not to interrupt its work, and it continued in being throughout the Hundred Days of Napoleon's resumed rule in France with the result that the Treaty of Vienna was signed in June before the Battle of Waterloo and was not altered as a result of the Second Treaty of Paris.

The Congress consisted of sovereigns and representatives from 'all the powers engaged on either side in the present war'. The most important of these were Russia, Britain, Austria and Prussia; and at the beginning of the Congress their representatives declared 'that the conduct of the business must practically rest with the leading powers'. In fact, however, Russia and Britain were foremost among these powers. They had played the most important part in defeating Napoleon and were now each in their own way, in an outstanding position at the Congress. Russia's armies had swept across Europe in 1813 and 1814, and she had previously been strengthened by victories over Sweden and Turkey. She was the decisive military power on the Continent with an army of almost a million men in 1815. Britain alone had withstood France undefeated throughout the wars and had emerged with her superiority in industrial development, worldwide trade and naval strength increased. On the other hand, neither Austria nor Prussia could rival them in power and influence. Austria had suffered a series of military setbacks at the hands of France followed by harsh treaties and accompanied by mounting economic problems. She had not taken a leading part in the overthrow of Napoleon's empire and was regarded as unlikely to remain a leading power. Prussia had collapsed after her defeat by Napoleon at Jena in 1806, and although she had made a remarkable recovery, she was the least among the important powers in terms of territory, resources and influence.

Thus the representatives of Britain and France at Vienna were well placed to get what they wanted during the negotiations, particularly as they generally neither wished nor were able to oppose each other. This did not mean, however, that the resulting treaty was devoted entirely to their interests. Other states were able to benefit from their policies, especially as they both shared a common wish to settle the problems of Europe as a whole.

The British representative was Lord Castlereagh, who had spent most of his life in public office since being appointed by William Pitt the Younger to his cabinet in 1798. He was at the War Office during the Peninsular War, when he gave the Duke of Wellington his first military command in Spain, and he had been Foreign Secretary since 1812 in

Lord Liverpool's government. From Pitt he had inherited the idea of establishing peace in Europe on the basis of a 'just equilibrium' of power among the states. And he knew that this was what was required by British interests and public opinion. Having been engaged in warfare for so long, Britain looked for a peaceful, settled Europe from whom she need fear no threat to her enormous and vulnerable empire and with whom she could pursue without hindrance the international trade by which, as an increasingly industrialized country, she had to live. To defend these interests she relied upon maintaining her naval supremacy. She had no wish to extend her land frontiers in Europe. Her colonial policy aimed at exploiting natural resources—particularly tropical ones—rather than establishing settlements such as had been lost to her in North America. These considerations governed Castlereagh's attitude during the negotiations for both the Treaties of Paris and the Treaty of Vienna. 'It is not the business of England', he wrote, 'to collect trophies, but to restore Europe to peaceful habits.'

Castlereagh was always responsible to the British government, parliament and public opinion, but the Russian Tsar, Alexander I, was under no such restraints. He always regarded himself at Vienna as the sole representative of his state and deviser of its policy. He was a complex enigmatic figure. Napoleon called him 'the sphinx' and 'the cunning Byzantine'. During the wars he had allied himself alternately with Britain and Napoleon, a policy which had finally brought him triumph and glory. Some accused him of deceit, while others suspected him of instability. Yet, when he came to Vienna, there were some who hoped that he would display an idealism that would raise him above the other statesmen there because he had been influenced by both the liberalism of the eighteenth century Enlightenment and the more recent religious revival in Europe. They hoped that he would consider the wishes and interests of the peoples of Europe and be less concerned with territorial gains for his country. Nevertheless, during the Congress he was as determined as any previous Russian ruler to achieve the traditional objectives of the country's foreign policy: expansion towards the Balkans and the Baltic and, above all, in Poland.

Though King Frederick William III of Prussia was present at Vienna, his Chancellor, Prince Hardenburg, usually acted for him. He was bound to continue the traditional Hohenzollern policy of intrigue and negotiation, which since the seventeenth century had contributed to the rise of his country from a small, weak German princedom to an important European state. He wanted Prussia to regain the power and prestige she had lost through her defeat by Napoleon. However, he was not in a position to demand that Prussia should either be restored to her previous lands or be given new territory. He could only hope to get as much as possible by making use of the policies of the other powers for his own ends.

The Austrian Emperor, Francis I, also did not take an active part in the peace-making at Vienna. He was largely content to enjoy the prestige of having the Congress in his own city and entertaining the statesmen lavishly. He left most of the diplomatic work to Metternich, who was consistently conservative in his outlook (*see page 42*). Francis was the first Habsburg ruler to be Emperor of Austria. He had taken that title when Napoleon abolished the Holy Roman Empire and seized the territories over which the Emperor traditionally claimed authority. This authority had diminished over the centuries, and at the Congress there could be no question of Austria gaining any real predominance in Germany. Metternich looked instead for the creation of Austrian power over the several states of Italy, insisting that this was essential for the preservation of Habsburg influence in Europe, and he tried to persuade the other powers that peace and good government in the peninsula would not be established without this.

Though France and Austria had been old rivals for influence in Germany, Metternich believed that the two countries now had much in common in their foreign policy, and he had particularly supported the making of peace with France which meant that, though defeated, she could attend the Congress. Since Louis XVIII did not come to Vienna, France was represented by Talleyrand, who was determined to make his voice heard in the discussions, though much of the treaty would inevitably be unfavourable to her. He especially wished to oppose the strengthening of Prussia on her eastern frontier and knew that Metternich was opposed to this too.

(c) The Principles of the Congress

Though much of the Treaty of Vienna, like all such settlements, was a compromise between the rival aims and ambitions of the great powers, there was also a considerable degree of general agreement at the Congress about its purpose and the principles by which this should be achieved. The statesmen were ready to combine to restore what they thought of as the 'ancient public law of Europe', which had been violated by Revolutionary and Napoleonic France. They wanted a settlement which would provide stability in Europe and prevent the outbreak of another general war. This benefited Austria. She had a supreme interest in the establishment of international agreement and peace because her empire would be in grave danger of collapse and disintegration without this. The allies, therefore, were ready to preserve and strengthen the Austrian Empire as a safeguard against threats to a settled, pacific Europe.

French domination of Europe had, in fact, been ended at Moscow and Waterloo, but this was not yet recognized in 1815. The allies still saw her as the country whose ambitions since the seventeenth century had involved her in continual wars of aggression, and they wished to safeguard against this in the future. Just as at Paris Britain's small colonial gains from France had been designed to prevent any further attempts at overseas expansion by her, so now at Vienna the allies planned to make territorial arrangements upon her frontiers to prevent any aggression in Europe.

As early as 1701, the *London Gazette* had spoken of the 'glorious design of re-establishing a just balance of power in Europe', and this was what Pitt meant when he spoke of the need for a 'just equilibrium' among the nations. This principle of eighteenth-century diplomacy held that international peace would best be maintained if no state was in a position to threaten the independence of the rest. The statesmen at Vienna accepted this as a rule to guide their decisions. They believed that it would be the best way of obtaining the Europe that they wanted in the future, and they attached much importance to it in deciding upon the territorial settlement. Moreover, it was then a realistic course to follow as it was consistent with the foreign policy and interests of the leading powers at the time. Britain and France did not come into conflict within the areas covered by the provisions of the Treaty, and Austria and France then accepted the settlements in Germany and Italy, though they both had interests there. It was not foreseen that a stronger Prussia would accept this balance during the course of the century.

Talleyrand put forward at the Congress what he called the 'sacred principle of legitimacy' by which he meant that the 'rightful' rulers should be restored to their 'legitimate' inheritance. This he claimed was recognized by the 'ancient public law' which the allies wished to establish throughout Europe. He saw that it would clearly benefit the French Bourbons, and it did also appeal to the allies as they naturally wished to uphold dynastic rulers who had suffered from revolution and aggression since the 1790s. Talleyrand was not as successful as has sometimes been supposed, however, in obtaining the acceptance of the principle at the Congress. It was never of supreme importance in the making of the settlement. Frontiers were redrawn and previously independent states extinguished in defiance of it, and Talleyrand had to agree that it should be subordinate to the more important principle of the balance of power.

(d) The Treaty of Vienna (1815)

When the Treaty of Vienna was signed, its territorial settlement largely reflected the relative power of the four leading allies represented at the Congress. Britain and Russia achieved the aims they desired, while Prussia and Austria were dependent upon the wishes of the other two powers, who were not always in agreement.

Territorial Changes

to Austria	Lombardy and Venetia; Dalmatia; Galicia
to Prussia	Posen and Thorn; Swedish Pomerania; Rhinelands; three-fifths of Saxony
to Russia	greater part of the Grand Duchy of Warsaw
to Britain	Malta; Ionian Islands; Heligoland; Cape of Good Hope; Ceylon; Trinidad; British Guiana
to Sweden	Norway (from Denmark)
to Holland	Austrian Netherlands

Table 2. The Treaty of Vienna (1815)

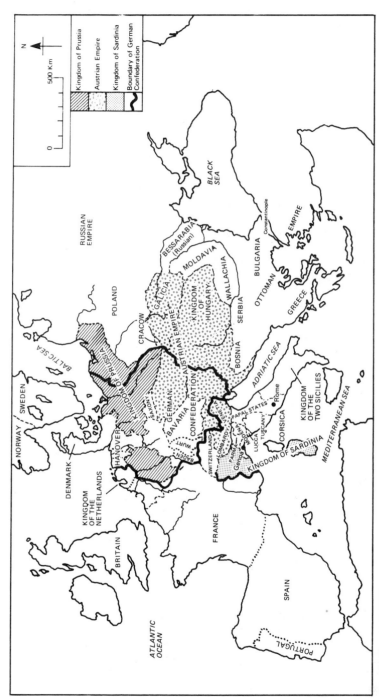

Map 3 Europe in 1815

13

During the wars, Britain's naval power had enabled her to make considerable overseas gains, including colonies belonging to France and enemy-occupied Spain and Holland. Castlereagh insisted that the Congress should not concern itself with the question of overseas possessions and that it should be settled by a series of separate treaties with the countries concerned. Nevertheless, he wished Britain to make only limited colonial gains at Vienna. She kept the Dutch colonies of the Cape of Good Hope and Ceylon, which were of obvious strategic value for the protection of her Eastern trade routes. Malta and the Ionian Islands, which Napoleon had used in his attempt to conquer India, were also kept to strengthen the British position in the Mediterranean. So too was Heligoland, an island off Schleswig-Holstein, occupied by Britain during the wars and now valued for its strategic value in the North Sea. In the West Indies, the Spanish island of Trinidad was retained as a centre of trade with South America. In South America itself, British planters persuaded Castlereagh not to return Demerara, Essequibo and Berbice to the Netherlands because they had invested £15 million in coffee, cotton and sugar estates there, and they became British Guiana.

Just as he had already relinquished Guadeloupe, Martinique and other French West Indian colonies, so Castlereagh now gave up the rich Dutch East Indies. When British merchants protested at this, he told Lord Liverpool, 'I am sure our reputation on the Continent as a feature of strength, power and confidence is of more real value to us than any acquisition thus made'.

Two of the territorial changes made on the Continent were also desired by Britain for strategic reasons. The transfer of Norway from Denmark to Sweden benefited her because the entry to the Baltic was no longer controlled by a single state (which had persistently supported Napoleon), and the Union of Holland and Belguim into a united kingdom placed the mouths of the Rhine and the Scheldt in the possession of a neutral state. To enable this new state of the Netherlands to check French aggression, Britain arranged that the £6 million which she paid to the Dutch government for the loss of its colonies was to be spent on fortifying the frontier with France. This was in accordance with Castlereagh's idea that colonial questions should influence the wider European situation in the interests of peace and stability.

The way in which the British government had to take account of opinion at home was shown by Castlereagh's introduction of the subject of the slave trade at the Congress. Britain had already abolished this in 1807, and the failure of the Treaty of Paris to compel France to do the same had caused a considerable outcry in the country. William Wilberforce, the parliamentary anti-slavery leader, said it was 'the death-warrant of a multitude of innocent victims, men, women and children'. The government was, therefore, anxious to rescue its reputation at Vienna, but other slave-trading powers were not affected by the emotions now moving the British people. The most Castlereagh was able to do was to persuade France, Spain, Portugal and Holland to declare that it was 'repugnant to the principles of humanity and universal morality' and to agree in the 'wish of putting an end to a scourge which has so long desolated Africa, degraded Europe and afflicted humanity'. They would not fix a date for its prohibition.

Tsar Alexander kept the gains he had already made during recent fighting—Finland (from Sweden) and Bessarabia (from Turkey); and he claimed the Grand Duchy of Warsaw and proposed that Prussia should be compensated for the loss of her Polish territory by annexing the whole of Saxony. His justification for this treatment of Saxony was that she had been an ally of Napoleon, even though other German states had been too. The only difference between them and Saxony was that she had been late in deserting him in 1813.

Castlereagh and Metternich feared that to give way to the Tsar's demands would undermine the balance of power in Europe. They, therefore, proposed the revival of the Third Partition of 1795 which had divided Poland between Russia, Prussia and Austria. But Russian troops occupied both Poland and Saxony. Alexander was determined not to give way. 'Poland is mine,' he said. 'There can be little negotiation with 600 000 men.' Hardenburg was equally determined to get Saxony for Prussia if he could.

This was the most critical stage in the proceedings of the Congress, and it gave Talleyrand his most effective opportunity to intervene on behalf of French influence and prestige. He insisted that the King of Saxony should be protected by the principle of legitimacy from being deposed in this way. Since France still remained, next to Russia, easily the strongest power on the Continent, he was able to persuade Britain and Austria to join her in forming a defensive Triple Alliance to oppose Russia. 'France is no longer isolated in Europe', he triumphantly told Louis XVIII. The threat forced Alexander to compromise. Prussia was given the Polish province of Posen and the city of Thorn and about three-fifth's of Saxony's territory which contained about two-fifths of her population; and Austria received the Polish province of Galicia. Alexander kept what was called 'Congress Poland' and agreed to grant it a constitution which would enable it to govern itself.

Despite this failure to obtain the whole of Saxony, Prussia made relatively the greatest territorial and economic gains among the powers represented at Vienna. Although she got rather more Polish than Saxon territory, the part of Saxony assigned to her was rich and industrial and gave her additional German rather than Polish subjects. She also benefited from the desire of the allies to prevent France extending her influence into western Germany. She recovered her territory in the Rhineland, to which were added a number of small states in the area. In addition, she obtained Swedish Pomerania on the Baltic. She emerged from the Congress a potentially greater European power than ever before. She would have to take the lead in any future war against

France; and the distribution of her territories made it possible for her to establish economic and political control over Germany.

In place of the hundreds of states and free cities of the old Germany of the Holy Roman Empire, the Congress established a German Confederation of 38 states, which included the free cities of Lübeck, Bremen, Frankfurt and Hamburg, under the presidency of Austria (*see page 45*). For the allies, the main purpose of this again was to prevent the smaller states falling under French influence, particularly since they had found that their inclusion in Napoleon's Confederation of the Rhine, with its centralization and administrative efficiency, had brought them considerable advantages. Although the position assigned to Austria in this new Confederation gave her more influence in Germany than she had been able to exercise during the final years of the Holy Roman Empire, it was bound to be rivalled by Prussia, and Metternich, though himself a German from the Rhineland, had to accept this.

Fear of a renewal of French influence in Italy led the allies, however, to support Metternich's wish to gain compensation for Austria's inferiority in Germany and loss of the Netherlands by restoring and stengthening her position in the peninsula. Northern Italy was placed under her direct rule: she received back Lombardy and was given the former territory of Venice in Italy (Venetia) and in Dalmatia. She could assert indirect control of central Italy because the duchies of Parma, Modena, Lucca and Tuscany were placed under Habsburg princes. The restored Papal States remained outside her orbit as did Sardinia, which recovered Piedmont, Nice and Savoy and received Genoa, since the allies intended the enlarged kingdom to act as an effective buffer-state between France and Austria, lest they sought to come to terms over a division of Italy. In the south of the peninsula, however, Metternich succeeded in taking a step towards thwarting his fellow-statesmen in this respect. He was able to go behind the Congress (including Talleyrand) by making a separate engagement with Louis XVIII to ensure the restoration of the Bourbon rulers to Naples.

(e) The Significance of the Settlement

Later nineteenth-century historians strongly criticized the Treaty of Vienna because it ignored the great principles of nationalism and liberalism and made territorial changes solely in the interests of the great powers without giving any consideration to the wishes of the inhabitants. Contemporary critics were less certain and united in their condemnation of the settlement. Lord Byron was angry that the old regimes were restored. He wrote, 'Here we are retrograding to the full, stupid old system—balance of Europe—posing straws upon kings' noses instead of wringing them off.' None thought, however, that Italy and Germany should have been united. Wordsworth was roused because the republics of Venice and Genoa were extinguished and their people 'transferred to Austria, to the King of Sardinia and to the rest of those vile tyrants.' Prussia's annexation of Saxon territory filled Samuel Whitbread, the leader of the opposition in Parliament, with 'shame, remorse and disgust'. Whitbread, indeed, condemned the Treaty generally for 'forcing people to abandon their ancient governments', and this was a refinement of the principle of legitimacy which, if it had been followed by the Congress, would have fossilized the map of Europe. Castlereagh defended the Congress against accusation of illiberality. Like many others, he shared the outlook expressed by Edmund Burke in his *Reflections on the Revolution in France* in 1790. Burke had argued that the French revolutionaries, because of their enthusiasm and violence and their determination to sweep away the traditional institutions of Church and State and replace them by their new forms of government, would destroy the sense of confidence and security of the people and make them ready to accept tyranny and reaction as the alternative to anarchy and confusion. Castlereagh feared that such a European catastrophe might yet occur. 'It is impossible not to believe', he wrote in 1814, 'that a great change is coming on in Europe, and that the principles of freedom are in full operation. The danger is that the transition may be too sudden to ripen into anything likely to make the world better or happier. We have new constitutions launched in France, Spain, Holland and Sicily. Let us see the results before we encourage further attempts.' He regarded the new ideas as 'most hazardous'. The course of the French Revolution and the subsequent years of war had not proved Burke wrong. The experience had made Castlereagh fear that liberal ideas might produce a renewal of violence and aggression, and he believed that Europe needed a period of 'repose' to avert such a consequence. He hoped that the Treaty would provide this.

There were contemporary liberals who agreed with him. They too realized that the French Revolution had produced military tyranny and bloodshed, which people did not want to see repeated, and they believed that their cause would suffer badly if it were connected in the public mind with this. Not long after the Treaty of Vienna, the French liberal politician, Benjamin Constant, spoke to a learned society in Paris about ancient Greece and Rome, which had provided many liberal thinkers with their ideas. When he then condemned the liberty of the ancient world because it had subjected the individual to the community, he was thinking of the French revolutionaries. On another occasion he said, 'We do not want any revolutions.'

Nationalism was as new a force in 1815 as liberalism. It too owed its origin to the French Revolution (*see page 381*). In so far as the European statesmen of the time recognized and comprehended this notion, they considered it as dangerous as the idea of liberty, having been put forward by intellectuals and romantics and exploited by aggressive French governments, who had brought a new intensity to warfare by organizing the 'people in arms'. It was not to be expected that the Emperor of Austria, the King of Prussia, the Pope or any other rulers would have been ready to relinquish their authority in favour of any new national government; but, in any event, the idea of having a European settlement based upon the single principle that states must consist of self-governing groups of peoples having a common descent, history or language would have seemed impossible and undesirable to them.

Though the allied statesmen did not seek to redraw the map of Europe in the interests of liberty and nationalism, they did represent countries which had fought against a military power that had over-whelmed and subjected a large part of Europe. They wished to replace this neither by a new order of things nor by a complete reversion to the past, but by restoring international law, producing order out of chaos and creating a Europe in which recent events would not be repeated. Napoleon had been the only man to contain the revolutionary forces of Europe successfully, but none wished to emulate his ways. When the Treaty was signed, Metternich reflected in Vienna, 'Let us at least carry away the remembrance of having done some good—and in this respect I would not change with Napoleon.'

The twentieth century, which has become so sadly aware of the infinite difficulties of peace-making and settling frontiers, has seen the Treaty in a new light and come to be more sympathetic towards its makers. It has been inclined to judge the Treaty a success because it was followed by a century in which the peace of Europe, though disturbed by comparatively minor hostilities, was not upset by the outbreak of a general war.

It is doubtful, however, whether the peacemakers of Vienna really deserve this praise to such an extent. In international affairs, nineteenth-century European history came to be divided almost exactly in half. For about the first 50 years after 1815 there was no important war on the Continent. Peace was maintained despite the break-down of the congress system, which had been established to settle international affairs peacefully, and the potential danger from a number of problems during those years, particularly those raised by the Eastern Question. This was because the provisions of the Treaty were generally acceptable to all the great powers, including the defeated France. They accepted them and continued to accept them because they did not wish to challenge them by the use of force. If there were some changes they would have liked to make, they did not wish to upset the prevailing stability in Europe by provoking hostilities.

The situation changed, however, after the revolutions of 1848. Then the settlement was no longer seen to express political realities and ceased to contain irresistible new ambitions. A change of spirit took place among the rulers of Europe, particularly Napoleon III of France (*see page 228*). They were no longer prepared to maintain the terms of the Treaty, and the pacific agreement among them was destroyed by the wars of the 1850s and 1860s. The result of these wars was that the Vienna settlement was largely destroyed, but this did not result in a situation that led to the outbreak of a general war. Rather it was followed by a further period of comparative peace, which again lasted for about 50 years, and this was due, as it had essentially been in the first half of the century, to the policies of the great powers.

Bibliography

Harold Nicolson, *The Congress of Vienna* (Constable, 1946), and C.K. Webster, *The Congress of Vienna* (Bell & Hyman, 1919), deal with the organization and work of the Congress. The role of individual statesmen is considered in C.K. Webster, *The Foreign Policy of Castlereagh, 1812–1815* (Bell & Hyman, 1931), M. Walker, *Metternich's Europe, 1813–1848* (Harper Torchbooks, 1948), J.F. Bertrand, *Talleyrand* (Putnams, 1973) and P.K. Grimsted, *The Foreign Ministers of Alexander I* (Berkeley, 1969). The diplomatic ideas of the time are discussed in Edward Vose Gullick, *Europe's Classical Balance of Power* (Ithaca, New York, 1955).

Exercises

A   *This section consists of questions that might be used for discussion (or written answers) as a way of expanding on the chapter and testing your understanding of it:*

1   Why did Napoleon reject Metternich's offer of help in 1813?

2   Explain the meaning of the following terms used in the chapter: 'Dependent states'; 'annexed'; 'deposition'; 'restoration of the Bourbons'; 'indemnity'; 'Hundred Days'.

3   In order to clarify a complex sequence of events, construct a date chart and write down what happened (and the significance of that event) in each of the following months: June 1813; October 1813; May 1814; November 1814; February 1815; 18 June 1815; November 1815.

4   Complete the two diagrams below by adding the terms of the treaty affecting each aspect, and then comment on the differences between the two treaties:

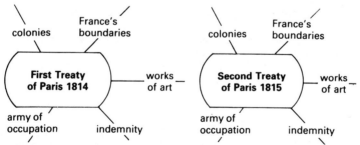

5   What do you understand by 'a just equilibrium of power among the states', and how might this be achieved?

6   What were the aims of (a) Castlereagh and (b) Alexander I in 1814–15?

7   Explain the major principles underlying the Vienna settlement.

8   'Prussia made relatively the greatest territorial and economic gains among the powers presented at Vienna.' How do you explain this in the light of the view that she was regarded as one of the lesser powers?

9 'Fear of French influence was the principle that *actually* dominated the Treaty of Vienna.' What arguments would you use to support this point of view?

10 From the point of view of a British observer in 1815, comment on the settlement, outlining the gains and losses that Britain has made in the light of her aims. (If possible, make clear either in a separate statement or from what you write, the political standpoint from which you are writing.)

11 What were the main criticims of the Vienna settlement made by (a) contemporaries and (b) later historians?

12 Why have more recent historians been more generous in their judgement of the settlement?

13 In what way is it possible to divide the nineteenth century into two halves?

B *Essay Questions*

1 'Much of the Vienna settlement was sensible and just and not vindictive, but where it attempted to wipe out the memory and effects of the last quarter century of history it was doomed to failure.' How acceptable is this judgement? (Cambridge, 1982)

2 Was the self-interest of the great powers the only 'principle' behind the Vienna settlement? (Cambridge, 1983)

3 To what extent did the terms of the Vienna settlement provide solutions to the problems facing the peacemakers of 1815? (SUJB, 1981)

4 Why can the Vienna settlement be described as a new approach to international relations? (SUJB, 1982)

5 'After the Napoleonic War France was still regarded as the greatest threat to the peace of Europe.' What evidence can you discover in the Vienna settlement to support this view? (SUJB, 1983)

6 How serious a factor was 'legitimacy' in the Vienna settlement of 1814? (Welsh, 1981)

7 'The period of stability which ensued was the best proof that a legitimate order had been constructed.' (Kissinger) Do you agree with this view of the Vienna settlement? (Welsh, 1981)

8 What were the aims of the peace-makers at Vienna in 1815? To what extent were their objectives achieved? (Welsh, 1983)

9 What principles guided the participants in the Vienna settlement of 1814–15? (Oxford and Cambridge, 1981)

10 Discuss the view that 'the Congress of Vienna solved every problem except the ones that mattered.' (Oxford and Cambridge, 1983)

11 'If the test of peace is that it should leave few unexploded bombs to go off in the face of posterity, then the peace of 1815 certainly deserves praise.' (AEB, 1981)

12 'Security, not revenge.' How far was Castlereagh's objective achieved by the Vienna settlement of 1815? (AEB, 1982)

13 On what principles was the peace settlement of 1814–15 founded, and how consistently did the peacemakers apply these principles in the drafting of the treaties? (London, 1981)

14 To what extent did the peace settlement of 1814–1815 impose effective restraints on further French expansion while avoiding policies of revenge? (London, 1983)

15 Examine critically the principles which influenced the statesmen in making their decisions in the Vienna settlement, 1814–15. (JMB, 1982)

C *Map exercise*

In order to familiarize yourself with the map of nineteenth-century Europe and to see the effects of the Revolutionary and Napoleonic War and Vienna settlement, compare the three maps on pages 5, 6 and 13. (Note that they are *simplified* maps and deliberately do not include all the details that would appear in, for instance, Muir's *Historical Atlas*.) To undertake your comparison,

1 Construct a chart, like that suggested below outlining the boundaries of each area:

Area	1789	1812	1815
Poland Prussia Italy etc.			

2 After completing such a chart in as much detail as possible, write some general conclusions drawing attention to the major changes that have taken place and comparing the overall results of the Congress of Vienna with Europe in 1792.

2 The Congresses

(a) The Holy Alliance (1815)

In September 1815, three months after the signing of the Treaty of Vienna, Tsar Alexander announced at a great military review in Paris that he had secured the agreement of the Austrian Emperor and the Prussian King to form with him a Holy Alliance. The three signatories had made themselves 'a true and indissoluble fraternity' and sworn to conduct their affairs' on 'the principle of that Holy Religion which the Divine Saviour has imparted to mankind, namely the rules of Justice, Christian Charity and Peace, which, far from being applied only to private concerns, must have an immediate influence on the councils of Princes. They will consider themselves as one and the same Christian nation.' And they invited other rulers to join with them in acknowledging the headship of 'God, our divine Saviour Jesus Christ, the Word of the Most High, the Word of Life.'

The Treaty of the Holy Alliance came to be regarded by liberals as a symbol of reaction and oppression, but this was not the intention of Alexander when he drafted it. It did not express the idea of a common policy of monarchical absolutism, but rather the beliefs of the romantic intellectuals of contemporary Europe, who now built their idealism upon the notion of a Christian order such as had apparently existed in the Middle Ages (*see page 388*). Alexander had moved from being a free-thinker to becoming a conservative evangelical. He said that the burning of Moscow in 1812 had 'enlightened his soul'; and before the end of that year he had founded the Russian Bible Society to print and distribute the Scriptures on the lines of the British and Foreign Bible

Society. In the following years he corresponded with and met the leaders of the religious revival on the Continent from whom he received guidance and encouragement.

It is not enough, however, to explain the Holy Alliance as the bizarre product of an intensely mystical phase through which the Tsar was then passing. As he had shown at the Congress of Vienna, however great his religious idealism, Alexander never forgot the immediate interests of himself and his country and, indeed, did not appear to find any conflict between his spiritual and patriotic aims. Napoleon's retreat from Moscow had been followed by events which made him the leader of a victorious military coalition, the universally welcomed 'liberator of Europe' and a powerful negotiator at Vienna who had made important gains for his empire. The will of God had brought him through the perils of war; now, as the leader of this new idealistic alliance, he expected that, working through the contemporary religious revival, he would be able to increase the influence of himself and his country on the Continent.

Other European rulers found themselves placed in a difficult position by the Holy Alliance. Austrian and Prussian adherence to it was a recognition of the value of retaining the Tsar's friendship and was only gained by him after Metternich had persuaded him to make a significant change in the text of the Treaty by which the fraternal call was addressed, not to 'the subjects of the three contracting parties', as originally proposed, but to 'the three contracting Monarchs', so that it was made clear that they alone directed government and policy. Before long all the rulers of Europe signed the Treaty except the Pope (who regarded the Tsar as a heretic tainted by liberalism), the Sultan (who for obvious reasons was not asked to join) and the King of Britain (who was incapacitated by illness).

It was natural that the statesmen of those countries, who had unwillingly joined the Holy Alliance, should seek to belittle it. Metternich, who particularly feared an extension of Russian influence over the German states, called it 'nothing more than a philanthropic aspiration, clad in religious garb', 'the overflow of pietistic feeling of the Emperor Alexander' and 'a loud-sounding nothing'. Castlereagh too had reason to suspect the Alliance. It might not only threaten the balance of power in Europe, but since it included the maritime and colonial powers, Russian support might enable them to challenge the British command of the seas. He called it 'a piece of sublime mysticism and nonsense' and found George III's illness a convenient way of avoiding both offending the allies by refusing to join and arousing opposition in Britain by accepting membership. He declared that the Prince Regent, though acting on behalf of the incapacitated monarch, was not constitutionally empowered to sign the Treaty, and he advised him only to write a personal letter to the Tsar expressing his hearty approval of its 'sacred maxims.'

(b) The Quadruple Alliance

On the same day as the Second Treaty of Paris was signed in November 1815 and two month's after the Tsar's proclamation of the Holy Alliance, the four allied powers (Russia, Austria, Prussia and Britain) agreed to continue their wartime union by signing the Treaty of the Quadruple Alliance. In this, the signatories undertook to uphold the settlement with France, prevent the return of Napoleon and maintain the army of occupation. In addition, Article VI stated that 'to ensure and facilitate the execution of the present treaty, and to consolidate the close relations which to-day unite the four Sovereigns for the good of the world, the High Contracting parties have agreed to continue at stated times, either under the immediate auspices of their Sovereigns, or through their respective ministers, the holding of conferences for the purpose of discussing the great common interests, and examining the measures which at each of these times will be judged the most salutary for the repose and prosperity of peoples and the maintenance of the peace of Europe.'

This was Castlereagh's idea. He wished to set against the Holy Alliance this Quadruple Alliance of the four great powers which had defeated Napoleon. They had shown themselves able to work together during the war, and this alliance would not contain any smaller states whom Alexander might bully or trick. Moreover, Castlereagh thought that meetings between the sovereigns or their ministers would make it more likely that international questions could be settled more quickly and amicably than through the ordinary diplomatic channels. He said that the Congress of Vienna had made him a firm believer in 'the habits of confidential intercourse, which a long residence with the principal actors has established, and which gives facilities to my intervention to bring them together.'

Alexander wished the business considered by these meetings to be restricted to matters arising out of the peace settlement itself. This would limit the influence of the Alliance; but Castlereagh argued that any European question could be brought up, and his view was accepted. The Duke of Wellington had said of the Holy Alliance, 'The British government would prefer something a little more precise,' but the Tsar wished its purpose to be expressed vaguely. Similarly, Castlereagh wanted, in opposition to Alexander, the Quadruple Alliance to be equally general and indefinite. Alexander and Castlereagh saw the Holy Alliance and the Quadruple Alliance as respectively their own instrument of policy. Each was, therefore, keen to restrict the influence and powers of the other, while keeping their own as free as possible to act and interfere in European affairs.

The result was that the Quadruple Alliance came into being to promote international co-operation and yet was not provided with any practical way of doing this. Historians often speak of its activities as the 'Congress System', but this never existed in reality. There was no organization set up through which the powers might make joint efforts to preserve European harmony and peace. Like the Holy Alliance, it was established in a situation of likely international ambition and rivalry, and the future of both would depend upon the turn the European situation took.

So, after 1815, there were two alliances, each claiming to have been founded to preserve concord in Europe. Ostensibly the Holy Alliance had the higher aims and more comprehensive membership, but it never had as good a reputation as the Quadruple Alliance. European liberals persisted in using it as a term to describe the repression of constitutional movements from 1820, but this was erroneous (*see Exercise C, page 36*). The repression was due to the policy of the Continental rulers and not to the formation of either alliance. It involved both the alliances, and it destroyed them both.

(c) The Congress of Aix-la-Chapelle (1818)

Alexander would have liked the first of the congresses of the Quadruple Alliances to have met at Basel, which was then an important centre of Protestant evangelism, but Metternich would not agree because this Swiss city was also a refuge for liberal political exiles from several countries. He did not think that they would provide an atmosphere congenial to his ideas of diplomatic negotiation, which he thought should be free from any threat of popular pressure. He was able to have the meeting-place at Aix-la-Chapelle (Aachen), which suited him better. It was now under autocratic Prussian rule and retained memories of former Habsburg greatness because it had been the northern capital of the original Holy Roman Empire founded by Charlemagne, who was born and buried there.

By the autumn of 1818, when the Congress met, France seemed to have become stable and tranquil under the restored Bourbon monarchy. The aims of the Ultras, the extreme Royalists, had been thwarted and the indemnity, imposed by the allies, entirely paid off (*see page 60*). When, therefore, the French government requested the withdrawal of the foreign army of occupation, the Congress agreed. France had been admitted to the peace-making process at Vienna with the intention that normal relations should be re-established as soon as possible with her, and so the Congress decided also to admit her into the Alliance (which now became the Quintuple Alliance) and to any further congresses.

Since the four powers had already agreed among themselves before the Congress to treat France in this way, the decision taken at Aix-la-Chapelle was in effect merely a formal one, and it was the only business transacted there. And since the Treaty of the Quadruple Alliance had been concerned mainly with maintaining the peace settlement imposed upon France, the admission of that country into the deliberations of the victorious allies meant that the new Quintuple Alliance had lost its original purpose.

This should have been the time when, as Castlereagh hoped, it could have found a new purpose aimed at preserving the stability of Europe;

but at Aix-la-Chapelle it began to appear that the disagreements among the great powers, which had already been apparent at Vienna, were now becoming more serious. The prospects for European unity seemed to be diminishing, and the divisions continued to centre upon the relations between Russia and the other powers.

To Metternich and Castlereagh, Alexander now appeared likely to become the most serious threat to the peace of Europe. Russian military power had hardly been reduced after the peace settlement. The Russian army was still the strongest in Europe, and though ten years later it was not to perform well against Turkey, it impressed the other powers, and Alexander retained his confidence in it to support his diplomacy. He was suspected of intending to pursue policies of his own aimed at extending Russian power and to persuade the other members of the Alliance to allow this to happen under the guise of continued international co-operation.

Both Metternich and Castlereagh were worried, therefore, when the Tsar proposed at Aix-la-Chapelle that the powers should undertake to guarantee 'the territorial status quo and legitimate authority' which then existed among the states of Europe. By this he meant that the Alliance should be used to keep intact the power and territory of existing rulers. He also wished the powers to hold regular meetings to keep the international situation in constant review and decide upon any action necessary to preserve both the frontiers and the established forms of government of Europe. Metternich foresaw that this might open the way for the further spread of Russian influence and even the movement of Russian troops across the Continent. His fears were made worse when this led Castlereagh, who did not frequent congresses to discuss such wideranging action under Russian leadership, to threaten British withdrawal from the affairs of Europe. Alexander was persuaded to accept an agreement limiting the idea of international intervention to the suppression of any revolution in France which might threaten the peace of Europe; but Castlereagh declared that the British government would not send representatives to any future congresses unless they were summoned only for specific reasons and occasionally. Already his hopes for the alliance were vanishing.

Further international deadlock was caused by the British attempt at Aix-la-Chapelle to secure common action against the slave trade and the Barbary pirates in the Mediterranean. The British government proposed that the slave trade should be suppressed by warships expressly authorized by the powers for the purpose with a reciprocal right of search which would deny slaving vessels the protection of national flags. This would inevitably be done almost entirely by the British navy, and Castlereagh rejected the Tsar's scheme for an international fleet based on the West African coast. Nor would he accept a similar Russian proposal to deal with the Barbary pirates. In both these instances, he suspected Alexander of wishing to threaten Britain's worldwide naval supremacy by gaining ports for Russian squadrons to operate in waters where they had not been before. And as the other countries did not want British cruisers to be licensed to interrupt their trade, they gave Castlereagh no support for his plan, and British public opinion was indignant that the Alliance would do nothing to remedy these two long-standing evils.

The combination of Russian aggression and British isolationism revealed at Aix-la-Chapelle, which threatened to destroy the Alliance, alarmed Metternich. Austria was in no position to stand alone on the Continent, but it was not easy to decide which side she should choose to join. By avoiding the taking of decisions on fundamental matters, Metternich had kept the Alliance in being, but the degree of dissension shown among its members at this congress did not augur well for the future. Its members were, in fact, about to regroup themselves in this post-war age.

(d) The Congress of Troppau (1820)

During the two years following the Congress of Aix-la-Chapelle, there was a succession of disturbances in Europe which were likely to have international consequences. Protests and revolts broke out in several countries against the governments which had resumed their power after the Napoleonic War. In 1820 a Spanish army, which was about to be sent to South America to recover the country's rebellious colonies, mutinied and brought about a successful revolution. Ferdinand VII, the restored Bourbon monarch, was compelled to re-introduce a constitution, which had originally been established in 1812 (being devised by the British envoy in Madrid, Lord William Bentinck, on the model of the French constitution of 1791) and was generally regarded by European liberals as an ideal for their hopes.

Portugal at this time was ruled from Brazil, where the Portuguese royal family had settled when it fled from Napoleon in 1807; and in 1815 Brazil had been given equal status with the mother country. In 1821 a Portuguese uprising established a liberal government, which persuaded King John VI to leave Brazil and return to Portugal. He left behind in Brazil his elder son, Pedro, as Regent, but an attempt to make the country subordinate to Portugal led to a revolt there, and in 1822 Pedro accepted the position of Emperor of Brazil, and the ties with Portugal were cut.

There were also disturbances in Italy and Germany. In Italy a secret political society, the Carbonari, was responsible for revolts in Naples and Piedmont in 1820 and 1821, which gained a constitution in both these states (*see page 51*). And in Germany, during the Wartburg festival of 1817, there were demonstrations by students for national unity; and two years later a journalist and suspected Russian spy, Kotzebue, was murdered (*see page 48*).

Alexander, indeed, had his agents not only in Germany, but also Spain, Italy and other countries, where they sometimes penetrated liberal movements, and in 1819 Metternich told Castlereagh of the 'proved conviction of Russia's falsehood and intrigue'. But by now Alexander was changing his attitude. The growing activities of the European liberal movements alarmed him, and he was to be profoundly shocked later in 1820 by the mutiny of a regiment of his household guards in Moscow, particularly since he believed the conspirators had been influenced by the Spanish revolt. Even before then he had wanted another congress to be called to consider the situation in Spain, but Metternich would not at first agree, fearing that the Tsar might be able to send Russian troops there. He declared for a policy of 'magisterial inaction'.

The revolt in Naples, however, changed the situation completely since this was a direct threat to Austrian influence in Italy (*see page 51*). Metternich would have preferred to have acted alone, but he could not afford to break with Russia in doing this, especially as Castlereagh had made a chilling pronouncement upon the European situation which made it clear that he would not consider British intervention in Naples. In his State Paper of 1820 he declared, 'We shall be found in our place when actual danger menaces the system of Europe; but this country cannot and will not act upon abstract and speculative principles of precaution. The Alliance which exists had no such purpose in view in its original formation.' It could well have been argued that this was the purpose of Article VI of the Treaty of the Quadruple Alliance, but now Castlereagh had no intention that it should do so.

In the autumn of 1820 Metternich agreed to the summoning of a congress at Troppau, the capital of Austrian Silesia. To this Britain and France each sent only an observer. Though this was not a meeting of the members of the Holy Alliance, Metternich presented to the Congress a declaration, known as the Protocol of Troppau, insisting that states, which had 'undergone a change of government due to revolution' and so threatened other states, ceased to be members of the Holy Alliance and that the assembled members had a duty to use coercion 'to bring it back to the bosom of the Alliance.' This was supported by the three eastern powers, but rejected by both Britain and France. Castlereagh let it be known that he considered the revolution in Naples to be a matter of domestic concern for Austria and that Britain would not oppose her if she intervened on her own responsibility. When Metternich would not do this, he announced that the British government would 'never consent to charge itself as a member of the Alliance with the moral responsibility of administering a general European peace of this description.' What Metternich called 'the great divide' had begun, and with it the failure of the congresses.

(e) The Congress of Laibach (1821)

The next business of the Congress was to consider directly the Neapolitan situation, but it was thought necessary to discuss the matter with the King of Naples himself. The aged Ferdinand I, however, could not travel as far as Troppau, and early in 1821, after an interval of three months, the Congress moved southwards to Laibach, the capital of the Austrian province of Carniola (and to-day Ljubljana in Yugoslavia).

By that time, Austria had concentrated 80 000 troops in northern Italy, and Russia was prepared to move 90 000 in that direction. Metternich persuaded Ferdinand to invite Austria to send an army into Naples to put down the revolt, but he had to agree that this intervention should be in the name of the Holy Alliance. Austrian troops now restored the former regimes in both Naples and Piedmont. Neither Britain nor France would support this move.

Metternich had hoped to preserve the formal unity of the Quintuple Alliance, but Castlereagh was completely opposed to the idea expressed in the Protocol of Troppau. The powers were now irretrievably divided into two great groups: Austria, Russia and Prussia as its eastern supporters; and Britain and France as its western opponents. This division was to persist during the century, though differences within each group were such as to ensure that it brought about only one open conflict between them—the Crimean War (1854–56), which did not involve Austria or Prussia.

(f) Greece and Spain

Shortly before the end of the Congress of Laibach, news reached it of a Greek national uprising in the Morea, the southern peninsula of the country, which was being brutally suppressed by the Turks. This raised those threats of discord among the powers which were always imminent in the Eastern Question, the term for the problems raised in south-eastern Europe by the decline of the Turkish Empire (*see page 78*). At this time the Turkish territories in Europe still comprised the Balkans south of the Danube (*see Map 4, page 29*) and included within its boundaries several Christian races who were determined to gain their national independence. The Turkish Empire was weak and badly-governed, which both added to the discontent of these races and made them hope that they could win their freedom. Austria and Russia, however, were already rivals in wishing to make territorial gains at Turkey's expense. This also provoked fear among other European powers, especially Britain and France, who foresaw a threat to their interests and to the balance of power if either country were successful. As early as 1774 Russia had gained by the Treaty of Kutchuk Kainardji the undefined right to make representations on behalf of the Christian inhabitants of the Turkish Empire, and it was generally expected that she would try to exploit this to her advantage when an opportunity arose.

Metternich did not want Russia to help the Greeks in their revolt. 'The complications which may ensue in the East defy all calculation,' he wrote. He wanted the revolt to 'burn itself out beyond the pale of civilization;' and he succeeded in getting discussion of the question postponed at Laibach. In Russia, the old ambition of taking Constanti-

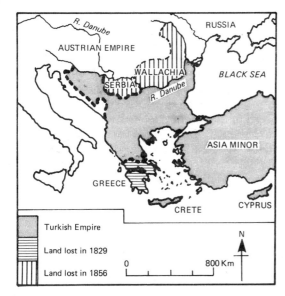

Map 4 The Turkish Empire in the Balkans, 1815–56

nople combined with sympathy for the Greeks, who shared with them the same Orthodox religion, to make many people favour such help; but Alexander was at first compelled by loyalty to the principles of the Protocol of Troppau to refrain from taking any action. The situation brought Metternich and Castlereagh together again. Both were prepared to see the Greek revolt fail because they wanted, above all, to stop Alexander establishing himself in the Turkish Empire. Castlereagh wrote a personal letter to the Tsar urging him to give no support to the Greek rising, which was merely 'a branch of the organized spirit of insurrection.'

Their task, however, was a difficult one. The Sultan, fearing that the Holy Alliance might mount a crusade against Moslems, resorted to terrorism against the Greeks. On Easter Eve 1822 the Patriarch of Constantinople was seized, immediately after morning service in the cathedral, with two of his bishops, and they were hanged in their vestments outside the patriarchal palace. The next year some 25 000 people of the island of Chios in the Aegean Sea were massacred, 47 000 people were sold into slavery and only 5000 escaped. Alexander spoke ominously of there 'being a limit to Russian patience'. Metternich said of him, 'He wriggles like a devil in holy water.'

Meanwhile, the situation in Spain had worsened. A royalist reaction against the revolution had produced a civil war in the northern provinces of the country. France was alarmed, and Alexander spoke of Russian intervention there also. Metternich saw that another congress would have to be held, and it met in 1822 at Verona in the Austrian province of Venetia in northern Italy.

(g) The Congress of Verona (1822)

Before the Congress met, however, Castlereagh had committed suicide. His death was a blow for Metternich, who had come to count on him as his 'second self'. Despite all that had happened, Castlereagh had continued to believe that there could still be circumstances which would make it possible for Britain to co-operate with the Continental powers. His refusal to withdraw Britain formally from the Quintuple Alliance had been widely interpreted in the country as approval of the despotic regimes in Europe and brought him parliamentary and popular hostility, but he would have regretted having to break completely with the great powers. During the Greek crisis he had made it clear that he wished to join in all possible steps to avert the danger of Russian intervention in the Turkish Empire.

Castlereagh was succeeded as Foreign Secretary by George Canning. It is commonly said that his replacement of Castlereagh made little difference to British foreign policy. This is arguable, although both were men of their time, controlled by membership of the same government and subject to the same influences from public opinion. Canning, however, belonged to a newer generation than his predecessor. Born without the advantages of inherited position and wealth which other statesmen enjoyed, he shared more strongly than Castlereagh the contemporary British outlook—the isolationist feelings, confidence in British naval and commercial power and growing dislike of the post-war period. 'For Alliance read England, and you have the clue to my policy,' he said in 1823, and also, 'Every country for itself, and God for us all.' Moreover, while Castlereagh was reserved by nature, could not express himself clearly at cabinet meetings and had an aristocratic dislike of publicity, Canning made outstanding speeches in the Commons which gave him control of the House, while he was the first Foreign Secretary to explain his policy at meetings outside Parliament and arrange for the immediate publication of his official despatches. He did not hesitate to take risks in foreign policy because he believed that a bold approach made him popular, though William Hazlitt said, 'Mr Canning has the luckless ambition to play off the tricks of a political rope-dancer, and he chooses to do it on the nerves of humanity.' He was very ready to oppose the ascendancy in European diplomacy of Metternich, whom he once described as 'the greatest rogue and liar on the Continent, perhaps in the civilized world'. Metternich, on his part, called him 'this malevolent meteor, this scourge of the world, a revolution in himself'; and Wellington commented in 1823, 'There are some people who like to fish in troubled waters, and Mr C. is one of them.'

At the Congress of Verona, France asked the Alliance to authorize her to invade Spain in support of the royalist cause. The Tsar now spoke of sending 150 000 Russian troops into the country. Metternich was alarmed by this and supported the French request. Canning, who knew that this would seem to many of his countrymen a reversal of the

Peninsular War, instructed Wellington, the British delegate, to say that Britain would not approve or support any intervention in Spain 'come what may'. This meant that the Alliance as a whole could take no action, but Britain was isolated, and Canning could do nothing to prevent France from acting on her own. A French army of 100 000 men entered Spain in 1823 and placed Ferdinand in control of his kingdom again.

This rebuff at the hands of France was a setback for Canning. He admitted that 'the entry of the French army into Spain was . . . an affront to the pride of England', but he welcomed the fact that it had not come about through 'an assumed jurisdiction of the Congress'. He rejoiced at what he thought would be the likely diplomatic outcome of the incident—'The issue of Verona has split the one and indivisible Alliance, and so things are getting back to a wholesome state again.'

Moreover, his defiance of the Alliance was very popular at home. When he scornfully rejected it as 'Areopagus and all that', he had the approval of the upper and middle classes whose classical education enabled them to understand that he was referring to the hill in Athens where the highest judicial had met, above and removed from the life of the city, in ancient times. Castlereagh had, indeed, already begun the dissolution of the Alliance in 1820, but he had never contemplated the possibility of this with anything other than regret.

(h) The Achievement of Canning

Canning could not have hoped to have done any better over the Spanish question, but he was more fortunate during the following years. He was presented with situations in parts of the world where British naval supremacy made it possible for him to act without being thwarted by any power or combination of powers.

In 1823 the newly-restored King of Spain invited the allies to a conference to discuss the future of the Spanish colonies in Central and South America, and there were rumours that the French government was ready to consider helping Spain to recover them. Canning not only refused to send a British representative to such a meeting, but also suggested to James Monroe, the President of the United States of America, that Britain and his country should make a joint declaration that they would not permit any European power to re-subjugate these newly-independent republics. Though Monroe was ready to do this, the prevailing anti-British feeling in America made it impossible. Canning proceeded to tell France that Britain would not tolerate any French intervention in that part of the world. Since the British navy alone could control the Atlantic, this warning could undoubtedly be enforced. 'If the barrier of the Pyrenees could not be defended by a British army, the gates of the Atlantic could be held by a British fleet,' Canning said. 'If France could humble Spain on land, England could humble France on the sea.' Monroe now felt able, therefore, to send an independent message to the American Congress, which became known as the Monroe Doctrine. It asserted 'that the American continents, by the free and independent condition which they have assumed and maintained, are henceforth not to be considered as subjects for future colonization by any European powers.' This action by Canning was popular in Britain, particularly as it was recognized that he took it, not to uphold republicanism and colonial revolt, but rather to protect British trade with South America. His well-known claim was typical and premature—'I resolved that if France had Spain, it should not be Spain with the Indies; I called the New World into existence to redress the balance of the Old.'

The next year Canning went on to recognize the independence of Mexico, Columbia and the Argentine Republic without any reference to the Quintuple Alliance. British trade with South America, which had increased tenfold in the past ten years, was safeguarded by treaties with these states; and British recognition of the independence of the Empire of Brazil followed in 1825. Such a combination of diplomatic principle with economic advantage for Britain gained him the continuing support of his fellow-countrymen, though abroad it was regarded as an example of British perfidy.

Canning was also able to make use of British naval power in his policy towards Portugal. In 1826 King John VI died. His legitimate successor was Pedro, the Emperor of Brazil, but he was opposed by his younger brother, Miguel. Pedro decided to renounce the throne of Portugal in favour of his eight-year-old daughter, Maria, with his sister, Isabella, as Regent, and he proposed that a papal dispensation should be sought to permit the marriage of Maria to Miguel. He also announced his decision to grant Portugal a constitution. But Miguel was absolutist in outlook and was supported by the reactionary party, who continued to try with unofficial Spanish help to get him on the throne in his own right. The constitutionalists appealed to Canning, who sent a fleet and 4000 troops to Lisbon. The Spanish government deserted Miguel, and the Portuguese constitution was saved.

By taking advantage of Portugal's maritime situation, Canning was able to prevent the sending of any Continental army into the country. The check he had suffered in Spain was not repeated there. As with South America, his intervention in Portugal was in the interests of British diplomacy. He was not primarily interested in saving the Portuguese constitution. He privately admitted that he did not admire 'paper constitutions'. He wished to make sure that, though French influence was established in Madrid, British predominance must prevail in Lisbon.

Meanwhile, the Greek War of Independence was providing him with a more complex problem. The Turkish atrocities, though the Greeks had replied by taking no prisoners in the fighting, had aroused indignation in Britain, where there was strong sympathy for the rebels. Romantic poets, liberal politicians and evangelical preachers saw the savage peasants of the Morea as the descendants of the ancient Greeks struggling against the barbarous Turks to establish a free Christian state. When Lord Byron went out to join the Greeks and died of fever in the swamps of Missolonghi in 1824, their cause gained an English martyr. In addition, much trade in the eastern Mediterranean, including British trade, was in the hands of the Greeks, and British banks had made loans to them. Canning recognized the Greeks as belligerents in 1823, but he would not listen to suggestions for further action which might bring Britain into conflict with Turkey. Neither the memory of a Greek general, who had defeated the Spartans, nor of the greatest of the Christian apostles would influence him. 'No war for Epaminondas or St. Paul,' he declared. He sympathized with the Greek cause, but was not prepared to support any European action intended to compel Turkey forcefully to accept a settlement.

This, however, was what the Tsar wanted to do. He wished to summon a congress to consider joint intervention for this purpose. Canning refused to allow Britain to be represented at it, stating he did not wish the country only to serve 'as a buffer between the colliding interests of Austria and Russia'. The other four powers met at St. Petersburg early in 1825, but the Congress broke up in disagreement between Metternich and Alexander.

The fighting in Greece seemed to have reached a stalemate for the Turks. Through their shipping, the Greeks had command of local waters. The Turks could not supply or reinforce their armies. Continuing Greek resistance seemed to assure their eventual success; but in 1825 two events changed the situation. In February the Sultan secured the help of his nominal vassal, Mehemet Ali, Pasha of Egypt, whose fleet conveyed an Egyptian army to the Morea, and this proceeded to reconquer most of the Greek mainland for the Turks. And in December Alexander died and was succeeded as Tsar by Nicholas I. The new Russian ruler was more ready than his predecessor to oppose Metternich actively and did not think that Russian assistance should be withheld from the Greeks for any longer.

Canning did not wish to intervene alone, and he now believed that joint action with Russia would be to Britain's advantage. He was also very ready to act independently of Metternich and to avenge the humiliation he had suffered in 1823 through Britain's diplomatic isolation. He sent Wellington to St. Petersburg, while he himself went to Paris. By July 1827 he was able to persuade France and Russia to join Britain in signing the Treaty of London, though Austria and Prussia refused to do so. This new treaty provided for the setting up by negotiation of a self-governing Greece under Turkish overlordship. It also, however, contained a secret article stating that if the Turks or the Greeks did not accept an armistice within one month of the signing of the Treaty, steps would be taken to bring the hostilities to an end by all the means that might 'suggest themselves to the prudence' of the three powers. A joint naval force was sent at once to Greek waters.

The Treaty of London was a triumph for Canning's policy. He had succeeded in depriving Metternich of the support of all the powers except Prussia, who had no influence in the Mediterranean. The new Tsar also was glad that he had been able to break away from Metternich's restraining influence. Metternich, however, saw the Treaty as an encouragement to Russia to intervene in the Turkish Empire, which would be as dangerous to Britain as it would be to Russia.

Canning, however, died that August—'It was Canning's temper that killed him,' said Wellington. He did not live, therefore, to see the results of an unexpected development in the crisis. Since the Turks refused to accept an armistice with the Greeks, the British, French and Russian fleet sailed in October into the Bay of Navarino, on the southwest coast of the Morea, and anchored opposite the Turkish and Egyptian warships which were stationed in the deep harbour. After some days, a Turkish ship fired upon a boat from the British flagship, HMS *Dartmouth*. Several British and French warships returned the fire. This produced a general engagement in which the entire Turkish and Egyptian fleet was destroyed. To Metternich this event was a 'frightful catastrophe'; it seemed to him to lay Turkey open more than ever to Russian designs. Wellington, who was now Prime Minister, was also alarmed. He had mistrusted Canning's policy. He believed that Britain's interests required the maintenance of a strong Turkey, free from foreign intervention. He described the Battle of Navarino as an 'untoward event', and the King's speech at the opening of Parliament 'lamented deeply the conflict with the naval forces of an ancient ally'.

The consequences of the incident did, indeed, at first sight seem likely to be very serious. Nicholas took advantage of the situation to invade Turkish territory. War between Britain and Russia seemed possible, but there was sufficient international co-operation to secure a settlement. The French government persuaded Wellington to agree that Russia should be allowed to intervene on the Danube, but not in the Mediterranean. Nicholas, whose troops were meeting serious reverses, agreed to this; and a French expeditionary force brought about the evacuation of Egyptian troops from the Morea. In September 1829 Russia and Turkey signed the Treaty of Adrianople, which recognized Greek self-government under Turkish overlordship. Both Wellington and Metternich wanted Greece to be completely independent. They thought that this would be the best way to prevent the country becoming a virtual Russian protectorate; but this was not to happen until 1832 (*see page 129*).

(i) The Collapse of the Alliance
Canning's policy had gained Greece her independence, but from the European point of view the result of the events was the complete and final collapse of the Quintuple Alliance and its congresses. The Congress of St. Petersburg was to be the last of these, and by 1830 nothing remained of the union of monarchs designed to preserve the Vienna settlement. British support for the South American republics and

Russian and French help in freeing Greece had weakened the idea of maintaining the existing arrangements in Europe. 'The ministry of Mr Canning marked an era in the history of England and Europe,' remarked Metternich bitterly as late as 1831.

Canning had given the Alliance its virtual death-blow, but nevertheless both Castlereagh and Alexander had made its breakdown almost inevitable by their policies even before 1820. There was, in fact, so little basis for co-operation among the great powers that the chances of this attempt at united action ever succeeding were bound to be slight. The effort to settle the affairs of Europe by international conferences only served to reveal the fundamental differences between the member states and made the British government determined not to take part in an arrangement in which it would always be outvoted.

Metternich correctly foresaw that such a situation was likely to benefit the European revolutionary movements. They were encouraged by the events in South America and Greece, and there was now no alliance to oppose them. His response was to seek to bind Russia and Prussia to Austria. He still wanted to help them put down revolutionary movements because, in some parts of Europe, these might threaten the existence of the Austrian Empire; but a much greater threat to Habsburg rule was the possibility of a general war which Austria might very well not survive. The ambitions of Prussia in Germany and of Russia in the Balkans made both these powers potential enemies of Austria. To avoid the outbreak of such a war, Metternich's policy was to emphasize the points upon which they agreed and might be able to co-operate; and both Russia and Prussia were ruled by conservative monarchs, who were afraid of the consequences of nationalism. Canning's foreign policy had caused him to despair, and he regarded his death as a divine miracle which averted complete disaster in Europe at the last moment. Metternich's policy was now preserved and, by continuing beyond his own time, was to safeguard Austria's position for nearly another 40 years.

Bibliography

The period of the congresses is dealt with generally in F.B. Artz, *Reaction and Revolution, 1814–1832* (New York, 1934) and H.G. Schenk, *The Aftermath of the Napoleonic Wars* (Routledge & Kegan Paul, 1947). For the statesmen (in addition to the books mentioned on page 19), there is C.K. Webster, *The Foreign Policy of Castlereagh, 1815–1822* (Bell & Hyman, 1963) and H.W.V. Temperley, *The Foreign Policy of Canning, 1822–1827* (Bell & Hyman, 1925). Also concerned with the subject are Roger Bullen, 'The Great Powers and the Iberian Peninsula,' in Alan Sked (ed.), *Europe's Balance of Power, 1815–1848* (Macmillan, 1979); and E.S. Forster, *A Short History of Modern Greece, 1821–1956* (Methuen, 3rd. edn., 1957).

Exercises

A *This section consists of questions that might be used for discussion (or written answers) as a way of expanding on the chapter and testing your understanding of it:*

1 What do you understand by 'a common policy of monarchical absolutism' and the 'beliefs of the romantic intellectuals of contemporary Europe'?
2 How would the Holy Alliance satisfy Alexander I's spiritual and patriotic aims?
3 Why did other European powers dislike the Holy Alliance?
4 Why did Castlereagh see the Quadruple Alliance as a balance against the Holy Alliance?
5 What was the significance of Article VI of the Quadruple Alliance?
6 What do historians mean by the 'Congress System'?
7 What were the main (a) decisions and (b) areas of disagreement at the Congress of Aix-la-Chapelle (1818)?
8 List the main crises that arose between 1818 and 1820 and explain the attitude of the Tsar Alexander I to them.
9 Why did the Congress of Troppau (1820) reveal 'the great divide'?
10 What did the Alliance do for the King of Naples?
11 Why did the Quintuple Alliance split between the eastern and western powers?
12 What do you understand by the 'Eastern Question'?
13 Why was Alexander I prepared to help the Greek revolt against the Turks?
14 What difference did Castlereagh's replacement by Canning actually make to British policy?
15 What was the Monroe Doctrine, and why did Canning see it as advantageous to Britain?
16 Why did the other European powers disapprove of British policy towards South America?
17 Why was the Battle of Navarino so significant?
18 Why had Canning 'given the Alliance its virtual death-blow'?

B *Essay questions*

1 How far did the problems of either (a) Greece in the 1820s or (b) the Iberian peninsula in the 1820s and 1830s, affect the relations between the European powers? (Oxford, 1981)
2 'Self-interest rather than differences of principle caused the break-up of the Congress System.' How far do you agree with this view? (Oxford, 1983)
3 Explain what is meant by the 'Congress System'. How did this system influence international relations in the decade after 1815? (SUJB, 1981)
4 Why did so many countries support the Greeks in their struggle for independence? How far did this support influence the outcome of their struggle? (SUJB, 1982)
5 'The Concert of Europe was doomed from the outset due to the conflicting aims of its participants.' How far do you agree? (Welsh, 1982)
6 With what justification can the 'Congress System' be acclaimed as an enlightened experiment in international cooperation? (AEB, 1983)
7 'The rebellion of the Greeks, and the international involvements which followed from it during the 1820s, well illustrated the various facets of the problem which came to be known as the Eastern Question.' Discuss. (London, 1981)

8 What international complications resulted during the 1820s from the Greek struggle for independence? (London, 1983)

9 'An admirable and enlightened example of international cooperation.' Does the Congress System (1815–25) deserve to be so described? (JMB, 1981)

C *An assessment of the Congress System*
Some contemporaries saw the congresses as a means of upholding the traditional, conservative European governments at the expense of liberal and nationalist movements. This exercise tests that theory by requiring you to examine the role of the European leaders in the crises of the 1820s. Draw out and complete a chart like the one below (but larger):

Date	Area concerned	Major Powers involved	Outcome of crisis (side supported by Powers, etc.)
1820	Spain: army mutiny & King forced to give constitution.		
1821	Portugal: uprising against John VI & loss of Brazil.		
1820–1	Naples & Piedmont: liberal revolts & constitutions granted.		
1821–7	Greece: revolt against Turkish rule.		
1821–3	Spain: royalist opposition to revolt & civil war.		
1823	South America: future of Spanish colonies.		
1826	Portugal: succession to John VI disputed.		

Once your chart is completed, you should be able to return to the original question and answer it on the basis of evidence provided by the chart: Was the Congress System a means of upholding traditional, conservative governments?

D *Interpretations*
In this section, European statesmen have been quoted on a number of occasions. Explain what they meant by each of the following:

(*i*) '. . . nothing more than a philanthropic aspiration, clad in a religious garb. . . .' '. . . the overthrow of pietistic feeling of the Emperor Alexander. . . .' (Metternich, *page 22*)

(*ii*) The British government would 'never consent to charge itself as a member of the Alliance with the moral responsibility of administering a general European peace of this description.' (Castlereagh, *page 27*)

(*iii*) 'There are some people who like to fish in troubled waters, and Mr C. is one of them'. (Wellington, *page 30*)

(*iv*) 'I resolved that if France had Spain, it should not be Spain with the Indies; I called the New World into existence to redress the balance of the Old.' (Canning, *page 32*)

(v) 'The ministry of Mr. Canning marked an era in the history of England and Europe'. (Metternich, *page 35*)

E *Essay-writing skills 1: narrative and analysis*
Throughout this book, you will find sections on essay-writing. They are intended to help you to improve this most vital aspect of your work and may be taken entirely separately from all other exercises. They also work from a simple to a more complex level, so that you should find this opening exercise relatively straightforward. (If you are also studying nineteenth-century British history, you will find a similar exercise in the Open University Humanities Foundation Course Unit 7, 'Basic Problems of Writing History', on political reform.)

Imagine you are faced by the title:

'An admirable and enlightened example of international co-operation.' Does the Congress System (1815–25) deserve to be so described?

It is most important in writing an essay at this level to avoid simply writing a history of what the Congress System was and did between these dates. If you do this—'tell the story'—you are writing only a *narrative* of events. Rather, you should be attempting to answer the question asked—*was* the System 'an admirable and enlightened example of international co-opera-tion'? In other words, you should be *analysing* the actions of the Congress System in an effort to draw a conclusion. As you will see, there is an important place for narrative factual information in essays, but at this stage you are only required to identify the difference between the two types of statement. Below are ten sentences about the Congress System between these dates—identify which of them are narrative statements of fact and which are analytical statements presenting arguments in answer to the question.

(i) Some of the weaknesses and divisions of the Congress System were clearly visible by 1820.
(ii) The Congress of Laibach opened in January 1821.
(iii) That the Congress System was indeed 'an enlightened example of interna-tional co-operation' is suggested by the agreement reached in 1818 at Aix-le-Chapelle.
(iv) When the Greeks revolted in 1821, the great powers had different opinions on what action to take.
(v) The Protocol of Troppau (1820) stated that 'States which have undergone a change of government . . . cease to be members of the European Alliance.'
(vi) Only in its earliest years did the Congress System match this description.
(vii) At Aix-la-Chapelle in 1818, the Congress Powers agreed on several matters relating to France, but did not set up an international army nor take any action over Spain's colonies in America.
(viii) Britain's premature departure from the Congress of Verona in 1822 was a clear indication of the failure of the System as one of 'international co-operation'.
(ix) By the early 1820s, it was clear that national self-interest was a more important motive than the unity of the Congress System.
(x) In 1825, three Congress Powers—Austria, Prussia and Russia—met at St. Petersburg and discussed further the Greek problem.

3 Metternich's System

(a) The Austrian Empire

When Napoleon formed the Confederation of the Rhine in 1806, he assumed the position of its Protector and announced its withdrawal from the Holy Roman Empire, which had, indeed, by then ceased to have any real authority in Germany. The Holy Roman Emperor, Francis II, who had already declared himself hereditary Emperor of Austria in 1804 when Napoleon became Emperor of the French, now gave up his old Imperial title and became the Emperor Francis I of Austria.

The Austrian Empire as such was, therefore, only of recent origin in the period after the Napoleonic War, but its provinces were those which the Habsburg family had secured in the course of centuries and were settled by the Treaty of Vienna. These comprised extensive territories astride the middle Danube, extending into northern Italy and facing the Adriatic. As well as present-day Austria and Hungary, the Empire included Bohemia, Moravia, Galicia, Slovakia, Transylvania, the Bukovina, Croatia-Slavonia, Carniola, Gorizia, Istria, Dalmatia, Lombardy and Venetia (*see Map 5*). These were without any geographical or economic unity, and, moreover, were inhabited by some 11 groups of peoples of varying nationality, language, customs, religion and cultural level (*see Map 9 page 198*). The Austrian Empire has, indeed, been described as 'a Europe in miniature'. Though one of the large Continental powers, it was alone in lacking a national foundation such as was becoming increasingly important for unity and

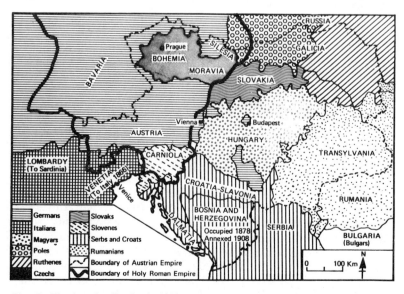

Map 5 The Austrian Empire in 1815

stability in the nineteenth century. And the Imperial government feared that if it made any concession to the wishes of its subject peoples, the whole existence of the Empire would be threatened. 'My realm resembles a worm-eaten house', said Francis to a Russian diplomat. 'If one part is removed, nobody can tell how much will fall.'

Though the condition of the Austrian Empire made the establishment of effective central government difficult, the age-long tradition of Habsburg rule was autocratic. Its provinces were their family lands, belonging to them and to be administered by German-speaking Austrian officials from Vienna. Francis, who had become the ruler of this Habsburg territory in 1792 at the age of 24, believed that its government should depend solely upon the monarch's will, and that the supreme duty of all his subjects was to obey him unquestioningly. This belief was strengthened by the events of the French Revolution and the subsequent wars in which Austria suffered severely. He was afraid of the spread of liberal ideas which might undermine his position. 'I want not scholars but good citizens,' he informed the teachers and professors in the schools and universities of his lands. 'Whosoever serves me, must teach according to my orders. Whosoever is not able to do so or starts new ideas going, must go or I shall eliminate him.' To teach the pupils and students in the way he wanted, he relied mainly upon the Roman Catholic Church; it was largely given control of education for which it received financial assistance, but was kept in subordination to the Imperial government. Attempts were made to increase the effectiveness of the censorship of the press, and spies and informers were employed to keep watch upon the professional and educated classes whom he mistrusted most because they were likely to hold and express notions that threatened him.

Maria Theresa 1740–1780
Joseph II 1780–1790
Leopold II 1790–1792
Francis II 1792–1835 (1804 Emperor Francis I of Austria)
Ferdinand 1835–1848 (abdicated)
Francis Joseph 1848–1916

Table 3. The Habsburg Rulers (1740–1916)

Francis, however, was far from being a completely absolute ruler. During the second half of the eighteenth century, two successive Habsburg rulers, Maria Theresa and her son, Joseph II, had tried to introduce reforms and innovations, centralize the government in Vienna and Germanize the other peoples of their dominions. Under Maria Theresa, the teaching of the German language was made compulsory in schools and its use enforced in all government offices; a universal income tax and a graduated poll tax were introduced; and councils to deal expertly with administrative and financial business were set up together with royal commissions of enquiry (including one directed by her to consider the possibility of preventing improper love-making). Joseph proclaimed the whole of his dominions to be a single state divided into 13 districts, each under the rule of a governor, made German the only official language and established a supreme court of appeal at Vienna, which could review decisions made by law courts throughout his lands.

These changes strengthened the Habsburg monarchy and enabled it to survive the defeats and losses of the first years of the nineteenth century; but they also aroused great resentment and opposition so that Joseph had died in 1790 amid widespread demonstrations of unrest and rebellion. Francis had no wish to provoke such a dangerous situation in his reign. Reform and change were not for him. He would have liked to have made the Imperial government a more efficient and complete absolutism, but shrank from making further attacks upon local rights and privileges. He even did not enforce his authority as effectively as he might have done. Imperial decrees might be ignored; many officials were allowed considerable independence; and nationalist societies and publications enjoyed widespread toleration in practice. For the whole of his reign the government of the Empire remained in what has been described as 'a condition of suspended animation'.

In every part of the Empire, the peasants formed the greater proportion of his subjects. Joseph had released them from serfdom, and they had obtained possession of their lands, but the nobility still enjoyed the right to judge them according to feudal law in the manorial courts. The nobility, indeed, were wealthy and powerful and controlled the life of both town and countryside as well as filling all the higher ranks and posts in the army and diplomatic service. They were loyal supporters of the monarchy, and so also were the Roman Catholic clergy, who shared the Emperor's fear of liberalism. There was as yet no important middle class of merchants, industrialists and financiers to challenge the power of the nobility and clergy. In other words, the government of the Austrian Empire and its social system still largely rested upon the old aristocratic society of the eighteenth century, which had been little changed by the newer ideas and developments such as were making themselves felt in other parts of Europe.

Among the Habsburg lands, the kingdom of Hungary had been most able to resist the move towards imperial centralization and was, in fact, the only part which still possessed any measure of self-government. The Magyar nobility were its ruling class; they continued to enjoy their exemption from taxation, to possess almost unlimited rule over their peasants and to control local administration. Past Habsburg rulers had been obliged to make concessions to them in order to protect their power over the rest of their territories, and Magyar noblemen were now appointed, together with Austrian noblemen, to foreign embassies and other big offices. Moreover, while the Habsburgs had been able to restrict the powers of the diets (local parliaments) in Bohemia, Moravia, Styria and other provinces, the Hungarian Diet remained important and was controlled by the Magyar nobility. When Francis ceased to summon the Diet from 1812 to 1825, the nobility retaliated by refusing to send the troops and supplies needed to assist in the suppression of the revolts in Italy in 1820 and threatened to take other measures. The Emperor had to summon the Diet regularly from that time and make further concession to it, which included the recognition of the Magyar language for some official purposes. Such continued conciliation of Hungary was to lead to the establishment of the Dual Monarchy in 1867 (*see page 324*).

(b) The Metternich System

During the years after 1815, Metternich dominated not only European diplomacy, but also the affairs of Austria and Germany. He was not a native of Austria, but was born in 1773 at Coblenz in the Rhineland and was educated at the universities of Strasbourg and Mainz. The invading armies of the French Republic compelled him to flee to Austria in 1792, and three years later he married the granddaughter and heiress of Prince von Kaunitz, the chief minister of Maria Theresa. The marriage brought him both large estates and a prominent position at the Habsburg court. After serving as Austrian ambassador in Dresden from 1801 to 1803, in Berlin from 1803 to 1806 and in Paris from 1806 to 1807, he first achieved a European reputation in 1809 when he was made Foreign Minister and negotiated the marriage between Napoleon and the Archduchess Marie Louise, the daughter of the Emperor Francis, as a means of obtaining a respite for Austria from French hostility. Despite having made peace with Napoleon, Metternich gave him only nominal help during his Russian campaign of 1812; and when Metternich refused to accept his terms for an alliance after the disastrous French retreat from Moscow, he brought Austria into the Fourth Coalition. He presided over the Congress of Vienna in 1814 and 1815, and in 1821 the Emperor of Austria made him Chancellor as well as Foreign Minister.

Metternich became hated by European liberals as an arch-reactionary, and as historians have mostly supported the liberal cause, he has not been favourably written about by them. He was, however, neither cruel nor unintelligent. He was a product of the Enlightenment of the eighteenth-century Age of Reason, believing in politics as a systematic branch of knowledge and in time-tested orderly government. And he acquired a wide experience of practical politics which convinced him that he had a better understanding of his age than other statesmen. 'Men regard me,' he wrote, 'as a lantern to which they approach in order to illuminate a dark night.' He was conservative, monarchical and aristocratic in his outlook. He believed that absolute monarchy was the natural form of government likely to preserve the social order, which like monarchy itself was divinely ordained, and that the aristocracy existed to advise the ruler and assist him in governing wisely. As an aristocrat—his father had been a Count of the Holy

Roman Empire—he thought of himself as a member of the leading European class, which was international in its character and outlook; he told Wellington in 1824 that Europe was like a fatherland to him. He was no democrat and was completely opposed to the idea of popular sovereignty and any form of government which sought to put it into practice. 'The people let themselves be duped easily enough,' he once said. 'You cannot exaggerate the goodness of the people, I might even say of all peoples, but their ignorance is great, and therefore they must be led.' But the greatest danger, he believed, came not from the mass of the people. It came from individuals, who had no knowledge of political reality and were deluded by the popular, passing abstractions of the time. 'Two words are enough to create evil,' he said, 'two words which, because they are empty of all real meaning, enchant the dreamers by their emptiness. These words are "Liberty" and "Equality".'

He thought that a state must uphold stable and orderly relations between its subjects as strongly as he accepted the idea of the balance of politics in international politics. He believed that the highest duty of statesmanship must be to preserve firm and steady government and feared that the aims of the liberals and reformers threatened its destruction and might bring about a revival of the anarchy of the French Revolution. He was too cynical and humane to believe that change should always be prevented; he told the French statesman, Francois Guizot, in 1827, that he thought of himself as a 'socialist-conservative'. Reform, he thought, was possible and desirable, but it was essential that it came about in the right way; it must be natural, gradual and in conformity with the normal development of political institutions. The French Revolution and its consequent wars had left Europe in a condition of moral instability, which required the suppression of would-be revolutionaries until a new generation, accustomed to the normal stability of peace, could undertake the necessary changes with a calmer outlook. Except for the developments in literature and science, he disliked all that had happened in his own age, which he regarded as a time of uncertainty and turmoil between two greater ages. 'My life,' he reflected, 'coincides with an abominable period. I have come into the world either too soon or too late. . . . I should have been born in 1900 with the twentieth century before me.'

Probably his greatest weakness was that, despite his humanity and rationalism, his policy was in practice a negative one of blind repression. He did not distinguish in his actions between the revolutionaries and moderate reformers. His repressive measures increased rather than diminished opposition to his rule. 'If Metternich would only leave people a little alone.' Lord Palmerston once said, 'he would find his crop of revolutions . . . soon die away on the stalk.' Though it is hardly likely that this would have been so, the fact remains that always his only answer to liberalism or radicalism in the end was unconstructive suppression which probably made the explosion more violent when it came.

As with his foreign policy, Metternich's political outlook was naturally affected by the peculiar circumstances of the Austrian Empire. Nationalist and liberal ideas were that empire's greatest internal threat and were even more serious to the Habsburgs than they were to other European rulers. In the Austrian Empire, as elsewhere, the most numerous supporters of these ideas were—in Metternich's words —'paid state officials, men of letters, lawyers and individuals charged with education', and there were also some among the army officers and the small commercial class. As in other states, these men resented the lack of opportunity and initiative which they suffered under autocratic government, but in the Austrian Empire there was also the hatred of the subject nationalities at being ruled by the German-speaking administration in Vienna. They included the Hungarians, Croats, Slovaks, Rumanians and Poles and also the Italians in the provinces of Lombardy and Venetia, which were made part of the Austrian Empire in 1815. At the same time, German nationalists were opposed to the Austrian presidency of the newly-created German Confederation.

To preserve the Austrian Empire and maintain the authority of the house of Habsburg in the face of such disruptive forces, the Chancellor evolved the 'Metternich System', as his policy came to be called, though he himself always denied that any such thing existed. Nevertheless, the policy he adopted in the Empire had a definite intellectual basis, and it again went back to the Age of Reason. It was essentially that of Enlightened Despotism, which was the attempt in the eighteenth century to justify monarchical absolutism as a reasonable form of government rather than one that existed because it had been instituted by God. Monarchs realized that the belief that they ruled by divine right was fading, so they wished to establish the rightfulness of their rule by its wisdom, popularity and efficiency. It was a paternal form of government, that is to say, it regarded a king as ruling over his people as a father governed his family, who recognized that he directed, instructed and even chastised them for their own good.

Maria Theresa and Joseph II had both been recognized as Enlightened Despots, and the measures by which they sought to make their rule more reasonable had included such reforms as religious toleration and equality before the law as well as their administrative improvements; but Metternich was faced by Francis I's continual refusal to follow their example (*see page 41*). The Imperial government remained to a large extent unco-ordinated, inefficient and unable to enforce its commands firmly or uniformly. Metternich could do nothing about this; he once told a Russian general that were he to diverge from the will of the Emperor, he would be without a job within 24 hours. The result was 'an absolutism tempered by slovenliness,' as a socialist called it. During Metternich's post-war years of office, the government's expenditure annually exceeded its income; and the elaborate censorship of the press, which sought to control all publications from newspapers to school textbooks, was never as effective as Metternich would have wished. 'I have sometimes ruled Europe,' he declared with typical polished cynicism, 'but I have never governed Austria.'

He could not aim at strengthening the power of the Imperial government or making it more acceptable to the peoples of the Empire or establishing a greater measure of unity over its diverse provinces. He had to achieve his purpose of preserving the Empire as a safeguard against anarchy, lawlessness and strife by continuing the traditional policy of 'divide and rule', which was the method by which the Habsburgs had largely retained control of their subject peoples in the past. These peoples were divided by mutual jealousies, resentments and conflicting ambitions over such issues as territory, language and trade, which were later to contribute to the failure of the risings of 1848 (*see page 158*). The policy of 'divide and rule' set out to exploit and exacerbate these so as to make united action against the Imperial government impossible. It also involved never allowing the contingents of the Imperial army to be stationed in their native provinces so that, for instance, Venetian towns were garrisoned by Hungarian regiments and Bohemian towns by Austrian troops. It meant too the preservation of the German Confederation as a loose alliance of autocratic princes whom Austria might hope to control.

(c) The German Confederation

The German Confederation, set up by the Treaty of Vienna in 1815, consisted of 39 states (including Austria). Geographically it was identical with the Holy Roman Empire in 1792, which it replaced. This meant that it contained important non-German minorities—the Czechs in Bohemia and Moravia, Slovenes in Styria and Carniola and Italians in the South Tyrol (*see Map 6*). It meant also that, though Austria and Prussia were members of it, not all their territories were included within its boundaries. Its focus was the Diet, but this represented the rulers and not the people. It met at Frankfurt-on-Main under the permanent presidency of the Austrian delegate. The six largest states (Austria, Prussia, Saxony, Bavaria, Hanover and Württemberg), comprising nearly five-sixths of the population, had 24 votes, but the remaining states had 47 votes in all. Minor matters could be decided by a majority vote, but others required a two-thirds majority, and decisions concerning the constitution of the Confederation had to have a unanimous vote.

The Congress of Vienna had established the Confederation to meet a practical need: the provision of some sort of a framework to replace the defunct Holy Roman Empire. Though federalism was accepted as the basis for its organization, the German rulers were determined to retain their independence, and the Confederation was, in fact, little more than an alliance of practically sovereign states and the Diet an assembly of ambassadors. Since the German states were thus regarded as free and self-governing, they could wage war and make treaties with foreign

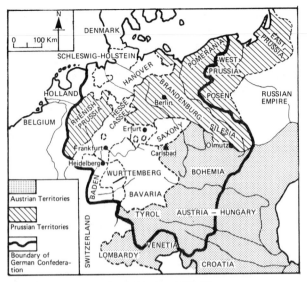

Map 6   The German Confederation, 1815–66

powers, though the constitution stated that neither must be directed against other members of the Confederation. There were no federal laws or executive, no common currency or safeguards for personal rights and no provision at all for economic co-operation or even consultation. The Diet did agree in 1821 to build federal frontier fortresses and form an army of ten corps, three from Austria, three from Prussia, one from Bavaria and three from the other states, but from the start these defence plans were seriously weakened by disagreement over questions of command and cost.

Metternich supported (with Russian approval) the setting up of the Confederation in this form because he believed that it would enable Austria, despite the strengthened position of Prussia, to retain a measure of influence in Germany. Austrian presidency of the Diet provided him with a way of strongly affecting German affairs. Austria could veto in the Diet any attempt to change the constitution of the Confederation, and the allocation of votes meant that she could gain the support of the smaller states most likely to fear Prussia. In addition, Napoleon had replaced the patchwork of free cities, prince bishoprics and other petty sovereignties in southern Germany by four enlarged states (Bavaria, Württemberg, Baden and Hesse-Darmstadt) to counteract the power of Prussia. This arrangement was not changed in 1815, and these four states usually supported Metternich.

As well as intending to oppose the power of Prussia, Metternich wished also to check the advance of liberalism in the German states. Several princes in central and southern Germany, including Baden,

46

Bavaria, Württemberg, Hesse-Darmstadt and Saxe-Weimar, did establish constitutions in their states, but these were not very liberal in their provisions. They guaranteed certain civil rights, granted a limited franchise and established assemblies with slight control over the governments. The rulers in most states were more or less autocratic and governed with the assistance of their noblemen. In 1815 German liberals had hoped for reforms in the government of Prussia, but these were not forthcoming. The state's diverse and scattered post-war territory would have made their introduction difficult; but King Frederick William III was nevertheless at first ready to consider giving Prussia a written constitution with an elected assembly until Metternich persuaded him against it.

(d) The Zollverein (1818)

The Diet did discuss the possibility of arranging a general German tariff, which would provide for free trade among them and impose a common customs duty upon foreign goods entering the territory of the Confederation; but its constitution did not provide for any economic planning, and each state continued to levy duties on both German and foreign imports, and some of the larger ones even had internal customs barriers. Prussia, with her provinces scattered across northern Germany from Aachen to Königsberg, could not continue in a situation in which 67 different tariffs hindered trade within the state and prevented protection against British manufactured imports. In 1818 she abolished all duties on trade between her provinces and simplified those on goods from other states, so making Prussian territory a large free-trade area. This *Zollverein* or economic union not only strengthened Prussian unity, but also imposed her domination upon the small neighbouring states which, between 1819 and 1822, were compelled to join it. Other states had formed unions of their own by 1828, notably the Union of Bavaria and Württemberg, the Central German Union (under Saxony) and the Tax Union of Brunswick, Hanover and Oldenburg; but by 1834 these had been compelled to join the *Zollverein* by Prussia's superior economic resources and her geographical position across most of the north-south waterways and trade routes which enabled her to tax heavily goods in transit along these routes. It then consisted of 17 of the 39 states of the Confederation, which contained between them over two-thirds of both its area and population. Within the next ten years, all the German states joined except Hanover, which was still united with the British crown, and the three northern trading cities (Hamburg, Lübeck and Bremen) which were under British influence.

Austria did not join the *Zollverein*. Her backward industries required the protection of high tariffs if they were to survive. The consequence of this was that German trade inevitably turned from the Danube Valley to the ports of the North Sea, and Austria was increasingly excluded from the economic life of Germany. Metternich vainly opposed the formation of the *Zollverein*. He warned Britain that Prussia wished to 'set up a miniature Continental blockade'; and it did indeed enable Germany to protect its industries against the post-war flow of British goods into the Continent. Prussia naturally gained most economic benefit from the *Zollverein*, particularly as her government had at the same time set out to establish improved communications to unite her newly-acquired dominions. By 1828 some 4500 kilometres of new roads had been built, and steamships were speeding up traffic on the Rhine. Still more important was the coming of the railways. The first small line was opened in 1835 and the first freight line two years later. During the following years, when a network of lines was established in Germany, the existence of the *Zollverein* ensured that these were built with a uniform gauge and made it natural that Berlin should become the centre of the railway system.

The political and psychological effects of the *Zollverein* were probably, however, more immediately important than the economic results, which were considerably slower in taking place. Having assumed economic leadership in Germany, it became increasingly to be expected that Prussia should take up political leadership as well. And the German people were more ready to accept this than the rulers of the states.

(e) The Wartburg Festival (1817) and the Carlsbad Decrees (1819)

Economic unity, while encouraging the German liberals and nationalists, did not satisfy their ambitions. The educated and professional classes particularly resented being deprived of the political, administrative, legal and other openings which a large united Germany would have offered them in a way that the small, autocratic states never could. It is not surprising, therefore, that the spearhead of resistance to the Vienna settlement in Germany should come from the students at the universities, who formed themselves into nationwide patriotic fraternities (*Burschenschaft*). In 1817 the students at the University of Jena organized a festival at Wartburg in Saxony to commemorate the tercentenary of Luther's defiance of the Papacy, which began the Reformation, and also the anniversary of the victory at Leipzig over Napoleon in 1813. Patriotic speeches were made in praise of the 'Christian-German Fatherland', and reactionary books, together with objects which included an effigy of Metternich, were burnt on a bonfire in imitation of Luther's burning of the papal bull condemning him for heresy. And in March 1819 a student of the same university stabbed to death an anti-liberal journalist, August von Kotzebue, who was suspected of being a secret agent of Tsar Alexander.

The murder of Kotzebue was, as Metternich admitted, the opportunity for which he had been waiting. He could now represent the liberal and nationalist movement, which he feared would destroy the stability of Germany, as subversive. He dissuaded Frederick William of Prussia from granting a constitution to his kingdom. He also called a meeting of representatives of several German states at Carlsbad in Bohemia, where he persuaded them to draw up a series of decrees, which were submitted to the Diet of the Confederation and passed, despite opposition from the more liberal states. These Carlsbad decrees called upon the German rulers to co-operate in enforcing counter-measures against any form of revolutionary activity. They prohibited political meetings, ordered a strict censorship of the press, placed university teaching under close inspection, forbade students' associations without permission and required the expulsion of pro-fessors and students if they expressed dangerous views.

The German rulers accepted Metternich's interpretation of the situ-ation and put the Decrees into force in their states. A permanent commission was set up at Mainz, which was in Hesse-Darmstadt but was garrisoned by Austrian and Prussian troops, to supervise their enforcement and to collect evidence, with the help of police spies, against liberals and other revolutionaries. Police spies were particularly active in the universities, where they kept files on students which were later used if they wished to become government officials. Many political leaders were imprisoned or exiled. Among the publications banned by the Prussian censors at Cologne was the *Rhineland Gazette*, edited by Karl Marx, and also an edition of Dante's *Divine Comedy*, which they condemned for making fun of sacred matters. These repressive measures continued to be applied in Germany for 30 years; and the so-called Final Act of 1820 gave the Diet the right to intervene with armed force in the domestic affairs of member states to suppress revolts against monarchical government. The liberal movement declined. There followed what German historians call the 'quiet years' until the general outburst of revolutions in Europe in 1848.

Metternich had, indeed, been able to turn the aims of the nationalists against themselves by increasing the power of the Confederation for reactionary instead of liberal policies. The Carlsbad decrees gave it in effect a greater central authority than had been envisaged at the Con-gress of Vienna. This would not have been possible without agreement between Austria and Prussia, and it emphasized the fact that Metternich could only make use of the Confederation in this way as long as Prussia remained unopposed towards Austria and could be persuaded to accept his policy.

(f) Conspiracy and Reaction in Italy

Although Italy was destined by the Congress of Vienna to be the area to compensate Austria for her loss of territory and influence elsewhere, Metternich was never able to exercise as complete a control over the peninsula as he could over Germany. Italy had not even got a loose federal organization like the German Confederation. When Metternich tried to form something like this throughout the peninsula, Piedmont and the Papacy successfully resisted him, and they also refused to make separate treaties with Austria which would have placed them under her protection. Metternich's influence was naturally strongest in the provinces of Lombardy and Venetia, where he appointed Austrians and Slavs to the most important administrative posts and stationed Imperial troops (the hated 'whitecoats') to garrison the towns; but he also had considerable power in the Habsburg duchies of Parma, Modena and Tuscany. Otherwise his sway over Italy was most assisted by the fact that all the rulers in the divided country were despots, determined to maintain their power and independence, quick to suppress all opposition within their states and aware that Austrian assistance was the best guarantee of their being able to do this. Ferdinand I of Naples was the most ready among these rulers to recognize his dependence upon Austrian goodwill. He was prepared to make a separate treaty with Austria. In return for an Austrian guarantee of his throne and territory, he agreed not to alter the constitution of his kingdom without first consulting the Austrian government and in the event of Austria being involved in a war to provide her with an army of 24 000 men.

During these post-war years, national resentment against Austria was probably greater in Italy than in Germany. Italy had known a greater degree of unification and measure of efficient government under Napoleon, and had a larger middle class, at least in the northern provinces directly ruled by Austria. There were a number of secret societies in the peninsula. Some of these went back to the eighteenth century, particularly the Freemasons, who were rationalist and anti-clerical. They had been condemned as early as 1738 in the Bull *In Eminenti* issued by Pope Clement XII (or rather his advisers as he was incapable by then). During the nineteenth century, societies influenced by freemasonry, but with political objectives, were founded. The most important of these was the Carbonari ('charcoal-burners') founded in Naples after the restoration of the Bourbons in 1815. It aimed at the overthrow of existing Italian governments and the expulsion of the Austrians, but it contained a wide variety of members—monarchists and republicans, clericals and anti-clericals, conservatives and radicals. Consequently, it was not well-organized and almost completely without definite plans to gain its objectives.

The first uprising took place in 1817 in the Papal States, where the enforced resignations of government officials, appointed before 1814 by the French, to make way for priests, had caused widespread resentment. The plot, however, was betrayed to the ecclesiastical authorities, and large numbers of conspirators were sentenced to long terms in prison or in the galleys. That these sentences were imposed by a court of priests, presided over by a cardinal, aroused strong anti-papal and anti-clerical feeling among Italian nationalists.

In 1820, following the revolution in Spain, the Carbonari led a rising in Naples and were supported by officers of the royal army, who disliked the Austrian military instructors recently sent to train them. Ferdinand was forced to grant a constitution, modelled upon the Spanish one of 1812, which included the ending of noble and clerical privileges, the abolition of the Inquisition and the establishment of an elected parliament. Ferdinand took an oath in the private chapel of his palace to uphold this constitution and accepted the new government, which allowed him to go to the Congress of Laibach 'to obtain the sanction of the powers for our newly-acquired liberties': but instead he there secured Austrian troops to restore him to his former position in the kingdom (*see page 28*).

Soon afterwards, the Carbonari took the lead in a similar revolt in Piedmont. King Victor Emmanuel I, who could not bring himself to crush the rebellion, abdicated in favour of his brother, Charles Felix, who at the time was out of the country. The King's nephew, Charles Albert temporarily acted as Regent and granted a constitution. When Charles Felix returned, however, he revoked the constitution, and Austrian troops defeated the insurgents at the Battle of Novara in 1821.

The Austrians also put down revolts which had broken out in their own provinces of Lombardy and Venetia. Hundreds of Italian nationalists were now in prison as the result of these risings, which had demonstrated the failure of the Carbonari to organize effectively any step towards unity and independence. Metternich had observed with satisfaction that the revolt in Piedmont was 'a terrible confusion'. He was also highly satisfied with the results of Austria's 'protective intervention' in Italy. He was pleased too with the support this action had received from the Continental powers. At the close of the Congress of Laibach, he told its members that 'never, perhaps, had the spirit of the allied sovereigns been manifested under an aspect more consoling for the human race and more reassuring for the Italian courts.' And, indeed, the continuance of Austrian supremacy in Italy depended upon the Habsburgs receiving such foreign support in the future and the nationalists being deprived of it.

Bibliography

For Austrian history, see A.J.P. Taylor, *The Habsburg Monarchy 1809–1918* (Hamish Hamilton, 1948) and C.A. Gulick, *Austria from Habsburg to Hitler* (Univ. of California Press, 2 vols., 1948). Metternich's policy is discussed in A.Milne, *Metternich* (Hodder & Stoughton, 1975) and Alan Sked, 'The Metternich System 1815–1848' in Alan Sked (ed.), *Europe's Balance of Power 1815–1848* (Macmillan, 1979). An aspect of German history during this period is considered in W.O. Henderson, *The Zollverein* (CUP, 1939).

Exercises

A *This section consists of questions that might be used for discussion (or written answers) as a way of expanding on the chapter and your understanding of it:*

1 In what ways was Austria different from other European powers?
2 Why did Austria's government remain 'in a condition of suspended animation' during the reign of Francis I?
3 In what ways did Hungary remain different from the other provinces of the Austrian Empire?

4 Outline and discuss Metternich's political views.
5 Why was there more opposition to the central government in Austria than in other European countries?
6 What do you understand by the 'Metternich System'?
7 What was the German Confederation, and what did Metternich see it as being?
8 What was the *Zollverein*?
9 Why did the smaller German states join the *Zollverein* while Austria remained outside it?
10 Why did the murder of Kotzebue provide Metternich with 'the opportunity for which he had been waiting'?
11 Compare the Carlsbad Decrees with measures approved by the British government in the same period.
12 How was Metternich able to maintain Austrian influence in Italy?
13 Why were the revolts of the Carbonari so unsuccessful?

B *Essay questions*
1 Who was the better 'European': Castlereagh or Metternich? (Oxford, 1982)
2 Explain how Metternich gained an ascendancy in Europe after the treaty of Vienna. (SUJB, 1982)
3 What was the 'Metternich system', and what were the chief threats to it? (Oxford and Cambridge, 1982)
4 'Metternich had every reason to be satisfied with the outcome of the peace settlement of 1814–1815, but international events during the ten years which followed brought him little more than anxiety and dismay.' Discuss the truth of this statement. (London, 1982)

C *Essay-writing skills 2: creating an essay plan*
This essay aims to improve your essay writing skills by guiding you through an essay and developing your ability to avoid narrative and concentrate on analysis (*see page 38*). The title under consideration is:

What were the political views of Prince Metternich, and how did he attempt to implement these views at home and abroad?

(a) Below are a number of sentences; some of these would provide a direct and relevant answer to this question, while others only state facts broadly associated with Metternich. Write down those that you consider relevant.

(i) Metternich had served as Austrian ambassador in Dresden from 1801 to 1803, in Berlin from 1803 to 1806 and in Paris from 1806 to 1807.
(ii) To oppose revolutionary ideas in Germany, Metternich was instrumental in having the Carlsbad Decrees approved and enforced.
(iii) In 1815 the German Confederation was founded, consisting of 39 separate states.
(iv) In the international arena, too, Metternich did his best to oppose liberal and nationalist movements.
(v) He was an unremitting opponent of revolutionaries and unable to distinguish between them and those seeking moderate reform.
(vi) Metternich opposed the Carbonari and other revolutionaries in Italy by a variety of methods.

(vii) Metternich felt that government efficiency, together with policies that were for the benefit of the bulk of the people (a sort of nineteenth-century Enlightened Despotism), was desirable.

(viii) In 1821 Austrian troops defeated the rebels of Piedmont at the Battle of Novara.

(ix) The *Zollverein* was established when Prussia abolished all customs duties between the separate provinces under her rule.

(x) In general terms, Metternich may be characterized as a political reactionary.

(xi) Troops of the Imperial army were never based in their own provinces, but were stationed instead in other parts of the Empire.

(b) Consider the sentences that you have selected in relation to the question as a whole; what aspects of the question remain unanswered? Write similar appropriate sentences to cover these aspects. You should now have between seven and nine sentences that will serve as suitable first sentences of paragraphs in answer to the original question.

(c) Now place your introductory sentences in the most appropriate order to answer the question logically.

(d) Below are four sets of data that will provide the supporting material for four of your sentences. When fully explained, these will form the remainder of each of four of your paragraphs; decide with which introductory sentences each of these four goes:

A Support for Ferdinand I of Naples.
   Victory at the Battle of Novara.
   Support for the petty despotic princes of Italy.
   Suppression of revolt in Lombardy and Venetia.

B Metternich's regrets about the inefficiency of Austria's government.
   Metternich's desire to continue the reforms initiated by Maria Theresa and Joseph II.

C Opposition to democratic ideas.
   His view that the people were too ignorant and easily led.
   Hostility to the ideas of 'Equality' and 'Liberty'.
   Support for gradual and moderate reform.

D Influence over the Protocol of Troppau.
   Hostility to Canning and British policy in Greece.
   Support for French intervention in Spain in 1823.
   Desire to draw Russia and Prussia closer to Austria.
   Hostility towards South American revolutionary movements.

(e) Next, create similar sets of data for your other sentences.

(f) If you have now created an extremely detailed essay plan of the kind that is essential in these early stages of study, it should now be possible to write a relevant and accurate answer in essay form to the question originally posed.

4 The Restored Monarchy in France

(a) Louis XVIII (1814–24) and the Charter

The Bourbon monarchy was restored in France in 1814 through the initiative of Talleyrand (*see page 8*). The allied rulers, for whom the establishment of a republic was out of the question, accepted this as the settlement most likely to succeed; and royalist demonstrations among the war-weary French people suggested that it met with approval there.

The new King was a brother of Louis XVI and had taken the title of Louis XVIII in 1795 after the death in prison of his ten-year-old nephew, who had been recognized by Royalists as Louis XVII when his father was executed in January 1793 (*see Diagram 1*). Having spent the years of revolution and war on the Continent and in England, the 60-year-old monarch was stout, gouty and lazy (and Talleyrand had wished that Napoleon had been lazy in the later years of his reign), but well-meaning and conciliatory. In his very appearance he represented the *ancien régime*; he still dressed in the fashion that had gone out with the Revolution—a powdered wig, knee-breeches and three-cornered hat. He did indeed believe firmly in the divine hereditary right and absolute power of the Bourbon monarchy, but he also understood that national unity required that he should rule as a moderate constitutional monarch. He told his brother that he was resolved not to be the king of 'two peoples'. He wished to avoid recriminations against both Republicans and Bonapartists, and he realized that neither the French people nor the allies would countenance an attempt to return to pre-1789 days. He wished to commend the monarchy to the French people by linking it with Henry IV (1589–1610). His statue was re-erected in Paris; his head replaced that of Napoleon on the cross of the Legion of Honour, the order instituted by the Emperor for distinguished services to the state; and instead of the Imperialist *Chant de Départ*, the national anthem became *Vive Henri Quatre*. He had as his chief ministers both Talleyrand and Joseph Fouché, who had been Napoleon's minister of police, but had been dismissed in 1810 for intriguing with the exiled Bourbons. Since both men had served successfully in the governments of both the Republic and the Empire, it was to be expected that they would share his understanding about the need for toleration and comprehension by the restored French monarchy.

In 1814, when Napoleon's defeat seemed to be near, Louis had crossed from England to Ghent, where he drew up with Talleyrand's assistance a Charter laying down a constitution for a renewed French kingdom; and he proclaimed this when he assumed the throne. This was to remain (with a few small changes made in 1830) the constitution of France until 1848. It was a compromise, designed either to satisfy or to placate the differences of political belief in the country, but it was also the most liberal on the Continent. The principle that all power belonged by right to the monarchy was retained, and the constitution

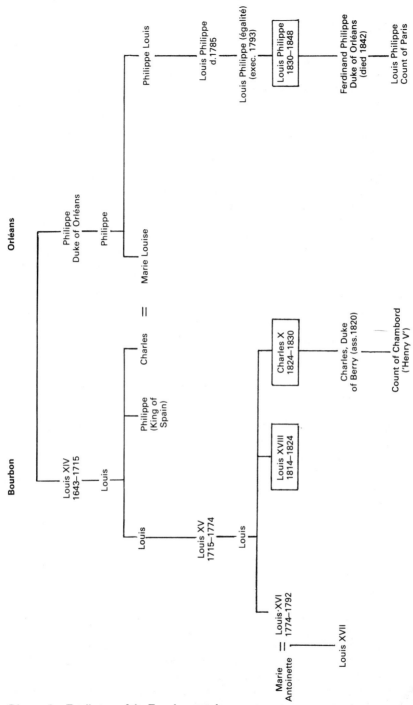

Diagram 1. Family tree of the French monarchy

55

was granted by the King as a concession to his people, like the Edict of Nantes which Henry IV had issued in 1598 to establish religious toleration in his kingdom. The Charter stated that the King was to govern through his ministers, but he retained considerable powers. He was to command the army and navy, declare war and make treaties, appoint to the public service and the Chamber of Peers and to be the sole proposer of legislation. He could also dissolve the Chamber of Deputies, create peers, alter the electorate and rule directly by ordinances in times of emergency. There was to be an Assembly consisting of a Chamber of Peers, some of whose members were hereditary noblemen and some appointed for life by the King, and a Chamber of Deputies, the members of which had to be over 40 years old and to pay 1000 francs a year in direct taxes. A fifth of the deputies were to come up for election each year, and the electors had to be over 30 years old and pay 300 francs a year in direct taxes. These restrictions meant that only 90 000 men in a total population of nearly 25 000 000 could vote, and only 12 000 men were entitled to stand as candidates. Though only the King could propose laws, the Assembly could refuse to pass them or to levy taxes.

Year	Deputies' tax	Deputies' age	Years of tenure	Elector's tax	Elector's age	Type of constituency	Number of seats
1814	1000 francs	40	5 (⅕ elected yearly)	300 francs	30	Single-member	258
1815		25					402
1815							395
1816		40					258
1817					25	Multi-member	
1820						Single-member	430 (172 more elected by chief taxpayers)
1824			7 (no ⅕ elected yearly)				

Table 4. Bourbon electoral system (1814–1848)

Though inspired by the British example, this was not a parliamentary constitution, since governments could be formed by the King and would not depend upon a majority in the Assembly. It was conservative by the standards of the later years of the Revolution, but it was a radical change for a restored Bourbon to make and showed that he planned to rule on the lines of the moderate constitutional monarchy of 1789 rather than the age-long absolutism of the past French kingdom. And though Napoleon's constitution had provided for universal adult male suffrage, the voting merely produced a list from which the First Consul or his nominees selected the members of the Legislative Body. The Charter did make it possible for a small proportion of the French people to take part in the political life of the country, but the number able to do so effectively was very limited. More than half of the people were illiterate, and about three-quarters of them were peasants, living in small isolated villages and much under the influence of the Church.

Besides setting up a form of government, the Charter also accepted the legal and administrative developments which had taken place during the revolutionary and Napoleonic periods. The law codes and the centralized system of administration devised by Napoleon were retained. The cherished personal rights of the Revolution were also preserved. All Frenchmen were to be equal before the law, to be secure from arbitrary imprisonment and to be eligible for civil and military appointments. There was to be trial by jury, freedom of the press and religious toleration, the position of the Roman Catholic Church being still regulated by the Concordat made by Napoleon with the Papacy in 1801. Pre-revolutionary privileges were not restored, the Napoleonic nobility was not recognized, and those who had bought confiscated ecclesiastical or noble property had the title to their possession confirmed.

The chief gainers from the Revolution had been the middle class, who were still mostly to be found in the professions and government service rather than in commerce and in industry. Now the Charter had given the wealthiest of them the possibility of political power. They were to show themselves determined to retain and even extend this and to oppose any attempt to restore the position of the nobility or the Church at their expense.

(b) The Hundred Days (1815)

Napoleon's return to France from Elba for nearly a hundred days between March and June in 1815 was a disastrous episode for the restored Bourbon monarchy, which never recovered from its consequences. It intensified the difficulties which the new regime had to face in any event and diminished the chances of overcoming them.

Napoleon succeeded in gaining control of the country during the Hundred Days mainly because of the support he received from the army, which was embittered by defeat and resented the events of the peace. The loss of territory suffered by France through the peace treaty (*see page 8*) had made its victories useless. The Royal Bodyguard, which only noblemen could join, was revived, and *emigré* officers, who had fought on the side of the allies, were given half pay and then promoted, but 14 000 Imperial officers were summarily retired; an English traveller met a captain who was working as a waggoner. And, while Napoleon's regiments had continued to fight under the French revolutionary flag, the tricolour, the new regime restored the royalist white fleur-de-lis flag. 'They imposed on us', wrote one of Napoleon's marshals, 'the flag under which they had fought us.'

When Napoleon landed on the French coast, he was not only welcomed by the soldiers. The officials of the old Imperial administration renewed their loyalty to him as readily as they had recently given it to the new monarchy. And most of the people remained passive and inactive. As Napoleon proceeded on his way through the countryside from the south of France to Paris, he did his best in his speeches to win over as many sections of the population as possible. He made himself out to be a liberal constitutionalist, a champion of the Church, a defender of the peasants' lands and a man of peace, but there was no sign that the nation wanted to live again under his rule in any guise. When he arranged a plebiscite to confirm a new constitution he had granted and elect a fresh legislative body, there was widespread abstention among the voters. Yet, at the same time, there was no decisive royalist resistance to him, and Louis XVIII had to flee the country.

The Hundred Days showed how insecure was the position of the restored monarchy, which had no genuine popular movement to support it. When the First Restoration of 1814 put Louis XVIII on the French throne, it had been possible to represent him as having come as the result of an invitation by a provisional government on behalf of the nation. But when the Second Restoration of 1815 brought him back again after the defeat of Napoleon at Waterloo, it was not as easy to deny the accusation of his enemies that he had been returned 'in the baggage wagons of the foreigner'. Moreover, though the terms of the Second Treaty of Paris were still moderate, they were not as favourable to France as those of the First. Public opinion resented the surrender both of French Savoy to Piedmont and of the Saar to Prussia (which meant the final abandonment of the Rhine frontier) and blamed the King for it. Already there was widespread regret at the passing of the great days of the Republic and the Empire when French armies had overrun the Continent and dictated terms to the nations. There was no possibility of suggesting that the people had gladly returned to the obedience due to their rightful monarch.

In addition, the Hundred Days upset the general reconciliation in France which Louis XVIII had wanted and damaged the chances of success for the constitutional government which he had granted. The nation became yet more sharply divided. The exasperated Royalists wanted to avenge themselves upon all who had supported Napoleon during his adventure. The loyalty of the old Imperial administrators could no longer be trusted. Many of them now found themselves debarred from office and replaced by appointments made from the *émigré* nobility and clergy, who could be relied upon as faithful supporters of the regime. And so the Bourbon monarchy found itself having to face more widespread opposition than had seemed likely in 1814.

(c) The Ultras and the White Terror

It had not been possible to hold a general election for the Chamber of Deputies before the Hundred Days. It took place in August 1815. Louis XVIII had been persuaded to increase the number of seats from 258 to 402 (though this was soon reduced to 395 after the territory lost through the Second Treaty of Paris) and to lower the age of eligibility for membership from 40 to 25. The result of this election in the harsh climate of opinion prevailing after the Hundred Days was the return of a Chamber which contained a large majority of young, inexperienced and extreme Royalists—the Ultras as they came to be known. Louis himself called this '*la Chambre introuvable*' (meaning that he had never thought that a Chamber so royalist could have been found). The Ultras (who formed the only strongly organized and coherent political party) were led by the King's brother, the Count of Artois. He was the heir to the throne and had been a prominent *émigré* who had fought against the Revolutionary and Napoleonic armies. Many of the Ultras were themselves *émigrés*, the noble and wealthy refugees from the Revolution, who had fled from France and lived abroad until the Restoration and now returned with a bitter hatred of all that had happened since 1789. They wished to restore as much as possible of the *ancien régime* in France by regaining for the nobility and the Church their former powers and privileges. As a step towards this, they planned to set up a censorship of the press and to place education under the control of the Church. And, since under the Charter they could only do this through the Assembly, they were prepared to make common cause with the liberals to compel ministers to accept its authority.

Talleyrand and Fouché had tried hard to secure the return of moderate deputies, and their failure made it impossible for the King to keep them in office to contend with a hostile Chamber. Since he was not required by the Charter to appoint ministers whom the Chamber favoured, he replaced them in September by a ministry headed by the Duke of Richelieu, who had spent his years of exile in the service of the Russian government, becoming governor of the newly-conquered territory of the Black Sea and founding the town of Odessa. Talleyrand described him scornfully as 'the man in France who knows most about the Crimea', but Wellington said of him that his word was equal to a treaty. It was, indeed, probably an advantage that he had not been involved in either the service of Napoleon or the intrigues of the *émigrés* in allied courts and armies, and he was respected for his upright and disinterested character. He saw that one of the most serious problems facing the new regime was 'the violence of passions, the store of hatred, the insatiable thirst for vengeance' among contemporary Frenchmen.

Indeed, that summer of 1815 produced a situation approaching civil war. This was the time of the 'White Terror' when the Royalists, enraged by the Hundred Days, sought reprisals against the Bonapartists. These began immediately after the Battle of Waterloo. At Avignon one of Napoleon's marshals was beaten to death by a crowd, and when his coffin was being taken to burial, it was seized and his body thrown into the River Rhône; and two other marshals were murdered. Religion too provided a motive, and Protestant men and women were publicly flogged at Nîmes. Altogether acts of violence resulted in some 300 deaths throughout the country. Richelieu was unable to resist the pressure from the Chamber to agree to a series of emergency laws allowing the imprisonment of suspects without trial and the setting up of military courts from which there was no appeal. This was the 'Legal Terror'. Sentences of imprisonment and exile were imposed, and a number of high-ranking officers were executed, the best-known being Marshal Ney, a hero of the Russian campaign, who had taken the oath of loyalty to Louis XVIII in 1814 and then welcomed Napoleon on his return from Elba.

The activities of the Ultras made the peasants fear that they might lose their land. They revolted in Grenoble. The allied governments were alarmed at the situation, and so too was Louis. He dissolved the Chamber of Deputies in 1816 and ordered another general election for which he restored the number of deputies to 262 and their qualifying age to 40 as laid down in the Charter. This election gave Richelieu a working majority of moderates who supported him. Under him the indemnity imposed on France after the Hundred Days was paid off, and the country now seemed to have such a stable government that in 1818 the allies withdrew the army of occupation and admitted France to the Alliance (*see page 24*).

(d) The Failure of Conciliation

The post-war period until 1820 saw indeed an attempt to establish constitutional government in France. Louis hoped not only to check the extreme wishes of the Ultras, but also to gain for the monarchy the support of those whose sympathies were with the Revolution, but this was made difficult by the changing balance of power within the Chamber brought about by the elections for a fifth of its members each year. In 1817 there was a majority in the Chamber which wanted a reform of the electoral system, and the King agreed to do this. Under the Charter, there were small, single-member constituencies, which allowed the wealthier landowning class to exercise a considerable influence over the voters. In 1817 the change was made to larger, multi-member constituencies, and the qualifying age of the voters was reduced from 30 to 25. Under this new system, the elections in the autumns of 1817 and 1818 increased the strengths of the liberals, which alarmed Richelieu so much that he wanted to cancel the electoral changes and to seek an agreement with the Ultras. The result, however, was a split in the ministry, and since the regime was still a monarchical and not a constitutional one, Louis could take advantage of this to replace him in December 1818 by a personal favourite.

He was the Duke of Decazes, who had become minister of police after the Hundred Days. This had brought him into close contact with Louis, who wrote to him daily in such terms as, 'Come to receive the tenderest embraces of thy friend, thy father, thy Louis.' That this brought him political advancement did not make him popular. The French people, it was said, preferred 20 mistresses to one favourite. He believed that he should try to conciliate the rising liberals, and he did achieve some early success in this policy, especially after he had persuaded the King to enoble some 60 of his supporters to gain him a majority in the Chamber of Peers. In 1819 he secured the abolition of the censorship of the press and the granting to journalists of the right of trial by jury to protect them from arbitrary government action. This made possible, for a short time, the rise of flourishing liberal newspapers and magazines.

It did not, however, gain him more support for his ministry. On the contrary, liberal politicians and journalists now attacked it unrestrainedly. It was clear that many liberals were abandoning any idea of compromise with the monarchy. Decazes, in his turn, was alarmed. The ministry could have mounted a campaign of repression which might have crushed this sort of opposition out of existence, but this would have placed it in the position of having to rely upon the Ultras, as thorough supporters of the Bourbons, and not being likely to be able to control them. His room for manoeuvre between the two contending groups was, therefore, limited. The further success gained by the liberals in the elections in the autumn of 1819 was a bitter blow to him and led him to consider reviewing the electoral law; but the final stroke came in February 1820 when the Duke of Berry, the King's nephew, was murdered by a republican workman.

This aroused such a storm of indignation among all royalist opinion that Louis had reluctantly to part with his favourite and recall Richelieu to power. He set about to control the reviving political activity in the kingdom by restoring the censorship of the press and permitting the imprisonment of suspected persons without trial. He also changed the electoral system again, restoring the smaller, single-member constituencies and giving the highest taxpayers among the voters an additional vote to return a further 172 deputies to the Chamber. The results of the first elections held under this arrangement in 1820 considerably strengthened the Ultras in the Chamber at the expense of the moderates, and the elections of 1821 gave them a large majority in it. And when the Ultras joined with the liberals to oppose Richelieu, he resigned because the King, now weakened by age, showed no readiness to support him.

He was again succeeded by a new favourite. The King now had a mistress, the young Countess of Cayla, though his age and infirmity limited her activities to playing chess with him and writing him a daily letter in the composition of which she was helped by his new favourite, the Count of Villèle. He had made his fortune in the West Indies as an *émigré* and was a natural choice to head a new ministry, particularly as he was also the leader of the Ultras in the Assembly. His ministry was entirely composed of Ultras, who accepted the guidance of the Count of Artois.

This development resulted in revolutionary liberal action. Secret societies were formed, such as the Charbonnerie, which had connections with the Carbonari in Italy, and their members were encouraged by the revolutions in Spain and Naples. In 1821 and 1822 there were a number of risings in different parts of France, but they achieved nothing. The best-known conspirators were four sergeants of the garrison of La Rochelle, who were tried and executed for a hopeless attempt to subvert their regiment. Repression and internal quarrels brought about the dissolution of the Charbonnerie by the end of 1822; it had never had more than 40 000 members and had attracted little working-class support. These incidents indicated, however, that extremism was gaining ground on both sides of the opposition to the regime, and the moderates, upon whom the success of the constitution depended, were rapidly declining in numbers and effectiveness.

Though they failed, the liberal risings caused many people to fear that the country might be drifting into anarchy, and this assisted the Ultras. Villéle tightened the censorship and placed secondary education under the supervision of the clergy. But that was not all. He was an able and industrious administrator. He completed the reform of the French financial system, which had been beyond the Controllers-General of the *ancien régime*, but had been begun by Napoleon. An annual estimate of revenue and expenditure and close control of government spending gave the country financial stability at last. At the same time, he sought the support of industrialists by raising the tariff considerably and general popularity by a vigorous foreign policy. In 1823 a French army put down the revolution in Spain, though Canning compelled the abandonment of any attempt to regain for Spain her colonies in South America (*see page 31*).

To strengthen its power, the government held a general election in the spring of 1824, which was an overwhelming success for the Ultras. The new Chamber was so like '*la Chambre introuvable*' of 1815 that it was called '*la Chambre retrouvée*'. The liberal opposition had been reduced from 110 to 19 members. Later in the year, the government again changed the electoral law, doing away with the annual partial elections to the Chamber and decreeing that it should last for seven years without a dissolution. The way in which the electoral system had been constantly changed during these years was one of the most serious signs of the failure of the constitution.

By now Louis XVIII's health was declining, and so were his powers of independent judgement. Since he had been compelled to abandon his policy of conciliation in 1820, he had been more and more influenced by the Countess of Cayla, who sympathized with the Ultras, and accepted advice from the Count of Artois. He died in September 1824. Had he been younger and more energetic, his prudence might have enabled him to control the Assembly with its select membership and limited power, and to restore royal absolutism by making the crown the arbiter of the political situation so that it became accepted as the best means of preserving peace and order. The Bourbon monarchy had been able to do this during the fierce political and religious rivalries of sixteenth and seventeeth France, but, as it was, he had relinquished the crown's independence to an extreme, sectional party.

(e) Charles X (1824–30) and Religious Policy

Louis was succeeded by the Count of Artois. The new King was not as intelligent as his brother, but possessed a more pleasing and gracious personality and was more active despite his 67 years. He announced his attachment to the institutions of the constitution and restored the freedom of the press. The country as a whole seemed to welcome his accession.

The first important measure undertaken by the Assembly during his reign was a project to compensate *émigrés* for the loss of their estates during the Revolution. This had been planned in the previous reign, and a settlement of the question was desired by others as well as the *émigrés*. Ever since the restoration of the French monarchy, the position of such land had been uncertain. There was a constant possibility that the *émigrés* might succeed in getting it back. Consequently its value remained lower than that of other land, since purchasers did not know how long they might retain possession of it; but if the former landowners were to be indemnified, they could no longer retain any claim to it. The money, about 1000 million francs, was raised by reducing the interest on the national debt, which meant that middle-class investors largely financed the measure, and during the debates in the Assembly bitter memories were revived of the losses investors had suffered through inflation and confiscation in the days of the Revolution.

The French Church was strongly influenced in renewed zeal and increasing ordinations by the widespread revival which Europe had been experiencing since the early years of the nineteenth century. Many of its members, moreover, were Ultramontanes, who, that is to say, looked 'beyond the mountains' to Rome and were ready to uphold papal authority and traditional doctrines (*see pages 294, 390*). Since 1820 government policy had largely favoured the influence of the Church in France, and Charles X's own views supported this. Louis XVIII had not been physically strong enough to submit to the traditional five-hour coronation ceremony of the French kings, and so he had not been crowned at all; but Charles was determined not to let this lapse. He was crowned, as custom required, in Rheims Cathedral with the full ritual of the old ceremony, which emphasized the sacred character of the monarchy and the close support which Crown and Church gave each other. Soon both sacrilege and criticism of the divine right of kings were made crimes. Religious orders, including the Society of Jesus, were allowed to resume their activities which had been forbidden since the Revolution. New religious societies were formed. These included the *Congrégation*, which organized religious propaganda throughout the country, and the *Chevaliers de la Foi*, a secret Royalist society (whose existence remained unknown until 1949) dedicated to restoring the Church to its old position during the *ancien régime*. A cleric was made Minister of Education, and the bishops were allowed to appoint all the teachers in primary schools. There was even talk of abolishing the Concordat which Napoleon had made with the Papacy. The Revolution had deprived the French Church of the land from which it drew its income. Under the Concordat, the Papacy accepted the nomination of bishops by the state in return for it paying the salaries of the clergy. The attempt, however, to restore the Church to the privileged, landowning position it had possessed under the *ancien régime* did not get the support of the Papacy, which considered the terms of the Concordat too favourable to be abandoned.

France, however, was acutely divided over the religious issue. The nobles supported the Church, as did some intellectuals, while the peasants remained attached to the Roman Catholic faith. Yet rationalism and anti-clericalism were still strong, even among some Ultras, and the newly-rich classes were alarmed at any possibility of the Church recovering its privileges and lands. Such a policy also alienated some royalists, who maintained the ancient ideas of Gallicanism, the belief that the Crown should control the Church. The liberals were able to benefit from this widespread anti-clericalism and exploited the situation to form a powerful combination against the government. In 1826 alone no fewer than 5000 anti-clerical pamphlets were published. The government's response was to abolish the freedom of the press, imprison journalists and publishers and dissolve the National Guard, the predominantly middle-class, part-time militia established in Paris during the early days of the Revolution. Late in 1827 Villèle decided upon a general election in the hope of taking the opposition by surprise and retaining control of the Chamber for another seven years however unpopular the government might become. His gamble failed completely. The liberals had a majority of 60 in the new Chamber, and early in the next year he had to resign.

(f) The Mounting Crisis (1828–30)
The religious issue was to be a primary cause of the downfall of the Bourbon monarchy. Charles X was bitterly disappointed by the result of the election and the fall of Villèle. He was determined not to compromise with the liberal opposition on this question, but he lacked

the political skill to do this. Other ministers persuaded him that Villèle should be succeeded by the Viscount of Martignac, a lawyer from Bordeaux, who was a moderate, anti-clerical Ultra. He hoped to make the situation less dangerous for the government by a conciliatory policy. The censorship of the press was again lifted, and the growth of ecclesiastical control over education was checked, but this policy showed no signs of placating the opposition, and Charles disliked it. He dismissed Martignac in 1829.

Charles too had a favourite whom he wanted in office. He replaced Martignac by his friend, Prince Jules de Polignac, a member of an ancient aristocratic family and an uncompromising Ultra, who had long been his trusted adviser. He declared that his aims were 'to reorganize society, to give back to the clergy their weight in state affairs, to create a powerful aristocracy and to surround it with privileges.'

Yet, for six months, while the opposition organized itself for a contest, the government did nothing. Political societies were formed, including one with the name of 'Help Thyself and Heaven will Help Thee', and new liberal newspapers appeared. The liberals in the Chamber gained confidence and in March 1830 succeeded in passing a resolution reminding the King that 'the permanent harmony of the political views of your government with the wishes of your people is the indispensable condition for the conduct of public affairs.' The opposition was now insisting that the ministry should be responsible to the majority in the Chamber and not to the King. The answer of Charles was to dissolve the Chamber in June and order a general election. He himself did all he could to persuade the voters to support the government's candidates, but they lost 60 seats. Even the restricted electorate was opposed to the King and expected him to appoint a new government acceptable to the Chamber.

(g) The July Revolution (1830)

Polignac suggested that he should take some liberals into his ministry, but Charles was determined to uphold his prerogative. 'I would rather earn my bread than reign like the King of England,' he declared. He resolved not to yield, though both the Tsar and Metternich advised him to make concessions. The government, in search of prestige, had sent a military expedition to Algeria, and when news reached the country of early successes there, it was encouraged to stand firm. Acting in accordance with the Charter, the King declared a state of emergency and issued the Ordinances of St. Cloud, which forbade the publication of newspapers without the government's permission, dissolved the newly-elected Chamber, restricted the franchise to the 25 000 of the wealthiest existing voters and arranged for another general election. Then he went to Rambouillet to hunt.

While Charles was doing this, Polignac was having repeated visions of the Virgin Mary in which she always promised him success. Perhaps this assurance of divine aid was the reason why once again the forces of the opposition were given time to organize themselves. The government took no steps to concentrate troops for an emergency, occupy all strategic points in and around the capital or even arrest potential leaders of the oppostion. Neither the King nor Polignac expected the opposition to respond to their challenge. They did not, indeed, even realize that they had made one; but to refuse any compromise at all was bound to provoke a revolutionary response.

The appearance of the Ordinances of St. Cloud brought about immediate disturbances in Paris. Liberal and Bonapartist politicians organized protest meetings; students and workmen raised barricades. Circumstances favoured the opposition. There had been an economic recession since 1826. During the post-war years, Paris had gained its first pavements, omnibus services and gas lighting, but now there were also many unemployed in its streets. The Paris mob supported the raising of the barricades. The National Guard, though disbanded, still had their weapons and came out into the streets with them. The King now decided to send in troops, but it was too late. They lost control of the city during the fighting of the 'Three Glorious Days' (27–29 July), when some 1800 rioters and 200 soldiers were killed. By the end of the fighting the rioters had captured the Louvre and other important buildings, and the army was retreating, many men deserting to the rebels. From the terrace at St. Cloud Charles saw through a telescope the tricolour flying from the Cathedral of Notre Dame. He vainly dismissed Polignac and withdrew the Ordinances. A mob set out to search for him. He moved again to Rambouillet, where he abdicated early in August in favour of his grandson, the Duke of Bordeaux. He himself went to England and then to Scotland, being allowed to spend the rest of his life at Holyrood House in Edinburgh. He had nearly £500 000 in gold, which had been deposited in a London bank by Louis XVIII in 1814 in case of such a development.

The combination of the extremism of the Ultras, the organization and propaganda of the liberals and the political ineptness of the King and his ministers had destroyed the Bourbon monarchy. But the insurgents were now divided among themselves. Once they had defeated the Bourbons with the assistance of the Paris mob, the politicians quickly subdued the disturbances. Many liberals wanted a republic and proposed to offer the presidency to the aged Marquis de Lafayette, who had commanded the French troops sent to fight with the colonists against the British in the American War of Independence (1775–83) and been the first commander of the National Guard in 1789. The professional and commercial classes, however, feared that this might endanger private property and damage international relations with the great powers. Having prevented the clergy and nobility from regaining their position as the ruling classes, they believed that they could establish a middle-class monarchy which could maintain their political power and promote their interests. So the July Revolution of 1830 was a disappointment to the republican minority in the country, and they were never prepared to accept its outcome; but it was a triumph for the middle class, who had finally gained the political and social supremacy for which they had contended since 1789. Aristocratic and ecclesiastical power could never assert itself again in French politics.

Louis Thiers, an able, active journalist, placarded the walls of Paris in favour of the establishment of a kingdom under Louis Philippe, Duke of Orleans, who belonged to a younger branch of the Bourbon family (*see Diagram 1, page 55*). His father, Philippe, Duke of Orleans, had remained in France during the Revolution and adopted the name of *Philippe Egalité*, but had later been guillotined. Louis Philippe himself had fought in the Revolutionary armies in the early 1790s, but soon afterwards deserted to the Austrians and spent the rest of the war years in England, Switzerland and the United States of America. From 1815, his Paris home, the Palais Royal, had been the centre of middle-class liberal opposition to the Bourbon monarchy. He was, therefore, well-known and popular in those political circles, and he gained republican support when, soon after Charles X's abdication, he went to the Hôtel de Ville and, beneath an enormous tricolour, was embraced by Lafayette, who himself preferred the idea of a monarchy to the dangers of republicanism. Not long afterwards, Louis Philippe accepted the offer of the throne from the two Chambers of the Assembly.

Bibliography

General histories of France are Denis Brogan, *The French Nation from Napoleon to Petain* (Hamish Hamilton, 1957), J.P.T. Bury, *France 1814–1940* (Methuen, 3rd. ed. 1954) and Alfred Cobban, *A History of Modern France* (Penguin Books, 3 vols., 1957–65). On this period are F.B. Artz, *France under the Bourbon Restoration 1814–1830* (Harvard UP, 1931), V.W. Beach, *Charles X of France of France* (Colorado, 1971) E.L. Woodward, *French Revolutions* (OUP, 1934).

Exercises

A *This section consists of questions that might be used for discussion (or written answers) as a way of expanding on the chapter and testing your understanding of it:*

1 In what ways was the new French constitution liberal and in what ways reactionary?

2 How were the following affected politically by the Bourbon restoration — the Church, the Napoleonic nobility, the middle classes, the nobility, the peasants?

3 What effects did the Hundred Days have on the position and prestige of Louis XVIII?

4 Why was '*la chambre introuvable*' so called?

5 Why did Louis XVI replace Talleyrand and Fouché?

6 Who were the *émigrés* and why were they likely to become Ultras?

7 Why did Decazes fall between two extremes?

8 What reactionary measures did the Ultras take betwen 1821 and 1823?

9 Why was the question of the *émigré* land so important, and how was it settled?

10 What was the significance of Charles X's coronation?
11 What measures did Charles X take to restore the power and influence of the French Church?
12 Why did the position of the Church in France arouse such strong feelings?
13 Why was Polignac so unpopular?
14 What were the Ordinances of St. Cloud?
15 What were 'The Three Glorious Days'?
16 Why was the July Revolution a triumph for the middle classes?
17 What was the significance of Louis Philippe embracing Lafayette under the Tricolour?

B *Essay questions*
1 'He had learned nothing and forgotten nothing and his accession sealed the fate of the Bourbon Restoration.' Comment on this judgement on Charles X. (Cambridge, 1983)
2 Why did Charles X manage to retain the throne of France for only six years? (Oxford, 1982)
3 Explain the decision to place Louis XVIII on the throne of France. Did the events of his reign justify this decision? (SUJB, 1982)
4 Why did the regime of either (a) Charles X or (b) Louis Philippe come to a sudden end? (Welsh, 1981)
5 How far were Charles X and the Ultra-Royalists responsible for the downfall of the Bourbons in 1830? (Oxford and Cambridge, 1981)
6 Why was the rule of the restored Bourbons in France, 1814–30, so brief? (Oxford and Cambridge, 1982)
7 Why was the Bourbon restoration so short-lived? (AEB, 1981)
8 Analyse the causes of the French Revolution of 1830. (AEB, 1982)
9 'The Bourbon monarchy was swept away in 1830 because Charles X and his ministers had no understanding of the economic and social changes which were occurring in France.' Discuss. (London, 1982)

C *Political trends in Restoration France*
1 Study and discuss the diagrammatic view of political trends in France from 1814 to 1824 opposite.
2 Create a new similar diagram to cover the period from 1824 to 1830.
3 What do these diagrams reveal about the downfall of the Bourbon monarchy in 1830?

D *Debating points*
Consider each of the following statements and decide whether or not you agree with each. Then write down arguments and evidence to support and/or refute each statement.

    (i) Louis XVIII was eager to restore the authority of the Bourbon monarchy and made few concessions to changes that had taken place since 1789.
    (ii) The period 1816–1820 saw increasing stability and moderation in France.
    (iii) Louis XVIII proved able to maintain the power and authority of the monarchy and prevent it falling into the hands of any one sectional interest.
    (iv) The pre-eminence of the French Church was restored during the reign of Charles X.

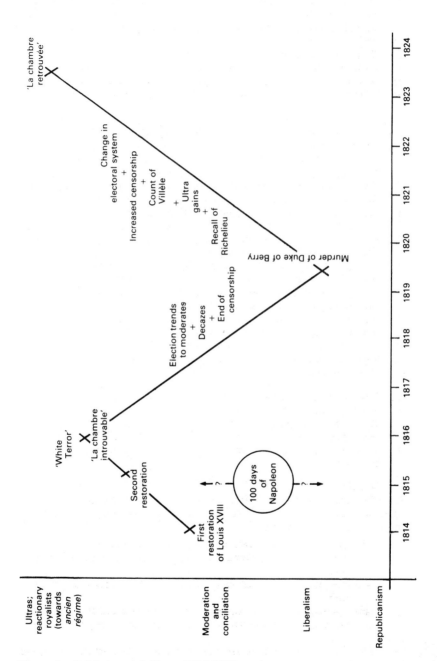

Diagram 2. Political trends in France (1814–1824)

69

(v) By 1830 the opposition in the Chamber were seeking to fight Charles X on new grounds.

(vi) The July Revolution might have been prevented if Charles X and Polignac had shown greater political acumen.

E *Documentary evidence*

Charles X has been described as 'an ultra-royalist King'. Examine the extracts from documents from his reign reproduced below, and answer the questions that follows them.

Source A. Law of Compensation of Emigrés, 1825—a contemporary report on the bill from *Annual Register*, 1825, pages 136–7, reproduced in Kertesz, *op. cit.*, pp. 48–49.

'. . . the minister brought forward three measures of the greatest importance. The first related to the settlement of the civil list; the second proposed a plan for indemnifying the emigrants or the royalist proprietors who suffered by the excesses of the Revolution. . . .

. . . The law of indemnification gave rise to a great variety of opinion. Some dissented from the principle of the measure as too antirevolutionary; others conceived that it did not go far enough; the ultra royalists thought that the emigrants were only half-compensated if what they received was not taken from those who had been gainers by their spoils; and all who disliked the financial alteration with which it was coupled wished for its failure. The debates, though protracted, were of little interest; and M. de Villèle carried his scheme triumphantly through both chambers. . . .'

Source B. Law for the Punishment of Sacrilege, 1825, from *Annual Register*, 1825, page 139, quoted by Kertesz, *op. cit.*, p. 49.

'Another ministerial measure, which excited considerable interest, especially in England, was a law introduced for the punishment of sacrilege. The law first defined the crime, which it sought to coerce, in the following manner:

"The profanation of the sacred utensils and of the consecrated hosts is the crime of sacrilege. Every overt act committed voluntarily and through hatred or contempt of religion on the sacred utensils or the consecrated hosts is declared a profanation. . . .

The profanation of the sacred utensils shall be punished with death.

The profanation of the consecrated wafers shall be punished in the manner of parricide."

This law passed the Chamber of Deputies by a majority of 210 to 95; and, though the severity of the enactment was somewhat mollified, there was in its provisions, such as they were when it received the final sanction of the legislature, no deviation from the principles stated above.'

(Profanation means to treat without due reverence; parricide means the murder of a father or close relation).

Source C. Proclamation of Charles X before the Elections, June 1830, from *Annual Register*, 1830, pages 177–8, quoted in Kertesz, *op. cit.*, pp. 50–1.

'The elections are going to commence at all points in my kingdom—listen to the voice of your King, and maintain the Constitutional Charter, and the institutions on which it is founded, which I will preserve with my utmost efforts; but to attain this object, I must freely exercise, and cause to be respected, the sacred rights which belong to my Crown, which are the guarantee of public peace and of your liberties, as the nature of government will be altered if the culpable attempt to invade my prerogative succeed, and I shall break my oath if I submit to it. Under this Government, France has become flourishing, and she owes to it her credit and her industry. France does not envy other states and only aspires to the preservation of the advantages which she enjoys. Remain assured of your rights, which I unite with mine, and which I will protect with equal solicitude. Do not let yourselves be deceived by seditious persons, enemies to your repose; and do not yield to unfounded fears, which may excite serious disorders. Electors, hasten to join your colleagues; let the same sentiment animate you, and rally under the same standard. It is your king that demands it—it is the call of your father—fulfil your duties, and I shall fulfil mine.'

1 What evidence is contained within the documents that (a) supports and (b) refutes the view that Charles X was an ultra-royalist King?
2 It is not difficult to find fault with Charles X's political views, especially given the fate that befell him and our late twentieth-century perspective. It is much harder to defend the views which he held and the policies which he followed. Using these documents as a starting point, write a defence of his political outlook.

II The Threat to the Settlement 1830–1848

1 France under Louis Philippe

(a) The July Monarchy

Louis Philippe's supporters made sure that several steps were taken in 1830 to give the new monarchy a popular aspect. To indicate that, as an elected monarch who derived his authority from a majority of votes in the Assembly, he had broken with his hereditary predecessors, he was designated, not Louis XIX nor Philip VII, but Louis Philippe, and he was proclaimed as 'King of the French by the Grace of God and the will of the nation' and not by the traditional title of 'King of France and Navarre by the Grace of God' as both Louis XVIII and Charles X had been. The tricolour again became the national flag in place of the old white royalist ensign. These changes were meant to associate the Orleanist monarchy with the Revolution and not the Bourbons.

Nevertheless, the actual constitutional changes made in 1830 were not extensive and, in fact, changed the regime only very superficially. This was, indeed, to be expected since they were made by the last Chamber of Deputies of Charles X's reign from which only the Ultras were excluded. By the revised Charter of 1830 the royal power of issuing ordinances and suspending laws was abolished, and the Assembly could now propose legislation. The Chamber of Peers was to consist only of life members. The number of deputies was raised to 459; their tax qualification was lowered to 500 francs, their qualifying age to 30 and their length of tenure to five years. The tax qualification for voters was lowered to 200 francs; this approximately doubled the size of the electorate to 200 000 out of a total population of 35 000 000. The National Guard was reinstated; it was to elect its officers and to be under the control of the civil authorities—the mayors of towns and the prefects of departments; and both these arrangements increased its middle-class character. The censorship of the press was abolished. Roman Catholicism was no longer described as 'the religion of the State', but as that 'professed by the majority', and its influence over education was restricted.

These provisions were in accordance with the objects of the men who had taken control of the July Revolution. They wanted to prevent a return of the absolutism and clericalism threatened under the restored Bourbon monarchy; but they wanted also to preserve public order and private property. They disliked and feared the ideas of democracy and republicanism. The revised Charter only slightly extended the franchise qualification and maintained the existence of an electorate which was only a small fraction of the nation. The great majority of the voters and of those they elected were landowners, many of whom had made their wealth during the Revolution and had invested it in property. They proposed to maintain their position through the constitution and with the aid of the revived National Guard.

A great question facing the new regime was whether the less wealthy middle class, which was growing in numbers and importance, would remain content with this arrangement. The ruling class hoped that they might keep themselves in power by representing the Orleanist monarchy, despite its restricted constitution, as a middle-class monarchy in character and purpose. It was not aristocratic, but sympathetic towards the aims and wishes of the middle class. They trusted that this would satisfy the middle class though they did not possess any real political power.

Louis Philippe seemed to be a suitable monarch for such a regime. He was shrewd and subtle, tolerant in religious matters, little attracted by art or literature, but otherwise had wide interests and was fascinated by all aspects of industry. He was simple and unaffected in his habits and tastes. Disliking the finery and display of the aristocracy, he genuinely preferred and adopted the outlook of the middle-class. He sent his children to middle-class schools, while the young Duke of Bordeaux, who remained the Bourbon claimant to the throne, followed the princely tradition of employing private tutors. When Louis Philippe wore a uniform, it was commonly that of the National Guard. Otherwise, wearing a top hat and frock-coat and always carrying an umbrella, he became a familiar sight strolling round the Parisian shops and boulevards. He discarded the pomp and etiquette of the Bourbon court and was always ready to receive popular delegations. State occasions had no appeal for him, especially after he had been shot at several times. Nevertheless, he consulted a teacher of deportment in order to learn the best way of bowing to the crowd in acknowledgement of their sympathy after an attempt on his life. He lit his own study fire and shaved himself every morning, liked soup and was proud that he had learnt how to cut wafter-thin slices of ham from a waiter with whom he had shared lodgings when he was in exile. The old royalists despised such popular habits, but they appealed at the time to the middle class.

Yet beneath Louis Philippe's outward show of modesty and good nature, there lay a desire for royal power. He was thoroughly un-scrupulous and cleverly opportunist, knowing how to win popularity for his own advantage. He was not prepared to be a mere regal figure-head and wanted to take an active part in politics. He was as determined as any of his predecessors to govern France and was ready from the very start of his reign to assert his will despite the constitutional limitations placed on the royal prerogatives. 'They may do what they like,' he said, 'but they shall not prevent me from driving my own coach.' Though he proceeded cautiously, this ambition was in the end to lose him the support not only of the middle class, but also of nearly every other section of French political life.

(b) Parties and Disturbances (1830–32)

The July Monarchy rested upon a very narrow basis. Though the middle class probably did not yet amount to as much as a tenth of the total population, only the very wealthiest of them had the vote. Moreover, the new regime had not the support either of the hallowed traditions of the historical monarchy or of any form of popular approval. It was not suprising, therefore, that its first years were troubled ones. Political and social opposition to it was strong. The ideas and passions produced by the events of 1830 only gradually died down. They were expressed by political activity of all sorts, particularly by the rise of parties, which were not prepared to accept the Orleanist settlement as final and wished either to revive the past or to put new beliefs into practice, to recover their hold on power or to reverse its denial to them.

For the first time in French history, the condition of the industrial workers became a political issue. Though the numbers employed in large-scale industry did not yet total a million, the Industrial Revolution was developing in France (*see page 81*). This was producing the same conditions as in Britain—crowded, unhealthy urban slums, long hours of work, widespread female and child labour, low pay and uncertainty of employment, especially as the economic recession of the later 1820s was slow in improving. There were serious riots by the silk-workers of Lyons demanding a minimum wage in 1831 and 1834. The government suppressed them with the National Guard and regular troops and then passed laws forbidding workers to form organizations and attempt collective bargaining. Socialist ideas began to spread rapidly among the working classes (*see page 83*).

Among the political parties, the Legitimists, who wished to place a descendant of Charles X upon the throne, hoped to take immediate advantage of the monarchy's insecurity. In 1832 the Duchess of Berry, the Duke of Bordeaux's mother, was persuaded to land in the south of France and proclaim her son as Henry V, but few royalists supported her. The rising was quickly suppressed, and the Duchess was imprisoned in a fortress where she soon gave birth to a daughter. She had to confess that the year before she had secretly married a minor Italian count, who was her secretary. The embarassed Legitimists disowned her and abandoned any further direct attempt upon the throne. Nevertheless, they remained an important political force, still possessing the support of many of the clergy and the nobility.

Another party, the Bonapartists, seemed, however, to be of much less consequence. Their aim was to restore the Empire with a descendant of Napoleon as its ruler, but in 1832 their plans were completely upset by the premature death in Vienna of Napoleon's only son, the Duke of Reichstadt, whom they called Napoleon II. The new head of the family, Napoleon's young nephew, Louis Napoleon Bonaparte, was insignificant in appearance and hardly seemed worthy of such a great name. No one would have foreseen that he was to come to power 16 years later.

The most dangerous opposition to the July monarchy came from the Republicans. They held to the ideas of the Revolution and wanted to make France a republic again. Their resentment at having been robbed of power in 1830 led them to make great efforts to gain popular support—no less than 6 000 000 copies of their pamphlets were distributed in six months. Their proclamation of a form of government in which the supremacy of the people was to prevail attracted much support from the poorer classes. There were violent anti-clerical and anti-royalist demonstrations in Paris. In 1831 a mob demolished the Church of St. Germain l'Auxerrois and the fine thirteenth-century Archbishop's Palace, next to Notre Dame, and burnt its great library. The next year there was a rising in the city which was only crushed after two days' bitter fighting by the National Guard. This brought such mass action to an end, but almost every year there were attempts to assassinate the King. During a royal procession in Paris in 1835 two republican fanatics shot at him with a device which fired 24 muskets simultaneously from a shuttered window. The hail of bullets mowed down 41 people in front of Louis Philippe, but he was only grazed on the chin. 'It is only in hunting me that there is no close season,' he commented.

(c) The King's Triumph (1832–35)
To add to the new regime's early difficulties, it began with an uncertain government. Its leader, Jacques Lafitte, a banker who had assisted the liberals in the period before the July Revolution, seemed unable to deal with the problems facing him—public disorder, continuing unemployment and popular demands for intervention on behalf of the national risings in Belgium, Italy and Poland. He had to resign in March 1831 and was succeeded by Casimir Périer, a successful businessman, who proved to be an energetic and forceful minister. Aided by a conservative majority produced in the Chamber by the elections later that year and an improvement in the economic situation, he was able in just over a year to put the monarchy in a firm position, before he suddenly died of cholera, which was raging for the first time in the insanitary towns of both Britain and France.

Périer's achievements and early death prepared the way for Louis Philippe himself to rule, as he had always intended he would, through a succession of amenable, docile ministers. From Périer's death in May

1832 until October 1840 he had no less than ten chief ministers. Only as long as a minister was content to carry out the King's wishes could he expect to remain in office. If he showed a wish to have a policy of his own, he was soon dismissed. At the same time, the King retained control of the Chamber by resorting to bribery and corruption; deputies were made administrative officials and influential voters received government contracts. Between 1830 and 1847 the number of deputies who were also officials rose from 142 to 193, which was between a third and a half of the total membership of the Chamber.

He was also determined to take crippling action against the opposition parties. The freedom of the press, which had greatly assisted their activities, was curtailed. Journalists who criticized the government were tried in special courts without a jury. The Law of Associations of 1834 made illegal the formation of societies wishing to overthrow the government, and the next year, following an attempt on the King's life, another law forbade even the discussion of any other form of government and made it an offence for anyone to declare himself a supporter of a former ruling family in France. By 1835 the enforcement of these laws against Republicans, Legitimists and Bonapartists alike had largely driven the opposition underground to operate through secret societies and hidden printing presses. Louis Philippe seemed to have secured the personal control over the government which he wanted, though only by putting into effect measures which recalled the methods of the Ultras in the previous reign.

(d) Foreign Policy (1830–48)

Louis Philippe considered that his life abroad in exile had given him a special knowledge of European affairs, and from the beginning of his reign he took a prominent part in the conduct of foreign policy, which he thought was of vital importance to the success of his regime. He was aware that France had been very successful since 1815 in regaining her influence as an important power. He knew too that Frenchmen believed that their country could re-establish for itself the Continental supremacy which it had held since the days of Louis XIV in the later seventeenth century and that they would support a government able to secure French prestige and power.

At the same time, the July Revolution placed him in a difficult position. The overthrow of the Bourbon monarchy, whose establishment was part of the Vienna settlement alarmed Continental governments, especially when the events in Paris encouraged risings and demonstrations in other parts of Europe. This unease was increased by French republican demonstrations in favour of insurgents and liberals elsewhere. Louis Philippe did not wish to engage in dangerous adventures abroad. He wanted first to convince other European governments that the July Monarchy would be a responsible and stabilizing influence in foreign affairs. Then he hoped to avoid a policy that would increase the fears and suspicions of the great powers, particularly

Britain, whose foreign policy was directed by the energetic and aggresive Lord Palmerston during most of this period. Moreover, he knew that his middle-class supporters wanted French commercial prosperity to be encouraged and that this depended upon the preservation of peaceful conditions abroad. There was, therefore, a contradiction in the aims of his foreign policy which he was never able to succeed in resolving.

At the start of his reign, though the presence of many Polish exiles in Paris and the dramatic and romantic nature of the Polish rising aroused very strong sympathy in France for this hopeless cause, Poland was too remote to present him with a difficult foreign policy (*see page 132*). On the other hand, the events in both Belgium and Italy did require decisions on his part, and he emerged eventually from these situations with considerable success and increased prestige.

Immediately he came to the throne, he was faced by the problems presented by the Belgian revolt (*see page 97*). This occurred in territory adjacent to France and, moreover, in a part of Europe towards which French foreign policy had long-established expansionist objectives. Ever since the seventeenth century, when this country had been first the Spanish Netherlands and then the Austrian Netherlands, conquering French armies had invaded it. Flemish towns, such as Dunkirk and Lille, had been made French, and Napoleon's seizure of the whole of the country had been popular in France. Louis Philippe, however, resisted French interventionist opinion on this occasion and took his part in bringing about a satisfactory solution to the problem, although his opponents did not hesitate to accuse him of having yielded in order to placate Europe and especially the British government.

In the Belgian question, Louis Philippe had, indeed, wished particularly to establish friendly relations with Britain. He similarly had no desire to clash with Austria over the situation in Italy. When revolts broke out in 1830 in Central Italy, he declared that his government was opposed to all foreign intervention in the peninsula, but when Metternich sent Austrian troops to suppress the insurgents, he took no action. When, however, another rising took place in the Papal States two years later, he felt firmly established enough at home and abroad to do something to assert French interest in Italian affairs and oppose their complete domination by Austria. After the Papacy had again called in Austrian troops, he replied by occupying the Adriatic port of Ancona (*see Map 8, page 113*). The French soldiers remained there until the Austrians withdrew from the Papal States in 1838. This was a successful demonstration on behalf of French prestige and the balance of power, though again it brought him criticism in France for not having acted with sufficient determination on behalf of the Italian nationalists.

During the 1830s, however, Louis Philippe's ministers supported his foreign policy, but Thiers, who became his chief minister in 1840, wanted it to be more aggressive and adventurous, and the King was ready to listen to him after the criticism he had met through his handling of the Belgian and Italian questions. At this time, the opportunity for more forceful action arose in the Near East. In 1832 Mehemet Ali had seized Syria (*see page 129*); but in 1839 the Sultan of Turkey took advantage of Syrian discontent to make a vain attack upon him. France had maintained a close interest in Egypt ever since Napoleon's expedition there in 1798 and had already secured a dominant position in the country by sending officers, teachers and traders and making loans to the government. So French opinion supported Mehemet Ali; and if he succeeded in defeating the Turks, France could become supreme in the Near East. Thiers favoured French military intervention on his behalf, but Palmerston regarded this as a threat to Britain's vital interests in the Mediterranean. Palmerston was able to get Austria, Russia and Prussia to agree that Mehemet Ali must give up Syria, a decision that was enforced by an allied fleet (*see page 131*). French opposition was aroused. There was talk of France abandoning the Treaties of 1815 and fighting the new 'Quadruple Alliance' in the Rhine. Thiers too was furious and still urged action by France; but Louis Philippe was alarmed at France's isolation and did not want to risk war with the great powers. Instead, he dismissed Thiers in October 1840.

To succeed Thiers, the King appointed Francis Guizot, a learned historian, and austere Protestant and a liberal who was prepared to co-operate with conservatives. He was to be in office for the remainder of Louis Philippe's reign. He believed that France must accept the borders imposed upon her in 1815 if she were to establish good relations with the other European powers. He agreed with Louis Philippe in wishing to save France from diplomatic isolation, particularly by gaining an understanding with Britain. His task was made easier by the replacement of Palmerston by Lord Aberdeen between 1841 and 1846. Aberdeen trusted him and formed a close and friendly relation with him. For a time it looked as if a better understanding had been formed between the two countries; but 1846 brought another crisis in their relations with each other.

This arose over the subject of the marriage of the young Queen Isabella of Spain, which aroused in Britain the same fears of a union between the French and Spanish crowns that had led to the outbreak of the War of the Spanish Succession (1701–13), though neither country offered such a threat to Britain as they had done then. Aberdeen, indeed, said that the issue was no adequate cause for a national quarrel. He was prepared to recognize the French ascendancy in Madrid, but he had been succeeded as Foreign Secretary by 'Firebrand' Palmerston, who distrusted both France and Guizot. He wanted a Saxe-Coburg prince, a cousin of the Prince Consort, to marry the Spanish Queen, but Louis Philippe supported the claim of his youngest son, the Duke of Montpensier. In the end, it was unofficially agreed between the British and French governments that the Queen should marry her cousin Francis, but Guizot, who resented the British change of policy, could not resist attempting a sensational coup. He arranged that, simultaneously with the Queen's wedding, her younger sister should marry Montpensier. Since the Queen was not expected to have children, it seemed that an Orleanist heir would eventually ascend the Spanish throne.

Guizot's involved and underhand policy over the Spanish Marriages was inspired by his belief that France should maintain her position in the Mediterranean if she were to remain a great power. Many Frenchmen greeted his action as a diplomatic victory which had enabled France to recover from the setback she had suffered in 1840, but it infuriated Palmerston and threatened France again with isolation. Moreover, since the Queen soon had a son, it was an empty victory, and there were no further French triumphs to compensate for it.

Meanwhile, the conquest of Algeria, begun in Charles X's reign, was proceeding. At first, French occupation was confined to the coast, but from 1827, for reasons of security, French troops began to take over the interior, which involved campaigning for some ten years. By 1848 Algeria had some 109 000 Europeans, about half of whom were French, and was organized as three outlying departments of France (*see page 231*). It was the beginning of the new French Empire and was supported by Guizot, who saw French occupation of North Africa as part of his Mediterranean policy. Louis Philippe, however, had done little to encourage it, seeing in it some prestige, but little profit. 'It is our opera box,' he is reported to have said, 'but a terribly expensive one.'

Guizot's foreign policy was not successful because he could not convince the European powers that he really accepted France's position on the Continent under the Vienna settlement. He was, therefore, no more successful than Louis Philippe in rescuing the country from diplomatic isolation. Moreover, he failed to reconcile his countrymen to the new order in Europe. Unaware of the slow but inevitable decline in French power that was taking place, they remained staunchly revisionist in their attitude towards the peace settlement, and they did not believe that any overseas colonial ventures could atone for the country's lack of success in European affairs.

(e) The Napoleonic Legend

The Bonapartists were strong advocates of revisionism, and it has been said that disillusion with Orleanist foreign policy was favourable to the growth of Bonapartism and the appeal of the Napoleonic Legend during the later years of the July Monarchy. It is, however, unlikely that this was so. Neither Bonapartism nor the Napoleonic Legend had much political importance at any time during Louis Philippe's reign. The Bonapartists remained a very small party, and it never seemed likely that they could ever hope to regain political power and make France an Empire again.

Napoleon himself had begun the construction of the Napoleonic Legend when he was Emperor and had set out to develop it during the

Hundred Days and then when he was captive in St. Helena through his correspondence and the *Mémorial de Sainte-Hélène* which he dictated there. It had subsequently been preserved and elaborated by his followers until, as the Duke of Wellington remarked, 'Napoleon was not a personality but a principle.' It represented Napoleon, not as a military conqueror and despotic ruler, but rather as the national leader who had given France law and order, prosperity, efficient administration and a great empire, and who also, if he had not been prevented by defeat at the hands of his enemies, would have brought Europe peace and liberty and helped its peoples to gain independence and unity. By 1830 all this held an attraction for a few French people, but even for them as part of their national history and hardly as a relevant factor in contemporary politics which actively concerned them.

Indeed, the Napoleonic Legend seemed so harmless that Louis Philippe and his ministers actually encouraged it in the hope of bathing themselves in the reflected glory of the Empire and so gaining much-needed prestige from it. The Arc de Triomphe in Paris, on which Napoleon's victories were inscribed, was completed, and Napoleon's statue was placed again on top of its column in the Place Vendôme in 1833. The uncomfortable, expensive Palace of Versailles was re-linquished by the monarchy as a royal residence and handed over to the state as a museum of national glory. And in 1840 the body of Napoleon was disinterred from its grave in St. Helena and taken to Paris to be enclosed in an elaborate marble sarcophagus in the Invalides with a ceremony of solemn splendour (the Duke of Wellington having said, when asked by the British government whether he objected to this, that he did not care 'a tuppenny damn' what happened to his former adversary's corpse). The only contribution made by Louis Napoleon himself to the furtherance of the Bonapartist cause was to make a fool of himself in two ignominious attempts to seize power and the publication of a number of undistinguished writings, which hardly circulated beyond the faithful (*see page 146*). Bonapartism as a political force never seemed important at any time during Louis Philippe's reign.

The Bonapartists tried to represent Napoleon as a compelling myth, a figure of immense glamour and energy, and to look back romantically to the Empire in a way that made it seem more inviting than the dull days of the middle-class monarchy under which Frenchmen were then living, but few could be persuaded to think of him in this way. To most Frenchmen, Napoleon was the great betrayer—the man who, accepting service under the Republic, had first set out to fulfil the Revolution in France and then spread its liberating ideas throughout Europe, but who had abandoned these very beliefs which had once inspired him and brought about the destruction of the Republic. They did not find attractive, therefore, the notion of another Napoleonic regime as an alternative to the July Monarchy.

(f) The Economic Situation

'France is bored,' said the radical poet, Alphonse Lamartine, in 1839—words which are often quoted to show how the failure of Orleanist foreign policy cost the regime the support of the people. Undoubtedly the absence of military glory and diplomatic prestige during these years did gradually erode its popularity. Several generations of defeat in wars against Britain during the eighteenth century had contributed towards the downfall of the *ancien régime* in the Revolution. The episode of glory and power of the Revolutionary and Napoleonic Wars now seemed to shine in contrast to the failures of post-war foreign policy and strengthened the revisionism which Guizot was unable to counter. But it is doubtful whether this contributed most to the downfall of the July Monarchy.

'What has been done during the last seven years?' asked an opposition deputy in the Chamber in 1847. 'Nothing! Nothing! Nothing!' He was speaking not about foreign policy, but rather about the economic and social circumstances at home which were increasingly attracting the critical attention of French thinkers and writers and causing despair and frustration among the mass of the people. It was described by Pierre Joseph Proudhon, the socialist, as the disease of *'immobilisme'*. And it was this, together with the inability of the government to improve the situation, that brought about the sequence of events that led to the collapse of the regime.

During Louis Philippe's reign, the industrialization of France proceeded, but at a slower rate than might have been expected in a country of her size and resources. Apart from northern France with its textiles, coals and iron, she had no considerable industrial areas, and her industrial stagnation was shown by the difference in the rate of growth in size between British and French towns.

	Britain	France
1801	23.3	9.5
1851	39.5	10.6

Table 5   Proportion of population in towns of over 10 000 (percentages)

France made an early start in railway building. Her first railway was completed in 1832 and ran from the coal-mines of St. Etienne to Lyons, but the first important line to be opened was from Paris to Saint-Germain in 1837, which Thiers said might be worth constructing as an amusement for the Parisians. And, indeed, France was slow to realize the importance of railways. Her system was backward compared not only with Britain, but also with disunited Germany. By the end of Louis Philippe's reign, it was both small and fragmented.

Her industrial output was still larger than that of all the other Continental countries put together, but Britain had moved ahead of her in manufacture and trade. In 1830, though French exports were the

81

	Britain	France	Germany
1850	10 653	3008	6010
1870	24 935	17 700	32 180

Table 6. Length of railway track (in kilometres)

most valuable on the Continent, British exports were double in value. Moreover, Germany was soon to mount an industrial challenge to her; and France was never to become a leading industrial country in the nineteenth century as did these two countries. The signs of this were already apparent in Louis Philippe's reign in the comparative figures of the production of pig-iron, which was the best indication of industrial strength in the first half of the century.

	Britain	France	Germany
1830	670 000	265 735	45 275
1850	2 214 450	393 680	211 605
1870	5 865 830	1 771 560	1 377 880

Table 7 Output of pig-iron (in tonnes)

Another aspect of the situation in France at this time was her relative decline in population. In 1789 France was, as she had been for a long time, the most populous state in western Europe. By then Britain was beginning to overtake her economically, but her population was about two-thirds that of France. Then the French birth-rate began markedly to fall well in advance of that of other countries. The reasons for this are not clear. It is likely to be connected with the destruction of old traditions by the Revolution and the relaxation of former moral beliefs which lessened opposition to birth control. It was probably due also to the social structure then established in France. The peasants had gained the abolition of the feudal obligations to which they had been subjected, and many of them had possession of their land; but the civil law as laid down by Napoleon in his Code required a holding to be divided equally among the owner's sons on his death, and the peasants consequently limited the size of their families. Whatever were the reasons, the French population increased more slowly than that of any other single country in Europe. There was no rapidly-growing, landless population to provide abundant labour for the new factory-towns. And after 1890 Britain overtook France in population, a development which would have seemed impossible at the beginning of the century.

Again, both the ruling class and the electorate under both the Bourbon and Orleanist monarchies were for the most part landed proprietors (*see page 72*). They were not interested in industrial development, and when they had money to invest, they were more often ready to put it into flourishing foreign enterprises than rather less attractive domestic ones. Large-scale French capitalism could not

	Britain	France	Italy	Austria	Germany	Russia
1815	18	29	18	27	26	43
1830	24	32	21	31	30	50
1840	26	33	22	33	31	55
1850	28	36	24	35	36	57
1860	29	37	25	32	38	63
1870	31	38	26	36	41	77
1880	35	37	28	38	45	89
1890	38	38	30	41	49	95

Table 8 Populations of European countries (in millions)

thrive in such difficult and unrewarding circumstances. In 1848 three-quarters of the population were still engaged in agriculture, and in Paris, where there were nearly 65 000 industrial undertakings, only 7000 employed more than ten workers.

Indeed, France's industrial production increased even more slowly than her population. Manufacturers still found it more profitable to produce luxuries instead of cheap, standardized goods for mass consumption. Though there was a general rise in the standard of living under the July Monarchy, the way of life for many of the working-class was precarious. A poor harvest or an economic recession was likely to have serious consequences for the poorer people.

(g) Discontent and Socialism

Labour relations remained bad in France, perhaps as bad as anywhere in Europe. In addition to the riots at Lyons in 1831 and 1834, there were working-class disturbances in Paris in 1832, 1834 and 1839 and in Lille, Clermont and Toulouse in 1840. In 1833 and again between 1844 and 1846 there was a particularly large number of strikes throughout the country. The attitude of the government to these demonstrations of discontent went little beyond suppression.

Writers and thinkers, however, paid more attention to the situation. This was not because poverty was now worse in France than it had been in the past, but because the greater numbers of the poor and their concentration in the towns made their misery more apparent. The social conscience of these intellectuals was affronted by the contrast between the conditions of these poor people and the wealth of the ruling propertied class. They were led to adopt a critical attitude towards the social order as a whole, including such institutions as property, inheritance and even marriage and the family. They came to wish to reorganize society anew, and from about 1830 the name of Socialists was applied to them (*see page 384*).

The pioneer among the French socialist thinkers was Henry, Count of Saint-Simon, who died in 1825. He wished society to be organized by experts, who would replace 'the exploitation of man by man' by considering the common good and ensuring a fair distribution of wealth to everyone—'to each according to his abilities, to each ability according to its works.' Among others were Charles Fourier, who proposed the establishment of co-operative communities, each of some 1800 people, whose profits would be shared according to the value of each person's work or the capital he invested; and Pierre Joseph Proudhon, who went as far as completely condemning private property in a pamphlet in 1840 in which appeared his well-known epigram 'property is theft'. But the most influential Socialist in Louis Philippe's reign was Louis Blanc, who was the son of a government official and as a young lower middle-class man resented his exclusion from political power. Eventually he became a tutor in the family of a rising manufacturer, a position which aroused his interest in industry, and he believed that the poverty of the workers was because of the intense competition between employers which encouraged low wages and insecurity of employment. He published a book, also in 1840, *The Organization of Labour*, in which he insisted that every man had the right to work and that the State should organize 'socialist workshops' to make this possible.

(h) The Collapse of the July Monarchy (1846–48)

The social agitation of the 1830s had gained some results from the government. In 1841 a law was passed to regulate child labour; in 1843 a uniform scale of wages replaced the mutual bargaining which had usually favoured employers; and in 1845 workers' associations, hitherto disguised as mutual benefit societies, obtained legal recognition. Such measures, however, did not satisfy either the working class or the social reformers, who both became convinced that only political power would enable them to secure their demands. At the same time, though the limited franchise of the regime gave political power to the growing class of new, rich factory-owners, it continued to exclude the greater part of the middle class, who grew evermore resentful at the situation.

The year 1846 was fatal for the July Monarchy. It produced the circumstances which led to its collapse. Not only did it see the fiasco of Guizot's venture into foreign policy, but it also brought the economic crisis which was bound to cause severe distress in France. The country shared in the consequences of the widespread bad weather of 1846 and 1847 which resulted in poor corn harvests and blighted potato-crops in northern and western Europe. As prices soared in France, crowds of starving people began looting the bakeries and food-shops, spreading terror throughout the countryside, while in the towns businesses failed and factories closed bringing about mounting unemployment.

At the same time, the disclosure of a number of government scandals gave the opposition an opportunity to launch a campaign for constitutional reform. Several of its leaders, including Thiers, introduced in the Chamber at the beginning of 1847 an amendment to the electoral law which would lower the tax-qualification for voters to 100 francs. Guizot was convinced that the safety of the state required that political power should remain in the hands of the upper, propertied classes, who had most to lose from any breakdown of order. He was inflexible in this

84

attitude, and it was entirely shared by Louis Philippe. He, therefore, had the proposal defeated in the Chamber by a large majority and refused to make any concessions to the opposition. The King supported him, and he felt secure in his control of the Chamber with its large proportion of deputies who either received government pensions or held official posts. He felt certain also of the support of the existing electorate and knew that they would not want the franchise reformed. It was to bind them to him that he made his well-known remark, 'Never, never, will the time come for universal suffrage.'

Finding that they could make no progress in the Chamber, the liberal opposition decided to carry their campaign to the country in the manner of the successful Anti-Corn Law League in England. Political meetings were forbidden by law, but throughout 1847 they organized a number of 'reform banquets' at which the diners paid for a meal followed by speeches denouncing the government and demanding constitutional reform. Numbers and cost, however, made this a limited form of propaganda, and both diners and orators were moderate, well-to-do men. They did not want radical changes. Their chief aim was to get themselves into power instead of Guizot and his supporters. When the government banned a large banquet to be held in Paris on 22 February 1848, its organizers showed their moderation by unprotestingly cancelling the arrangements.

By now, however, the government was faced with wider and more determined opposition from other classes, and the situation got beyond its control. The price of wheat had now more than doubled, and as bread became dearer, the industrial depression grew worse. This was taking place elsewhere in Europe, but conditions in France were made worse by over-speculation and the tardy development of the railways which caused a financial crisis. As companies became bankrupt, and half-completed lines were abandoned, unemployment and discontent became nationwide. The abandonment of the banquet in Paris was followed by a large demonstration near the establishment where it was to have been held. Rioters, waving red flags, appeared in the streets. Over a million paving stones were torn up and more than 4000 trees cut down. By the morning of 23 July over 1500 barricades had been erected. The National Guard, when it was called out, was reluctant to support the monarchy against the demonstrators, but a frightened patrol fired a chance volley into the crowd, killing or wounding about 40 people. The rioters began to arm themselves with weapons seized from the barracks. Later in the day Louis Philippe dismissed Guizot and promised reforms, but the regime could not now be saved by constitutional changes. The violence of the mob, encouraged by re-publican orators, was increasing. There were demonstrations outside the Tuilleries. The King lost his nerve, abdicated on 24 February and fled to England, landing at Newhaven under the name of Mr Smith. Three days of rioting in Paris had brought the monarchy to an end.

A second attempt to establish a constitutional monarchy in France had failed, and fundamentally for the same reason as in 1830. The King had been determined to establish his personal rule, and the middle class, largely excluded from political power, had not been prepared to tolerate this. And when economic recession roused the working class to revolt, the Orleanist monarchy had alienated the class which might have saved it.

Bibliography

In addition to the books mentioned on page 67, there is T.E.B. Howarth, *Citizen King: The Life of Louis Philippe* (Eyre & Spottiswoode, 1961), D. Johnson, *Guizot: Aspects of French History, 1787–1874* (Routledge & Kegan Paul, 1963) and L.C. Jennings, *France and Europe in 1848* (OUP, 1973).

1814	April	Abdication of Napoleon
	May	First Treaty of Paris
	June	Charter of Louis XVIII
1815	1 March	Napoleon lands in France
	18 June	Battle of Waterloo
	8 July	Second Restoration
		Ministry of Talleyrand and Fouché
		'White Terror'
	August	Election of *la Chambre introuvable*
	September	Resignation of Talleyrand and Fouché
		Ministry of Richelieu
	November	Second Treaty of Paris
	December	Execution of Marshal Ney
1816		General Election
1818	November	End of Allied Occupation
	December	Ministry of Decazes
1820	February	Murder of Duke of Berry
		Recall of Richelieu
1821		Death of Napoleon
		Charbonnerie
	December	Ministry of Villèle
1822		Plot of Sergeants at La Rochelle
1823		Expedition Sent to Spain
1824	March	Election of *la Chambre retrouvée*
	September	Death of Louis XVIII
		Accession of Charles X
1825		Law against Sacrilege
		Emigrés compensated
	May	Coronation of Charles X
1827	November	General Election
1828	January	Ministry of Martignac
1829	August	Ministry of Polignac
1830	June	General Election
	July	Capture of Algiers
	27–29 July	'Three Glorious Days'
	2 August	Abdication of Charles X
	7 August	Acceptance of Throne by Louis Philippe
		Ministry of Lafitte
1831	February	Riots in Paris
	March	Ministry of Périer
	August	French Expulsion of Dutch from Belgium

	October	Revolt in Lyons
1832		Death of Duke of Reichstadt
		Attempt of Duchess of Berry
		French troops sent to Italy
	May	Death of Périer
1834		Revolt in Lyons
		Law of Associations
1840		Reburial of Napoleon in Paris
	March	Ministry of Thiers
		Mehemet Ali Crisis
	October	Ministry of Guizot
		Louis Blanc, *The Organization of Labour*
		Pierre Joseph Proudhon, *What is Property?*
1846	October	Spanish Marriages
1847		'Reform Banquets'
1848	22 February	Riots in Paris
	23 February	Dismissal of Guizot
	24 February	Abdication of Louis Philippe

Table 9. Date chart of French history (1814–48)

Exercises

A *This section consists of questions that might be used for discussion (or written answers) as a way of expanding on the chapter and testing your understanding of it:*

1 What symbolic changes did Louis Philippe make to indicate that his regime was to make a fresh start?
2 What changes were made to the Constitution by the Charter of 1830?
3 Why was Louis Philippe regarded as a 'bourgeois monarch'?
4 Who or what were the 'hallowed traditions of the historical monarchy'?
5 List the groups that opposed Louis Philippe and explain their opposition and aims.
6 What actions did Louis Philippe take in the early 1830s to secure personal control over the government?
7 What effects did Louis Philippe's suppression have on the opposition?
8 What was the underlying contradiction in the aims of Louis Philippe's foreign policy?
9 Assess the role that Louis Philippe played in the Belgian and Italian revolts.
10 Why was Thiers dismissed?
11 Examine the relations between Britain and France in the period 1830–1848 (this could be done in the form of a chart, indicating both the events that took place and the degree of friendship between the states at each stage).
12 Why was there 'disillusion with Orleanist foreign policy'?
13 What was the 'Napoleonic Legend'?
14 Why was France's economic development relatively slow?
15 Who were the main socialist thinkers of the period, and what were their chief ideas?
16 Why was 1846 a fatal year?
17 Why were Louis Philippe and Guizot so determined to make no concessions to demands for political reform?
18 What part did working-class dissatisfaction play in the 1848 Revolution?

1   'Domestic, not foreign, issues were the causes of the downfall of the Orleanist monarchy in 1848.' Do you accept this view? (Cambridge, 1981)
2   What made French politics so unstable between 1815 and 1848? (Cambridge, 1982)
3   'Accidental and unexpected.' Discuss this verdict on the fall of the July Monarchy in 1848. (Oxford, 1983)
4   Why did the French welcome Louis Philippe as king in 1830, but reject him in 1848? (SUJB, 1981)
5   Was Louis Philippe's task more difficult than that of Louis XVIII? (Welsh, 1982)
6   How far do the shortcomings of the monarchs explain the ultimate collapse of either (a) the Restoration or (b) the July Monarchy? (Welsh, 1982)
7   What factors made for instability in France either under the restored Bourbon monarchy or during the reign of Louis Philippe? (Oxford and Cambridge, 1983)
8   'Inevitable yet accidental'. To what extent does this paradox explain the downfall of the July monarchy in 1848? (AEB, 1983)
9   Analyse and compare the revolutionary forces in France which overthrew Charles X in 1830 and Louis Philippe in 1848. (London, 1981)
10   'The fall of the July Monarchy in 1848 was due more to its own shortcomings than to the strength of its opponents.' Discuss this statement. (JMB, 1984)

C   *Essay writing skills 3: writing about causes and effects*

Introduction
So far you have been introduced to the distinction between narrative and analysis (*see page 38*) and to detailed essay planning (*see page 52*). This section aims to take your essay writing skills a stage further.

Most historical writing is concerned with one of four areas. Firstly, historians examine the causes and/or the effects of a particular event. They therefore write about the *reasons* for key events, such as the French Revolution, the outbreak of wars or the rise to power of a particular ruler. Similarly, they investigate the consequences of a particular event, period or individual, such as the Battle of Waterloo or the rule of Metternich. In the second part of this section, you will be investigating this type of question more fully.

In subsequent chapters, you will be examining in detail the other three types of writing; for now, you need only be introduced to them. Characters like Metternich and Garibaldi have been argued over frequently, as have the various factors influencing events. Consequently, you will find in examinations that you are often presented with a particular interpretation and asked your opinion of it. Such questions usually take the form of a quotation, followed by 'Discuss' or 'Do you agree?' The third area of concern is what might be called 'significance' or 'importance'. This approach investigates people and events slightly differently and seeks to assess their relevance to subsequent events, usually in comparison to other factors. Finally, historians compare and contrast different countries, periods or individuals and their relative performance, impact or causes.

Writing about causes and effects

If you are asked to write about the reasons for or the consequences of an event, you are essentially required to produce a *list* type of essay. It should consist of a number of paragraphs each identifying and explaining a separate cause or effect. It is generally easy to identify questions that seek such an answer, as they usually include 'Why?' or 'Account for' in the title if seeking reasons, or 'effects' or 'consequences' if examining that aspect. In this section, you will be concentrating on the first of these two kinds—causation essays—although much of the advice below applies equally to effects essays.

Since you are asked for reasons, it is imperative that you write paragraphs that explain reasons and do not simply give a narrative account of events. This sounds simple, but teachers and examiners will tell you how often this simple rule is ignored. Take this analogy. If you were asked, 'Why are you reading this book?', your answer is likely to be on the lines of 'Because I need to pass A level history' or 'Because I am interested in nineteenth-century Europe'. You are unlikely to say, 'I read the first chapter in September and took detailed notes on pages 12–15 at about midnight' or 'I took a very long time doing the essay exercise on Metternich, and I was very disappointed when I got a lousy mark for it.' The difference between these two sets of answers is glaringly obvious, yet many young historians, when faced by an essay title, take fright and start telling the story of events rather than analysing and writing about reasons.

One way of avoiding this pitfall is by careful use of the opening sentences of your paragraphs. Ensure that each of these provides an answer to the question asked by the title; you should be able to read the opening sentences of each paragraph and have an outline of your entire answer. Be especially careful not to state items of factual information in these opening sentences. You have to learn instead to *use* your factual knowledge to provide examples and to support the reasons you are writing about (*see page 239*). In this respect, you are working in the same way as a lawyer in court, who puts forward his arguments and supports each by reference to evidence. One way to avoid writing narrative and ensuring that you are writing about causes is to begin at least some of your paragraphs with phrases like 'One reason for. . . .', 'Another factor in. . . .', 'Thirdly. . . .' or 'The underlying cause. . . .'

In planning essays of this type, you will find it helpful to construct a planning sheet like the one shown below and on page 395. You will notice that space is provided for seven paragraphs—it is not essential to have this number, but it gives you an indication of the length that you will be required to write in examinations.

Students often find it difficult to give essays on causes a structure, and are concerned to avoid writing a 'list' too baldly. One way of structuring such essays is to categorise the causes. In *The Origins of the Second World War*, A.J.P. Taylor writes, 'Wars are much like road accidents. They have a general cause and particular causes at the same time. Every road accident is caused, in the last resort, by the invention of the internal combustion engine and by men's desire to get from one place to another. In this sense, the "cure" for road accidents is to forbid motor-cars.

Essay planning sheet:	
Title of essay:	
Summary of introduction (if any):	
Arguments/causes/effects (1st sentences)	Evidence to support argument
1)	
2) etc.	
Summary of conclusion:	

But a motorist, charged with dangerous driving, would be ill-advised if he pleaded the existence of motor-cars as his sole defence. The police and the courts do not weigh profound causes. They seek a specific cause for each accident—error on the part of the driver; excessive speed; drunkenness; faulty brakes; bad road surface. So it is with wars. "International anarchy" makes war possible; it does not make war certain. After 1918 more than one writer made his name by demonstrating the profound causes of the First World War; and, though the demonstrations were often correct, they thus diverted attention why that particular war happened at that particular time.'

This passage may be helpful to you in two ways. Firstly, Taylor's analysis may be adapted to events other than wars—revolutions, government changes and policies may be analysed in similar terms. Secondly, his approach offers a way of structuring essays on causation—immediate causes may be examined first, then intermediate and, finally, long-term reasons. Some students may find this the best way of approaching such essays.

In causation essays, it is also important to distinguish between the relative importance of different factors. An answer that simply lists a series of reasons, implying that they are all of equal significance, is not wholly satisfactory. You must endeavour to identify those causes that were especially important and distinguish them from lesser factors. This offers an alternative struture—an essay that starts with the most important factors and works its way down to lesser factors. Alternatively, the final, concluding paragraph can be used in this way to assess the relative significance of the causes.

Thirdly, list essays can be structured by examining various types of factors in turn. Most events in history are clearly the result of a number of reasons. Some may be defined as broadly geographical (especially if this term is broadened to include foreign policy)—for example, failures in foreign policy may lead to a country's downfall, or geographical considerations may lead to a country's desire to change its boundaries. Religious reasons also sometimes contribute to the course of events, although to a lesser extent in the nineteenth century than, say, in the sixteenth. Individual leaders, presidents and ministers also influence how and why things happen—think only, for instance, of the attitudes of Charles X. Most importantly, political and economic factors play a major determining role. You should ensure that you have at least considered, if not written about, each of these types of factors in your essay. They can readily be remembered by the initials: GRIPE, standing for Geographical, Religious,

Individual, Political and Economic. To these may be added a sixth—C—for Chance, as a way of recognizing that in certain circumstances chance factors, not readily foreseeable, also play their part.

GRIPEC may sound childish, but can be a valuable tool. It can act as a mental checklist whenever you approach an essay and thus improve the range of your answer and help you to avoid reverting to narrative. In particular, it can be relied upon to provide fresh inspiration when you 'run out of ideas'.

2 Belgian Independence

(a) The Division of the Netherlands

In 1798 William Pitt the Younger, who was then Prime Minister of Britain, was negotiating with the Russian government over the formation of the Second Coalition against France. He included among the war-aims, which he suggested the allies should adopt, the restoration of the Dutch Republic to its independence and its strengthening against future aggression by uniting it with the Belgian provinces to its south. This idea remained an object of British foreign policy throughout the remaining years of war.

Under the influence of Castlereagh, the First Treaty of Paris in 1814 contained an article stipulating that 'Holland, placed under the sovereignty of the House of Orange, shall receive an increase of territory.' A secret statement added to the Treaty made it clear what this meant—'The establishment of a just equilibrium in Europe demanding that Holland be constituted so as to be in a position to maintain its independence by its own resources, the countries comprised between the sea, the frontiers of France as defined by the present treaty and the Meuse shall be united in perpetuity to Holland (see Map 7). Castlereagh had also intended to strengthen the links between Britain and the Netherlands by a marriage between Princess Charlotte, heiress-presumptive to the British throne, and the Prince of Orange, but she wished to marry a Prince of the House of Saxe-Coburg-Gotha.

In urging the formation of such a United Kingdom of the Netherlands, the British government could claim that it had history on its side. In the past, from the time of the break-up of the Roman Empire, these lands had been combined into some sort of a political unit; but in 1814 they had been disunited for over 200 years. By the mid-sixteenth century, the ideas of the Reformation had spread into this part of Europe, and the Netherlanders, inspired by Protestantism and nationalism, revolted against Spain, the leading Roman Catholic power, which had gained control of their country through marriage earlier in the century. This produced, when peace was made, an independent Dutch Republic in the north, while the southern, Belgian provinces were retained by Spain until they became Austrian in 1713 as a result of the Treaty of Utrecht which brought the War of the Spanish Succession to an end.

This division of the Netherlands was not caused, as has often been thought, by differences of race and religion that distinguished the inhabitants of the two parts of the country from each other. In fact, Protestantism and resistance to Spain at first spread equally throughout the country. It was geographical factors, especially the influence of the great rivers of the land, which determined the final division of the country because they acted as natural strategic barriers to both sides during the revolt. In the later years of the fighting, the Spaniards could not advance beyond these rivers—the Scheldt, Rhine, Waal and Maas (Meuse)—to reconquer the northern provinces, while the Dutch could not wage war far enough across them to liberate the south. And so, when each side had to admit stalemate, the final frontier between north and south ran right through the Flemish-speaking area, separating the people of Flanders and Brabant from the Dutch and associating them with the French-speaking Walloons further south (*see Map 7*). The division of the Netherlands was, indeed, the cause of the differences between north and south rather than the result of it.

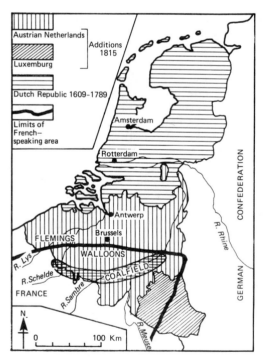

Map 7 The Netherlands in 1815

And by 1814 two centuries of such division had brought about very considerable differences between the Dutch and the Belgians, both French and Flemish-speaking. In the south, the Spanish Inquisition had destroyed Protestantism, which had been tolerated in the north, and so the Belgians were devoted Roman Catholics, while most of the Dutch were Protestants. The Dutch language and the Flemish dialect, once similar, had become almost as distinct as two foreign languages. The Dutch were primarily a sea-faring, commercial and colonizing people, depending upon imports for much of their requirements. The Belgians had no thriving sea-ports, but they had long farmed their fertile land and were now increasingly becoming a mining and manu-facturing nation. Belgium, indeed, was the first Continental country to achieve industrial development in any way like that of Britain. The population of Belgium was over three millions; that of Holland two millions. These decisive differences had resulted in animosities between the peoples of the two parts of the Netherlands. The Dutch despised the Belgians as subservient and backward; the Belgians hated the Dutch as prosperous heretics.

(b) The Settlement of the Netherlands (1815)
After the northern provinces had gained their independence from Spain, they became a republic under a Stadtholder, a post which was first held by William of Orange and became hereditary in his family. In 1795, when the French revolutionary armies invaded the country, the reigning Stadtholder, William V, fled to England, and the republic passed under French control until late in 1813. Then, Napoleon's troops, because they were threatened by an invasion of their own country by the allies, began to evacuate the territory of the Dutch Republic. A provisional government was formed in The Hague. William V was now dead, but it invited his son to return from exile. When he did so, he assumed the title of William I, instead of William VI, and declared himself to be Sovereign Prince of the Netherlands.

William was very anxious to bring about a union of Holland with Belgium and was encouraged by the support of the British government for this. He entered into secret negotiations about the plan with both Britain and Prussia even before the proposal was discussed by the Congress of Vienna. No decision about the idea had been reached by the Congress when Napoleon escaped from Elba. William took advantage of the Hundred Days to proclaim himself in March 1815 as King of the Netherlands without waiting for the formal approval of the allies.

Later that year, however, the Congress approved the establishment of the new United Kingdom. The allies insisted that it should restore the fortresses along the French frontier, which had been dismantled by the Austrians in the eighteenth century, though Castlereagh made an arrangement by which the British government helped with the heavy cost of this (*see page 14*).

In agreeing to the union of the Netherlands, the peacemakers were largely influenced by the British argument in favour of it—the need to contain France by the establishment of a strong state to the north-east of her. It could be justified, however, in other ways. The Belgians had never known independence, and since they were not a people with a common origin and language, it could be denied that there was a separate Belgian nationality. The Dutch East Indies and other colonies might provide Belgian industry both with raw materials and a market for its manufactured products. The idea of union was disliked by the Belgians, but a conciliatory attitude by the Dutch might make it succeed.

In establishing a united kingdom of the Netherlands, the Vienna settlement had laid down that the large Dutch public debt should be fused with the very small Belgian debt, and that there should be freedom of religion. Both these requirements were objectionable to the Belgians. The King appointed a mixed royal commission, half Belgian and half Dutch in membership. It was agreed that the country should be governed by a parliamentary monarchy. The Belgians succeeded in getting a States-General with two chambers—an upper chamber nominated by the King that would serve as a conservative check to the other chamber, which was to be elected. The Dutch, however, were able to insist that the number of elected members should be 55 for each part of the Kingdom, despite the difference in population, and that these should be elected indirectly by members of the provincial councils. The Dutch could generally reckon on having a majority in the lower chamber because there were several Belgian officials among its members who were dependent upon the King and the government for their posts. Moreover, the States-General had very limited powers, and the King could, if he considered that there was an emergency, ignore it by issuing orders of his own. The King could also appoint and dismiss ministers at his will; he controlled financial policy; and he personally ruled the overseas colonial possessions. And William, who combined a love of paying close attention to all the details of public business with an outlook very much like that of an eighteenth-century enlightened despot, was determined to rule as a powerful monarch. 'I can reign without ministers,' he stated. 'It is I alone who govern, and I alone am responsible.'

(c) The Difficulties of the Union

At first if seemed as if William's rule might be successful. He believed that if he could make his new kingdom materially prosperous, he would secure its stability and unity; and he followed an economic policy which brought him the nickname of the 'Merchant-King'. In order to put this policy into effect, he founded a number of financial institutions with which he maintained a close personal connection. As early as 1814, he founded the *Nederlandsche Bank* to control the national currency; and eight years later, in order to provide finance for industry, he established at Brussels the *Société Générale des Pays-Bas pour Favoriser l'Industrie Nationale*, nearly four-fifths of its capital being subscribed personally by himself. He also took a direct interest in encouraging new industrial undertakings. In 1817 he went into partnership with a British industrialist, John Cockerill, who established an iron foundry and machine-manufacturing works at Seraing in the old summer palace of the bishops of Liège, and it soon became the largest on the Continent. He continued this development, and some years later the Austrian Ambassador wrote to Metternich that special assistance was given to foreigners who wished to introduce useful industries into the country. Dutch trade with the East Indies had been strangled by the British naval blockade during the Revolutionary and Napoleonic Wars, and in order to revive it, the King set up at Amsterdam in 1824 a new commercial company, the *Nederlandsche Handelsmaetschappij*, in which he also made considerable personal investment. Through this company, Belgian cotton fabrics steadily came to dominate the market of the Dutch East Indies. He also founded other companies for various purposes, including the construction of new roads and canals to improve internal communications.

While these measures pleased businessmen throughout the new kingdom, other issues placed increasing strain upon its political life. From the start the religious question threatened the success of the union. The Roman Catholic Church in Belgium soon came into conflict with the government over the question of education. While in the Dutch Republic the schools were maintained by provincial and other authorities, these were entirely controlled by the Church in the Austrian Netherlands. The Belgian bishops wanted to preserve their direction of education, but William wished to have a system of state education in which, moreover, the teachers would be expected to influence the minds of their pupils towards an attitude favourable to the idea of a united Netherlands. So members of religious orders who wished to teach had to attend a special course of instruction given by professors appointed by the King, and candidates for the priesthood were not allowed to study at colleges at Rome or elsewhere abroad. William's conception of education was never accepted by the bishops, who continually refused to co-operate with it.

Nor was there complete agreement over the King's economic policy. Though the Belgian industrialists did enjoy the benefit of his measures and the increased overseas markets for their products as a result of the union, they wanted to maintain the duties on imports, which they had known under Austrian rule, to protect their manufactures, particularly from British competition. The Belgian farmers similarly wished for protection against imported foreign foodstuffs. The Dutch, on the other hand, looked for a return to the free trade, which they had previously experienced in the days of their Republic, since this would both bring them cheaper food and be beneficial to their commercial interests. In 1816 William introduced a high protectionist policy to assist industry in the Netherlands, but only five years later it had to be modified because of growing opposition from the Dutch merchants, and this was a compromise which left many of them dissatisfied. In addition, the new banks and companies were partly financed by fresh taxes on bread and meat which caused widespread discontent, especially among the growing Belgian industrial working classes.

Further discontent was caused by William's efforts to make the kingdom a powerful check to any further French aggression as was intended by the Vienna settlement. He considered that this could not be done satisfactorily merely be rebuilding the chain of fortresses on the southern frontier, however well this might be done. The Netherland's resistance to any French attack would be made much more difficult if the people on their side of the frontier sympathized with the aggressors. The people living on that border were the French-speaking Walloons, among whom French sympathies and culture had been strengthened during the wartime period of French occupation. William decided to try to reduce this influence by encouraging the use of the Dutch language throughout the Belgian provinces. He believed also that the adoption of a common language would promote a sense of national unity. In 1819 the knowledge of Dutch was required for appointment to all public positions, and in 1822 it was recognized as the national language and made official. This again brought the government into conflict with the Roman Catholic Church. The making of the Dutch language compulsory was strongly opposed by the Flemish clergy, who feared that it would mean the arrival of many Protestant officials, judges and teachers into the province. It also lost the government the support of the administrative and professional classes in the southern part of the country.

Indeed, the new kingdom never became truly united. It remained essentially a Dutch state, and no real attempt was made to give the Belgians a fair share in its government. The continual insistence that Dutch should be the official language of the whole kingdom threatened to make it impossible for most Belgians, whether Walloons or Flemings, to qualify for administrative posts even in their own part of the country. The government remained almost entirely Dutch. It had been agreed that the States-General should meet alternately in a northern and a southern city, but in practice it always met at The Hague, where all the ministries also remained. The Court of Appeal was there too, though it received five times more Belgian than Dutch appeals. Some years after the union, six cabinet ministers out of seven were Dutch and 35 of the 59 ambassadors. In the army, only 380 of the 1980 officers were Belgian, and all the nine generals were Dutch.

Apart from his belief about the way national unity should be established, it was natural and perhaps inevitable that William should place himself in this position at the very beginning of his reign. On his return from exile, the Dutch had welcomed him with the cry, 'Up the House of Orange!' To them he was the representative of the ruling family whose members were associated closely with their struggle for independence and later prosperity. The Belgians, however, had no such feelings for him. At the best, they were indifferent to him. He was bound to seek the support of his Dutch subjects, whose loyalty he could trust, and to wish to strengthen their influence in the kingdom as the best way of upholding his power.

The growing resentment that this aroused among the Belgians led the government to attempt to take action against it. Though the constitution guaranteed the freedom of the press, censorship was introduced by government decree as soon as 1815. The courts punished journalists who expressed the discontent of the southern provinces as well as bishops and priests who attacked the government's religious policy. Some suffered imprisonment and others fines, which were commonly paid for them by public subscription. By such a policy, the government aroused the opposition of both the Belgian clergy and liberals. At first, however, the Roman Catholic party, strong in the countryside, and the group of middle-class, anti-clerical republicans remained hostile to each other. It was not until the later 1820s that a united Belgian national movement became possible through the influence of the Liberal Catholicism proclaimed by the French priest, the Abbé de Lamennais (*see page 390*). A compromise was accepted by which the Roman Catholic schools were to be retained in Belgium and the freedom of the liberal press respected.

In 1828 the liberal journalist, Louis de Potter, wrote a violent article in his newspaper, the *Courrier des Pays Bas*, in which he called upon his readers to rally for action against the government: 'As we have formerly hunted down our enemies, let us now pursue the ministers.' He was fined and imprisoned for this, and two years later he was banished from the kingdom after publishing another aggressive article advocating the formation of an association to give active help to those who resisted the government. The agreement between Roman Catholics and liberals led him to become accepted as a national hero in Belgium, where feeling had now grown so intense that it seemed likely that some incident might at any time set it off into open rebellion.

(d) The Belgian Revolt (1830)

The incident which set off the events leading to the Belgian revolt was the news of the July Revolution in France. This caused great excitement in Brussels, where crowds were attending an exhibition of national industry. In August a performance of *La Muette de Portici*, a French opera dealing sympathetically with the revolt of the people of Naples against their Spanish oppressors in 1647, produced a demonstration in the theatre, which developed into rioting in the city and cries of 'Down with the Dutch!'

The King and his government were caught entirely by surprise. The riots became an uprising. The small Dutch garrison was expelled from the city. Other Belgian towns joined in the revolt, and in October its leaders, both Roman Catholic and liberal, formed a provisional government which proclaimed the country's independence.

The next month a National Congress, consisting of 200 members chosen by some 30 000 voters above the age of 25, met at Brussels to draw up a constitution. While excluding the House of Orange from the throne, it decided that the state should be governed by a monarchy. All forms of political and social liberty were guaranteed, and considerable powers of local government were assigned to the provinces. There was to be a legislative assembly, consisting of two chambers, to whom the ministers were to be responsible, though they were to be appointed by the monarch, who was also to control the executive. The franchise was extended, but only so as to give the vote to some 46 000 electors out of a population of 4 million. The Congress's aim was a parliamentary monarchy as in Britain. Many liberals, Belgian and foreign, praised the constitution, but the limitation of the franchise displeased others. Among them was Louis de Potter, who resigned from the provisional government and went to France.

William, meanwhile, had appealed to the signatories of the Treaty of Vienna. The Belgian revolt was, indeed, not only a clear violation of the settlement of 1815, but was also the first. It was bound, therefore, to be a matter of urgent concern to the great powers. William expected help from the three eastern powers at least, and their rulers were at first ready to give it to him. Metternich said that only such intervention to uphold the authority of the King over the whole of the Netherlands would arrest 'the universal shipwreck of Europe'. He would have liked immediate joint action to be undertaken to remove this first threat that the July Revolution in France would spread a disturbing influence over the Continent.

Louis Philippe, however, was anxious to begin his reign in agreement with Britain (*see page 78*). He gave the post of French Ambassador in London to the elderly Talleyrand—'that fabulous old man', Palmerston called him. Talleyrand was able to persuade the British government to accept the idea that the representatives of the five great powers should meet in conference to discuss the situation. The rulers of the eastern powers agreed to this because they hoped that such a conference would be ready to take steps to regain the whole of his kingdom for William.

However, soon after the conference met in London, the situation was completely changed by the sudden rising of the Poles against Russia in November 1830 (*see page 132*). The Tsar was now absorbed in its suppression, while the Austrian and Prussian governments had to take precautions against the possibility of a revolt in their own Polish provinces. Metternich had also to fear the danger of insurrection in northern Italy (*see page 112*). These developments now made any action in Belgium by these powers out of the question.

Though the union of the Netherlands had largely come about in 1815 as a result of British policy, Palmerston, who had recently become Foreign Secretary, believed that this had now failed irretrievably and that any international action would be dangerous and in vain. He said that, though 'it was for the interest of both England and Prussia that Belgium and Holland should have remained united', the British government had come to 'consider the absolute and entire separation of Belgium from Holland to be no longer a matter for discussion.' His main concern was to prevent that part of Europe being occupied by any great power. When, therefore, Louis Philippe, who was content with the dissolution of a state set up to contain France, suggested that the powers should accept the principle of non-intervention and recognise the independence and neutrality of Belgium, he readily agreed. The eastern powers now had to accept this decision, which was announced in January 1831. This was a situation which suited both Britain and France because its purpose was to prevent the use of Belgium by a hostile power to mount an attack on either of them.

There remained, however, the much more difficult problem of the territorial boundaries of the new state. The conference decided that it should have those possessed by the Austrian Netherlands in 1790, but the hardest question to decide was the future of Luxemburg, a small state bounded by France, Prussia and Belgium (*see Map 7, page 92*). This Duchy had been part of the Austrian Netherlands until it was annexed by France in 1795. The Vienna settlement made it a Grand Duchy and granted it to William I in compensation for his loss of family territories in the Rhineland which went to Prussia. It was then administratively incorporated within the Kingdom of the Netherlands, but William, as Grand Duke of Luxemburg, was one of the sovereigns of the German Confederation and a member of the Diet at Frankfurt; and the city of Luxemburg, known as the 'Gibraltar of the east' because of its strategic importance, was garrisoned by Prussian troops as a federal fortress. The people of Luxemburg, however, joined with the Belgians in the rising of 1830. Belgian troops occupied it, and representatives from it attended the National Congress in Brussels. The conference in London, however, since neither Austria nor Prussia wanted Luxemburg to be removed from the German Confederation assigned the Grand Duchy to the King of Holland.

By now a Belgian Assembly had been elected, according to the constitution, and it claimed Luxemburg as part of the new state. The issue also became linked with another question—the choice of a ruler for Belgium. The decision by the National Congress to make the country a hereditary monarchy had been taken on very practical grounds. The middle-class leaders of the revolt realized that the great powers of Europe would never recognize Belgium's independence if they set up a republic. As one of them said, 'As a monarchy, we will be a power; as a republic, we will be a scarecrow.' The Belgian Assembly offered the throne of the country to the Duke of Nemours, a son of Louis Philippe, in the hope that this would gain French support for the possession of Luxemburg by Belgium. Palmerston protested with his usual forthrightness, since he feared that France would bring Belgium within her control. He said that France should not have 'a cabbage-garden or a vineyard' in Belgium—the first of many such remarks with which European statesmen were to become only too familiar during the succeeding years. His words had their intended effect. Louis Philippe declined the Belgian offer, and on Palmerston's advice, accompanied by the promise of further negotiations over Luxemburg, the Belgian Assembly chose Leopold of Saxe-Coburg-Gotha as their King in June 1831. He was the widower of Princess Charlotte (*see page 91*) and was also an uncle of the future Queen Victoria.

William I, however, had not accepted the loss of Belgium. In July 1831 a Dutch army under his son, the Prince of Orange, invaded the country and advanced unchecked for ten days. The new King of Belgium appealed to Louis Philippe for help. The powers hastily authorized his intervention, which did something to enhance his prestige in France, although Palmerston again made it clear that the British government would not permit France to retain any permanent influence in Belgium. A French army occupied Brussels until the Dutch withdrew from the country. The Dutch continued, however, to retain the port of Antwerp until combined action by a French army and a British fleet compelled them to relinquish it in December 1832.

Eventually the details of the frontier were settled by the Treaty of London in 1839. Belgium was to retain Antwerp and the freedom of the navigation of the Scheldt, while Holland kept control of the mouth of the river. Belgium was given the western part of Luxemburg, which became the Belgian province of Luxemburg, the rest of the Grand Duchy remained with Holland, and the Prussian garrison was retained in the city. Holland had to recognize the Kingdom of Belgium by this same treaty. Britain, France, Russia, Prussia and Austria affirmed that Belgium was 'an independent and perpetually neutral state', and the fortresses built on the Franco-Belgian frontier in 1815 were to be demolished.

This formally ended the attempt by the European statesmen to unite into a single state two peoples who had once been ruled together, but now, as the events which dissolved the union showed, had been converted by history into foreign neighbours with more to separate them from each other than to form them into a single state again. That the dissolution of the Kingdom of the Netherlands took place without a serious threat to European peace was due to the co-operation of Britain and France on the one hand and the acquiescence of the three eastern powers on the other. The first had its difficulties, but was largely successful because the French government was prepared to recognize Palmerston's determination that Britain should have a foreign policy which upheld her interests, an attitude which France was not to maintain during the international crisis ten years later (*see page 78*). The second probably came about mainly through the preoccupation of the eastern powers with the problems of the Polish revolt, but perhaps also because Britain and France were restrained in their approach to this situation and to the risings in Italy.

Bibliography

Leon van der Essen, *A Short History of Belgium* (2nd. ed., Chicago, 1920), H. Van der Linden (trans. Sybil Jane), *Belgium: The Making of a Nation* (OUP, 1920), and George Edmundson, *A History of Holland* (CUP, 1922). In addition to the books about Louis Philippe mentioned on page 86, there is also Jasper Ridley, *Lord Palmerston* (Constable, 1970).

Exercises

A *This section consists of questions that might be used for discussion (or written answers) as a way of expanding on the chapter and testing your understanding of it:*

1 Why was Britain interested in creating an enlarged Dutch state in 1815?

2 Explain the meaning of the secret statement added to the First Treaty of Paris (1814).

3 What do you understand by 'the division of the Netherlands was . . . the cause of the differences between north and south rather than the result of it'?

4 Why did the Dutch and Belgians dislike each other by the early nineteenth century?

5 Why did William V's son call himself William I instead of William VI?

6 Were the powers at the Congress of Vienna persuaded to agree to the union of the Netherlands purely by strategic considerations?

7 When the United Kingdom was established, which aspects of the constitutional settlement were favourable to the Belgians and which to the Dutch?

8 How did William I hope to win support for his new kingdom, and what measures did he take to achieve this?

9 Explain how each of the following issues brought conflict between the Dutch and Belgian sections of the kingdom:
(a) the control of education.
(b) tariff policy.
(c) Dutch language laws.

10 How could the Flemings and Walloons claim that the new state 'remained essentially Dutch'?

11 Which aspects of William's policies towards the Belgians aroused most hostility?

12 Why did Metternich consider it so important that the great powers should intervene to support William?

13 How did the Polish revolt alter the attitude of the Eastern Powers towards Belgium?

14 Why was Palmerston prepared, in 1830, to go back on what had been British policy in 1814?

15 Why was the break-up of the new united Netherlands achieved relatively peacefully?

B *Essay questions*

1 Explain the importance of *two* of the following: (a) the Decembrist Revolt in Russia (1825); (b) the Polish Revolution (1830–1831); (c) the Belgian Revolution (1830–1839). (Cambridge, 1982)

2 What were the causes of the Belgian Revolt? Discuss the part played by the Great Powers in the 1830s in determining the future of Belgium. (SUJB, 1982)

3 Explain how and why the Belgians were able to set up an independent and constitutional state between 1830 and 1839. (JMB, 1981)

C *Extract question*
Some examining boards now include extract questions in their examinations. It is, therefore, important that you become familiar with the lay-out and nature of these. This was included in the London Board's 1981 paper.

BELGIUM IN THE 1830s
Study Extracts I, II and III below and then answer questions (*a*) to (*g*) which follow:

EXTRACT I

line
1   '. . . In sum, the whole of Belgium treated as a conquered Province or a Colony; everything, Gentlemen, made revolution *necessary*, and made it *inevitable*, and hastened its occurrence. *Grievances* so just and
5   genuine were bound also to ensure its success.
     We have risen against despotism in order to win back our rights; we were treated as Rebels by our tyrants. Our towns were burned, the most barbarous crimes were committed even against old men and women, the laws of humanity and the laws of war were trampled underfoot, and these
10   testify to the ferocity of *our Foes*, and at the same time sanctify *the victory of the People* which has *cleared them out of the land.*
     The fruit of this victory was Independence. The People has announced this through us.
     As the interpreter of its desires, the *Provisional Government* has called
15   you, Gentlemen, the elected representatives of the Belgian Nation, *to constitute this Independence* and consolidate it for ever.'
     (*A Message to the Belgian National Congress, 5 October 1830*)

EXTRACT II
     'Article I. *His Majesty the King of the Netherlands*, Grand Duke of
20   *Luxemburg*, engages to cause to be immediately converted into a Treaty with *His Majesty the King of the Belgians*, the Articles annexed to the present Act, and agreed upon by common consent, *under the auspices of* the Courts of Great Britain, Austria, France, Prussia, and Russia. . . .
     Article III. The Union which has existed between Holland and
25   Belgium, in virtue of the Treaty of Vienna of the 31st of May, 1815, is acknowledged by *His Majesty the King of the Netherlands*, Grand Duke of *Luxemburg*, to be dissolved.'
     (*Treaty of London, 19 April 1839*)

EXTRACT III
30   '(Our) policy was, in fact, at the same time liberal and anti-revolutionary. Anti-revolutionary without as within, for outside it sought the maintenance of the peace of Europe, within that of the constitutional monarchy. Liberal, because it accepted and respected the essential conditions of free government. . . . In fact, from 1830 to
35   1848 this double aim was attained. Exteriorly, peace was maintained, and I think even now, as I thought twenty years ago, that neither the influence nor the high standing of France in Europe was lowered.'
     (*François Guizot, 'Memoirs to Serve the History of My Own Time', English Translation, 1867*)

(*a*) State the nationality of 'our Foes' (line 9), and name (i) 'His (3)
Majesty the King of the Netherlands' (line 18), and (ii) 'His
Majesty the King of the Belgians' (line 20).

(*b*) Explain (i) 'Provisional Government' (line 13), and (ii) 'to (4)
constitute this Independence' (line 15).

(*c*) To what 'grievances' was reference made in line 3, and how (7)
far do you agree that they made revolution both 'necessary'
and 'inevitable' (line 2)?

(*d*) Comment on the claim that 'the victory of the People' had (3)
'cleared them out of the land' (line 10).

(*e*) What was the importance of 'Luxemburg' (lines 19 and 26) (3)
in securing a final settlement of the Belgian question in the
1830s?

(*f*) Why was this settlement 'under the auspices of' the powers, (3)
which are referred to in line 21?

(*g*) What policy towards the Belgian question in the 1830s did (8)
the government of France pursue, and how far was this
policy fittingly described by Guizot in Extract III?

D *Analysis: causes and effects*
In this section you will be considering in more detail three analytical
aspects of Belgian independence—the reasons why the 1830 Revolt took
place at all, the causes of its success and the international importance of the
event. In addition, you will be applying some of the ideas on causation
suggested in the exercise section on pages 89–91.

(*a*) *The reasons for the Belgian Revolt of 1830*
In the box below are suggested a number of reasons why the
Belgians revolted against the Dutch in 1830.

1 Study the list, adding to it any causes that you think have been omitted and
deleting from it any you consider irrelevant or invalid.

2 Now put the causes on your amended list into what you consider their
order of importance, placing the factor that you consider the most crucial
in bringing about the revolution at the top of the list, and so on down to the
least significant.

3 Having considered the importance of the different factors, *re-sort* your list
of causes into categories:
  (a) firstly, by chronology—place them into three groups—immediate
      causes, intermediate causes, long-term causes (*see page 90*).
  (b) secondly, divide them into five categories—political reasons, religious
      reasons, economic factors, geographical factors and 'individual'
      reasons (*see page 90*).

4 Write an appraisal of the three alternative approaches to causation that you
have just completed.

Causes of the Belgian Revolution, 1830

(i)	The constitutional and educational policies of the Dutch government after 1815, leading to resentment among their Belgian subjects.
(ii)	The increasing separation of the Belgian and Dutch people after the seventeenth century, so that by the nineteenth century they could be considered two separate peoples, with little in common.
(iii)	The impact of the July Revolution in Paris and the response of people in Brussels to this revolt.
(iv)	The attempts of William I to reorganize the Dutch economy and the alterations he made to tariffs.
(v)	The wholehearted determination of the Belgian liberals to establish their own Kingdom and their untiring efforts to achieve this.
(vi)	The different attitudes of the Dutch and Belgians towards the House of Orange and of the new King towards them.
(vii)	The United Kingdom of the Netherlands was a false creation anyway, put together by the great powers in 1815 as a bastion against the French.
(viii)	The deliberate suppression of Belgian opposition, including the censorship of the press and the punishment of the clergy.

(b) *The reasons for the Belgian success*

Using the ideas suggested by the diagram below, write a list (similar to that in the box above) of reasons for the success of the Belgians in the 1830s. Having written such a list, repeat the same four exercises as in (a) above—i.e. sort out your causes by importance, chronology and category.

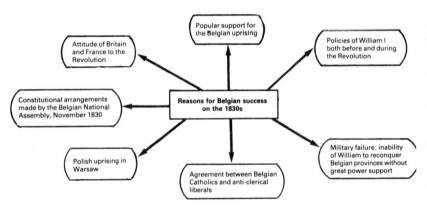

(c) *The international significance of the Belgian Revolution*

It is difficult to assess the importance of an event while you are studying the period for the first time, as you often require a broad chronological perspective to see its true significance. Indeed, it is often better to return to questions of this kind at the end of your course. However, it is also important to have some ideas about an event's importance, so that you can keep it in mind while studying subsequent events elsewhere. In this section, therefore, you will be introduced to some aspects of the significance of the Belgian Revolution. This is intended to be a discussion paper, and down the left-hand side are suggested some points you may discuss. It is also intended to illustrate by example some of the aspects of essay-writing (especially the use of first sentences) referred to on page 89.

Paradox?	In the first place, the crisis revealed both the strength and the weakness of the Congress System. The great powers worked together, reached agreement by negotiation and imposed a settlement on the Netherlands and Belgium, even to the extent of deciding who should be King. In this way, they prevented a local problem having international consequences, which could
Such as?	have led to war between the great powers as, indeed, apparently minor matters were to do over the next hundred years. For this success, the diplomats of Europe, such as Talleyrand and Palmerston, must take some credit, although it may be argued
For example?	that their success was equally due to other events and accidents as well as to their own skills.

At the same time, the great powers could be said to have failed. They had originally created the United Kingdom of the
When and Why? Netherlands, and at the same time had decided to uphold the political status quo of Europe and to come to the aid of the 'legitimate' rulers of Europe. When the Belgians revolted in 1830, the immediate reaction of the Eastern powers was to help William I to suppress the revolt. However, under the influence of the Western powers and events in Poland, they decided not to
Why the Change? do this and, in effect, reversed their policy, supporting instead the rebels and imposing a settlement that clearly went against the principles they had so clearly enunciated only 15 years earlier. On the other hand, it might be argued that in these circumstances, the great power diplomats were showing their flexibility
How so?
Such as? and their preparedness to react to events and trends that had taken place over the period since the Congress of Vienna.

See page 380 In particular, it may be argued that Belgian independence had important effects for the cause of liberalism in Western Europe. The Belgians had removed a ruler who was more inclined to autocracy than liberalism, and who had imposed on them laws and policies that were against their interests. They had replaced him with a new form of government that guaranteed individual rights and liberties and reached a compromise on the position of the Church in the State. Though the franchise was limited, the new constitution was 'the envy of
Where was this example followed? liberals throughout Europe'. (Anthony Wood, *Europe 1815 to 1945*, p. 81.) The Belgians had, therefore, provided Europe with an example of how liberalism could succeed, both in removing an autocratic ruler and constructing a new state.

The place of the Belgian revolution in the rise of nationalism
See page 381 is more debatable. On the one hand, it may be argued that the new state was not a national one. The people of Belgium had, for several centuries, been ruled over by a variety of political masters, had never been independent and had more loyalty to their individual provinces than to any national entity. Nor were
What makes a nationality? they of a single nationality or religion. On the other hand, William I had clearly tried to impose an alien nationality on these people by a variety of policies. The Belgian opposition to
Such as? these policies may be described as nationalist, in that it objected to a new form of nationality being introduced. The Revolution

led to creation of a new, small state and was thus in keeping with the nationalist trend away from a limited number of major, multi-national states. Again, its success can be seen as providing an example to other national groups in Europe, especially those that were objects of similar policies of 'integration.'

Such as?

Meaning?

Finally, Belgian independence had important geopolitical consequences. Firstly, it settled for the rest of the nineteenth century the boundaries of an area that had been disputed and changed hands a number of times since the sixteenth century. The area was of clear strategic importance, lying immediately north of France, west of the Empire and incorporating Channel ports that could be regarded as a threat to Britain. The new state and its neutrality were also guaranteed internationally. Thus, the international position of Belgium remained until 1914, when Germany's invasion of France through Belguim provided Britain with the *casus belli* to join the First World War. Secondly, the Belgian episode was the first of a process by which, throughout the nineteenth century, other disputed areas of Europe were to be settled, either by peace or war. Ominously, by the end of the century, only the Balkans remained a geopolitical vacuum.

Why?

Such as?

3 The Challenge to Metternich

(a) The Failure of Imperial Government

The Emperor Francis had constantly supported Metternich on condition that the idea of his personal, unrestrained rule should be upheld unquestioningly. Other Continental rulers believed in this for themselves, but Francis believed in a particular way that loyalty to the Emperor was the most effective way of retaining the obedience of his diverse dominions. As national unity was impossible in a multinational empire, its place had to be taken by *Kaisertreue*, personal devotion to the Emperor and the Habsburg family. He once asked a question which summed up his attitude. When a distinguished official of the Empire was recommended to him as a worthy patriot, he asked, 'But is he to be a patriot for me?' And when in 1809 the Tyrolean patriot, Andreas Hofer, led an insurrection against the French and Bavarians to maintain the union of his country with Austria under the imperial crown, Francis gave him no support and acquiesced in his execution by the French. Other rulers might hope to harness national feeling to the support of their throne, but he did not wish to encourage nationalism in Austria or any other part of his Empire. He believed that acceptance of the rule of the head of the Habsburg family alone could unite his multi-racial and weakly-governed dominions.

This monarchical ideal had now been widely challenged by the French Revolution, but even when widely held in past European history, it had depended for its practical effectiveness upon the character of the particular ruler; and when Francis died in February 1835 and was succeeded by his son, Ferdinand I, it was seriously threatened in the Austrian Empire. His parents were first cousins, and he was descended through his maternal grandfather from the unstable Neapolitan Bourbons. He was a mental and physical defective. He has been remembered because he said, 'I am Emperor, and I *will* have dumplings', but that is not his only coherent remark on record. He wished to rule, but since he was incapable of reading documents or following an argument, he was incapable of doing so. 'To govern is easy, but to sign one's name is difficult,' he is reported also to have said. Palmerston realized the danger presented to the Austrian Empire by his accession. 'How can an empire stand in these days without an emperor at its head?' he wrote to the British Ambassador at Vienna. 'And by an emperor I mean a man endowed with intellectual faculties suited to his high station. A mere man of straw, a Guy Faux, like the present Emperor, may do very well in quiet times.' And Ferdinand's reign was not a quiet time. It is commonly known as the 'pre-March' period, when the frozen post-war years were fast dissolving into a spring thaw which was bound to end in floods sooner or later.

Though Ferdinand's unsuitability for the imperial throne had long been apparent since he was forty-two when he succeeded his father, there was no desire in official circles to interfere with the hereditary nature of the monarchy or to exclude him from the succession. It was likely that this would have been difficult, particularly since Ferdinand had been crowned King of Hungary five years previously in an attempt to gain Magyar loyalty to the throne; and the most likely prince to replace him, his younger brother, Charles was only slightly more intelligent. There seemed, therefore, no reason for abandoning the strict hereditary principle in the Habsburg family.

Metternich never seems to have thought of opposing Ferdinand's right to the throne. This may have been because he thought that the incapacity of the new Emperor would increase his own authority over the Habsburg lands and enable him at last to strengthen the power of the central government. Francis, despite his attachment to the idea of personal imperial rule, had not really been able to exercise it and was unwilling to support the constitutional changes needed to make it possible. Metternich had long wanted to make the Emperor more than a symbol of unity; he wanted to use his position as a means of effective government (*see page 44*).

Metternich had done his best to make sure that he retained his power during Ferdinand's reign. On his deathbed, Francis signed a political testament, drafted by Metternich, in which he urged his son to 'change nothing in the foundations of the structure of the State' and to rely upon Metternich, 'my most loyal servant and friend'. The new reign did not, however, turn out as Metternich had hoped. The other members of the imperial family and rival politicians, being no longer restrained by Francis, both intrigued against him. Power ceased to be entirely in his hands, but passed to the Council of State. This consisted of himself; the narrow-minded Archduke Louis, the previous Emperor's younger brother; and Count Francis Kalowrat, a Bohemian nobleman, who had been Minister of the Interior since 1826 and gained great prestige by his financial ability, but had no general gifts as an administrator. Kalowrat was intensely jealous of Metternich as a 'foreigner' from the Rhineland. He sought popularity by posing to favour liberal ideas, while Metternich came increasingly to reply upon the support of the Roman Catholic Church. The struggle for influence between these two men was encouraged by the Archduke Louis, who disliked them both, and the result was that the Council of State became more and more ineffective.

This situation made it impossible for Metternich to achieve any of his projected constitutional reforms, which lacked support from any class or party in the Empire. Even his plan to strengthen the idea of loyalty to the person of the Emperor by the peoples of his lands failed. When the Austrian Empire had been proclaimed in 1804, no arrangements had been made for an imperial coronation, and Francis was never crowned, but Metternich now proposed that Ferdinand should be crowned Emperor of Austria in the presence of delegates from the provincial diets. The court, however, rejected this idea because it feared that even such a small measure of provincial co-operation would weaken the traditional Habsburg policy of 'divide and rule.' Having already been crowned King of Hungary, Ferdinand now merely participated in two further provincial coronations. In 1836 he was crowned King of Bohemia at Prague and in 1838 received the iron crown of Charlemagne at Milan as King of Lombardy. Both these events were performed with great pomp and ceremony and accompanied by the granting of amnesties to political prisoners, but they did nothing to bind the peoples of the Empire closer to the throne.

Not only would the bureaucracy not have been strong or efficient enough to carry out Metternich's reforms, it was not even able to manage the day-to-day government of the Empire at all forcefully. During these years the imperial administration remained as ineffective as ever before. Though its wish to prevent intercourse with the world outside the Empire led Palmerston to say that Austria was Europe's China, the censorship was unable to stop the circulation of liberal literature from abroad, mainly from Germany. Books in large numbers reached the University of Vienna, which became a centre of radical activity. Opposition parties existed with little interference, and liberal clubs advertized their meetings openly in the cities. Such an erosion of the government's restrictive measures gave a false impression that the regime was making occasional concessions to liberalism, while it was in reality obliged to give way through weakness. Outwardly the imperial system remained as oppressive as ever, and Metternich, though now unable to do anything to make it effective, was regarded by its enemies as responsible for its continuance.

(b) Social and Political Problems

These pre-March years were a period of important social changes in the Habsburg lands. By 1848 their population had increased by about 40 per cent since the end of the eighteenth century to bring it to a total of about 35 million (*see Table 8 page 83*). This situation encouraged some more enterprising landowners, notably in Bohemia and Moravia, to develop their estates so that they could profitably produce food for the growing number of people, but such improvements affected only a small part of agriculture. Most of the people in the countryside were peasants engaged in little more than subsistence farming, and in the Empire as a whole the increase of food production was very slow. Many peasant families, indeed, now had holdings which were not large enough to support them, and more were becoming landless.

Rural overpopulation, however, was not as great as in other European countries. In the 1830s it was estimated that the surplus labour of the Austrian Empire amounted to 1 in 25 of the total population compared with 1 in 6 in England. Nevertheless, it was a serious problem because there was not enough industry to provide work for this employable population. Industrial development was slow in the Empire. The first coke-fired furnace was only set up in the great Czech industrial centre of Vitkovice in 1836 and the first rolling-mill in Lombardy in 1840. The Empire had long suffered from inadequate roads, but the imperial government made determined efforts, partly for strategic reasons, to improve the situation. Between 1830 and 1847 the Empire (excluding Hungary) gained over 48 000 kilometres of roads, which multiplied its length of highway by two-and-a-third. Steam railways were introduced as early as in most Continental countries. The first line, the Kaiser Ferdinands Nordbahn, was opened in 1837 outside Vienna and ran from Floridsdorf to Deutsch-Wagram, though it was some years before it was completed to become a through route to Moravia. Indeed, although companies began the building of lines north and east of Vienna, where the country was suitable for easy railway construction, they found it difficult to raise capital, and more and more imperial help was needed. And the same difficulty was faced by the Austrian Lloyd Steam Navigation Company which was founded at this time.

A new wealthy capitalist class was slow to appear, and Austrian industry remained on a small scale. In the year 1836 the Empire (including Hungary and Lombardy) had only eight towns with a population of over 50 000, while Britain, with a total population of more than 10 million fewer, had twice as many. Nevertheless, the number of factory workers in the towns was steadily increasing. Many of them drew wages which were barely sufficient to keep them from starvation. In the autumn of 1847 Austrian industry was sufficiently large to suffer from the general economic depression in Europe. The unemployed industrial workers came to believe that they could only improve their situation if they gained political power, and they joined the opposition to the imperial system personified by Metternich.

More serious than these social problems as a threat to the stability of the Austrian Empire, however, was the growth of nationalism among the Magyars, Czechs, Serbs, Croats and other subject peoples. The peasants in the countryside were hardly influenced by this, but those who went into the towns began to provide nationalism with working-class support because they founded communities from the subject peoples there, which were sufficiently large and cohesive to resent the predominance of the German language and officials in their everyday life. Among all the peoples, leadership continued to come from the intellectual and professional classes, but they now gained the support of the landowning nobility, who saw it as a means of increasing their own rights and privileges. The local diets, which they controlled, became centres of opposition to the imperial government and put forward demands for provincial (though aristocratic) liberties. For instance, the Bohemian Diet in 1840 claimed the right to reject as well as to discuss proposals which were placed before it by the central government, and in 1846 it insisted that it should vote the taxes of the country. Other diets made similar attempts to regain for themselves those powers which the Habsburgs had taken away from them during the sixteenth and seventeenth centuries. The response of the imperial government to this was again to seek to 'divide and rule' by supporting one linguistic group, as an ally, against others.

(c) **Hungarian Ascendancy**
The linguistic group that the imperial government supported was usually the Magyars since Hungary continued to be the one part of the Austrian Empire that was capable of making terms with the central government. During the reign of Francis, the Magyar nobility had been able to defend their privileges and to revive the Hungarian Diet after a period of eclipse (*see page 41*). They now wished to go further. They had demands for the future which were based upon the past. They saw themselves as the equals of the Germans in the Empire because they looked back to the time before the Battle of Mohacs in 1526 when the last native King of Hungary had been killed by the Turks and his lands passed to the Habsburgs. This union of crowns had formed a lasting basis for Habsburg power, but now the Magyar nobility wanted to make Hungary a separate national kingdom within the Empire.

As a step towards this, they wanted to gain further official acknowledgement of the Magyar language, which would distinguish Hungary in an important way from the other provinces of the Empire where no such recognition was given to national languages. The common language used in Hungary for all government business, including the deliberations of the Diet, was Latin. They were able to show that this was becoming increasingly out-of-date and impractical for such purposes and insisted that the only alternative to it was their own language. In 1840 the Diet adopted Magyar as its official language and ordered that all registers of births, marriages and deaths were to be kept in it; and in 1844 it completely abolished the use of Latin in Hungary, including Latin lectures at the University of Budapest, and established Magyar as the exclusive language of the kingdom. The Imperial government had to accept this, being only able to obtain the concession that German was to be the language used for correspondence with the imperial authorities. Few German officials, however, could now be sent to Hungary because Magyar was a difficult language to learn and was not widely spoken like German, French or English.

Magyar, in fact, was the language of only a minority of the people of Hungary. Only about 4 500 000 of the 11 000 000 inhabitants of the kingdom spoke it. Other linguistic groups, such as the Croats of Zagreb, the Serbs of the Voivodine, the Saxons and Wallachs of Transylvania and the Slovaks of the northern hills, were now all compelled to use Magyar for official purposes. (*see Map 5, page 39*).

The man who came to dominate Hungarian nationalism during the pre-March period was Louis Kossuth. He was of Slovak origin and had a mother who could never speak Magyar. Though he himself owned no land, he belonged to a lesser family of the Magyar nobility, whose members, since by Hungarian law all the sons of a nobleman assumed aristocratic rank and inherited an equal share of his land on his death, now numbered some 600 000, many of whom, however, were no better than titled peasants. He became a journalist, identifying himself with the Magyar nobility, and bitterly attacked Austrian rule over Hungary, which deprived the noblemen of their power in the country. At the same time, he sought wider support by advocating every kind of liberal and democratic reform in his passionate, ruthless speeches and writings. He edited a journal which, owing to the law, was not printed but transcribed; and the issue of a lithographed paper led to his imprisonment for treason by Metternich from 1837 to 1840, when he was released because the international crisis precipitated by Mehemet Ali made it necessary to conciliate Hungary again (*see page 78*).

From then the decline of imperial authority and the continued need to appease the Magyars combined to enable Kossuth to establish himself as a national hero among them. In 1841 he founded a newspaper, the *Pesti Hulap*, the first important Hungarian journal ever to appear, and in this he advocated political and economic freedom for the kingdom. He urged also freedom of the press, trial by jury, the abolition of serfdom and other liberal reforms, though these were to be enacted by the Diet with strict political safeguards to preserve the supremacy of the nobility. The establishment of the official position of the Magyar language in 1844 made him still more influential, and despite his lack of connection with the land, he was elected to the Diet in 1847. Here his fiery, nationalist, anti-Austrian speeches aroused enthusiastic support for his revolutionary programme, which included, however, coercive measures against the minority peoples in Hungary.

111

(d) The Italian Risorgimento

The July Revolution in France aroused high hopes among Italian nationalists in 1830, but the resulting small insurrections, in which the Carbonari again took a leading part, were no more successful than ten years previously in dislodging the Austrian control of the peninsula, which Metternich had established during the age of the Congresses (*see page 51*).

This time the disturbances took place in Central Italy, where the conspirators planned to unite the small duchies and the Papal States into a single constitutional kingdom. They hoped for help from both Louis Philippe and Francis IV, the Duke of Modena, who was known to be ambitious to become a king and rule over a larger state. But they were immediately disappointed in this, and the lack of agreement among the leaders and the indifference of the common people made it easy for the Austrians to put the risings down.

When the conspirators took action in Modena in February 1831, Francis decided that they were likely to be unsuccessful and attempted to suppress the rising. When, however, it spread, he had to flee from his state, as also did the Duchess Marie Louise from Parma and the papal pro-legate from Bologna in the Romagna, the northern part of the Papal States (*see Map 8*). Delegates met at Bologna and proclaimed the establishment of an independent United Provinces of Central Italy. The Pope appealed to the Austrian government for help, and Metternich, who feared that there might be uprisings at any moment in Lombardy and Venetia, immediately sent troops across the River Po into the territory of the newly-proclaimed state. Louis Philippe contented himself with sending an expeditionary force to occupy the port of Ancona (*see page 77*). The inhabitants of the Romagna disarmed the insurgent troops of the two neighbouring states when they retreated into papal territory. The Austrians overcame the last resistance before the end of March. Francis returned to Modena and hanged a number of the leading conspirators; and the capitulation of the rebels in the Romagna, though it had been accepted by the legate, was later cancelled by Pope Gregory XVI because he held that they had been pardoned under duress. A number of the insurgents managed, however, to escape abroad and were later to become prominent nationalist leaders.

The revolts of 1820 and 1830 thus followed the same course. On both occasions, Metternich sent, with Prussian and Russian approval, troops to quell risings in states that were close to the Austrian provinces in northern Italy and succeeded in restoring the existing regimes there. The only significant difference in 1830 was that another power, France, intervened in the affairs of the peninsula. This brought no immediate help to the nationalists, but it foreshadowed the way in which the Austrian hold over Italy was eventually to be loosened.

The suppression of the risings of 1830 discredited the Carbonari and the other secret societies and brought their activities to an end. They

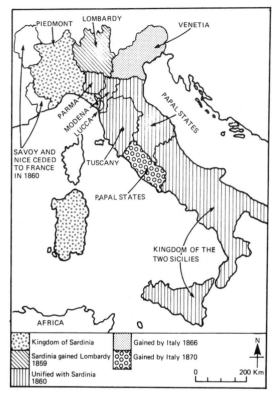

Map 8 The unification of Italy, 1815–70

had not succeeded in extending their membership beyond a proportion of the middle classes and in times of revolt had got little support from the armies of the peninsula. They were essentially plotters, lacking any long-term constructive policy to bring about a revolution in Italy by means of a popular movement. Their activity was consequently limited to isolated, sporadic conspiracies set off by events abroad, and their efforts to secure liberal constitutions in individual states or limited areas had inevitably brought about their defeat and resulted in bloodshed and severe reprisals. Such methods now seemed hopeless.

From 1830, therefore, Italian patriots turned from attempts to obtain liberal reforms to a search for Italian unity. The leader of the most radical group within this movement was Giuseppe Mazzini, who gave new life and unity to its struggling aspirations by his idealism. He was born at Genoa, the son of the Professor of Anatomy at the University, where he himself studied law and first entered politics by joining student demonstrations against the incorporation of the Genoese Republic into the Kingdom of Piedmont by the Congress of Vienna. His

113

thoughts were turned to the liberal cause when he saw the defeated refugees from the battlefield of Novara passing through Genoa to seek safety in foreign exile in 1821. From that time he believed that he should accept the 'duty to fight for the freedom of one's country'. His revolutionary activities began when he joined the Carbonari in 1829, only to be betrayed within six months, imprisoned and then banished from Piedmont.

He settled in Marseilles, where he gathered 40 other exiles around him and founded the Association of Young Italy. The failure of the risings of 1830 had destroyed his confidence in the Carbonari because of their local revolts and lack of any general plan. He wished to inspire the people to think not only of their own district, but also to regard the whole of Italy as their native country. 'Never rise in any other name,' he said, 'than that of Italy and of all Italy.' He hoped also to be able to 'place youth at the head of the insurgent multitude.' His plan was for an Italian republic which would be 'independent, united and free'. Twice already had civilization been given to the world from Rome—Rome of the Caesars and Rome of the Popes—but there would be a Third Rome, a Rome of the Italian people, which would usher in the Era of the Peoples everywhere. He called upon his followers to discipline themselves and unite to expel the Austrians from Italy without foreign help, so that the several petty despotisms would collapse and a single national state be created. 'The tree of liberty does not fructify,' he declared, 'unless it is planted by the hands of citizens and rendered fertile by the blood of citizens and guarded by the swords of citizens.' He believed in humanity and progress, being convinced of the virtues of 'the people' throughout the world, who had only to be liberated to 'accept genius and virtue as their guides' and live together in perfect peace and harmony. It was an idea particularly acceptable to middle-class intellectuals.

Young Italy was a secret society, but one that combined political conspiracy with a high moral purpose and for the first time used the press as a political weapon. It secretly printed its own newspaper, copies of which were smuggled into Italy in barrels of pitch and bales of drapery. Mazzini's words attracted the patriotism and idealism of Italians and gave them a lasting vision of their country. He was the first to have a vision of an Italian state, which would make the Italians like other nations. People began to turn away from seeking judicial changes, the freedom of the press and other reforms within their own states and to consider the demands of Italian nationalism. By 1832 Young Italy had some 60 000 members with local organizations in all the chief Italian towns. In that year the ship on which Giuseppe Garibaldi was a sailor, put into a Black Sea port. There he met an Italian, who told him about Young Italy, and the news changed his whole life as it did that of many other Italians too (*see page 188*). Metternich considered Mazzini 'one of the most dangerous men' and decreed that membership of the Association in Lombardy and Venetia was high treason punishable by death.

Mazzini's romantic idealism, however, proved to be too vague for the demands of the situation. Though he wished his movement to be more constructive and universal than the Carbonari, he had little knowledge of practical politics and human nature, and he adopted the same conspiratorial methods and local risings as the secret societies. In 1834 he considered that the time for action had come. Taking several hundred supporters to Switzerland, he planned an armed invasion of Savoy, which he was convinced would inspire a popular rising, making possible the overthrow of Charles Albert, who had become King of Piedmont in 1831, and the establishment of a constitutional government able to reorganize resistance to Austria throughout Italy. The attempt was a complete failure. Charles Albert was as afraid of nationalism as Metternich, and he acted with greater severity than the Austrians had in 1830. Drugs and torture were used to compel arrested conspirators to betray their comrades, and a number were shot. Mazzini escaped and had to take refuge in England. The episode, which confirmed Mazzini in his republicanism, was a bitter disappointment to him. Young Italy was discredited and ceased to be an active force in Italian politics. Mazzini had not realized that the peasantry, who made up 90 per cent of the population of the peninsula, were indifferent to his cause, and, indeed, most of them had never even heard of the word 'Italy'. Nationalism and liberalism continued to draw its leadership from the professional middle classes.

Mazzini's failure, however, caused many of the middle class to turn away from Young Italy. Though they were beginning to think in national terms, they mistrusted the revolutionary radicalism of the Association and disliked the idea of any violent upheaval. Many of them gave their support to the Federalists, who were founded in the mid-1830s. Their most influential figure was a priest, Vincenzo Gioberti. His book, *On the Moral and Civil Primacy of the Italians*, published in 1843, had an immediate effect upon many Italians who thought that his ideas were more realistic than those of Mazzini. He argued that Italy could recover the primacy, which she had once enjoyed among the nations, if the princes of her existing states were to unite in a confederation under the sovereignty of the Papacy. In this way Austrian supremacy could be destroyed and Italian influence made international through a strengthened Roman Catholic Church. This plan appealed to middle-class opinion which hoped that the Papacy might in such a way achieve the unification of Italy without the destruction of existing political and social institutions.

In 1846, when the hitherto little-known 54-year-old Bishop of Imola in northern Italy became Pope as Pius IX, the Federalists believed that their opportunity had come. The new Pope was an excitable and impetuous man, who had suffered from epilepsy in his youth. He was also a kindly, gentle cleric with a handsome presence and a fine voice. As a Cardinal, he had been distressed by the bad relations which had hitherto existed between the papal government and its subjects. Under

115

his predecessor, Gregory XVI, discontent with the government of the Papal States had not only brought about revolt, but had also caused the five great powers—Austria, Russia, Britain, France and Prussia—to urge reform in its administration. By the time of his death, little had been done. Dissatisfaction was still rife, and the papal finances were in disorder owing to the heavy expenditure involved by the upkeep of a strong military force. Pius issued an amnesty to convicted criminals, as had been customary for new popes, but he also included in it thousands of political prisoners and exiles. Metternich warned him of the danger of such a general amnesty—'Amnesty is, in effect, none other than a declaration of *forgetting*. . . . God never grants amnesties. . . . The mercy of God is only extended by way of pardon, and repentance is the condition necessarily required for pardon.'

Pius had probably regarded his amnesty as a local act of mercy in his own state, but the news of it was received with widespread demonstrations of delight. These flattered Pius, who enjoyed popularity, and at the same time persuaded him to further action. He authorized the construction of railways (Gregory XVI had forbidden them because they would 'carry fewer goods than ideas'), gas-lighting in the streets of Rome, the establishment of a Council of State to share authority with the College of Cardinals in the administration of the Papal States and the creation of a municipal council for the city of Rome itself in which Jews were for the first time to be tolerated. These in themselves were moderate reforms, designed to do no more than meet the accusations of papal misgovernment and to bring the administration of the Papal States more in accordance with nineteenth-century ideas and give them the advantages of recent inventions; and the Pope showed himself politically naive in failing to appreciate the inevitable interpretation of his actions in Italy at that time. There was really little to justify the belief that these actions were signs that he was a supporter of Italian liberalism and nationalism, but throughout the peninsula he was proclaimed as such at political meetings and demonstrations. Even Metternich was astonished and alarmed. 'We were prepared for everything except a liberal Pope,' he said. 'Now we have got one, there is no answering for anything.'

By now, however, other nationalists were looking to Piedmont and not Rome for leadership towards a united Italy. Piedmont had a historic belligerent tradition, resting upon her control of the great and lesser St. Bernard Passes through the Alps and possession of the strategic Duchy of Savoy on the French frontier. Charles Albert, though no liberal, was the only native Italian ruler, and he hated Metternich, who believed that he was ambitious enough to wish to become King of Italy. When some of his ministers urged him to follow the Pope's example and introduce similar reforms in his kingdom, he thought that this might enable him to lead the nationalist opposition to Austria's supremacy in Italy. Between the autumn of 1847 and the spring of 1848, he gave greater freedom to the press, reduced police action, expanded his army and brought down the price of salt to help the poorer people. These actions were greeted with excited demonstrations in Turin, the Piedmontese capital, at which anti-Austrian speeches were made.

These developments also encouraged nationalists who had already looked for leadership in this direction. In 1843 a Piedmontese writer, Count Cesare Balbo, argued in *Hopes of Italy* that the two-fold ecclesiastical and temporal position of the Papacy made it unable to govern Italy. He advocated a federation under the Piedmontese monarchy and expressed the opinion that this would be possible because Austria would soon turn east to gain a sphere of influence in the declining Turkish Empire and would abandon Lombardy and Venetia.

Another Piedmontese nobleman, Count Camillo di Cavour, also advocated this solution, though he believed that Austria would have to be defeated militarily with foreign assistance before Italian independence could be achieved. Cavour was educated at the Military Academy of Turin and entered the army as an officer in the engineers, but he soon resigned because of his liberal opinions. He then proved his practical ability by amassing a fortune through the careful management of his family estates and the introduction of new agricultural methods. He also travelled widely in Europe and came to admire especially the British system of parliamentary government and to support the building of railways for the same reason that Pope Gregory had condemned them. In 1847 he founded a newspaper to express his ideas, *Il Risorgimento* ('Resurrection'). This had been used as a literary term in the eighteenth century by Italians who wished to revive their cultural past, which had declined since the Renaissance of the sixteenth century, and to establish an Italian national language to replace French, which was spoken by the upper classes, and the numerous regional dialects used by the ordinary people throughout the peninsula (*see page 263*). Cavour widened this term to apply it to the movement for Italian unification. And it was to be achieved in the way he advocated.

(e) German Constitutionalism

Metternich's power was least challenged in the German Confederation during this period. The calm of the 'years of quiet' was still hardly broken. National and liberal sentiment continued to gain strength among the intellectual and professional classes and was encouraged by the success of the Greeks in gaining their independence. Its supporters, however, were neither well-organized nor numerous, and their activities did not go beyond meetings and banquets, speeches and resolutions. There seemed, as yet, to be little support for the idea of national unity, though liberal political groups continued to exist in the German states despite the Carlsbad Decrees.

The fall of the Bourbons in France in 1830 had few consequences for German politics. There was a small number of uprisings, and these were only successful in four minor states—Saxony, Hanover, Hesse and Brunswick—where the rulers were compelled to grant constitutions,

117

but Duke Charles of Brunswick soon recovered his authority; and in 1837, when the Duke of Cumberland succeeded William IV of Britain as King of Hanover, he suppressed its constitution. Otherwise the German rulers, including the cautious Frederick William IV of Prussia, continued to support Metternich's policy.

The greatest revival of liberalism in Germany took place among the students. By 1830 the *Burschenschaft* had been revived in several universities, and other secret clubs were founded. The most notable demonstration occurred at Hambach in the Bavarian Palatinate on the left bank of the Rhine, which had been part of France for 20 years and still retained French sympathies. In May 1832, at a meeting in the castle of Hambach, which flew the red, black and gold flag of the students' associations, a number of professors and students, lawyers and writers, Frenchmen and Polish refugees from the rising of 1830, made speeches in favour of constitutional government and German unity.

Metternich acted as he had done after the Wartburg Festival 15 years earlier. He persuaded the princes to agree at the Diet of Frankfurt in June 1832 to the imposition of decrees, known as the Six Articles, which further strengthened the Carlsbad decisions of 1819. All political meetings were banned, and the wearing of the colours of the students' associations, even in neckties and scarves, was forbidden. The rigid control of the universities continued. In 1837, seven professors, among whom were the brothers Jacob and Wilhelm Grimm, already famous for their researches into German folklore, were expelled from the University of Göttingen for protesting against the abolition of the Hanoverian constitution by the new King. The strict censorship of the press was maintained to suppress 'revolutionary agitation'. The writings of Heinrich Heine, the poet, and George Büchner, the dramatist, and others who criticized political conditions in Germany, were banned in 1835 as subversive. And pressure was put on Thiers to expel the large number of German political refugees who had gathered in France. The only attempt at resistance to the acts of oppression occurred in 1833 when a small band of students stormed the guardhouse at Frankfurt with the intention of arming the people and proclaiming a republic, but they received no support, and the soliders quickly rounded them up. The Metternich System seemed as strong as ever in Germany.

Nevertheless, economic conditions were inexorably promoting German unity. The growing effect of the *Zollverein* and the railways continued to be particularly important (*see page 48*). Already in 1828 Goethe was saying to his friend Eckermann that he had no fears that Germany would not be united; its good highways and the future railways would see to that. In the 1840s railway construction in Germany was well ahead of that in France and was beginning to rival the mileage of the British lines (*see Table 6, page 82*). At the same time, however, the growth of industry, as elsewhere in Central Europe, was slow, and the few manufacturers in Germany faced serious competition from British goods.

Some Prussian heavy industry had already been established in the Rhineland, Ruhr and other areas and were comparatively prosperous, but older industries were decaying. In 1844–5 the textile workers of Silesia revolted (*see page 168*), but after being suppressed by the army the sentences imposed upon 80 of the rioters totalled 203 years of forced labour, 90 years imprisonment and 330 lashes of the whip. More influential politically was the demand of the middle classes for a share in the government of the state. This found expression in 1840 when Frederick William III died and was succeeded by his son, Frederick William IV. The new King was always eccentric and was soon to become mad. At the time of his accession, he had a romantic, visionary interest in the religion and life of old Germany, and many liberals hoped that this would inspire him to be sympathetic towards the encouragement of German nationalism and unity. His accession to the throne and the international crisis of 1840 was followed by an outburst of national feeling and the composition of two patriotic songs, *Die Wächt am Rhein* (The Watch on the Rhine) and *Deutschland, Deutschland über Alles* (Germany, Germany over All), which encouraged Prussians to think of the importance of their new Rhineland provinces and the position of their state in Germany.

Frederick William IV's reign began, indeed, in a way that raised liberal hopes. He released a number of political prisoners, relaxed the censorship of the press, gave the brothers Grimm posts in Berlin and even appointed some liberals among his ministers. He himself, however, was far from being a liberal. He was a religious and humane man, but he had no conception of the political effects of the changing economic and social conditions of the time. He liked to think of himself as a traditional, paternal monarch with the duty to rule his people benevolently because he had been placed over them by the will of God. Moreover, his absorption in German history led him to accept Habsburg supremacy as a traditional part of German political life.

Those who trusted in him were soon disappointed. There was a growing demand for a united national Diet composed of representatives of the eight diets of the individual Prussian provinces. The King temporised. He did not summon such an assembly until 1847 and then refused to allow it any real powers. It demanded that redress of grievances should precede the voting of any money to the government. After a few months of debating, during which a young count, Otto von Bismarck, gained prominence as a supporter of the crown, the King dissolved it without any promise that it should meet regularly in the future. Nor would he consider a written constitution for his kingdom. 'Never will I consent,' he declared, 'that a written paper should intrude, like a second Providence, between our Lord God in Heaven and this country, to govern us through its paragraphs.'

Bibliography

In addition to the books on Austria and Metternich previously mentioned on page 51, there is Alan Sked, 'Metternich's Enemies or the Threat from Below,' in Alan Sked (ed.), *Europe's Balance of Power, 1815–1848* (Macmillan, 1979). A general history of Italy is A.J. Whyte, *The Evolution of Modern Italy, 1715–1920* (Blackwell, 1944), and for particular aspects of this period there are Derek Beales, *The Risorgimento and the Unification of Italy* (Longman, 1981), S.J. Woolf, *The Italian Risorgimento* (Longman, 1969), and E.E.Y. Hales, *Mazzini and the Secret Societies* (Eyre & Spottiswoode, 1956). General histories of Germany are G. Mann (trans. M. Jackson), *History of Germany since 1789* (Chatto & Windus, 1968) and E.J. Passant and others, *A Short History of Germany, 1815–1945* (CUP, 1959), and there is also T.S. Hamerow, *Restoration, Revolution, Reaction: Economics and Politics in Germany, 1815–1871* (Princeton, 1958).

Exercises

A *This section consists of questions that might be used for discussion (or written answers) as a way of expanding on the chapter and testing your understanding of it:*

1 Why did the Emperor Francis allow Hofer to be executed?
2 Why did the Austrian court accept the succession of a 'man of straw'?
3 How was Metternich's position weakened by the death of Francis?
4 What did Metternich hope to achieve by an imperial coronation, and why was his plan opposed?
5 List the economic developments that took place in early nineteenth-century Austria, and explain what political effects these had.
6 What aspects of nineteenth-century liberalism can be identified in Austria and Hungary at this time?
7 What do you understand by 'they (the Magyars) had demands for the future which were based upon the past' (*page 110*)?
8 What was the significance of the Hungarian Diet's laws regarding the Magyar language?
9 Would you describe Louis Kossuth as a nationalist? And as a liberal?
10 Why did the Italian risings of 1830 fail while the Belgian revolt succeeded?
11 What impact did the failure of the Carbonari in 1830 have on Italian revolutionary movements?
12 Compare Young Italy with other liberal and nationalist movements.
13 Why was Metternich so hostile to Young Italy?
14 Why did many middle-class Italians turn to the Federalists rather than to Young Italy?
15 Why might Pius IX be described as 'politically naive'?
16 Outline the broad aims and plans of each of: (a) the Carbonari; (b) Young Italy; (c) the Federalists; (d) Pius IX; (e) Balbo and Cavour.
17 Why was there little support for liberalism in the German states?
18 What do you understand by 'economic conditions were inexorably promoting German unity'?
19 Why were Prussian liberals soon disappointed by Frederick William IV?

B *Essay questions*

1 How serious was the threat to the Austrian Empire from students and intellectuals between 1815 and 1849? (Cambridge, 1983)

2 'Austria is a quite imaginary name. It describes neither a self-ruled people, nor a land, nor a nation.' What then held the Habsburg monarchy between 1815 and 1849? (Welsh, 1983)

3 'I ruled Europe sometimes, but I never governed Austria.' How accurate is Metternich's assessment of his influence in the period 1815–1848? (Welsh, 1983)

4 What was the 'Metternich system', and what were the chief threats to it? (Oxford and Cambridge, 1982)

5 How far can it be argued that the German Confederation was totally under the control of Metternich throughout the first thirty years of its existence? (London, 1981)

6 'In the period 1815 to 1848, I governed Europe occasionally but Austria, never.' How seriously can you take this claim of Metternich? (JMB, 1982)

C *Factors underlying the challenge to Metternich*
You have read how Metternich's authority and system were challenged in a number of countries by a variety of people. However, several common ideas and developments underlay this opposition. Draw out a chart like the one below, and then complete it by writing a comment in each box; one or two have already been completed as examples.

Factor	Austria	Hungary	Italy	Confederation	Prussia
Political consequences of economic developments					
Desire of nobility to retain privileges and authority					
Influence of liberal ideas regarding constitutional government				Uprisings in 1830—constitutions in Saxony, Hanover, Hesse and Brunswick, but short-lived & overthrown. Revival of *Burschenschaft* & Hambach demo.	
Taking the opportunity to challenge a weak ruler					
Nationalist sentiments: desire for national unity & autonomy		1840s— Magyar language laws & *Pesti Hulap*— Kossuth's Magyar paper.			
Influence of events in other countries					

4. Russia and Poland

(a) Holy Russia

At the opposite extremities of Europe, Russia and Britain were both markedly unlike the other countries of the continent, but in very different ways. Russia was now an important European power, but this huge Slav country was set apart in its way of life from the rest of the nations. Russia in Europe, including the Grand Duchy of Finland and the Kingdom of Poland, formed only a small part, not more than a quarter, of the area of the whole Russian Empire, but it contained some six-sevenths of the population, which had reached 50 million by 1830. (*See Table 8, page 83.*) Russia was the greatest of the European states in population, but it was also the least densely populated. It had only six towns with a population over 50 000; and a German merchant, travelling to Moscow, declared, 'The Tsar's realm is no more than an empire of villages.'

It was also in many ways the least developed economically and culturally. About 45 million of the Russian population, which included peoples of many different races and languages, worked on the land, and over half of these were serfs owned by individual noblemen or by the state. Russia, indeed, was the one European country where serfdom had become more extensive and severe during the eighteenth century. Since the reign of Peter the Great (1682–1725), the power of the nobility over the serfs on their estates had been increased and had also been imposed upon peasants who had been previously free. Russian serfs were now practically without rights. They were bought and sold, compelled to labour without restriction and flogged with the knout and otherwise punished as their masters chose. 'The negroes on the American plantations are happier than the Russian serfs,' a Russian writer considered in the early nineteenth century.

Though the possession of their estates and power over their serfs, as well as positions in the military and civil service, made the nobility a privileged class, they were nevertheless subservient to the Tsar. They had no right to be appointed to places in the central government, and even in their own parts of the countryside were inferior to the provincial governor appointed by the Tsar. Consequently, they had few interests beyond their estates. They took no part in local administration. The provincial assemblies of the nobility, which were supposed to advise the governors, were rarely effective beyond protecting their own interests. Officials were corrupt and badly-paid and had no real concern for local matters.

Unlike some other European monarchs, the Tsar had no restrictions imposed upon him by a constitution. He ruled as a despot, governing his vast empire by imperial decrees through favourite ministers, an inefficient, conservative bureaucracy and a more effective secret police. He appointed to all important posts in the state, decided what direct and indirect taxation was to be levied and controlled foreign policy at all levels. He was the 'Autocrat of all the Russians' and the 'Little Father' of his people. He was also the 'Chosen One of the Almighty'. 'The Lord has placed the Crown on thine head,' declared the bishop at his coronation, and resistance to his will was regarded as sinful.

Uniquely, he was as powerful over the Russian Orthodox Church. Unlike rulers in western Europe, the tsars had never had to contend with the claims of the Papacy or of Protestant congregations to control the Church in their lands. The affairs of the Russian Church were managed by a Synod, headed by a lay official whom the Tsar nominated. In every village, the parish priest acted as an agent of the government and assisted in the promulgation of imperial decrees. Moreover, since most Slavs outside Russia also belonged to the Orthodox Church, 'Holy Russia' claimed to be the centre of the faith, and ever since the early sixteenth century Moscow was regarded as a 'holy city' and the 'Third Rome' (the first being Rome, which was sacked by the barbarians in A.D. 410, and the second Constantinople, which was captured by the Turks in 1453). And the tsars, after the Treaty of Kutchuk Kainardji in 1774, claimed the right to act as the protector of the religious rights of Orthodox Christians in other lands (*see page 28*).

Russian agriculture had to depend upon a substantial use of serf labour because its methods were primitive and its output poor, which meant that there were terrible famines in some years. It also had a serious effect upon the general economic condition of the Empire. Though there was some economic growth, notably in the textile industries around Moscow and Lodz in Poland, during and after the Revolutionary and Napoleonic Wars (1792–1815), Russian industry remained very backward. This was partly due to the almost complete absence of a banking system and the lack of capital, but also to the difficulty of obtaining labour. Peter the Great had introduced industrial serfdom in both private and state mines and factories, but this was now inadequate, and it was difficult to obtain free workers to expand the labour force; the surplus labour of the Russian Empire in the early 1830s was only 1 in 100 of the population. Transport and communications were inadequate as well. The first railway in Russia was built in 1837 from St. Petersburg to Pavlovsk and Tsarskoe Seloe, but after that the development of railways proceeded very slowly indeed. By 1850 Russia, with a population of 57 million, had 595 kilometres of track compared with over 13 675 kilometres in the United States of America with a population of 18 million. The Tsarist government had the same fear of railways as other European rulers. The Minister of Finance declared in 1843 that they were dangerous because they encouraged 'frequent purposeless travel, thus fostering the restless spirit of the age.'

The majority of the Russian population remained illiterate. The 'middle class' was composed of individuals who did not really form a class. They were a small group of merchant-manufacturers, coming from the peasant serfs; they often remained the serfs themselves of a factory-owner, though they managed his labour force, and were only able, after years of toil, to purchase both their liberty and the factory in which they worked. There was in Russia, therefore, no strong middle class, such as existed in other European countries, sufficiently numerous and forceful to demand liberal reforms and representative institutions.

The most cultured group were the higher nobility, who had been encouraged since Peter the Great's time to westernize themselves through education and foreign travel. This had made many of them aware of their country's social and political backwardness. They wanted such changes as the abolition of serfdom, the establishment of political liberty and the reform of the government. The experiences of wartime officers, who had served in the Russian armies in Germany and France, increased the numbers of those reformers, and they found support among the small but important administrative, professional and intellectual classes in the towns.

(b) Alexander I and the Arakcheyevshchina

In 1801 the hopes of Russian reformers had been raised by the accession of Alexander I, the son of the 'mad Tsar', Paul, at whose murder he had himself connived. Alexander had been educated by a Swiss tutor, who was a disciple of Rousseau, and he was familiar with western ideas and spoke both English and French better than he did Russian. During the first years of his reign he did introduce a number of reforms. Landowners were empowered to free their serfs (about 400 did so in the next half century); serfdom was abolished (without any grants of land to the peasants) in Livonia, Estonia and a few other non-Russian provinces; and serfs were not to receive more than 15 lashes of the knout (a limitation ignored on most estates). In 1807 he was attracted by the abilities of an administrative official, Michael Speransky, the son of a country priest, and entrusted him with the task of drawing up a comprehensive system of constitutional government for Russia. His only reform to take effect, however, was the establishment of a Council of State of ministers and other advisers appointed by the Tsar to be the supreme advisory body on legislation. His ideas alarmed many noblemen and bureaucrats as renewed war against France became imminent, and so in 1812 Alexander dismissed and exiled him not long before Napoleon's invasion of Russia.

In doing this, Alexander lost a unique opportunity of undertaking some of the reforms that Russia needed most. He would have been assisted by the great devastation caused by the French invasion and the surge of patriotism which for a time drew Russians together, but he did not seem capable of undertaking this on his own. He was unstable and vacillating—as his allies, during and after the wars, found out (*see page 10*). He became restless and unsettled as the years passed, travelling ceaselessly from one European conference to another or in Russia

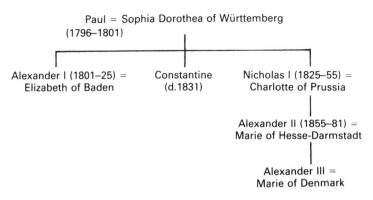

Diagram 3. Family Tree of the Russian Royal Family (Romanovs)

driving rapidly from one province to the next, until people began to say that Russia was being governed from the back of a post-chaise.

He also steadily abandoned his liberal and reforming ideas, a process seemingly hastened by his religious conversion (*see page 21*). His 'liberal phase' was not completely over by the end of the war; he gave both his new Kingdom of Poland and Grand Duchy of Finland very liberal constitutions (*see page 132*). The signing of the Treaty of Troppau marked his final repentance from his 'liberal delusions' (*see page 27*).

During the last five years of his reign, he came increasingly under the influence of General Arakcheyev, and this short period of Russian history is known as the *Arakcheyevshchina*. The General was responsible for the establishment of a system of 'military colonies' by settling regiments and their families in villages to work with state serfs. They were established near St. Petersburg and in the Ukraine, facing respectively the strategic threats posed by Sweden and Turkey (who might become allies of Britain and Austria). Their object was to provide a military reserve which was supported by agriculture and at the same time to improve the efficiency of farming and the welfare and education of the population. The colonies possessed considerable advantages. They received liberal grants of money which brought about better crops, excellent housing, good schools and hospitals and improved sanitation. Foreign visitors were invariably impressed; but the colonies were disliked by their inhabitants. The commanders were often unimaginative and brutal men. The soldiers had to work on the land as well as drill and manoeuvre. Military discipline was imposed on the villagers, who were regarded as part of the martial establishment, and married women were even fined or birched if they did not add annually to their families to provide soldiers for the future. Revolts in these villages and in other places throughout the Empire were brutally put down, many of the rebels being knouted to death. 'Nearly the whole of Russia groaned under blows,' wrote one of Arakcheyev's junior officers of this period.

125

The mutiny of the Semenov guard, news of which reached Alexander while he was at Troppau in 1820, finally convinced him of the perils of liberalism (*see page 27*). He supported Arakcheyev's repressive measures and instituted stricter control of the press and the universities.

This did not prevent the growth, however, of secret dissident societies, mostly directed by aristocrats, within the army and even at the court. Some of these had close connections with freemasonry, which in Russia had always challenged orthodoxy and autocracy. Eventually nearly all these societies amalgamated into the Northern Society, led by officers of the guards in St. Petersburg and Moscow, and the Southern Society, led by the most remarkable of all the conspirators, Colonel Paul Pestel, a staff officer who was the son of a Governor-General of Siberia and had distinguished himself in the campaign against Napoleon. Some of the conspirators wished to rid the Tsar of his 'evil counsellors', especially Arakcheyev, in the belief that 'Alexander the Blessed' would return to his old liberal idealism, but Pestel and others believed in revolution and not reform. They wanted the establishment of a Russian republic with a constitution which would prohibit serfdom. Such differences over aims and methods inevitably weakened the movement and lost it wider support.

(c) The Paternalism of Nicholas I

In December 1825 Alexander died from malaria at the early age of 48, not in the Winter Palace at St. Petersburg, surrounded by his family, court and guards, but at Taganrog, a village on the shores of the Sea of Azov, where he had taken the ailing Tsarina. His mystical reputation and the circumstances of his death gave rise to a legend that his burial in the richly-decorated Cathedral of St. Isaac of Dalmatia, which he had erected in St. Petersburg, was a sham and that he lived for many years as a revered, pious hermit in Siberia. But the immediate effect of his death was to cause grave political confusion.

Since Alexander had no son, the heir presumptive to the throne was his elder brother, the Tsarevitch Constantine, the Commander-in-Chief of the Polish army, who was supposed to hold liberal views. In 1820 he had divorced his wife and married a Polish countess, but only the members of the imperial family knew that Alexander had agreed to this marriage to someone outside the European royal families on condition that he renounced his succession to the throne in favour of his younger brother, the Grand Duke Nicholas. Uncertain of the loyalty of the guards to himself, Nicholas swore allegiance to his brother, but meanwhile Constantine had already sworn allegiance in Warsaw to Nicholas. In London *The Times* commented that Russia was 'in the strange predicament of having two-self denying Emperors and no active ruler.'

Messengers sent by Nicholas to Warsaw failed to persuade Constantine to come to the capital and either accept the crown or formally abdicate. After three weeks, Nicholas decided that such a dangerous situation could not continue any longer. He proclaimed himself as Tsar. This faced the secret societies with a crisis. They had intended, as soon as Constantine arrived in St. Petersburg to assume his position as Tsar, to arrange an armed demonstration and present their political demands to him; but now they had to act quickly. The result was the Decembrist Conspiracy.

The leaders of the Northern Society brought out several guards regiments in an attempt to seize power and prevent the accession of Nicholas. They raised the cry of 'Constantine and Constitution', but many of the 3000 soldiers knew so little about their purpose that they thought that Constitution must be Constantine's wife. Nicholas had them dispersed by artillery fire, and a rising led by the Southern Society in the Ukraine was also crushed. The conspirators got no support from either townspeople or peasants anywhere. Pestel and four other Decembrists were hanged, some 120 sent to Siberia and many soldiers flogged.

The Decembrist Conspiracy was the first organized insurrection in Russia with definite political aims. Its leaders were drawn from the westernized, educated nobility (*see page 124*), who were serving in the army. The main reason for its failure was that they had little sympathy for their ideas from the rest of the nation. Not only the peasantry, but also the small urban middle class were not attracted by liberalism. Their political outlook was still bounded by traditional Russian loyalty to the autocratic tsardom. The Decembrists took too much for granted. They made no effort to gain popular support for themselves and could not even command the loyalty of their regiments. The Conspiracy was the first and last political revolt by army officers, who henceforward remained loyal to the tsars.

The Conspiracy, however, had a powerful effect upon Nicholas I's policy. Unlike his predecessor, he was a straightforward soldierly character, who never had any sympathy with liberalism and was nicknamed the 'Nebuchadnezzar of the North'. He believed that the prompt action he had taken against the Conspiracy had saved the country from ruin. Though, compared with previous tsars, he had punished the conspirators with clemency, he was determined that it should never happen again. 'Revolution is at the gates of Russia,' he said, 'but I swear that it shall not enter as long as I have a breath of life left within me.'

The Conspiracy made him deeply mistrustful of the westernized aristocracy. For the rest of his life, he kept an annotated list of the Decembrist noblemen always close at hand. He was determined not only to exclude them permanently from public office, but also to replace their ideas with 'good principles' which upheld the traditional aristocracy. The censorship of the press was used to achieve this. Forbidden books might neither be printed in Russia nor be imported from abroad, and even to possess such a book might mean exile to

Siberia. In 1826 the secret police were reorganized as the Third Section of His Majesty's own Chancery, and the force was provided with numerous agents and spies and placed beyond the ordinary processes of the law. Foreign travel was forbidden, even to the wealthy, except under rigid conditions through a passport system. Secondary education was restricted to the children of the gentry and of government officials, so that as few as possible should understand western ideas. And in 1835 the universities were reorganized to bring them completely under government control. The number of students was reduced in all faculties except theology and medicine, and the whole emphasis of instruction was changed from the promotion of scholarship to training for the enlarged bureaucracy. And in classics less emphasis was placed upon Greek philospophy, from which liberal ideas were derived, and more to Roman government, which stressed central control and strict orders. Independent organizations and societies were dissolved, including the Bible Society founded by Alexander I.

At the same time, Nicholas wished to follow the traditional paternalistic conception of the Russian monarchy (*see page 122*), and this led him to embark upon several reforms. He dismissed Arakcheyev and recalled Speransky, who set out to codify (but not rewrite) the laws, a task which he completed in 45 volumes by 1833. The military colonies were made less fearful, though they continued to be established in the Ukraine and the Caucasus into the 1850s; and personal freedom was granted to serfs on state lands in 1838.

Yet the reign was one of increasing social discontent. The situation of the peasants did not improve. The public sale of serfs was forbidden in 1833, but the landowners refused to accept any limitation on either the amount of weekly work required from them or the sum they had to pay to buy their freedom. The Tsar's prohibition of punishment by the knout was ignored on numerous estates, while it was used so extensively as a penalty for all manner of offences by the law courts that he was nicknamed 'Nicholas Flogger'. Moreover, the continued, though slow, development of industry brought an increase in serfdom in the factories and mines, where men, women and children, brought in from the countryside, worked long hours under brutal and dangerous conditions, which factory laws decreed by Nicholas I did nothing to improve. During his reign there were over 400 peasant risings, three-quarters of which occurred after 1840. After each was suppressed, its leaders were deported in chained columns to Siberia, where they were joined by writers and other intellectuals. Some 150 000 people of all classes were sent there during the reign of Nicholas.

(d) Nicholas I's Foreign Policy

Nicholas I's paternalistic and despotic outlook also influenced his foreign policy. He wished both to extend Russian power and influence and to uphold the authority of the established rulers of Europe. These two aims were not easily reconciled, particularly in connection with the

Eastern Question, where he wished to establish Russian control over the Slavs in the Balkans (which had been the desire of all Russian rulers since the princes of Kiev in the tenth century) and to obtain a southern sea outlet through the Bosphorus, the strait throught Turkish territory connecting the Black Sea with the Sea of Marmara and so with the Mediterranean (*see Map 4, page 29*). The success of such a policy would give Russia the warm-water ports that she lacked; but its pursuit was always likely to bring her into conflict with the existing international settlement and make her relations difficult with the western powers.

Nicholas came to the throne amid the crisis caused by the Greek revolt (*see page 33*). This immediately presented him with a situation in which his legitimist principles were opposed to Russian interests. The Greeks were rebels, but Russia was likely to benefit by upholding their cause. He reversed Alexander's policy and supported the Greeks against the Sultan. He believed that the Turkish Empire could not last much longer and that the Greek revolt was a sign of its imminent collapse. He wanted to get what he could for Russia, and to gain influence in an independent Greece would place his country in a powerful position to begin to do this.

Canning believed that co-operation with Russia was the best way of solving the crisis. Nicholas joined with the British and French governments in signing the Treaty of London in July 1827, but his allies would not agree when he proposed that more active measures should be taken to help the Greeks. The Battle of Navarino, however, gave him an opportunity to attack Turkey the next year. The war proved to be a difficult one for Russia, and he did not think that this was a favourable opportunity to attempt a large-scale campaign against Turkey. He made peace with the Sultan, therefore, at Adrianople in September 1829. The Treaty, in addition to making Greece self-governing under Turkish overlordship, gave the Danubian Principalities of Moldavia and Wallachia the same status and ceded some Turkish territory in Asia to Russia. It was a moderate settlement, which Nicholas trusted would not produce any international repercussions.

Nevertheless his policy had alienated Austria and, still more, Britain. The governments of both these countries feared that he intended to intervene in the affairs of the newly-created autonomous states within the Turkish Empire (Greece, Moldavia and Wallachia). In face of this and of the outbreaks of the European revolts of 1830, which extended to Poland, Nicholas was ready to adopt a conciliatory policy that would remove their suspicions. He accepted Britain's invitation to join with her and France in signing a second Treaty of London in 1832, which recognized Greece as completely independent from Turkey.

He had not, however, abandoned his intention of intervening in Turkish affairs when a suitable occasion arose. This came with the crisis precipitated in 1832 by Mehemet Ali (*see page 78*). The Sultan had promised Mehemet Ali the governorship of Crete and Syria in return for sending troops against the Greeks, but in 1830 he gave him Crete only. Accordingly, in 1832, Mehemet Ali conquered Syria and even threatened to attack Constantinople. The Sultan appealed to Britain for help, but this could only have been given through the Royal Navy, which was now fully engaged in blockading Holland to compel William I to recognize Belgian independence and in supporting Queen Maria of Portugal against the continued attempt of her uncle, Miguel, to seize power (*see page 32*). Nor was help forthcoming from France, which continued to favour Mehemet Ali. The Sultan, therefore, had to turn reluctantly to the Tsar and accepted the help of a Russian expeditionary force on the Bosphorus.

Britain and France, now thoroughly alarmed, insisted that the Sultan made an immediate peace with Mehemet Ali, even though this meant recognizing Egyptian control of Syria. In July 1833, however, Nicholas compelled Turkey to agree to the Treaty of Unkiar Skelessi, which established a defensive alliance between the two countries for eight years. Russia was to help Turkey if she were attacked, but if Russia were attacked she would merely require Turkey to close the Dardanelles to foreign warships, 'not allowing any foreign vessels of war to enter therein on any pretext whatever.' From the Russian viewpoint, this was a defensive treaty, designed to prevent the British and French navies in the Mediterranean from threatening Russia's vulnerable southern coast. Nicholas did not intend to send his ships from the Black Sea into the Mediterranean, but Palmerston and Guizot both believed that he did, and they were alarmed at the way in which the Treaty reduced Turkey to dependence upon Russia. In Palmerston's words, it made 'the Russian Ambassador at Constantinople the Chief Minister of the Sultan.'

Such hostility caused Nicholas to look elsewhere for support. In September 1833, little more than two months after the signature of the Treaty, he met Francis I of Austria at Münchengrätz in Bohemia, where the two monarchs agreed to maintain the existence of the Turkish Empire under the Sultan, to protect it again if necessary from Mehemet Ali and to act together if it seemed about to collapse. Also at the meeting was Metternich, whom Nicholas greeted as his 'master', and he was pleased with the Tsar's attitude. He wrote, 'We acquit Russia of any aggressive views with regard to the Turkish Empire.' And Nicholas showed that he wanted co-operation with Austria, even at the cost of some sacrifice by Russia. In 1834 Russian garrisons were withdrawn from the Danubian Principalities where they had been maintained since 1829, though Turkey had not yet fully paid the war indemnity promised in the Treaty of Adrianople.

Palmerston was resolved to bring the agreement made at Unkiar Skelessi to an end whenever he could. His opportunity came in 1839, when conflict was renewed between the Sultan and Mehemet Ali (*see page 78*). The Egyptians completely defeated the Turkish troops attempting to reconquer Syria, and a Turkish fleet deserted to

Alexandria. Once again Constantinople was threatened; and France supported Mehemet Ali. Nicholas, however, did not want to intervene on behalf of Turkey this time and arouse British hostility again. He agreed in 1840 to join with Britain, Austria and Prussia in a Quadruple Alliance, which sent an allied fleet to the eastern Mediterranean to compel Mehemet Ali to submit. By the Treaty of London of 1841, Mehemet Ali had to restore Crete and Syria to Turkey, but was made hereditary Pasha of Egypt under only nominal Turkish overlordship; and in London in 1842 the powers of the Quadruple Alliance and France signed the Convention of the Straits by which the Dardanelles were to be closed to all foreign warships while Turkey was at peace.

The settlement of this crisis was a triumph for Palmerston. It seemed to be a set-back for Nicholas, but he had secured the defensive purpose of the Treaty of Unkiar Skelessi without being bound by an alliance with Turkey. He had refused to agree to a British suggestion that he should guarantee the territorial integrity of the Turkish Empire. He would not do this because he was still convinced that its collapse was imminent, and he still wanted to make the greatest gain he could for Russia. At first he had thought that he could do this alone, but the diplomatic isolation, which the Treaty of Unkiar Skelessi threatened to bring upon Russia, alarmed him. He judged it impossible to renew this treaty and wished to use the crisis of 1839–42 to bring to an end the 'liberal alliance' between Britain and France. The successful negotiations, which settled the Syrian question, now convinced him that he was more likely to achieve his aim by co-operation with Britain, who would always wish to reach a peaceful solution when any crisis arose. He did not understand, however, that no British government would be willing to allow Russia to strengthen herself at the expense of Turkey, and this failure to realize that co-operation with Britain would only be forthcoming to maintain the integrity of the Turkish Empire was to lead to the outbreak of the Crimean War a dozen years later (*see page 201*).

(e) Congress Poland

Palmerston described the Polish question as 'that sad inheritance of a triumphant wrong.' During the eighteenth century, Poland had been a vast kingdom, including not only the eastern and central parts of present-day Poland, but also much of Lithuania, Latvia, White Russia and the Ukraine. Three partitions in 1772, 1793 and 1795 between the three great neighbouring powers of Russia, Prussia and Austria wiped the state of Poland off the map, and in 1815 Poland again disappeared, most of the territory going to Russia (*see Map 3, page 13*). The Vienna Settlement gave Russia the Austrian and Prussian shares of the partition of 1795 and about half the Prussian share in that of 1793, while Russia regained all her shares (*see page 15*). And while Germans, Hungarians, Italians and other nationalities in Europe were able to make good their claims to nationhood during the nineteenth century,

Polish attempts to do this were marked by disaster, and by the end of the century the Poles seemed to be further away than ever from the recovery of their independence.

From the Polish territory he received at the Vienna Settlement, Alexander I created a Kingdom of Poland with himself as its ruler. 'Gentlemen,' he said to the Poles at Vilna on his way back from Paris in 1814, 'yet a little patience, and you will be more than satisfied with me.' He had, indeed, felt a sympathy for Poland since his youthful days when he had come under the influence of the nationalistic ideas of the French Revolution. And though this 'Congress Poland' was to be indissolubly linked to Russia through the personal union of the crowns, he gave it in 1816 a constitution of its own, which owed much to the Napoleonic form of government in the Grand Duchy of Warsaw and aroused bitter envy among Russian reformers.

The constitution provided for an Assembly or Sejm elected under a wider suffrage than that prevailing in Britain in 1832 or in France before 1848. The Napoleonic Code was retained, freedom of the press and protection from arbitrary arrest were guaranteed, and the Roman Catholic religion and the Polish language were officially recognized. There was to be a separate Polish army, and the country was to be administered by Polish officials. While the power of the Sejm was, in fact, restricted to the right of petition, and ultimate authority rested with an executive council under the direction of a Viceroy appointed by the King, the Polish constitution was a remarkable concession and in many ways the most liberal in contemporary Europe.

In the first years after 1815, the Polish laws were reformed, the University of Warsaw was established, and by 1821 over a thousand primary schools were in existence. Yet, though Poles had little to complain of in the government of their country, there was a strong nationalist opposition to any form of Russian control among Polish army officers, noblemen and intellectuals. Secret societies in the universities and plots in the army led to repressive measures on Alexander I's orders, which included the deportation of suspects to Russia.

(f) The Polish Revolt (1830)

On his accession, Nicholas I promised to maintain the Polish constitution, but he made no pretence of his contempt for its form of government and was incensed by reports that the Decembrists had Polish connections. He established his newly-founded Third Section in the kingdom and gradually replaced Polish by Russian officials and instituted a censorship of the press. In 1828 he ceased to summon the Sejm because it refused to declare that arrested members of the secret societies were guilty of high treason. Mounting resentment at these measures found expression when the Tsar mobilized the Polish army in 1830 for possible intervention against the French and Belgian revolutionaries. In November young officers at the Military Academy in Warsaw gained control of the garrison of 10 000 in the city and compelled Constantine to flee from the country. From such promising beginnings, however, the revolt failed to become a national movement. The landed aristocracy supported it and so did most of the urban population of Warsaw, but the peasantry did not follow them, and the middle class was still too small to be of any importance. Moreover, the nationalists were seriously disunited. The 'Whites', who controlled the administrative council set up to replace the Viceroy, wanted moderate reforms and a compromise with Russia; but the 'Reds', who had a majority in the Sejm, demanded complete independence and the restoration of the Lithuanian provinces which Russia had taken in 1772.

Nicholas was determined to crush the insurgents and not negotiate with them. 'Russia or Poland must now perish,' he told Constantine. At first the Polish forces, which soon numbered 70 000, were able to hold off the Russians, but by the spring of 1831 Nicholas invaded the country with an army twice as large. The Sejm issued a declaration of independence and an appeal to the world which insisted that Poland had a much better historic right to national independence than Greece or Belgium. The only hope of success for the Poles, indeed, lay in foreign help, and they expected to get it, but Austria and Prussia closed their frontiers with Russia and sent troops to the border areas to prevent their own Polish subjects rising in revolt. British and French opinion sympathized with Poland, but the country lay outside their sphere of action, and neither Palmerston nor Louis Philippe contemplated giving her any assistance. Both wanted Russian goodwill during the settlement of the Belgian crisis.

After inflicting a decisive defeat upon the Poles, the Russians besieged Warsaw. The Reds tried to fight on, but their situation was hopeless. That summer cholera first appeared in Europe from the East. It ravaged both armies, but the Poles, lacking in reinforcements, were weakened the most. In September the city surrendered, and soon afterwards the remaining 20 000 Polish troops marched over the frontier and surrendered to the Prussians.

Nicholas abolished the Sejm and gave the kingdom a new constitution, which on paper preserved the Polish legal code, language and local administration, but in practice government was by military decree. All civil rights were immediately suspended except by the grace of the Tsar, and there was no safeguard against the intensive policy of Russification put into effect during the following years. About a tenth of the land was confiscated and distributed to Russians. The Russian language was to be taught in all schools, and the Universities of Warsaw and Vilna were closed. The Polish army was merged into the Russian forces, and the sons of the insurgents were sent to Russian military academies. All important posts were given to Russians, and the Russian language was made compulsory for administrative purposes. A strong citadel, erected at the gates of Warsaw, with its dungeons for prisoners and cannon directed against the town, was one aspect of Russian policy towards Poland, and the impressive new Orthodox cathedral, built amid the ancient Roman Catholic city churches, was another.

133

Some 80 000 Poles were exiled to Siberia, and nearly 10 000 fled to western Europe, mostly to France. Among them was the young Frederick Chopin, who had gone in 1830 to study at Vienna, having already won fame both as a performer and composer in Warsaw, but now, instead of returning to Poland, settled in Paris. The politically active among the exiles formed secret societies and engaged in continual and intense propaganda against the Russian government.

Their activities, however, merely worsened the situation in Poland. The Russian policy of repression continued unabated, and any attempt at defiance was ruthlessly punished. The Napoleonic Code was curtailed, and the Russian criminal code was introduced. Foreign opinion became hostile to Russia, which was henceforward regarded as the 'gendarme of Europe'. Metternich was replaced by Nicholas I as the chief champion of tyranny in the eyes of European liberals. In France, the Chamber of Deputies passed an annual resolution of sympathy for Poland during the whole of the time of the July Monarchy. In Britain, Parliament voted the Polish exiles a grant of £10 000, which was renewed every year until 1852, and the British press gave full publicity to Russian activities in Poland. Queen Victoria was urged to protest to the Tsar over the particularly notorious case of Madame Kalergi, a member of a distinguished aristocratic Polish family, who was knouted in Warsaw in 1846 for aiding a pro-French friend to escape from the secret police of the Third Section.

Foreign pressure, however, seemed to have no effect upon the Russian government nor to bring any help to the Polish cause. When the revolutions of 1848 broke out in western Europe, although the Poles received sympathetic expressions of support from the several nationalist movements and assemblies, and Polish exiles assisted both the Viennese and the Hungarians in their risings against the Austrian government, no revolt took place in Poland itself.

Bibliography

B. Pares, *A History of Russia* (Rev. edn. Cape, 1955), J.D. Clarkson, *A History of Russia from the Ninth Century* (Longmans, 1962) and R. Hare, *Portraits of Russian Personalities between Reform and Revolution* (OUP, 1959). Norman Davies, *God's Playground: A History of Poland* (2 vols., OUP, 1981) is the most up-to-date history, while W. Reddaway (ed.), *The Cambridge History of Poland* (2 vols, CUP, 1941–50) still has some useful chapters.

Exercises

A   *This section consists of questions that might be used for discussion (or written answers) as a way of expanding on the chapter and testing your understanding of it:*

1   In what ways was Russia 'markedly unlike the other countries of the continent'?

2   Why was local government in Russia inefficient?

3 What was autocracy?
4 How did the Orthodox Church reinforce the powers of the Tsar?
5 Why was industrial development in Russia so slow?
6 What reforms did Alexander I introduce, and how far-reaching were they?
7 What evidence is there, from his part in international affairs, that Alexander I was 'restless and unsettled'? (*see page 124*)
8 What do you understand by Arakcheyevshchina?
9 Why was there no revolution in Russia during the reign of Alexander?
10 Why did the Decembrist conspiracy of 1825 fail?
11 What effects did the Decembrist conspiracy have on Nicholas I?
12 How was Russia likely to gain from the Greek revolt?
13 Why did the treaty of Adrianople anger Austria and Britain?
14 Why did Nicholas help the Sultan against Mehemet Ali in 1833, but join the Quadruple Alliance in 1840?
15 In what ways were the treaty of London (1841) and the Straits Convention (1842) 'triumphs for Palmerston'?
16 In what ways was Congress Poland given preferential treatment?
17 Why were the Poles therefore dissatisfied?
18 Why did the Polish Revolt of 1830 fail?
19 How was the government of Poland altered after the suppression of the revolt?
20 Why were the Poles unable to improve their position in relation to Russia?

B *Essay questions*
1 Why did the Belgian revolution of 1830 succeed and that of Poland in the same year fail? (Welsh, 1981)
2 Discuss the reasons for the failure of Congress Poland. (Welsh, 1981)
3 'The principal instrument of preventing progress and causing revolution to fail.' How far do you agree with this view of Tsar Nicholas I? (Welsh, 1982)
4 How do you explain the different results of the revolutions of 1830 in Belgium and in Poland? (Welsh, 1982)
5 How strong and how organized was the internal opposition to Tsar Alexander I and Tsar Nicholas I? (Oxford and Cambridge, 1981)
6 What were the main aims of the domestic policies of Alexander I and Nicholas I of Russia? (Oxford and Cambridge, 1983)
7 'Merely repressive.' To what extent is this an accurate comment on the personality and policies of Nicholas I? (AEB, 1981)
8 'Tsar Nicholas I, on his death bed, could look back with satisfaction on a reign in which he had fulfilled almost all of his objectives.' How far do you agree? (London, 1981)

C *Biographical study: Tsar Alexander I*
As E.H. Carr wrote, History 'is a continuous process of interaction between the historian and his facts, an unending dialogue between the present and the past.' That is to say, each generation is inclined to interpret the people and events of the past in the light of its own values and interests. At its simplest level, this argument can be used to explain the shift from the concentration of historians on constitutional issues and 'great men and women' in the first half of this century to their later preoccupations with social conditions and the way in which the lives of ordinary people have changed. In this 'unending dialogue', one of the

hardest tasks for student historians is to understand rulers with completely different values, interests and aspirations from those of the late twentieth century. By studying one such ruler in some detail, you may be able to gain some insights into such a ruler and, at the same time, undertake a different aspect of historical study, biography.

Firstly, review in outline the facts that you know about Alexander, both as Tsar of Russia and as an international statesman. This could be done by constructing a summary date chart, divided into a series of sub-sections.

Date	Domestic policies	Relations with Poland	International policies

Next, consider Alexander's personality and the principles that underlay the actions he took. To do this, you will need to do some personal research, in which you should attempt to identify at least five aspects of Alexander's approach to government and international affairs (e.g. liberal or reactionary? influence of religious ideas?) that appear to you to be dominant. To help you with this research, you will find reprinted below some sources and extracts that will act as starting points:'

Source A. From *From Vienna to Versailles* by L.C.B. Seaman

'Yet that the problem of Poland occupied any time at all in 1815 was due solely to the equivocal desire of Alexander of Russia simultaneously to liberate Poland to satisfy his conscience, and to keep it to satisfy his Romanov pride. One might well apply to Alexander and his Polish plan the remark once made about Lord John Russell—"he always has such excellent motives for doing himself a good turn". . . . What Alexander was trying to create was a Polish client-state by means of which he would extend Russian influence farther into Europe than ever before. His appeal to Polish patriotism was even more fraudulent than the similar appeal made by Alexander II in 1878 to the patriotism of the Bulgars.'

Source B. Tsar Alexander to the Metropolitan of Novogorod and St. Petersburg. 1st January 1816, from Alexandre 1er. et sa Sainte-Alliance. (Librarie Fischbacher. 1975) p.175. (Translated by L.W. Cowie)

'From my first entry into Paris, I wished to have at the end of this sacred war a monument which could be to the glory of this religion which has conquered the world and also to the glory of the Supreme Leader, who grants victories and crowns them, Christ the Saviour! It is with this intention that I send you these sacred vessels made in Paris by my order for use in the service of the Holy Sacrament. Place them on the altar of the cathedral, the church consecrated to the Holy Mother of God; on this altar, at the foot of which I began and accomplished my travels which have been accompanied by so many favours from Providence. May this offering in recognition of the Giver of every perfect gift make it known that in the vast temple which forms this universe, the Lord alone gives to each vessel, inspired by his goodness, the power which enables him to execute His unchangeable decrees. May this gift be a silent appeal to all those who come in this temple to glorify there the Almighty and strengthen their trust in Him alone.'

Source C. From *Europe 1815-1945* by Anthony Wood (p.9)

'[At the Congress of Vienna], Tsar Alexander never relied entirely on any single one of his advisers and the other Powers could never be sure that he would not revoke what his subordinates had just negotiated. Alexander, his round cherubic face shining with benevolence, his tight-fitting uniform almost bursting at every seam, was a strange unpredictable character, oscillating wildly between authoritarianism and liberal gestures, a complicated psychology in which pious aspiration often blended with deep cunning.'

Source D. from *A History of the Modern World* by R.R. Palmer and Joel Colton (p.385)

'Alexander was the grandson of Catherine the Great, educated by her to be a kind of enlightened despot on the eighteenth-century model.⁴ The Swiss tutor of his boyhood, La Harpe, later turned up as a pro-French revolutionary in the Helvetic Republic of 1798. Alexander became tsar in 1801, at the age of twenty-four, through a palace revolution which implicated him in the murder of his father Paul. He still corresponded with La Harpe, and he surrounded himself with a circle of liberal and zealous young men of various nationalities, of whom the most prominent was a Polish youth, Czartoryski. Alexander regarded the still recent partitions of Poland as a crime. He wished to restore the unity of Poland with himself as its constitutional king. In Germany many who had first warmed to the French Revolution, but had been disillusioned, began to hail the new liberal tsar as the protector of Germany and hope of the future. Alexander conceived of himself as a rival to Napoleon in guiding the destinies of Europe in an age of change. Moralistic and self-righteous, he puzzled and disturbed the statesmen of Europe, who generally saw, behind his humane and republican utterances, either an enthroned leader of all the "Jacobins" of Europe or the familiar specter of Russian aggrandizement.

Yet Alexander, more than his contemporaries, formed a conception of international collective security and the indivisibility of peace. He was shocked when Napoleon in 1804, in order to seize the duke of Enghien, rudely violated the sovereignty of Baden. He declared that the issue in Europe was clearly between law and force—between an international society in which the rights of each member were secured by international agreement and organization, and a society in which all trembled before the rule of cynicism and conquest embodied in the French usurper.'

Having examined both what Alexander did and what sort of person he was, you should now be able to construct a biographical study. Avoid writing this as a purely narrative account of the events of his life, followed by a summary of his personality and attitudes. Rather, endeavour to weld the two together, so that you are concentrating on features of his personality and attitudes, and *illustrate* how these affected his policies and actions by reference to the events of his life and government.

D   *Essay writing skills 4: Discussion essays*
On page 89 you were introduced to different types of essays, and 'list' essays were discussed at some length. In this section, you will be concentrating on discussion, or 'yes/no', questions. In these, a statement

—usually in quotation marks—is presented to you, followed by the words 'Discuss', 'Comment' or 'Do you agree?'. Sometimes, the wording and format is different, but this question type, unless it incorporates 'Discuss' or 'Comment', can *logically* be answered by the word 'yes' or 'no'. Consider these two examples.

(a) 'They learned nothing and forgot nothing.' Does this adequately explain the collapse of the restored Bourbon dynasty in France?
(b) 'A period of repression, militarism and gloom'. How far is this an accurate description of the reign of Nicholas I?

It should be clear that a one word answer 'yes' (or 'no') would make sense in answer to (a) but *not* in answer to (b); thus (a) is of the type under consideration here, whereas (b) is not (for this type of question, see page 180). Here are four further examples of discussion type questions, on topics you have already studied:

(c) 'An admirable and enlightened example of international cooperation.' Does the Congress System (1815–1825) deserve to be so described?
(d) 'Its prospects for survival were good until 1824 but negligible after that date.' Would you agree with this assessment of the restored Bourbon monarchy in France?
(e) 'Virtually indistinguishable from his Bourbon predecessors.' Discuss this verdict on Louis-Philippe.
(f) Was Louis-Philippe's task more difficult than that of Louis XVIII?

It is more helpful to think of this question type as 'Yes/No' than as 'discussion' questions, as this will ensure that you adopt the correct approach in planning and writing your answer. As with all A level essays, you must avoid writing a purely narrative essay that just 'tells the story'. Rather, you should aim to put forward all those arguments that support the statement made—the 'Yes' arguments—and then those that refute it—the 'No' arguments. Using a planning sheet of the type below and on page 396 should help you to do this. It is essential that you do consider both sides of the argument; it is almost *never* the case that there is only one side—the examiners would not ask a question if it were not a topic that provoked some debate.

Essay planning sheet: discussion essay				
Title of essay:				
Summary of introduction (if any):				
Yes arguments		No arguments	
Arguments	*Supporting evidence*	*Arguments*	*Supporting evidence*
1)			
2) etc.			
Summary of conclusion:				

You should make sure that you come to a conclusion at the end of your essay, in which you explain which side of the argument you ultimately favour, and why. You should avoid opening your essay by clearly choosing one side or other, as examiners are generally more concerned to see that you can create a *balanced* argument.

When a quotation is used, it will often point to the key debate between historians on a particular issue, and will sometimes be taken from a leading writer. You should therefore do all you can during your course to keep up with the areas of academic debate in your subject. Journals such as *History*, *Past and Present* and *History Today* are often the most helpful places to do this, as are book reviews, both in these journals and in papers like *The Sunday Times*. Student historians often find it difficult to see the wood for the trees—they become so involved in learning up all the factual material that they fail to see the *purposes* of knowing all the facts. One purpose is historical interpretation, which is what questions of this kind are aiming to test. Thus you should try to show the examiner that you are familiar with the historical debate over a subject and are able both to refer to some of the best known interpretations and to reach your own conclusions. If you do so, you will certainly put yourself above the rank and file of A level candidates.

Finally, 'yes/no' essays are often the easiest of all to write, since the planning of them is already partly done for you by the title. The essay automatically has to be broken into two parts (yes and no) of, say, three or four paragraphs each. If the assertion contains two or more parts, then the arguments for and against each part have to be considered, thus further breaking down the essay for you. If you were asked, for example, 'A period of repression, militarism and gloom'; is this an accurate description of the reign of Nicholas I? (Note the change of wording from (b) above), you would have to consider each of the following:

1 Arguments to support the view that it was a period of repression (Yes 1)
2 Arguments to support the view that it was a period of militarism (Yes 2)
3 Arguments to support the view that it was a period of gloom (Yes 3)
4 Arguments to refute the view that it was a period of repression (No 1)
5 Arguments to refute the view that it was a period of militarism (No 2)
6 Arguments to refute the view that it was a period of gloom (No 3) (You may approach each of 4, 5 and 6 by comparing the reign of Nicholas with what went before and after it.)
7 Conclusion

Thus your essay is almost planned for you by the very question asked. (Incidentally, it would be quite acceptable to write the essay above in the order 1, 4, 2, 5, 3, 6, 7).

With these ideas in mind, answer the following question on Nicholas I:
'Was the reign of Nicholas I merely repressive?'

III The failure of the revolutions 1848–52

1 The Second Republic in France

(a) The Provisional Government

The fall of Louis Philippe in February 1848 had been precipitated by the demonstrations of the working classes in Paris and not by the speeches and banquets of the unenfranchised middle class. As in 1830, the political opposition had wanted reform and not revolution. They were dismayed by Louis Philippe's complete failure of nerve and his flight, which had brought the monarchy to an unexpected end. Moreover, the Parisian working class were now more powerful and vocal than in 1830. Freedom of the press and of public assembly immediately resulted in the appearance of hundreds of revolutionary newspapers and political clubs. It seemed that for the first time the working class were no longer content to accept the leadership of middle-class liberals, but wanted a complete reconstruction of society in their own interests. Marx and Engels, who were writing their *Communist Manifesto* at this time, believed that the time of the proletarian revolution had come (*see page 386*).

The French middle-class politicians had, therefore, to act with greater caution than in 1830. It seemed as if they had no immediate choice but to co-operate with the authors of the revolution whose aims they suspected and feared. They hoped, however, that by manoeuvering and temporising they might yet find the opportunity to direct the course of politics in the way they wanted. Louis Philippe had abdicated in favour of his nine-year-old grandson, the Count of Paris (*see Diagram 1, page 55*). The Chamber of Deputies, wishing to accept the boy's accession to the throne, received with acclaim his mother, the beautiful Duchess of Orleans, whom they proposed should act as Regent; but a crowd broke into their meeting-place, shouting '*Vive la République*', and took control of the proceedings. Lamartine, who was then at the height of his popularity as a symbol of the idealism of the time, made an eloquent speech urging the setting up of a republic. Seven Republican deputies were nominated to form a Provisional Government. The mob then swept Lamartine away to the Hôtel de Ville, where the Republic was proclaimed, and the Socialists insisted upon the addition of four of their members (including Louis Blanc and a workman named Albert) to the Provisional Government. Lamartine did, however, successfully demand that the national emblem should be the tricolour, which had 'gone round the world in triumph', and not the red flag of socialism, which he condemned as a banner of blood and hatred.

The Provisional Government, which was temporarily to administer the Second Republic and arrange for the election of a Constituent Assembly to draw up a constitution, was thus from the beginning a compromise between two mutually opposed and suspicious groups —the Republicans (who accepted 'the Republic') and the Socialists (who wanted a 'social Republic'). They were able, however, in February and March to reach agreement in arriving at three important decisions. They made it possible for all classes to join the National Guard; they declared the right of all citizens to work and set up National Workshops for the unemployed as demanded by Louis Blanc and his followers; and they ordered the immediate holding of elections for the Constituent Assembly on the basis of universal manhood suffrage, which increased the electorate from a quarter of a million to nine million. Thereafter their relations became increasingly contentious, and the only social reform secured by the Socialists was the reduction of the working-day to ten hours in Paris and 11 in the provinces.

(b) The April Elections

Both Republicans and Socialists became anxious as the time for the elections approached. Lamartine said, 'The people must be left free to make mistakes,' but the Socialists did not feel so complacent about the likely outcome. They knew that their main support came from the urban working class, who were a minority of the new voters. They wanted to postpone the elections so that they might have time to spread their ideas. They organized mass meetings and demonstrations in towns throughout France, which sometimes drew crowds as large as 100 000 to hear well-known speakers like Louis Blanc. Such activities, however, brought them little contact with the peasants of the countryside, where the Church was also strongest.

The Republicans and Socialists eventually agreed to postpone the elections for a fortnight so that they were held on Easter Day at the end of April. The result was not pleasing for either party. It was a reminder that France was still a predominantly rural country, where the largely illiterate peasants were traditional and conservative in outlook, staunch supporters of property and order and suspicious of the politicians in Paris who might take their land and who favoured the factory-workers. They were ready to follow their local clergy and landowners and ignored the school-teachers who were often anti-clerical and radical. The very day chosen for the elections favoured the opponents of the Provisional Government. In many parts of the country, the parishioners

141

attended the early festal mass, where they heard the priest in the pulpit recommend candidates to them (often from an approved list sent by the diocesan bishop) and then marched in procession behind him from the church to vote, while notably fewer set out from the town hall or school-house for the same purpose.

A poll of 84 per cent elected a conservative, traditional Constituent Assembly. Its members were lawyers, professors, landowners and army officers, four-fifths of whom were over 40 years of age. The Assembly contained 900 members altogether, and the diagram shows the approximate strengths of the parties. Half were monarchist (Orleanists or Legitimists), and the majority of the rest were Republicans, mostly middle- class men, who wished to uphold the newly-established regime, but were also pledged to suppress disorder and to restore financial stability in France. There were only about 30 middle-class members and no peasants among them. No less than 165 were former deputies of the July Monarchy.

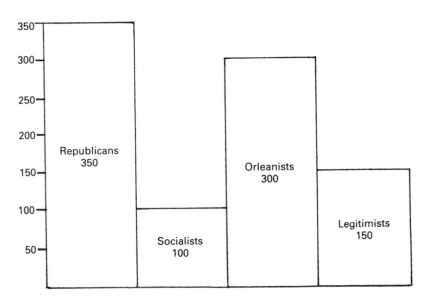

Diagram 4. French Political Parties (1849).

(c) The National Workshops

The first action of the Constituent Assembly was to replace the Provisional Government by an Executive Commission of five moderate Republicans. The frustrated Socialists made an attempt to overthrow this by stirring up the mob to demonstrate in Paris. They proclaimed a government of their own at the Hôtel de Ville; but they were easily suppressed by regular troops and the National Guard. The only result was that the Socialists lost nearly all their leaders. Some were imprisoned; others, including Louis Blanc, escaped to England.

Soon afterwards, the National Workshops, which Louis Blanc had inspired, also disappeared. They had never attempted to put into effect the scheme of his 'socialist workshops'. He had planned that in these workshops the workers would both own and control the processes of production and share the profits among themselves. The government would provide them with the initial capital and buy premises, machines and materials, but later part of the profits would be set aside to establish more workshops so that industry would be expanded, employment created and an increasing part of the country's economy conducted on socialist lines.

The National Workshops, however, had been set up hastily under Socialist pressure in the face of the alarming increase in unemployment in Paris brought about by the general economic dislocation caused by the Revolution. The unemployed of the city were instructed to register and received a small dole. By June 1848 some 120 000 were on the register, which was then closed to the exclusion of perhaps another 50 000. Work was found for about 12 000 men, who received a small wage as well as extra food, cheap clothing and free medical care. Some performed useful tasks, including the reconstruction of the hall to be used by the Constituent Assembly, but most were set to work levelling the Champ de Mars, which led a journalist to say that they might have well been engaged in bottling the waters of the Seine. No attempt was made to select men for tasks according to their skill or to find work which would make a profit. Most of the members of the Constituent Assembly had no intention of giving serious support to a scheme that might threaten private property and business enterprise.

After the April elections, the economic situation had grown worse. The government's financial position was critical. It tried to raise a loan, but the future was so uncertain that appeals to the patriotism of investors had little effect. Yet an increase in taxation could not be considered. Before the elections, the Provisional Government had imposed new taxes, which had fallen mainly on the peasants, whose resentment had influenced their votes. A reduction in government spending seemed to be the only alternative.

The National Workshops had now become objects of public ridicule and scorn. When it became known that a number of the workers employed by them had taken part in the disturbances of May, the Executive Commission decided that economy required their abolition. In June the Constituent Assembly closed the workshops. Young men were offered the choice of dismissal or military service in Algeria. The rest had either to accept what work could be offered by private employers or go to labour on public enterprises in the provinces, such as draining the mosquito-infested swamps of Sologne in Central France.

(d) The June Days

The result was the 'June Days', a rising by some 20 000 workers who barricaded off the large industrial districts of Saint-Marcel and Saint-Antoine in Paris. Lamartine, who had opposed the abolition of the

National Workshops, went round the city and pleaded with the rebels, but only gained the mistrust of both sides. The alarmed Constituent Assembly hastily empowered General Eugène Cavaignac, a conservative-minded Republican and veteran of North Africa, to put down the revolt. For the first time in French history he used the railway to move his troops, taking more than 30 000 into the city, and crushed the insurrection after six days of bitter street fighting. The official number of insurgents killed was given at as 1460, but at least as many were executed without trial, and no count was made of those who died in hospital or were buried immediately. Among the casualties was the Archbishop of Paris, who was shot dead while attempting mediation. After the fighting, 15 000 people were arrested, and 4000 of these were deported, mostly to Algeria. A few were able to flee abroad.

The June Days enabled the Republicans to assert themselves over the Socialists and deprive them of their means of propaganda. Their newspapers were suspended, and their clubs were placed under police supervision. And in September the length of the working-day was increased to 12 hours and became longer in many occupations during the following years.

The political consequences of the June Days were lasting. The Paris mob had not this time been able to determine the course of French history. The nobility, middle classes and peasantry, supported by the army, had overcome it. The downfall of the Second Republic was made inevitable. It had destroyed the hopes which the urban working classes had placed in it, and they never forgave its leaders for the ruthless suppression of the rising. At the same time, these leaders and those who had put them in power had finally lost confidence in its ability to maintain order and protect their interests.

(e) The Republican Constitution

Nevertheless, a restored monarchy was impossible. The supporters of the Bourbon and Orleanist claimants to the throne, the Count of Chambord and the Count of Paris (*see Diagram 1, page 55*), could not reach any agreement. And, moreover, the Assembly feared that the abolition of the Republic might produce a much more serious insurrection than the June Days. The Assembly, therefore, continued its work of drawing up a constitution for the Republic, which it had completed by November. This specifically did not mention any right to work, but it was set on liberal lines.

It provided for a Legislative Assembly consisting only of a single Chamber of Deputies with 750 members, elected by universal manhood suffrage for three years and not to be suspended or dissolved before then even by itself. Deputies could not be ministers or public officials. It was to pass laws, and a vote of three-quarters of the deputies was to be required to amend the constitution. Executive power was to be in the hands of a President, who also was to be elected by universal manhood suffrage for a term of four years, but was not to be eligible for immediate re-election at the end of his period of office. The President was to appoint his own ministers, control the armed forces and was not to be responsible for his actions to the Chamber.

The constitution resembled in important respects that of the United States of America because it followed the idea of the separation of powers as the best way of preventing despotism, but it did not define the precise relationship between the President and the Assembly, both of whose power was based upon universal suffrage. Lamartine, who himself was ambitious to be President, had successfully argued against the proposal that the President should be appointed by the Assembly, saying that an Assembly would be unreliable, but 'a nation is as incorruptible as the Ocean'. There was, indeed, a general fear that extreme factions might gain control of the Assembly, and for this reason strong executive authority was given to the President so that he might be able to oppose it should this happen. Giving such power to the President, however, whose elected position enabled him to claim that his power rested upon popular support, was to make it possible for him to bring about the destruction of the Republic.

(f) Louis Napoleon (1808–73)

Louis Napoleon's father was Louis Bonaparte, Napoleon I's third brother, whom he made King of Holland in 1806, but four years later ejected because he thought his rule was too liberal. Louis Napoleon's mother was Hortense, the daughter of Napoleon I's Empress Josephine, by her first husband; she wrote the air of *Partant pour la Syrie*, which replaced the *Marseillaise*, briefly adopted by the Second Republic, as the official anthem of the Second Empire. Louis Napoleon was born prematurely and was so weak that he had to be revived with wine-baths and wrapped in cotton wool; and his health remained uncertain throughout his life.

Being exiled from France after 1815, Louis Napoleon was educated at Augsburg, so that ever afterwards he spoke his native language as a German. He studied artillery and engineering at a Swiss military camp in Thun, where he was convinced of his own military genius. In 1831 he and his elder brother joined the Carbonari and took part in the nationalist rising in the Papal States. His brother died there. He himself caught measles. Hortense found him in Ancona, nursed him secretly back to health and took him in her coach, dressed as a footman, past the Austrians out of Italy. The next year, Napoleon I's own son, the Duke of Reichstadt, died. The two deaths made Louis Napoleon the heir to the Bonapartist succession and legend.

He was ill-fitted to assume the Napoleonic inheritance. In appearance and character he was supremely unlike his uncle. He lacked most of his qualities, particularly his energy and efficiency, ruthlessness and genius. All his life he was an intriguer rather than a governor, a plotter rather than an administrator. This was the impression he made upon those who came to know him after he achieved power. Prince Albert

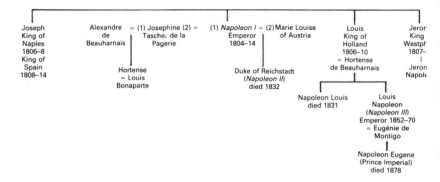

Joseph King of Naples 1806–8 King of Spain 1808–14	Alexandre de Beauharnais	= (1) Josephine (2) = Tasche; de la Pagerie	(1) *Napoleon I* = Emperor 1804–14	(2) Marie Louise of Austria	Louis King of Holland 1806–10 = Hortense de Beauharnais	Jeron King Westph 1807– Jeron Napol
	Hortense = Louis Bonaparte		Duke of Reichstadt (*Napoleon II*) died 1832			

Napoleon Louis died 1831

Louis Napoleon (*Napoleon III*) Emperor 1852–70 = Eugénie de Montigo

Napoleon Eugene (Prince Imperial) died 1878

Diagram 5. Family tree of the Bonapartes

said he was 'an amateur', and Palmerston considered that 'his mind was as full of schemes as a warren is full of rabbits.' He had, however, two valuable assets—his name and his unfailing belief in his destiny which inspired him to persevere after every setback.

Having first learnt about it from his mother, he did his best to identify himself with the Napoleonic Legend (*see page 79*). Unable to be in France, he wrote books designed to gain him the support of both the French people and the French army —*Rêveries Politiques*, insisting that, though he himself was a republican, freedom in France would best be safeguarded by an imperial form of government, and a *Manuel d'Artillerie*, which he was able to get into the hands of French officers. But Hortense insisted that literary propaganda alone would not gain him France. She urged him to exchange the pen for the sword.

His attempts at action, however, were ludicrously disastrous. In 1836 he established himself in Germany at a convenient distance from Strasbourg, where he tried to win over the garrison with the assistance of the commanding officer's mistress. But when he entered the town, dressed as a general in the French artillery, he could not even make a good enough speech to convince the soldiers that he was not an imposter. After a scuffle, he was arrested and deported. He went first to the United States and then to England, where in 1839 he wrote his most ambitious book, *Des Idées Napoliennes*, in which he attempted the difficult task of depicting his uncle as a peacemaker and social reformer.

Action, however, still called him. The next year he hired a Thames paddle-steamer, the *Edinburgh Castle*, and landed at Boulogne with 50 men in second-hand French uniforms. They were scattered by the National Guard. The Prince tried to escape in a small boat, but it capsized, and he was rescued rather than apprehended. He was sentenced to imprisonment for life in the fortress of Ham in the marshland of the Somme, where the climate began that decline in his health which was to be so disastrous in the later years of the Second Empire. While there, he wrote a pamphlet, *L'Extinction du Paupérisme*, in which he advocated government action to deal with unemployment, and it brought him support from the followers of Saint-Simon as well as a visit from Louis Blanc. He escaped in 1846 disguised as a workman. Back in London, he became a lively favourite of the ballet-girls, and in 1848, during the Chartist scare, he patrolled Bloomsbury as a special constable.

(g) From Republic to Empire
When Louis Philippe lost his throne, Louis Napoleon did not go to France until after the June Days and so escaped being identified with any of the factions of the troubled beginnings of the Second Republic when he decided to stand for the Presidency. Nevertheless, his chances of success did not at first seem great. His black clothes and heavy moustache, pale features and expressionless eyes, thick accent and clumsy speech, all convinced experienced politicians that he would make no impression during the electioneering. But soon he gained powerful support. Thiers and other ambitious politicians, who had failed to achieve office after the Revolution they had done so much to stimulate, hoped to use him to regain power. Royalists believed that he could be a temporary substitute for the monarchy until the Legitimists and Orleanists resolved their differences and enabled France to have a king again. The clergy and army alike expected him to uphold their privileges. Some Frenchmen were attracted to him as a president who would be above the intrigue and vacillation of recent politics; others as one who would be opposed to the Vienna Settlement. The working class in the towns, who would not vote for Cavaignac—the 'Butcher of June'—and could expect nothing from the discredited Socialists, hoped that they would benefit from his interest in social reform. Above all, the peasants throughout the countryside believed that he stood for strong, orderly government and would be a safeguard against their ever-present fears of socialist schemes for the nationalization of the land.

The result was that the presidential election in December 1848 gave Louis Napoleon 5 400 000 votes and Cavaignac 1 500 000. Lamartine got only 17 000. When the Revolution had taken place, Lamartine was its most popular leader, but now the ineffectiveness of the Provisional Government, the June Days and the continuing economic depression had led the country to reject him and other Republicans. In April 1849 Louis Napoleon strengthened his popularity with the clerical party and the peasants by sending a French army, not to help the Italian nationalists in whose ranks he had once fought, but to re-establish the

Pope in Rome (*see page 189*). The leaders of an attempted insurrection in Paris and several provincial towns in support of the Roman Republic were imprisoned or had to go into exile; and the trees of liberty, which had been planted in Paris during the revolutionary eras of 1790 and 1848, were cut down by the military in January 1850.

The elections for the Legislative Assembly the next month showed that the peasants, despite their support for Louis Napoleon, mistrusted the old politicians, since there was only a poll of 50 per cent. Legitimists, Orleanists, Bonapartists, Catholics and other conservatives made up some 500 of the deputies. There were only about 70 Republicans, but 180 Socialists, who had gained nearly a third of the votes cast.

The unexpected success of the Socialists alarmed the conservative parties. As soon as the Chamber met, they passed two measures designed to limit their influence. An education law allowed religious orders to conduct schools and also gave prefects the right of appointing and dismissing teachers in the state primary schools. And an electoral law required all voters to have lived in their constituency for three years and never to have had any court convictions, even for the most trivial offence. This disfranchised over 3 million of the poorer voters. Radical leaders in Paris tried to arouse the people against these measures, but they were thwarted by memories of the suppression of the June Days and a fierce cholera epidemic which was killing several hundred people a day in the city.

Louis Napoleon spoke against the restriction of the franchise. He wished to represent himself as the champion of all the French people. 'Other French governments have ruled with the support of perhaps one million of the educated masses', he said. 'I have called in the other 29 million.' And soon he was to override the constitution of the Republic to make it possible for him to place himself in such a position.

Yet it would be wrong to suppose that he always intended to use the Presidency as the means of re-establishing a Bonapartist empire. This credits him with more determination and resolution than in fact he possessed. He was satisfied with his position as President in all respects except two—the inadequacy of his income for his extravagant expenditure (which included gifts to workpeople and soldiers as well as entertainment and sport) and the impossibility of his tenure of office extending beyond 1852. In 1850 the Assembly refused to increase his annual income from 1 500 000 francs to 3 500 000 francs; he thereupon borrowed 500 000 francs from the Spanish Ambassador and ostentatiously sold his race-horses by auction. And in July 1851 his motion to change the position of the President in the constitution failed to obtain the necessary three-quarters of the votes of the deputies in the Chamber. Not until after that did he listen to the urging of Bonapartists leaders that he should take steps to change his situation in the state.

If he had persevered, he might still have persuaded the large conservative majority in the Assembly to have revised the constitution in his favour. They had reasons for negotiating with him terms on which he could remain President because they still thought of him, in the words of Thiers, as 'a noodle whom anyone could twist around his finger'. But Louis Napoleon did not wish to become completely dependent upon the Assembly; and despite the years of futile plotting in exile, he still loved intrigue and conspiracy. He carefully prepared to gain control in a way modelled upon the *coups d'état* which had brought the first Napoleon to power. Throughout France, prefects, officials, judges and generals (including the commander of the garrison in Paris) were replaced by men upon whom he could depend. He undertook a series of tours in the provinces, making speeches designed to attract whatever audiences he addressed, promising encouragement for building and trade to financiers and businessmen, farm subsidies and higher agricultural prices to landowners and peasants, greater military expenditure and new weapons to the officers of troops whom he reviewed; and at mass meetings, where he spoke of the need for firm government and public order, his supporters shouted, as instructed, '*Vive l'Empereur!*'

Then, in the early hours of 2 December 1851, the anniversary of his uncle's coronation as Emperor of France in 1804 and of his overwhelming victory over the Austrians at Austerlitz in 1805, Louis Napoleon slipped away from a splendid reception at the Elysée Palace to give the orders, in packets labelled 'Rubicon' (*see page 203*), which brought about, as Queen Victoria wrote to her Uncle Leopold at Brussels, 'the *wonderful* proceedings in Paris, which really seem like a *story* in a book or play'. Police arrested a number of deputies, and troops occupied the main buildings of the city. Placards announced the dissolution of the Assembly because it had been 'forging arms for civil war', and the restoration of universal suffrage.

Unlike the Coup d'Etat of Brumaire by which Napoleon I had established the Consulate in 1799, Louis Napoleon's *coup d'état* was not bloodless. Sporadic risings in Paris and the provinces were crushed by the army with two or three hundred casualties; tribunals sentenced some 10 000 people to terms of imprisonment and about as many to deportation to Algeria or Guiana. Some politicians and writers, including Victor Hugo, went into voluntary exile. A fortnight later, voters were asked to declare whether they wished 'to maintain Louis Bonaparte in authority and to delegate to him the necessary powers to establish a constitution.' He gained what he wanted by 7 500 000 votes to 600 000. Though the opposition were under arrest or intimidated, the result probably accurately reflected the continuing popular disenchantment with the Republic and hope for firm stable government under him.

The amendment of the constitution was carried out the next year. It gave Louis Napoleon much the same position as his uncle had possessed as First Consul between 1799 and 1804. The President was to hold office for ten years and possess full executive powers. A Council of

State, appointed by the President, prepared the laws which he wished to propose. These were discussed and passed by a Legislative Chamber consisting of 260 members elected every six years by universal adult male suffrage (for the first time in France), meeting for only three months a year and not allowed to publish its proceedings. Laws were to be examined, to see that they did not conflict with the constitution, by a Senate, whose 150 members were appointed for life by the President.

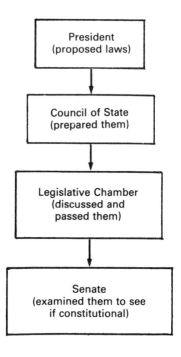

Diagram 6. Law-making under the French Constitution (1852)

For some months, Louis Napoleon initiated social reforms such as housing-schemes and the building of baths and hospitals, and he continued his tours around the provinces and chief towns. He now wished to follow the example of his uncle by replacing the transformed Republic by an Empire. Before the end of the year, he had no difficulty in persuading the Senate to vote for a Bonapartist restoration. Since the Bonapartists regarded the Duke of Reichstadt as Napoleon II, he was proclaimed as Napoleon III on 2 December 1852. The voters endorsed his action by 7 800 000 to 253 000. In both plebiscites, however, over 2 million voters abstained. There was still strong republican and socialist feeling in the south-eastern departments and the larger towns.

Bibliography

Events in 1848 are considered in George Duveau, *1848: The Making of a Revolution* (New York, 1966) and Roger Price, *1848 in France* (Thames & Hudson, 1975), which has instructive illustrations of the revolution. The later developments are discussed in Roger Price, *The French Second Republic: A Social History* (Ithaca, N.Y., 1972), F. le Luna, *The French Republic under Cavaignac, 1848* (Princeton, 1969) and D. McKay, *The National Workshops* (Cambridge, Mass., 1965). For Louis Napoleon, there are two general biographies, A.L. Guerard, *Napoleon III* (Cambridge, Mass., 1943) and T.A.B. Corley, *Democratic Despot: A Life of Napleon III* (Barrie & Rockliffe, 1961). The best treatment of his early years is in F.A. Simpson, *The Rise of Louis Napoleon* (3rd. edn., Longmans, 1951).

Exercises

Additional exercises on aspects of this section will be found on page 195, where aspects of the 1848 revolutions as a whole are considered, and on page 238, where the reign of Napoleon III as a whole is examined.

A *This section consists of questions that might be used for discussion (or written answers) as a way of expanding on the chapter and testing your understanding of it:*

1 In what ways did the 1848 revolution appear to differ from the earlier revolutions?

2 Why did the middle-classes fear the aims of the authors of the revolution?

3 What is a Constituent Assembly?

4 Why were both the Republicans and the Socialists anxious about the outcome of the elections of April 1848?

5 Why did the Socialists fare so badly in the elections for the Constituent Assembly?

6 In what ways did the National Workshops 'threaten private property and business enterprise'?

7 What effects did the June Days have?

8 What do you understand by ' . . . the idea of the separation of powers as the best way of preventing despotism . . .' (*page 145*)?

9 Why was Louis Napoleon ill-suited to inherit the 'Napoleonic legend'?

10 Comment on Louis Napoleon's efforts to seize power in the 1830s.

11 Given their backgrounds, account for the success of Louis Napoleon and the failure of Lamartine in the presidential election of 1848.

12 Why did the Socialists succeed in the 1849 elections, and how did the Assembly respond to this success?

13 Why did Thiers regard Louis Napoleon as 'a noodle whom anyone could twist around his finger' (*page 149*)?

14 Why did Louis Napoleon decide on a *coup d'état* in December 1851?

15 Why was there so little opposition to this coup?

B *Essay questions*

1 How far did political change in France reflect social change between 1815 and 1851? (Welsh, 1983)

2 Account for the failure of the Second French Republic, 1848–51. (Welsh, 1983)

3 Why did the 1848 Revolutions succeed in France and fail elsewhere? (Oxford and Cambridge, 1982)

C *Extract question (London, 1982)*
Study Extracts I, II, III and IV below and then answer questions (*a*) to (*g*) which follow:

EXTRACT I

line
1 'It seems that the *election* will not be as good as was expected. Socialism has made the most alarming strides; in several of the *departments* the Red candidates will be successful, and even if the moderates succeed in others, their majority will be so small that the moral effect will be
5 disastrous. If this happens there will be nothing left to do but to pack our things, get up a civil war and ask the cossaks to come and help us!

The Empire is the only thing that can save the situation. Some of the leading politicians have been nibbling at the idea.'
(*A letter written by M. Mornay, 16 May* 1849)

EXTRACT II

'France neither wishes for a return to the old order of things, in no
10 matter what form that may be disguised, nor for ventures into dangerous and impractical *utopianism*. It is because I am the natural enemy of both these alternatives that *France* has given me its *confidence*. . . . Indeed, if my government has not been able to bring about all the improvements it had in mind, that must be blamed on the
15 devious conduct of various factions. For three years, as you will have noted, I have always had the support of the assembly when it has been a question of combating disorder by repressive measures. But, whenever I have wanted to do good and *improve conditions for the people*, the assembly has denied me its support.'
(*A speech by Louis Napoleon, May* 1851)

EXTRACT III

20 'Events speak for themselves!
Who exactly is in revolt at present?
Who is causing bloodshed in our *departments*?
Who else but the barbarous militia of the secret societies, that is to say, of communism and terrorism.
25 The decent folk in all the parties were at first abashed by *the astonishing events of 2 December*. Yet they have seen the truth of the matter in the sinister glare of the fires and crimes of every description committed by bands of insurgents. . . . Louis Napoleon Bonaparte, from the supreme position in which he is placed, had seen and judged
30 the situation in France before they had realised what was wrong. Appreciating the magnitude of the peril he has chosen appropriate measures to deal with it.'
(*L'Union, 30 December* 1851)

EXTRACT IV

'The Bonaparte dynasty represents not the revolutionary, but the conservative peasant; not the peasant that strikes out beyond the
35 condition of his social existence, the small holding, but rather the peasant who wants to consolidate this holding, not the country folks who, linked up with the towns, want to overthrow *the old order* through their own energies, but on the contrary those who, in stupefied seclusion within this *old order*, want to see themselves and
40 their small holdings saved and favoured by the ghost of the empire.'

(*Karl Marx*, '*The Eighteenth Brumaire of Louis Bonaparte*')

	(Maximum marks)
(*a*) When, and how, did 'France' first give 'its confidence' (line 12) to Louis Napoleon?	(2)
(*b*) Explain the sense in which *each* of the following terms is used in these Extracts: 'departments' (lines 2 and 22); 'utopianism' (line 11); 'the old order' (lines 37 and 39).	(5)
(*c*) To what 'election' (line 1) was M. Mornay referring, and how justified was he in the fears he expressed concerning this election in lines 1 to 6 of Extract I?	(3)
(*d*) What were 'the astonishing events of 2 December' (line 26)?	(3)
(*e*) What do Extracts I (lines 1–8) and IV (lines 33–40) reveal of the social tensions which existed in France during the Second Republic?	(4)
(*f*) How would you make use of *each* of these four Extracts in explaining why Louis Napoleon eventually became the Emperor Napoleon III?	(7)
(*g*) In what ways, and to what extent, both before and after he became Emperor, did Louis Napoleon seek in his domestic policy to 'improve conditions for the people' (line 18) of France?	(7)

D *The failure of the 1848 Revolutions in France*

In this section two key analytical questions are examined in more detail, and may also serve as a background to the exercises on pages 194–196 on the failure of the revolutions as a whole.

(a) *In what sense was the Revolution a failure?*

The 1848 Revolution is usually regarded as a failure, but what exactly do historians mean by this? Below are suggested four ways in which it may be considered such. Consider the validity of these interpretations and add to them your own ideas on its failure:

1 The Republic that was established by the Provisional Government after the overthrow of Louis Philippe was itself overthrown and replaced by the Second Empire of Napoleon, a dictatorial regime that did little for the people of France.

2 The National Workshops, the one innovation made for the benefit of the working classes, were closed down.

153

3 No substantial or long-term political, social or economic changes were brought about as a result of the revolution.
4 The leaders of the revolution were either imprisoned or fell from power, losing such influence as they had in the government of the country.

(b) *What were the reasons for the failure of the Revolutions?*
In this section, a number of reasons *why* the Revolutions failed are suggested. Again, you should

  (i) consider the validity of each suggested reason
 (ii) add other reasons of your own
(iii) rank the list of reasons into what you consider their importance, explaining your order.

  (i)   The Provisional Government proved ineffective and unpopular: it was unable to agree on policies, introduced few policies of any worth, damaged the French economy and led to violent swings in electoral fortunes.

 (ii) The underlying rural conservatism of France was such that a majority would cling to traditional ideas and follow the advice of landowners and priests.

(iii) The 'parties of the Revolution'—the Republicans and the Socialists—were always too divided to agree on common actions and policies and to accept a single leader.

(iv) Louis Napoleon was a skilful and determined politician who was able to exploit the weaknesses and divisions of his opponents to his own advantage, thereby bringing about the coup of December 1851.

 (v) Too many Frenchmen were fearful of the continued indecision and disorder that followed the 1848 Revolution. It was reminiscent of the periods that followed earlier revolutions, and they therefore welcomed the stability and discipline that Louis Napoleon offered.

(vi) A Republic was unacceptable to too many Frenchmen, as was a monarchy, and Louis Napoleon appeared the only answer: ' . . . the politicians supported him because they thought he could save them from the masses; and the masses supported him because they thought he could save them from the politicians.'

2 Nationalism in the Austrian Empire

(a) The Downfall of Metternich

The news of the French Revolution of 1848 produced risings throughout the Central European provinces of the Austrian Empire. Only their outbreak was sudden. They were, in effect, an explosion of the growing resentment fostered by the situation which had persisted in the Empire during the 30 years since the end of the Napoleonic War. The passing years had not, as Metternich had hopefully forecast, diminished the discontents and frustrations which had been apparent then. On the contrary, these had increased. Liberal propaganda had made the professional classes more aware of their situation and their desires. The demands and rivalries of the different nationalities were as strong and unsatisfied as ever. Behind them were thousands of impoverished and restless peasants as well as a resentful badly-paid or unemployed working class in the towns. Metternich's declining authority had made it increasingly difficult for him to deal with the situation. The materials for combustion were well-prepared; the news from Paris provided the spark that set them alight in several places.

As might be expected, the first reaction to Louis Philippe's downfall came in Hungary. On 3 March 1848 Kossuth made a violent speech in the Hungarian Diet, which met at Pressburg only 20 miles away from Vienna. 'From the charnel-house of the Viennese system,' he declared, 'a pestilential breath steals over us which paralyses our nerves and deadens our national spirit.' He urged the creation of a new constitution which would make Hungary completely equal to Austria and establish a separate Hungarian ministry. He wanted also to do away with the privileges of the nobility, abolish serfdom and secure the freedom of the press, of meeting and of association. The violence of his speech and the nature of his demands seriously alarmed the party of the nobility, but there were demonstrations in Budapest by students, who were supported by peasants visiting the city for the traditional March fair. The nobles had to accept a 'People's Charter', and the Diet gave effect to its principles by passing the so-called 'March Laws', which made Hungary, Transylvania and Croatia ('the lands of the Crown of St. Stephen') into a united state with a single, independent Diet and ministry. Kossuth called upon the Imperial government to recognize the legality of the Laws.

Meanwhile, Kossuth's speeches had stirred up trouble in Vienna itself. Here opposition first appeared at the University, which had formed links with the middle-class constitutionalists. On 12 March two professors presented the Emperor Ferdinand with a petition demanding a new government, democratic elections, the formation of a National Guard and the removal of the censorship of newspapers and books. The next day placards appeared on the Cathedral wall saying, 'Viennese! Liberate your good Emperor Ferdinand from the bonds of his enemies! All who desire the prosperity of Austria must desire the overthrow of its rulers!' This meant Metternich and his supporters; and students demonstrated against him as he stood with his family at the windows of the Chancellery. When troops opened fire, the disorder spread to the working-class suburbs.

Metternich urged the Council of State to stand firm and put down the rioting immediately so as to prevent the Emperor sharing the fate of Louis Philippe, but his enemies saw the situation as an opportunity to get rid of him. The Emperor was persuaded to dismiss him. He said simply as he did it, 'Tell the people that I agree to everything.' Metternich's comment was, 'This is what our liberal friends call the voice of God.' Baron Rothschild, who was already serving free meals to the student patrols in the city, made it possible for the 74-year-old statesman to escape with his wife and family. They left hidden in a laundry van and, travelling on forged passports, finally reached England where he passed a garrulous three years in London and Brighton until he was allowed to return to Vienna.

(b) The Success of the Revolutions

Neither the Austrian court nor the nobility, however, intended to change the Imperial system of government in any way that would weaken Habsburg power; and the departure of Metternich did not halt the agitation in the Empire. There were further demonstrations by students and workmen in Vienna on 15 March. The Emperor had to agree to the abolition of the censorship of the press and the establishment of a National Guard in Austria and to promise that an Austrian constitution should be drawn up. Soon control of the city of Vienna was taken over by a Revolutionary Committee of 22 members, among them representatives of the newly-formed National Guard and of a military organization of university students called the Academic Legion. In the suburbs workmen, under socialist influence, had formed their own committees.

Two days later, the Hungarian delegation, which had been sent to Vienna, was promised a 'responsible ministry', which was, however, to be 'subject to the preservation intact of the unity of the crown and of the link with the monarchy.' The Hungarian Chancellery in Vienna, from which the country had been largely governed, was abolished, and for the first time, a Hungarian government was created which was responsible to the Diet alone and not to the Emperor and had complete control of all administrative departments. The Diet proceeded to pass the 'April Laws', which transformed the political and social situation of the country. Foreign affairs and finance came under Hungarian control; and Hungarian regiments were withdrawn from the Imperial army to form a separate Hungarian army. Serfdom and manorial courts were abolished, and the nobility were deprived of their exemption from taxation. The Diets of Transylvania and Croatia were abolished, but the Hungarian Diet was to meet regularly at Budapest; it was to be elected by a uniform franchise extended to the middle class and wealthier peasants, and voting was to be direct instead of through the local courts as hitherto. Complete religious toleration (except for Jews) and freedom of the press was declared. To safeguard these constitutional reforms, a National Guard was established. A national flag was adopted, and Hungarian ambassadors were appointed to foreign countries. The aims of these measures, which Ferdinand accepted, was to make Hungary a modern, liberal state, bound to the Emperor only by nominal ties.

At the same time, similar events were occurring in other parts of the Empire. Before the end of March, the Austrians had been expelled from Milan and Venice, and the King of Piedmont had declared war with the purpose of driving them out of the whole of the Italian peninsula (*see page 185*). In Prague, some Czech radical intellectuals met at the Wenceslaus Bath, a café-concert-hall, and sent a delegation to Vienna, led by Francis Palacky, a historian at the University of Prague. The delegation demanded the fusion of Bohemia with Moravia and Silesia, which they claimed were 'the lands of the Crown of St. Wenceslaus', though half of the inhabitants were German, and in April nationalist leaders set up a provisional government in Prague and demanded a charter from Ferdinand. To all these demands the Imperial government had to agree. It seemed as if the Austrian Empire might be reduced to a collection of countries linked only by the loosest ties, and that Austrian rule in Italy might end completely.

In Vienna, lack of initiatives among the insurgents, enabled Kilowrat and other elderly court officials to delay taking action until on 25 April 1848 they eventually proclaimed a constitution of their own for the whole Austrian Empire, which they hoped would preserve the Viennese administration of the provinces as much as possible. The new constitution was not to apply to Hungary, Transylvania or Croatia, but the rest of the Empire was to be governed from the capital by Imperial institutions and German officials. The ministers were to be responsible to a Reichstag of two chambers, one of which would be elective, the vote being severely restricted by a high property qualification, and the Emperor was to have the right to veto its decisions.

The Viennese students, however, would not accept this. They were determined to press their own ideas upon the government, and on 15 May working-men, armed with spades and pick-handles, crowded into the centre of the city to support them. The government had to withdraw its constitution and to agree to the summoning of a single-chamber Constituent Assembly, elected by universal male suffrage, to revise the constitution. Meanwhile, the leaders of the movement set up a Committee of Public Safety to maintain order in the capital and find work for the unemployed.

(c) The Failure of the Revolutions

In May 1848 the revolutions were at the height of their success, but at the very moment when they seemed likely to carry all before them, the tide began to turn rapidly in favour of the Emperor. The first setback, which was to prove decisive, occurred on 20 May when the court decided to quit Vienna leaving a ministry in the city. The student patrols, which had made it difficult for Metternich to leave, offered them no opposition, which was a serious mistake. They were now removed from intimidation by the Committee of Public Safety and demonstrators in the streets. The Emperor and the archdukes with their families went to Innsbruck in the Tyrol and on the frontier. Here they were free to organize the defeat of the revolutionary movements, though this was to owe less to them than to the loyalty of the Imperial soldiers led by the three 'paladins', Prince Windischgrätz, Governor of

Bohemia, Marshal Radetzky, Governor of Lombardy and Venetia, and Count Jellaçic, Governor of Croatia.

Successful military intervention against the uprisings was made possible by divisions between the national movements inspired by racial or local differences. In May 1848 the Frankfurt Assembly met in Germany (*see page 173*). The deputies, who considered that Bohemia, Moravia and Silesia should be part of a greater united Germany, invited Palacky to attend, but he replied that he could not participate in a German assembly, saying, 'I am a Bohemian of Slav race.' He said also, 'If the Austrian Empire did not exist, it would be necessary for us to create it as soon as possible.' He wanted the nationalities of the Empire to achieve equality, but he believed that only if they were united under Habsburg rule could they escape German or Russian domination. To achieve this scheme (which was later called Austroslavism), he organized a Slavonic Congress in Prague, which included Slav representatives from all over the Austrian Empire as well as a few from Prussian Poland and from Russia, but it soon collapsed disastrously amid deep dissensions. It led to the wrecking of Czech hopes. It showed that even if the Habsburg government were prepared to grant self-government to their subject peoples, there was little chance of the Slavs reaching agreement within the Empire. Not only were they divided linguistically, culturally and religiously, but they feared and suspected each other. And the Moravian and Silesian Diets had already refused to submit to the provisional government in Prague.

The failure of the Slavonic Congress led a group of students in Prague, supported by some of the city's unemployed and workers (but opposed by the nationalist leaders) to make an irresponsible attempt to establish a Czech republic by revolution. Windischgrätz (who had not been allowed by the Imperial government to occupy Vienna), refused their demand for arms. There was a demonstration in front of his palace, during which a stray bullet shot his wife dead at a window. He took what he believed was the only way of putting down revolt —'Blood,' he had once declared, 'is the only remedy for all the ills of the century—communism, radicalism, impiety and atheism.' He withdrew his troops from the city to the hills outside, bombarded it for 12 hours and then occupied it after some street-fighting. Of the 100 000 inhabitants of Prague, less than 1200 manned the barricades and 800 of these were inexperienced students. Prague was put under martial law, the Bohemian Diet was forbidden to meet, and the leaders of the rising were imprisoned. The professors, including Palacky, resumed their teaching. The Frankfurt Assembly, which had discussed sending Saxon or Prussian troops to help Windischgrätz, offered him their congratulations.

Meanwhile, the Poles in Austrian Galacia had also risen. There had previously been disturbances there, which had led Austria to annex the Free City of Cracow, set up by the Congress of Vienna, in 1846 (*see Map 5, page 39*). Now there was another rising in 1848, but it was crushed by Count Stadion. And in July, Marshal Radetzky routed the Piedmontese troops under Charles Albert at the Battle of Custozza and regained control of Milan (*see page 185*).

These victories strengthened the nerves of the archdukes, and they brought the court back to Vienna. There the Committee of Public Safety had been no more successful than its counterpart in Paris in finding work for the unemployed. In August the ministry decided to relieve the economic problems of the city by reducing the industrial wages of women and children. There was an immediate working-class rising, which was crushed by the police and the National Guard. As previously in Prague, the peasants in the countryside gave no support to the insurgents; and in September, the Constituent Assembly, which was now sitting in the city, abolished serfdom throughout the Empire, so removing the only cause which might have inspired them to fight against the Habsburgs.

Radetzky's victory at Custozza had released troops for action against Hungary, and the opportunity to use them soon came. Elections in June had produced a Hungarian Diet composed mainly of noblemen with a few lawyers and others from the professional classes. The Croatian Diet, meeting at Agram, would not recognize its authority and refused to dissolve itself. It also declined to accept the Magyar tongue as the official language of Croatia. Jellaçic, who was a Croat, went to Innsbruck to assure the Emperor of his country's loyalty, and in September his troops crossed the River Drave in an advance on Budapest.

The Hungarians made this attack the reason for attempting a war of extermination against the Slovak minority in their lands. They also appealed to the Constituent Assembly in Vienna for support. But the Assembly contained far more Slavs than Germans, and there was complete disagreement among its members in the debates on the Hungarian approach. The German radicals favoured Hungarian independence since this would undermine Habsburg power and enable Austria to be part of a united Germany, and the Poles, who wanted to become an independent nation, agreed with them. The German conservatives, who wanted to maintain Austrian supremacy in the Empire, were supported by the Slavs, who sided with the Croats (and Slovaks) and also wished to preserve the Empire. The appeal of Hungary against the Croat invasion was, therefore, rejected by an overwhelming majority in the Assembly. The various Slav nationalities regarded Hungary as their persecutor and wanted an arrangement by which the Austrian government would recognize their rights and yet continue to protect them.

Two weeks after entering Hungary, Jellaçic's army was defeated and fled in retreat. The Imperial government decided to send troops from the garrison in Vienna to reinforce the Croats on 6 October, but a Viennese regiment refused to board the train. The railway station was surrounded by a crowd, composed mainly of students and workers, who began tearing up the rails and demolishing bridges to prevent the train leaving. Some Galician troops fired on the demonstrators. This precipitated a third rising in the city. The Minister of War was hanged from a lamp-post, and the court again fled from Vienna, going this time to Olmütz in Bohemia, where Windischgrätz could protect them. With them went many Austrian conservatives and the Slav members of the Constituent Assembly. The Imperial government ordered the Assembly itself to move to Kresmier, a small town not far from Olmütz, to continue its deliberations. The Viennese insurgents numbered about 40 000, but the city was soon encircled by the forces of Windischgrätz and Jellaçic, and a Hungarian army, sent by Kossuth to relieve it, was unable to break through. After a bombardment lasting three days, Vienna fell on 31 October. There was a great deal of looting, and some 2000 Viennese were killed in the capture of the city, but the Imperial government afterwards insisted on leniency, and only 24 men were executed.

Habsburg authority was now restored everywhere except in Hungary, but before subduing the Magyars, Windischgrätz secured the appointment of his brother-in-law, Prince Felix Schwarzenberg, to succeed Metternich as chief minister, a post that he was to hold until his death in 1852. Schwarzenberg was as determined as Windischgrätz to assert the authority of the Imperial government over the subject races by force. The Tsar Nicholas called him 'Lord Palmerston in a white uniform', and he was a man of considerable ability and diplomatic experience. One of his first measures was to arrange for the abdication of Ferdinand, whose personal acceptance of the April Laws would be an embarrassment in taking further action against Hungary, and to secure the renunciation of the throne by Charles in favour of his 18-year-old son, Francis (*see page 162*). He became the Emperor Francis Joseph, taking the additional name to identify himself with Joseph II, whose reforms had made his memory respected by the peasants (*see page 40*).

Schwarzenberg made the subjection of Hungary his immediate purpose. In January 1849 the forces of Windischgrätz and Jellaçic captured Budapest, but in the spring the Hungarians rallied under Kossuth, retook the city and even drove the invaders out of the country. In April the Hungarian Diet renounced the authority of Francis Joseph and declared the country to be an independent republic with Kossuth at its head. There seemed little chance that the Imperial forces would be able to extinguish Hungarian resistance in the future.

Schwarzenberg believed that it would be very dangerous for the authority of the Habsburgs if the Hungarians were not subdued immediately. Relying upon the terms of the Holy Alliance, he entered into negotiations with the Tsar Nicholas I, who was very ready to send troops into Hungary. He did not want an independent republic established so near to his discontented Polish dominion, and he wished to gain Austrian favour in order to have a free hand in his policy towards the Turkish Empire (*see page 197*). Any need for caution, because of the possibility of unfavourable international reaction to such foreign intervention, had now been removed by Louis Napoleon's successful expedition to Rome (*see page 148*). As with the Poles, geography made any foreign help for the Hungarians impossible, and in any event neither Palmerston nor Louis Napoleon wished to threaten the existence of the Austrian Empire.

In July 1849 three armies entered Hungary—the Austrians along the Danube from the west, the Russians over the Carpathians from the north and the Croatians across the Drave from the south (*see Map 9, page 198*). Altogether they comprised 280 000 men with 12 000 cannon. A cholera epidemic and difficulties of supplies at first hindered their progress, but they continued to advance, and the Hungarian forces, numbering 150 000 men and with only 500 cannon, had no chance of resisting them. By August the Magyar forces had surrendered, and Kossuth had fled into foreign exile. Martial law was established in the country under the Austrian commander, General Haynau, who had already achieved notoriety for being responsible for the flogging of women in Italy. Under Haynau, 13 Hungarian generals (later known as the Martyrs of Arad) were hanged, as were more than 100 other officers, 2000 men and women received long terms of imprisonment, and many more were flogged. Kossuth settled in England, where he was rapturously received, though he had brought about the summary execution of several hundred Slovaks. Haynau paid an official visit to London in 1850 to be called 'General Hyena' by the press and to be mobbed by the draymen (to Palmerston's great satisfaction) when taken on a visit to Barclay and Perkin's brewery in Southwark.

(d) The Imperial Reaction

Such expressions of liberal sympathies abroad, however, made more impression upon the Austrian government than they previously had upon the Tsar's policy in Poland. It was determined to make no concessions to liberalism in the Empire. It had already shown this by its attitude towards the constitution for the non-Hungarian lands of the Empire, which had meanwhile been produced by the Constituent Assembly in January 1849 at Kresmier. This proposed to make the Emperor a constitutional monarch ruling over a federal state. All titles were to be abolished, and complete religious equality was to be established. The Emperor was no longer to reign 'by the Grace of God' for it was stated that 'sovereignty proceeds from the people'. There was to be an imperial parliament with an upper house representing the provinces and a lower house elected by direct suffrage. This parliament was to exercise all the powers not explicitly assigned to the provinces, which were to have local diets and local autonomy. Though the Slav representatives had now broken away from the Assembly and refused to take any further part in its discussions, this constitution represented an attempt to put into effect a plan which would make the Empire a multi-national state such as Palacky's Austroslavism had envisaged.

Such ideas, however, were contrary to the Habsburg tradition which regarded the Empire as the family lands of the Emperor to be ruled personally by him, and were entirely unacceptable to Schwarzenberg. In March 1849 the Constituent Assembly was dissolved, and a new Imperial constitution was proclaimed. This was applicable to the entire Habsburg domain and made it for the first time into a centralized unitary state. The Hungarian kingdom was abolished and divided into new provinces based on national divisions; and Croatia, even though it had fought on the side of the Habsburgs, was also denied its wish to have a separate political existence and similarly made a province. All these provinces, together with those already in existence, were reduced to mere administrative subdivisions, which, perhaps most important, were united into a single customs union. The entire Empire was subjected to a uniform code of law, a uniform system of taxation and a uniform administration, and German was to be the official language everywhere. Provision was made for the establishment of an imperial diet, elected by direct suffrage, and a ministry under a prime minister which would be responsible to it; but the Emperor was 'provisionally' to rule by decrees. He continued to do this, and neither the diet nor the ministry came into being.

Francis Joseph had been brought up in the Habsburg tradition and firmly intended to follow it as Emperor. This gave him much the same paternalistic outlook as Tsar Nicholas. The inhabitants of the Empire were all his people, and he believed that it was his duty to rule them well and fairly, but he was entirely an absolutist, relying for his support in his mission, which he regarded as divine, upon the Imperial army and the Roman Catholic Church. He never intended to share his authority with any sort of representative institutions, and in December 1851 he revoked the constitution, declaring, 'Ministers are solely responsible to the monarch.' Henceforward, he alone was to govern the Empire with a nominated Imperial Council to advise him on legislation. In 1855 he made a Concordat with the Papacy which put the Roman Catholic Church in a strong and privileged position; it regained powers which had been taken away from it by Joseph II in 1781, including the control of education, the regulation of marriage and the restoration of the ecclesiastical courts. The revolutions of 1848 in the Austrian Empire were followed, therefore, by the establishment of an even more powerful absolutism wielded by the Habsburg monarchy. A socialist said that this absolutism depended upon 'a standing army of soldiers, a sitting army of officials, a kneeling army of priests and a creeping army of bureaucrats.'

The sole gainers from the revolutions were the peasants, for serfdom was not restored. They had never been roused by the ideas of nationalism and liberalism, and now they became persistent supporters of the Imperial cause. Their attitude was an important reason for the failure of the revolutions. At first the simultaneous outbreak of the revolts in different parts of the Empire, the helplessness of the semi-imbecile Emperor Ferdinand and the weakness of the ageing Metternich, enabled the revolutionaries to seize power and wrest concessions from the government. With the fall of Metternich and the abdication of Ferdinand, however, the Austrian ministers and generals were able to take advantage of the liberals' lack of support in the countryside and the ruthless national disagreements among them. The government was again able to 'divide and conquer' and take steps to crush the rising and nullify the constitutional concessions. Internal rebellion was not to overthrow the Habsburgs.

Bibliography
F. Eyck, *The Revolutions of 1848–49* (Oliver & Boyd, 1972), J.R. Rath, *The Viennese Revolution of 1848* (Texas, 1957), Alan Sked, *The Survival of the Habsburg Empire: Radetzky, the Imperial Army and the Class War, 1848* (Longman, 1979). Part III; and C.A. Macartney, *Hungary: A Short History* (Edinburgh UP, 1962).

Exercises
Additional exercises on aspects of this section will be found on pages 193–196, where aspects of the 1848 revolutions as a whole are considered.

A   *This section consists of questions that might be used for discussion (or written answers) as a way of expanding on the chapter and testing your understanding of it.*

1   How long after the revolution in Paris did revolt break out in Austria-Hungary?
2   What did the Hungarian rebels hope for?
3   Why did the Emperor dismiss Metternich?
4   How liberal were the Hungarian Diet's 'April Laws'?
5   Which three areas of the Austro-Hungarian Empire followed the Hungarians in making demands of the Emperor?
6   Why did the students not accept the Austrian Constitution of 1848?
7   What was 'Austroslavism' and how did it help to save the Empire?
8   What was the significance of the defeat of the Prague uprising?
9   Why was the court able to return to Vienna in August 1848 and suppress the revolt there?
10   Why did the Constituent Assembly reject Hungary's appeal for aid against the Croatian invasion?
11   Why was the Viennese uprising of October 1848 so short-lived?
12   Why did Schwarzenberg insist on Ferdinand's abdication?
13   Why was Schwarzenberg so determined to suppress the continuing Hungarian revolt in 1849?
14   Explain Schwarzenberg's refusal to accept the constitution produced by the Constituent Assembly in January 1849.
15   What do you understand by 'The revolutions of 1848 were followed, therefore, by the establishment of an even more powerful absolutism wielded by the Habsburg monarchy' (*page 162*)?

B *Essay questions*
1 How important was Russian intervention to the survival of the Habsburg Empire in 1848–9? (Cambridge, 1981)
2 Why did the Habsburg Empire survive the revolutions of 1848–9? (Oxford, 1983)
3 Explain (a) the success of the Belgians 1830–39, (b) the ultimate failure of the Hungarians, 1848–9, in their struggle for independence. (SUJB, 1983)
4 Illustrate and explain the early successes and later failures of the revolutionary movements within the Austrian Empire during the years 1848 and 1849. (SUJB, 1983)
5 Why were revolutionary activities so widespread in the Habsburg Empire in 1848, and why was the Empire again peaceful and intact at the end of 1849? (London, 1981)
6 Why was the Habsburg Empire able to survive the revolutions of 1848–9? (JMB, 1981)

C *Detailed investigation of the revolts*
The events you have studied are complex and sometimes difficult to follow on first reading. This section therefore suggests a variety of ways of investigating them further. It is not suggested that you attempt all the questions in this section, but rather that you select those that you might find most helpful.
1 In order to clarify the chronology of the revolts and to show the inter-relations between different aspects, construct and complete a date chart to cover the period from February 1848 to December 1851, and divide it into separate areas, as below:

Date	Austria	Hungary	Czechs	Italy	Elsewhere (including France)

2 Investigate the role of each of the following in the revolts: Kossuth, Emperor Ferdinand, Jellaçic, Palacky, Windischgrätz, Radetzky, Francis Joseph, Haynau.
3 Construct a chart to show the relative liberalism/authoritarianism of each of the constitutional documents listed below. This should take the form of a graph as shown below, and is similar to that constructed for France on page 69.
(a) Demands of Hungarians, March 1848
(b) Proclamation of Ferdinand, March 1848
(c) 'April Laws' of Hungarian Diet, April 1848
(d) Austrian Constitution, April 1848
(e) Constitution of Constituent Assembly, January 1849
(f) Imperial Constitution of March, 1849
(g) Francis Joseph's revocation of the constitution, December 1851

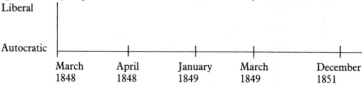

4   Two aspects of the Austro-Hungarian revolts seem to contradict 'general principles' and the experience of revolutions elsewhere. Comment on:

(a) the Imperial Court's fleeing from the capital

(b) the contrasting clemency of November 1848 and harshness of August 1849.

This should prompt you to discuss in more general terms how rulers should respond to revolutionary situations and how they should treat defeated insurgents.

D   *Documentary interpretation*

As C3 above has suggested, the Austro-Hungarian Revolt was a period in which constitutional arrangements were promulgated and withdrawn with almost alarming frequency. To increase your understanding of this aspect, study the three documentary extracts below and comment on *each* from the standpoint of:

(a) a Hungarian nationalist

(b) a foreign liberal observer

(c) a German conservative member of the Constituent Assembly

Source A. The Proclamation of Emperor Ferdinand, 15th March 1848 (from *Annual Register*, 1848, quoted in Kertesz, op. cit. page 122)

'By virtue of our declaration abolishing the censorship, liberty of the press is allowed in the form under which it exists in those countries which have hitherto enjoyed it. The National Guard, established on the basis of property and intelligence, already performs the most beneficial service.

The necessary steps have been taken for convoking, with the least possible loss of time, the Deputies from all our provincial states, and from the Central Congregations of the Lombardo-Venetian kingdom (the representation of the class of burghers being strengthened, and due regard being paid to the existing provincial constitutions) in order that they may deliberate on the constitution which we have resolved to grant our people.

We therefore confidently expect that excited tempers will become composed, that study will resume its wonted course, and that industry and peaceful intercourse will spring into new life.'

Source B. The demands of the Hungarian People, 15th March 1848 drafted by students and endorsed by a large meeting. (from *Deutsche Zeitung*, No. 84, 24 March 1848, Beilage, p. 4 translated by G.A. Kertesz and reproduced by Kertesz op. cit. pp. 125–6)

' 1. Freedom of the press; abolition of censorship.

2. A responsible ministry with its seat in the capital.

3. An annual parliament in Budapest.

4. Political and religious equality before the law.

5. A national guard.

6. Taxes to be paid by all.

7. Abolition of serfdom.

8. Jury system. Equality of representation.

9. A national bank.

10. The military to take an oath to the constitution; Hungarian soldiers not to be stationed abroad, foreign soldiers to be removed.

11. Political prisoner to be freed.
12. Union with Transylvania.'

Source C. The Austrian Constitution, 4 March 1849

'In October 1848 the Austrian government defeated a second revolution in Vienna; by the beginning of 1849, reactionary once more, it succeeded in establishing control over most of the empire (though not over Hungary). The time was considered to be ripe for counter-acting the nationalist, centrifugal tendencies of the revolutionary period and to strengthen the empire. A unitary centralized constitution was therefore imposed which, by applying to German and non-German peoples alike, finally precluded the participation of Austria in a united Germany, and thus effectively terminated the *grossdeutsch-kleindeutsch* controversy in the National Assembly at Frankfurt. Selected articles of the new constitution follow.

Source: *Annual Register*, 1849, pp. [319–24].

[The constitution began by a definition of the territory of the empire, which included the formerly independent areas, like Hungary.]

The Crown of the Empire, and of each single Crown land, is hereditary in the house of Habsburg-Lorraine, according to the Pragmatic Sanction and the Austrian family laws . . .

The Emperor is august, inviolable and irresponsible . . .

The Emperor proclaims the laws and publishes the decrees respecting the same. Each decree must have the counter-signature of a responsible Minister.

The Emperor appoints the Ministers and he dismisses them; he appoints to all offices in all branches of the Administration . . .

For all peoples of the Empire there is but one general Austrian citizenship . . .

Serfdom, no matter of what kind or denomination, is abolished . . .

All Austrian citizens are equal before the law and before the courts . . .

Public offices are open to all persons qualified for the same . . .

The General Austrian Imperial Diet shall consist of two houses— namely, of an Upper House and of a Lower House . . .

The Upper House is formed by deputies, to be chosen by the Crown lands from the members of their respective provincial diets . . .

The Lower House proceeds from general and direct elections. The franchise belongs to every Austrian citizen who is of age, who is in the full enjoyment of civil and political rights, and who either pays the annual amount of direct taxes fixed by the electoral law, or who, on account of his personal qualities, possesses the active franchise of a parish of an Austrian Crown Land.

The votes to the elections for either House are given by word of mouth and publicly . . .

The constitution of the kingdom of Hungary shall so far be maintained that the regulations which do not tally with this constitution lose their effect, and the equality of rights of all nationalities and of the languages of the country in all relations of public and civil life shall be guaranteed by institutions framed for that purpose . . .

In the kingdoms of Croatia and Sclavonia, . . . the peculiar institutions of these dominions shall be upheld within the union of those countries with the Empire, as determined by this charter of a constitution, but with the complete independence of the said countries from the kingdom of Hungary . . .

The constitution of the kingdom of Lombardy and Venetia, and the relations of that Crown land to the empire, shall be determined by a special statute.

All the other Crown lands are to have their own special constitutions.'

E *Causation and the 1848 Revolutions in Austria-Hungary*
It should be clear to you both from the chapter you have studied and from the examination questions above that the major aspect of these revolutions concerns causation—why the revolts happened, why they were successful at first and why they ultimately failed.

Why? —were there revolutions in Austria-Hungary in 1848?

were these revolutions at first successful?

were they then put down and Imperial authority restored?

These questions give you an opportunity to develop some of the ideas discussed in the section on causation essays on pages 88–91, and to practice that most vital skill—the rapid generation of a variety of ideas in answer to a question.

1 Write down as many answers to each of the 'why' questions as you can. Make these outline answers, and endeavour to think of them for yourself rather than looking back through the chapter. Students often seem to 'take fright' when they see a question, and dive into a textbook for security. This is often a false security, as it leads them to resort to narrative. It is much better to treat the question as a casual inquiry from a friend (if that is possible!), so that you have to answer it and explain your ideas in normal language, rather than 'textbookese'.

2 Taking each question in turn, develop your answer more fully, expanding on the reasons you have suggested and giving them some structure. It is an interesting exercise to attempt all three approaches to answering a causation question, i.e.
   (a) Rank your reasons by chronology: long-term, intermediate term and short-term reasons.
   (b) Place them in what you consider their order of importance.
   (c) Structure them by reference to different factors:
      Geographical
      Religious
      Individual
      Political
      Economic.

If you approach all three original questions in all three ways, you will not only cover the most important aspects of the revolts, but also develop your own approach to the writing of causation essays as a whole.

3 Liberalism in Germany

(a) The Constitutional Movement

The revolutionary events of 1848 had an effect also in Germany, but the situation there was not the same as in the lands of the Austrian Empire, where the subject races wanted to gain local liberties from the Habsburg government. By now German liberalism was beginning to revive after the quiet post-war years (*see page 117*), and its supporters possessed the common outlook of such people throughout Europe. They now joined these liberals in attacking the Metternich System (which was particularly exemplified in Germany by the Carlsbad Decrees) and the continuance of monarchical despotism and aristocratic privilege. And they shared with them a desire for constitutionalism and modern elected assemblies, freedom of the press and of association, trial by jury, equality before the law and national militias (*see page 379*). At the same time, national pride made many German liberals look beyond their own states and desire a greater measure of unification for the country.

The leaders of the German revolutions of 1848 were still the students and the professional and intellectual middle classes in the towns. As yet few of them were engaged in industry or finance. The Industrial Revolution had not yet got beyond its first stages in Central Europe. It was estimated that in 1848 there were 1200 steam engines of all kinds in Prussia (which is about as many as there were in England by 1800) and only 250 in Austria; and in 1846 London alone consumed more coal than was mined in the whole of Prussia. The German middle classes, therefore, were still mainly engaged in such occupations as medicine, law, education and administration, and most students were preparing for such academic or professional careers. They were more aware than other Germans of foreign ideas and events and resentful of the domination of the governments in their states by the princes and the conservative aristocracy.

The revival of liberalism in Germany coincided with the growth of discontent among both workers in the towns and peasants in the countryside. Such German factories as then existed were small, and the industrial workers, of whom there were only 600 000 in the whole of Germany in 1848, were relatively well-paid. There were still more handicraft workers, often making goods in their own homes, and they were being ruined by competition from cheap, mass-produced imports from Britain. There were disturbances as early as 1832 in Hesse-Cassel and the Palatinate, but the most serious was the revolt of the Silesian weavers in 1844 and 1845 brought about by the decline of the linen industry.

Equally serious was the condition of the many more numerous peasants. The post-war population of Germany had been rising rapidly and steadily since 1815 (*see Table 8, page 83*), but the proportion of town and country dwellers remained unchanged. In Prussia 73.5 per cent of the population was classed as rural in 1816 and 72 per cent in 1848. The result was increasing rural overpopulation, particularly in the south and west of the country. Peasant holdings were subdivided, but often became too small for efficient farming, and landless labourers became more numerous. In these circumstances peasants, who were still serfs, more and more resented having to pay their feudal dues and perform the services for the landowners.

On the eve of the revolutions of 1848, conditions deteriorated quite sharply in both town and country. In 1847 the first general economic crisis coincided with the last major famine in Europe. The potato harvests of 1845 and 1846 were ruined by blight, and the next year a sudden drought destroyed the grain harvest. The German peasants, whose circumstances had already been made so difficult, were particularly affected by this, and late in 1847 a cholera epidemic in Upper Silesia killed hundreds of people. During the early months of 1848, peasants in several parts of Central Europe refused to perform their services to the landlords and even attacked manor houses and castles, while others drifted to the towns where they added to the growing numbers of the unemployed. The disturbances of 18 March in Berlin, like those of 13 March in Vienna, were largely riots by the unemployed.

As elsewhere in Europe, however, there was little connection between the German political leaders and these signs of social discontent. The lower classes were doubtless influenced by the ideas of the revolutionary movements, but the middle-class liberals, though demanding more popular government and an extension of the franchise, refused, as did liberals elsewhere, to consider reforms which would bring about universal suffrage and economic improvement in the life of the people (*see page 380*). Their movement had constitutional and not social aims. They were prepared to use popular discontent to get political concessions from the princes, but they were determined not to make concessions to working-class leaders which they feared would deprive them of their own political power and even result in anarchy. Rather than do this, the liberals soon allied themselves with the princes, and they lost general support in Germany because their cause seemed to display no understanding of national needs.

(b) The Coming of the Revolutions (1846–48)

As liberalism regained its strength in Germany during the years before 1848, the ruler of nearly every state found himself facing opposition to his policy, and sometimes quite trivial, unpolitical incidents exasperated the discontent with their rule. The most remarkable and one of the earliest of these incidents occurred in Bavaria, where King Ludwig I ruled as an absolute monarch. In 1846 he became enamoured of a Scottish cabaret-dancer, who called herself by the Spanish name of Lola Montez (and who became even better-known for appearing in *Dolores, Our Lady of Pain* by Swinburne). Early in 1847 Ludwig asked his conservative, Ultramontane ministers to grant her Bavarian nationality, so that he could make her a countess. Shocked and indignant, they refused and resigned and were replaced by more tolerant ministers who agreed to the King's request. She was created Countess of Landsfeld and given a handsome annual allowance, but whenever she appeared in public, mud and stones were thrown at her. Early in February 1848 her tactless behaviour, which suggested that she thought she was the King's legal consort, cost her the support even of the students, who had previously been 'Lolamontaine'. Ludwig was very ready to close the University, which he disliked for its liberalism. This brought renewed rioting in Munich, and there were reports of general unrest throughout Bavaria. Eventually, the King had to reopen the University, summon the Bavarian Diet and banish the new Countess, who went on tour through the United States and Austrialia. The ridiculous episode badly damaged the prestige of the monarchy in Roman Catholic southern Germany and showed how vulnerable it might be to resistance and demonstrations.

Hardly had Ludwig's infatuation culminated in this result than news reached Germany first of Louis Philippe's abdication and then of Metternich's flight. Liberals were immediately stimulated to hope and activity. In state after state they began to assert themselves, demanding from their rulers the granting of a constitution and support for the summoning of a German parliament. The first state in which this took place was the Grand Duchy of Baden, early in March 1848. Here it was not really a revolution against the Grand Duke, who was himself liberally inclined, but rather a demonstration (which he looked upon with favour) against the Metternich System and the Carlsbad Decrees, which had so far prevented him from establishing in his state a responsible legislature and other liberal institutions. A mass meeting at Mannheim passed a resolution asking that he should now agree to these, and this was repeated in other towns. Within two days he granted the Duchy a constitution to the relief of moderate liberals, who feared the republican and social ideas of a group of radical reformers in the state.

The same pattern of events followed throughout Germany. Meetings and banquets, petitions and resolutions, persuaded princes to accept the demands of the liberals. Only in Bavaria did the ruler have to abdicate, and this was largely the result of continued popular dislike of his affaire. Everywhere else the princes remained on their thrones and granted constitutions or remodelled existing constitutions, often on the line of the Belgian constitution of 1831 (*see page 98*). The idea of popular sovereignty prevailed (though within the limits of a restricted franchise), and the lower houses of the newly-established legislatures, which were controlled by liberal deputies, claimed to possess the final authority in the management of the government of all these states.

(c) The Revolution in Prussia (1848–50)
The position of Prussia in Germany made the state of supreme importance in the events of 1848, and three circumstances led her to take a prominent part in the liberal and nationalist cause in the country. The

first was the disappearance of Metternich from the Austrian government, which subsequently became preoccupied with the revolts among its own peoples. This meant that Habsburg influence in Germany was temporarily suspended, and there was no power able to intervene in Germany in the face of events which threatened the balance of power in Central Europe.

The second circumstance was the transient liberalism of the eccentric Frederick William IV, who had become King of Prussia in 1840. Then his actions had aroused liberal hopes in his kingdom, but these had come to nothing (*see page 119*). His vacillating character was to be revealed yet more clearly during the events of 1848. In many ways he was like the Tsar Alexander I: he held a conservative view of his position and yet sentimentally wanted to be acknowledged as a liberal monarch. These contradictory qualities were to have an important effect during the revolution in Prussia and also, because of Prussia's importance, in the rest of Germany.

Thirdly, there was the economic depression and unemployment of this period. The situation was at its worst in the larger German towns, and Berlin, where a quarter of the population belonged to the working class, suffered particularly. The engineering works there dismissed some hundreds of its labour force, and landless peasants came from the countryside into the city in a hopeless search for relief. During the winter of 1846–47 serious disturbances—the so-called 'potato revolution' took place. Barricades were set up, grain transports attacked and market-stalls and foodshops looted; and the Crown Prince's palace was stormed. Eventually troops were called out to restore order. By the spring of 1848, the situation had not improved. Discontent remained as strong and prevalent as ever.

News of the rising in Vienna stirred this discontent into rioting, which on 18 March developed into street-fighting. Berlin's 'March Days' began. Troops pressed back the rioters, cleared the streets, blew up the barricades by cannon fire and began systematically to crush the revolt throughout the city. The rebels, however, resisted fiercely, throwing paving-stones and boiling water from the house-tops. The military commander wished Frederick William to go to his palace at Potsdam, 30 kilometres from Berlin, while the city was bombarded into submission, but his paternalistic feelings would not allow him to agree to this. Already many people had been arrested and about 300 (mostly from the lower classes) summarily shot by the angry soldiers. The King decided to capitulate. The next day he ordered the troops to withdraw from the streets, which they reluctantly did and were replaced by the patrols of a hastily-formed Civic Guard. A crowd thronged the palace courtyard in the centre of the city and forced him to stand bareheaded on the balcony while the corpses of some of those killed in the fighting were trundled past him on a furniture van. He afterwards said that this was the most terrible day of his life.

For the time being, however, he seemed to have joined the revolutionaries. On 21 March, surrounded by some of his generals and

171

newly-appointed liberal ministers, he rode in theatrical style through the streets of the city, beneath the new black, red and gold flag of the German nationalists. On the same day, he issued a royal proclamation addressed 'to my people and the German nation' in which he said that he would summon a Constituent Assembly to create a new representative united Diet for all his territory (*see Map 6, page 46*). He proposed also that this Prussian Diet should meet with other German diets to consider the establishment of a national German parliament. He ended the proclamation with his famous words, 'Henceforward Prussia will be merged in Germany,' which was a phrase that suited the ideas of the liberal nationalists throughout Germany. They were encouraged by the proclamation, and the King of Prussia's support for their cause enabled them to hasten the granting of constitutions by the rulers of the smaller states.

The proclamation also ended the March Days in Berlin. The Prussian revolution had, in fact, reached its climax and now began steadily to lose momentum. The victory it had gained in Berlin was really an illusion. The Prussian army was unbeaten and commanded by officers determined to have their revenge. Frederick William was beginning to regret his surrender to the liberals. A group of conservatives, led by Count Otto von Bismarck, urged him to put himself at the head of his troops and reassert his authority, but he could not bring himself to do this. Instead he sought the assistance of loyal politicians, officials and generals and soon gathered a powerful circle of supporters around him. His new liberal ministers did nothing to oppose this. They were alarmed by the way in which they had been put into power as the result of barricades, rioting and street-fighting. They had no wish to become the tools of a popular movement. They were ready, therefore, to uphold the Prussian crown and its advisers because they believed that their own authority depended upon such a policy. By the end of March, they had agreed that several infantry regiments should return to Berlin for the protection of the government.

The Constituent Assembly, elected by indirect universal suffrage, met in Berlin from May to December. It consisted of some 400 members, and its composition, which differed markedly from the recently-elected Constituent Assembly in France, showed how widespread was the popular discontent in Prussia. It contained very few noblemen and landowners, but there were many officials, lawyers and teachers and 68 peasants, mostly from East Prussia, where they were opposed to the Junkers, the group of Prussian landowners with estates east of the Elbe, who were politically conservative and closely connected with the crown and the army.

During its existence, the Assembly engaged in interminable debates about the new constitution for Prussia, while the situation in Berlin grew steadily more disorderly. Unemployment rose, and there were numerous demonstrations and processions. Radical leaders demanded that workers should be admitted into the Civic Guard. The government in alarm began to withdraw weapons from the city arsenal, which led to it being stormed by a mob in June. The middle-class liberals became hostile to the Assembly, which was estranging itself also from the monarchy. In October, after prohibiting the use of all noble titles and abolishing the judicial and financial privileges of the nobility, it deleted the phrase 'the the Grace of God' from the royal title. Encouraged by the re-establishment of authoritarian rule by Schwarzenberg in Austria and by Cavaignac in France, the King decided that the time had come to act. Early in November, he replaced his liberal ministers by a conservative government, which adjourned the Assembly and ordered it to meet in a fortnight's time at the town of Brandenburg, which was 60 kilometres away from Berlin. When it ignored this order and continued to sit in Berlin, 13 000 troops were moved into the city, which was placed under martial law, and the Civic Guard was abolished. There was no bloodshed or opposition from the more than 50 000 industrial workers in Berlin. Before the end of the year, the King finally dissolved the Assembly. He said, 'The Assembly wished to take from me my Divine Right. No power on earth is strong enough to do that. I shall hold it as I have inherited it from my ancestors.'

Frederick William now introduced by royal edict his own constitution, which came into effect in February 1850 and was to remain in force in Prussia until 1918. This provided for a Diet with an upper chamber, the Herrenhaus, comprising the princes, heads of the nobility, some life peers and a few representatives of provinces, large towns and the universities, and a lower chamber, the Landtag, of 433 members, chosen by open voting by electors. The electors were divided into three classes according to the taxation they paid, so that the workers and peasants, although they together comprised the vast majority of the electorate, only received a third of the seats, and the property-owners had many more. The Diet generally considered bills submitted to it by the King, who was empowered also to make laws himself and appoint his own ministers, and they were responsible to him alone and not to the Diet.

As a result of the Revolution, the government of Prussia was thus changed. It was changed by the will of the King and not the wish of the people, but the constitution was acceptable to many liberals, who did not want a repetition of the events of 1848. They had to accept the retention by the crown of its control over the government with the support of the nobility and the army. And Frederick William's triumph was important for the rest of Germany. Other rulers again took their example from him and withdrew the constitutional concessions they had made in their states.

(d) The Frankfurt Assembly (1848–49)
Meanwhile, the events early in 1848 had encouraged the German nationalists to invite all present or previous members of those diets which existed in the German states to meet on 31 March in a wide,

circular church, the Pauluskirche, in Frankfurt-on-Main as a preliminary assembly (*Vorparlament*) to discuss the setting up of a provisional executive and a central legislature for the whole country. Nearly 600 accepted the invitation and decided that elections should be held for a National Constituent Assembly by direct male suffrage throughout Germany and Austria. The Diet of the Confederation was obliged to sanction this, and the princes had to allow the elections to take place in their states on the basis of one member to every 50 000 voters, though most states limited the size of the electorate by imposing residential and other requirements. There was no great interest in the elections among the lower classes. In some states, as many as 30 per cent of them did not vote, and the membership of the resulting Frankfurt Assembly, which sat from May 1848 to June 1849, was very different from that of the Constituent Assembly in Berlin. It was drawn mainly from the professional middle classes. Of the 586 members, 106 were professors or schoolmasters, 95 lawyers, 157 magistrates and 124 government officials. There were six handicraft workers and only one peasant, who was a Pole from Silesia. Apart from a few who had been members of the Diet of the Confederation, their political experience was confined to the affairs of their states.

The chief division of opinion in the Assembly was between a radical group, consisting largely of lawyers and writers, who wished to overthrow the German princes and set up a democratic, centralized republic, and the moderate liberals, who were in the majority and wanted a federal constitution, which would preserve the existing states and provide for a limited monarchy where the powers of a legislative assembly and the rights of the people would be upheld in a written constitution accepted by the monarch. Before deciding about such a national constitution, however, the Assembly set about the establishment of some sort of a provisional government which would enable them to act with immediate authority. The moderate liberals wanted to choose a prince to head it, but they found it difficult to make a choice. Not until the end of June did the Assembly finally elect the Archduke John of Austria, the elderly brother of the Emperor Ferdinand, to the post of Imperial Vicar, the title given in the Holy Roman Empire to the Regent appointed after the death of an Emperor until a new Emperor was elected. The Archduke John was said to have liberal sympathies, but—as his title indicated—his appointment mainly expressed the belief of most of the members of the Assembly that German unity would best be achieved under the traditional leadership of the Habsburgs, who, since they were facing revolution in their own lands, might be expected to accept the authority of the Assembly.

The Archduke John did not take up his post until another month had passed. He then provided himself with a ministry, which included men of considerable talent, but had no real means of exercising its authority, though this was recognized by the Diet of the Confederation. The only money it had was a fund collected by the Diet in 1840 for federal defence, which had been banked with the Rothschilds. It could not create an armed force to defend the Assembly. The princes of most of the smaller states allowed their soldiers to swear an oath of allegiance to the Imperial Vicar, but the rulers of the larger states, including Austria, Prussia and Hanover, refused to comply with the request. It was becoming clear that, in fact, the power of the Assembly could only depend upon the attitude of the individual German states.

The Schleswig-Holstein question made this only too obvious. The Duchies of Schleswig and Holstein formed the southern part of the Jutland Peninsula, linking Denmark and Prussia (*see Map 6, page 46*). Since 1460 the King of Denmark had become Duke of both of them, though Holstein was almost entirely German and Schleswig partly so. In the 1840s the cause of the Duchies became a focal point for German national feeling. A South German liberal described them as 'a bulwark of the German empire' for which 'anyone whose heart burns for the German fatherland should be prepared to fight'; and nationalist demonstrations during these years invariably included anti-Danish speeches and the carrying of the red, white and blue flag of Schleswig-Holstein. In March 1848 the Duchies rose against Danish rule and asked for Prussian assistance. Frederick William, anxious to recover his prestige after the events in Berlin, intervened with an army, and the Frankfurt Assembly subsequently supported him. Both Britain and Russia, however, did not want Prussia to be in a position to control the entrance into the Baltic Sea. Their attitude and the strength of the Danish navy, which was capable of destroying Prussia's Baltic trade, induced him to withdraw amid bitter (but useless) protests from the Assembly.

Indeed, the episode seriously weakened the authority and prestige of the Assembly. It had failed as the champion of German nationalism. It could not pursue an independent foreign policy nor, in fact, act in any important way on its own. Its assertions were seen to be pretentious abroad. No foreign country recognized it except Hungary and the United States of America.

The rebuff suffered by the Assembly over Schleswig-Holstein came at a time when it was attracting popular discontent through its refusal to consider a social programme. In June, Karl Marx began to publish in Cologne his *New Rhenish Gazette*, which soon became influential, and petitions for reform were sent to the Assembly, particularly by Socialists; but the attitude of the liberals was expressed by one of its members—'We are dealing here only with civic equality, not with that crude, materialistic, communistic equality, which seeks to do away with all natural differences in intellectual and physical endowment and to neutralize their consequences in employment and in the acquisition of wealth.'

National resentment at the fate of Schleswig-Holstein combined with social discontent to bring about rioting in September throughout Frankfurt which developed into an attack on the Pauluskirche while the Assembly was in session. Hessian and Prussian soldiers, garrisoned at

Mainz, arrived just in time to prevent the mob breaking down the doors of the church and to rescue the members cowering in their pews. Bitter fighting followed in the streets, during which two conservative members were murdered by the insurgents, but the barricades were destroyed by artillery from Darmstadt, the red flags were torn down, and martial law was proclaimed in the town. The Assembly, saved by the soldiers of the existing German rulers, had failed to win popular support, and the liberals were alarmed by the revolutionary disorders. The September disturbances in Frankfurt had much the same consequences as the June Days in Paris.

The Assembly began to discuss a national constitution in October 1848, having already adopted a series of resolutions defining the fundamental rights of the German people, which included freedom of speech and publication, religious toleration, trial by jury, equality under the law and the abolition of all manorial rights and aristocratic privileges. On the constitution itself, the immediate problem to be considered was the extent of the territory to which it was to apply. Most members had assumed that this would include the German-speaking parts of the Austrian Empire, but these contained also large non-German speaking populations, and Palacky made it clear that the Czechs did not wish to be united with Germany (*see page 158*). Moreover, Schwarzenberg insisted that the whole of the Austrian Empire, including Hungary, Lombardy and Venetia, must be part of a new Germany. Some of the German princes welcomed this idea as it would provide a counterweight to Prussian influence, but the liberals believed that such a 'greater Germany' (*Grossdeutschland*) would be even more reactionary and repressive than the old Confederation. They had, therefore, to accept a 'little Germany' (*Kleindeutschland*) which excluded the Austrian Empire altogether and, therefore, left the predominant power to Prussia. Their majority in the Assembly secured the acceptance of this arrangement.

The Assembly also rejected the idea of a republic in favour of a federal empire, ruled by a hereditary emperor, but it was to have a liberal constitution which would give him only limited powers. There was to be a central legislature of two houses with a responsible executive, to which was to be entrusted the command of the armed forces, the conduct of foreign policy and all questions of peace and war. It was inevitable that the King of Prussia should be the Emperor of Germany, and on 28 March 1849 the Assembly elected Frederick William to this position, though without any great enthusiasm. About half the members voted for him, and the other half abstained. A deputation of members went to Berlin and offered him the imperial crown on 3 April.

Frederick William would have liked to have been Emperor of Germany, but not if it were offered to him by an elected, liberal assembly and restricted his authority. He rejected the offer, saying that he would not rule 'as a serf of the revolution,' nor 'pick up a crown of mud and wood from the gutter', which he would wear 'by the grace of bakers and butchers' and 'would be a dog-collar fastened round my neck by the sovereign German people.'

This marked the end of the Frankfurt Assembly. Frederick William's rejection of the proposed German constitution was followed by other German rulers, who also ordered the members from their states to leave Frankfurt. And as these rulers repealed the constitutions they had granted in 1848, there were disturbances in several states, which alarmed the moderate liberals. They too abandoned the Assembly, leaving only 130 radical members who aroused the hostility of the city authorities. They themselves moved to Stuttgart, the capital of the Kingdom of Württemberg, but were dispersed in June by the King's soldiers. In December the Archduke John renounced his title.

The Frankfurt Assembly failed because it possessed moral authority, which alone could not assert itself in Germany. The liberals hoped to get the support of the princes for the establishment of a united, constitutional Germany. For a time, most of these rulers judged it wise to make concessions to them, but when Austria and Prussia refused to accept the arrangements made at Frankfurt, the Assembly's chances of success disappeared. Moreover, radicalism and popular disturbances made the liberals increasingly dependent upon the princes and unwilling to persist with their cause. They could not conceive of political power being extended beyond the educated minority to which they belonged. The radicals had little success in appealing to the handicraft workers; Marx said that the revolutionaries had staff-officers and non-commissioned officers but no rank-and-file. And the peasants had no enthusiasm for the movement, especially as several states in 1848 and 1849 abolished feudal dues, manorial rights and other grievances felt by them. The professional middle classes, who had been the backbone of the Frankfurt Assembly, lost their political initiative forever. When industrialism began to develop in Germany, the new capitalist class looked to the established governing circles, which had retained their power in 1848, for the maintenance of the social order and effective administration which it desired in Germany.

(e) The Treaty of Olmütz (1850)

Frederick William of Prussia, after rejecting the imperial crown from the Frankfurt Assembly, did not wish to abandon the nationalist cause. He still wanted to rule Germany, but by agreement with the princes instead of under a liberal constitution. He proposed to them the idea of a federal Germany (still excluding the Austrian Empire) with a looser, more conservative constitution than that drawn up by the Assembly. It was to have a legislative assembly, elected on a limited suffrage, and its armed forces were to be under Prussian control. He succeeded in getting support for this from Saxony and Hanover with whom he signed an agreement known as the Three Kings' Alliance, and they were joined by several other German states. These sent representatives in March 1850 to an assembly which met at Erfurt in Prussian Saxony and formed themselves into the Erfurt Union.

By now, however, Schwarzenberg, after the suppression of Hungary, was ready to re-assert Austrian influence in Germany. He summoned the Diet of the Confederation to meet at Frankfurt in May, and ten other German states sent representatives. A trial of strength was now imminent between Austria and Prussia. The crisis came when the Elector of Hesse-Cassel withdrew the liberal constitution which he had previously granted to his state. The Diet of the state appealed to Prussia, while the Elector fled to Frankfurt and sought Austria's help. Both Prussia and Austria mobilized; but when Austrian troops entered Hesse, Prussia took no action. By the end of 1850, Prussia had to agree to the Treaty of Olmütz by which the Erfurt Union was dissolved, and the Confederation and its Diet were restored. The Diet set up a Reaction Committee to undo the work of the Frankfurt Assembly, and its Fundamental Rights were declared abolished in 1851.

The Treaty of Olmütz was described by many Prussians as the Humiliation of Olmütz, and it was, indeed, a triumph for Austria and a humiliation for Prussia. Frederick William had withdrawn because the Tsar Nicholas supported Schwarzenberg, and the Prussian army was not strong enough to take on by itself a possible alliance of Austria and Russia. If he had accepted the Habsburg challenge, his only chance of victory would have been to receive help from other German states and to submit to direction from the German nationalist movement. On the other hand, Austria's triumph was more apparent than real. She was not in a position to exploit her victory to the point of eliminating Prussia as her rival for supremacy in Germany. Her army was weak, and much of it was required to occupy Hungary and northern Italy. The Confederation was restored, therefore, to what had been its intention in 1815—an artificial means of prolonging Austria's influence in Germany. And she could only hope to preserve that position by diplomacy.

After 1850, indeed, a great change occurred in Austro-German relations. Between 1815 and 1848 Prussia had supported Austrian policy in Germany largely because Metternich had been able to persuade her rulers that they had mutual interests, particularly in their common fear of revolution. Now the mutual confidence between the two governments, which had hitherto upheld the Confederation, was destroyed and replaced by conflict. Prussia had given way militarily to Austria for the time being, but the *Zollverein* and the coming of industrialization in the 1850s gave her economic predominance in Germany, and the effect of Austrian policy was to make her want political supremacy as well. At this time the relations between the two governments, a German historian said, were like those between the two rival, bitterly-hostile ancient Roman generals, Caesar and Pompey.

Bibliography
In addition to the general histories of Germany mentioned on page 120, there are H. Friedjung (trans. A.J.P. Taylor & M.L. McElwee) *The Struggle for Supremacy in Germany* (Macmillan, 1935) and V. Valentin

(trans. E.T. Scheffauer), *1848: Chapters of German History* (Allen & Unwin, 1940).

Exercises
Additional exercises on aspects of this section will be found on page 194, where aspects of the 1848 revolutions as a whole are considered.

A *This section consists of questions that might be used for discussion (or written answers) as a way of expanding on the chapter and testing your understanding of it:*

1 What did German liberals want?
2 What were the reasons for discontent among townspeople and among German peasants?
3 Which classes led the German liberals, and what was the significance of the leadership coming from these classes?
4 What did the affair of Lola Montez illustrate?
5 What were the first effects of the liberal protests after March 1848?
6 Why did Prussia play such a prominent part in the German revolutions of 1848?
7 Comment on Frederick William's actions during the March Days in Berlin, especially in comparison with the Habsburgs at the same time.
8 Explain the significance of 'They (Frederick William's new liberal ministers) had no wish to become the tools of a popular movement' (*page 172*).
9 Compare the membership of the Prussian Constituent Assembly with the membership of those of France and Austria-Hungary.
10 Why did Frederick William dissolve the Constituent Assembly?
11 How liberal was the Prussian constitution of February 1850?
12 In what ways were the members of the Frankfurt Assembly divided?
13 What is the difference between a 'democratic, centralized republic' and a 'federal constitution with a limited monarchy' (*page 174*)?
14 Why was Archduke John selected as Imperial Vicar?
15 Why were the rulers of Austria, Prussia and Hanover reluctant to allow their soldiers to swear an oath of allegiance to the Imperial Vicar?
16 How did the Schleswig-Holstein question weaken the Frankfurt Assembly?
17 Why was the Frankfurt Assembly attacked in September 1848?
18 Were the decisions on 'little Germany' and a federal empire turning points in the life of the Frankfurt Assembly?
19 Why did Frederick William reject the Imperial title, and how important was his decision?
20 Why did his refusal lead to the collapse of the Frankfurt Assembly?
21 What was the Erfurt Union?
22 What was the significance of the Treaty of Olmütz?

B *Essay questions*
1 Why, both in France and the German Confederation, did the liberals of 1848 achieve only temporary success? (Oxford, 1981)
2 Examine the developments in (a) France and (b) Germany outside the Habsburg Empire in the years 1848–1851, and explain why most of the aims of the revolutionaries in the spring of 1848 were not permanently achieved. (SUJB, 1982)

3 Why did the revolutionaries in 1848 achieve so little in Germany and in the Habsburg Empire? (Welsh, 1982)

4 Why did Metternich's system collapse so easily in 1848? (Welsh, 1982)

5 Explain the failure of the Vorparliament and the Frankfurt Parliament to create a united Germany in the years 1848–49. (AEB, 1981)

6 In what ways did the revolutions of 1848 reveal the strengths and weaknesses of the movement for German unification? (AEB, 1982)

7 Why had German liberals and nationalists so little to show by the end of 1849 for their recent efforts to bring about change? (London, 1982)

8 Was it military men who chiefly determined the outcome of events in Germany and the Habsburg Empire in the years 1848–9? (London, 1983)

9 Explain the failure of the Frankfurt Parliament to unite Germany between 1848 and 1850. (JMB, 1984)

C **Essay writing 5—significance essays**

You have already been introduced to list and discussion essays (*see pages 88 and 137*). The third most common type of essay is the 'significance' type, in which you are required to assess the importance or significance of a particular event or person, either in general or in relation to an event or series of events. These essays are relatively easy to identify as they generally include one of the words 'important', 'significant' or 'extent' in the title, as these examples show:

(a) How important was Russian intervention to the survival of the Habsburg Empire in 1848–9?

(b) How great a force was the Roman Catholic Church in the politics of Europe in the nineteenth century?

(c) To what extent were Bismarck's problems inside Germany after 1871 of his own making?

(d) How far do the shortcomings of the monarchs explain the ultimate collapse of either (a) the Bourbon Restoration or (b) the July Monarchy?

An examination of these titles will probably suggest two things to you. Firstly, you might consider this essay type to be an extension of discussion essays. They appear to be asking you to say 'Yes, X was important . . .' and then 'No, X was not important. . . .' To an extent, this is the case, although in fact they require slightly more complex answers.

Secondly, significance questions very often approach problems of causation, but from a particular angle. They tend to identify one particular factor—such as the role of the monarchy in France in d) above—and ask you to examine it *in relation to* other factors. It is therefore important to ensure that you do not write only about the factor asked, but also assess its relevance as a whole. Thus your answers need to consist of three parts:

1) Yes, the factor concerned was important—in the following respects. . . .

2) No, the factor concerned was *not* important, in the following respects. . . . (this section is not always appropriate, and may well serve only as a link to 3)

3) Other factors were also important, such as . . . .

The essay planning sheet on page 397 will help you to achieve this structure.

It is often difficult to preserve balance (*see page 239*) in significance essays. On the one hand, you have to avoid concentrating wholly on the 'significant' factor, while, at the same time, avoiding writing too much about the 'other factors'. This is especially difficult when the question is almost designed to deceive, as in a) above: that is to say, Russian intervention was clearly relevant, but by no means vital, to the survival of the Habsburgs in 1848–9 and your answer would have to include a considerable amount on other factors.

Applying these ideas to the German revolutions of 1848–9, you will find a completed essay planning sheet below in answer to the question 'To what extent was Frederick William IV of Prussia responsible for both the initial success and ultimate failure of the German revolution of 1848–9?' Discuss, and above all criticize this plan (if you really want, write an essay on the basis of it!) Then re-work your knowledge and material to answer this question:

To what extent were the German revolutions of 1848–9 both caused and defeated by events outside Germany?

Essay planning sheet: significance question
Title: 'To what extent was Frederick William IV of Prussia responsible for both the initial success and the ultimate failure of the German revolutions of 1848–49?'
Introduction (if any): FW's background and personality, especially his vacillating nature (cf. Alexander I) and position as King of Prussia over extensive territory: therefore, likely to be influential?

A) Ways in which X was significant:

Arguments (1st sentences)	Evidence
1 FW certainly appears to have played an important part in the early successes of the Prussian revolution.	March 1848—withdrawal of troops, appointed liberal ministers, promised Constituent Assembly and talks on a national Assembly.
2 He also seems to have been responsible for the ultimate failure of the Prussian revolution.	Nov 1848—replaced liberal ministers, moved troops to Berlin; martial law and abolition of Civic Guard. Dissolved Constituent Assembly and 1850 Constitution—limited liberalism.
3 Equally, it can be argued that FW encouraged the Frankfurt Assembly.	Liberals were encouraged by events in Berlin, March 1848. FW did nothing to stop the Assembly (and could he have done?)

Arguments (1st sentences)	Evidence
4 Most clearly, FW was responsible for the failure of the Assembly.	1. 1848 refusal to allow soldiers to swear allegiance to Imperial Vicar. 2. Role in Schleswig-Holstein question. 3. 1849 refused title of Emperor—led to collapse of Assembly and revolutions.

B) Ways in which X was not significant:

1 However, his influence in the initial successes of the revolution was limited to Prussia.	Revolutions succeeded in other parts of Germany, e.g. Bavaria, Baden—without FW's influence.
2 In addition, it may be argued that the course of events was influenced by other factors.	(How important is one individual and how far can he alone influence events? Counter-factual argument —what if no FW?)

C) Other factors that were also significant:

1 The strength of liberal opinion in Prussia was such that some change was essential.	1. Background of anti-Metternich opinion 1815–48. 2. Events of Germany and Berlin 1848—extensive demonstrations etc. demanding change.
2 Events in other European countries also influenced the success of the German Revolution.	1. Revolts in France, Italy and, especially, A-H prevented intervention. 2. Concessions elsewhere also made change likely.
3 Similarly, it may be argued that the divisions of the liberals made ultimate failure likely.	Refusal of liberals to include radical demands, but also their insistance on a restricted Imperial authority —'falling between two stools'?
4 Other countries were also significant in bringing about the failure of the German liberals.	1. Again, experience of other countries and failures elsewhere. 2. Role of Britain and Russia in S-H question. 3. Influence of Austria at end?

Conclusion: FW a factor, but others of equal/greater significance?

4 The Risings in Italy

(a) The Outbreak of Revolt

At the beginning of 1848, the reforms of Pope Pius IX in the Papal States and of Charles Albert in Piedmont had encouraged the Italian nationalists (*see page 115*). The first risings in the peninsula, however, were in protest against local issues and were not inspired by a wider sense of Italian patriotism, which did not, in fact, exist among the great majority of the people. These risings also preceded the downfall of Louis Philippe in France, but were too peripheral to have the European effect that this revolution did.

The new year opened with the 'tobacco riots' in Milan, the capital of Lombardy. Austrian rule here and in her northern province of Venetia was not despotic, but the Italian professional classes continued to resent their exclusion from important government posts. At the same time, the urban lower classes blamed the foreign administrators for the economic situation. This had, as elsewhere in Europe, raised food prices and increased unemployment, but circumstances were particularly bad in Italy where the economy was backward and not doing well against British, French and Belgian competition. The Austrian administration drew a large part of its revenue from a highly profitable monopoly in the sale of tobacco. On 1 January the liberals in Milan organized a ban on smoking. Pickets were stationed outside tobacconists' shops, and would-be customers were greeted with shouts of 'Traitors! Traitors!'; people smoking in the streets were attacked, including Austrian troops who had a free issue of cigars. The lower classes then raised barricades, and rioting followed, which was finally suppressed by a cavalry charge and the loss of several lives. Impressive memorial services for the victims were held in both Milan and Rome.

The next rising, which was much more serious, broke out on 12 January in Palermo, the chief city and port of Italy. The resentment felt by Sicilians for many years towards the hated Bourbon rulers of the Neapolitan mainland had been increased by the severe hardships inflicted by the winter of 1848–49 upon the island where, as in the rest of the Italian countryside, the population was increasing and the standard of living falling. Moreover, the secret societies, including the Mafia, were well-organized and ready to take to violence. A crowd attacked and routed the garrison at Palermo. The wealthier classes then took over the leadership of the movement and forced King Ferdinand II to undo his recent union of the Neapolitan and Sicilian administrations, but when they went on to insist upon a fully constitutional government, he refused, and the fighting went on. By the end of January, a relieving force from Naples had been defeated, and royal authority no longer existed in most of the island. The insurgents re-established the old constitution of 1812 and declared Sicily's independence. Within a few days, Ferdinand hastily proclaimed a constitution, based on the French model of 1830, which included an assembly composed of two chambers, one to be elective and the other nominated by the King, with freedom of the press and individual liberty; and since there were now demonstrations in Naples as well, he granted it to the whole of his kingdom.

Though the Austrian government, now faced with difficulties of its own, could not support Italian despots as readily as in 1820 and 1830 (*see pages 51, 112*), political agitation would not have become as widespread and successful as it did in the peninsula during the spring of 1848 had it not been for the events which brought about the French revolution in Paris and the March revolution in Vienna. The news from abroad stimulated Italian liberals to make constitutional demands which the rulers had reluctantly to concede in their states. The Grand Duke of Tuscany, after demonstrations in the seaport of Leghorn, introduced representative government. Charles Albert promised the Piedmontese a two-chambered assembly and a civilian national guard and appointed Count Balbo as Prime Minister. Pius IX granted a constitution which provided for the government of the Papal States by a ministry containing a majority of laymen.

(b) War against Austria

The news of Metternich's downfall brought about fresh resistance to the Austrians in Milan, where after five days of street-fighting, the Habsburg Commander-in-Chief, Count Radetzky, had to withdraw his 20 000 troops, mostly Slavs and Hungarians, from the city. A separate rising in Venetia, led by Daniel Manin, a Jewish lawyer who was a descendant of the last Doge of Venice, compelled the Austrian garrison to abandon its barracks without a fight, and an independent Venetian Republic was established once more. Radetzky had to relinquish position after position in the two provinces, but he skilfully managed to retire with most of his exhausted forces into the Quadrilateral, a strategic district bounded by the Alps, the Mincio and the Adige Rivers and the four fortresses of Legnano, Peschiera, Verona and Mantua, which guarded Austria's easiest approach into Italy over the Brenner Pass (*see Map 12*). Map Godding 12 is of the Crimea.

The Milanese had appealed to Piedmont for help against Austria, and there was strong popular and ministerial pressure upon Charles Albert to act. He hesitated. The exasperated liberals nicknamed him 'King Wobble', but he found it difficult to decide upon war against Austria, whom Piedmont had long regarded as an ally. The ambassadors of Britain, Russia and Prussia urged him against action. He feared that, while getting little help from other states inside Italy and none from those outside, he was likely to incur papal opposition which would divide his subjects. He also had no wish to assist the cause of the revolutionary committee in control of Milan. And the Austrians might still recover and regain their provinces. After wasting precious days, during which he lost an excellent opportunity of overwhelming the retreating Austrian forces, he decided, however, that he must intervene if he wished to achieve his ambition of adding the Austrian provinces to his kingdom and securing the leadership of the nationalist cause in Italy. Moreover, Cavour and others warned him that further delay might bring about a republican-led revolution in his kingdom.

In a proclamation to the people of Lombardy and Venetia, he declared, 'We will support your just desires, trusting in the aid of that God who is visibly with us, of that God who has given Pius IX to Italy, of that God who, with such marvellous impulses, ensures Italy will make herself.' That final phrase—'Italy will make herself'—became the nationalist watchword of 1848. Charles Albert declared war on Austria on 24 March and adopted the tricolour of red, white and green, which by this time was accepted as the Italian flag. Four days later he moved with his army to join up with the Milanese rebels and advance swiftly across the Lombard Plain towards the Austrian army. At first it seemed as if the Italian war of liberation had really begun. Mazzini came hopefully to Milan and gave Charles Albert his grudging support. Nationalists appealed to other Italian states to support Piedmont, but even the new liberal governments had doubts about promoting Charles Albert's ambitions, and the assistance given was limited. Naples sent 14 000 troops (having promised 40 000). Tuscany, where a republic had now been established, sent 5000, and 9000 volunteers came from Rome. Charles Albert, on his part, was doubtful about accepting such recruits, many of whom were radicals or republicans, to his forces, and they met with hostility from the people in the countryside as they marched to battle. Many deserted before taking part in any fighting.

Nevertheless, the departure of the volunteers from Rome weakened the liberal opposition to Pius IX so much that he was able to be the first ruler to abandon the cause. As Pope, he could not support a crusade against such an important Roman Catholic power as Austria. At the end of April he issued a Papal Allocution calling upon the Italian people 'to abide in close attachment to their respective sovereigns.' Ferdinand of Naples followed his example. The continued unrest among the Neapolitan peasants, who wished to take over the large estates in southern Italy, alarmed the moderate liberals, and he was able to refuse to put his promised constitution into force and withdraw his troops from Lombardy to use them for the reconquest of Sicily.

So far the general weakness of the Habsburg government had made it possible for Charles Albert's forces to advance, and at the end of May he inflicted a defeat upon the Austrians at Goito. Then, however, he did not exploit his victory. Again he held back his troops. This time it was to pursue his private territorial ambitions. He wished to unite all northern Italy under his rule. He engaged in negotiating instead of fighting. By the beginning of July he had persuaded Lombardy and Venetia, together with the Duchies of Parma, Modena and Lucca to agree to union with Piedmont. But during that time Radetzky was able to obtain reinforcements for his army. On 23 July he took the offensive, routed the Piedmontese at the Battle of Custozza and compelled Charles

Albert to sign an armistice by which he withdrew his troops from Lombardy, Venetia and the Duchies.

During the months that followed, the liberal government failed to deal with the continuing economic crisis, and there was mounting discontent in the state. Cavour considered that a renewal of the war would be 'the only means of re-establishing order in the interior'; and in the spring of 1849, when the Austrian government was faced with renewed Hungarian resistance, Charles Albert desperately broke the armistice and again marched his forces into Lombardy, only to be defeated after a five-day campaign at the Battle of Novara. By the end of March, the 82-year-old Radetzky, who 35 years earlier had been Austrian Chief-of-Staff at the Battle of Leipzig, was completely victorious. In Vienna, Johann Strauss wrote the *Radetzky March* to commemorate his triumph. Charles Albert now abdicated in favour of his son, who became Victor Emmanuel II, and retired to a Portuguese monastery, where he died a few months later.

In Lombardy, the Austrians burned homes, imposed fines, confiscated property and executed some 900 people; and General Haynau ordered the public flogging of 15 men and two women in Milan. Radetzky was now able to reconquer both North and Central Italy. In April and May his troops entered Modena, Parma, Lucca and the Papal States, meeting with some resistance from the towns, but none in the countryside. The city of Rome still, however, opposed their advance.

(c) The Roman Republic

The Allocution issued by Pope Pius IX in April 1848 caused intense liberal disappointment throughout Italy, and during the spring and summer his persistent refusal to agree to war against Austria stiffened the opposition to him in Rome, where radical clubs were formed. Moreover, the economic situation had brought about large-scale unemployment. Papal finances could afford only a few public works to relieve this, and there was continuous unrest and outbreaks of violence during which the rioters shouted, 'Death to the priests!' However, in Rome too the liberal cause was weakened by disagreements between radicals and moderates. The reaction of the new ministry to the Allocution was to urge the separation of the government of the Papal States from the administration of the Church. They argued that constitutional government was impossible as long as the ruler of the state could claim to be bound by considerations that were superior to the wishes of the people. The Pope tried to silence this idea by appointing a more moderate ministry, but the radicals were now strengthened by the return of the volunteers from the war in Lombardy, and two months later the leading minister was murdered by a group of these men. Crowds attacked the Quirinal Palace, and a stray shot killed a bishop. The Pope had to replace the ministry by one that included prominent radical leaders, but soon afterwards, dressed as a simple priest, he left Rome in a nobleman's carriage and took refuge in a castle at Gaeta just across the frontier in the Kingdom of Naples. He told Ferdinand that he had gone into exile 'in order not to compromise our dignity or by our silence appear to approve of the excesses that have taken place and might take place in Rome.'

His departure left the radicals in power in Rome. In January 1849 they arranged for the election of a Constituent Assembly by universal suffrage. Like his predecessors, Pius IX believed that the Papal States were divinely his, as the successor of St. Peter, and he condemned the elections as 'abominable, monstrous, illegal, impious, absurd, sacriligious and outrageous to every law, human and divine.' These words led Mazzini to proclaim, 'An abyss has now opened between the papacy and modern society, and no human power can bridge it.' But the Pope's attitude encouraged large numbers of conservatives and moderates to abstain from voting. Out of an estimated 60 000 electors, only 23 000 voted, and some voted for Pius IX or even St. Peter.

The Constituent Assembly had consequently a large radical majority among its members. The next month it declared the Pope deposed and proclaimed the establishment of a Roman Republic. It proceeded also to abolish the tax upon flour, increase the number of public works including the building of railways, nationalize ecclesiastical property, divide estates among the peasants, abolish clerical control of the University of Rome, suppress the Inquisition and establish the freedom of the press.

Radical leaders now came to Rome from all over the peninsula, resolved to support the Roman Republic as the great hope of the united Italy they wanted. Among them was Mazzini. After the fall of Milan, he had gone to Florence and hitherto had received little support for his ideas. He was deeply moved by the news of the events in Rome and the challenge they presented to the Papacy. When he heard of the creation of the Roman Republic, he went to the city, where he hoped to realize his idea of the Third Rome (*see page 114*). He persuaded the Assembly to vote in favour of sending troops to assist the Piedmontese in their renewed war against Austria, but the next day they heard of the disaster at Novara.

The Assembly immediately appointed a Triumvirate with full powers to preserve the Republic. Mazzini was one of the three Triumvirs and from a small room in the Quirinal Palace virtually ruled the Republic. He continued the social reforms and the constitutional changes designed to give the Papal States a liberal, secular form of government, but he tried through moderation to preserve unity among the people. Only some of the land of the religious house was confiscated, and attempts to interfere with the religious work of the clergy were prohibited. He was faced, however, with insurmountable problems. Support for the Republic was practically limited to Rome, Bologna and the larger towns. Its activities were restricted by a chronic shortage of money. A forced loan imposed upon the upper classes brought in only a small yield, and the printing of large amounts of paper money increased the already desperate level of inflation. Some arms and munitions were bought from abroad, but its army was ill-prepared to meet an enemy.

The defence of the Republic was entrusted to Giuseppe Garibaldi, another exiled nationalist recalled to Italy by the events of 1848. A rough and uneducated character and the son of a Piedmontese fisherman, he became a merchant seaman and in 1833, at the age of 26, joined Young Italy (*see page 114*). The next year, when Mazzini was planning to invade Savoy, he took part in an attempt to seize Genoa for which he was condemned to death, but he fled to South America, where he fought for Uruguay in her war of independence and became adept at guerrilla warfare. There were many Italians in South America, and he organized from among them an Italian Legion of volunteers. For their uniform he bought cheaply a consignment of red shirts, which a Manchester firm had hoped to sell to the cattle-slaughterers in the Buenos Aires stockyards in the mistaken belief that the animals' blood would not show on material of this colour.

In 1848 he sailed to Italy with 169 volunteers to serve in the Piedmontese army, ready to abandon his Mazzinian republicanism if Charles Albert would defeat the Austrians. 'I was a republican,' he told a meeting of Young Italy, 'but when I discovered that Charles Albert had made himself the champion of Italy, I swore to obey him and faithfully to follow his banner.' Charles Albert was no more keen to receive him than he was to have other radical volunteers, and the Tuscan government did not want him either, but as the position of the Roman Republic became more dangerous, the Triumvirate accepted his offer of help. Garibaldi and Mazzini collaborated closely, though Garibaldi now regarded Mazzini as an impractical idealist, and Mazzini, anxious to prove that the Roman Republic respected law and order and private property, would not at first allow Garibaldi to bring his men into the city itself.

Meanwhile, Pius IX had appealed to the Roman Catholic powers to restore him to Rome and free his territory from 'the faction of wretches that exercise there the most atrocious despotism and every sort of crime.' In April 1849 the French troops sent by Louis Napoleon landed on the coast and advanced upon Rome. In the countryside they were welcomed by the people, who preferred them to the Spaniards who had occupied the mouth of the Tiber, the Austrians who were advancing from Tuscany, and the Neapolitans who had entered the Papal States from the south; but Mazzini and Garibaldi were determined to defend the city. Garibaldi had now gathered 5000 ill-trained and poorly-armed soldiers, but he defeated an attack by twice as many French troops. But by June, when the French had increased their numbers to 30 000, they broke through the city's defences, and the Triumvirate surrendered.

Before the city fell, Mazzini escaped and made his way to London, where for the next ten years he planned further unsuccessful risings in several Italian towns. Garibaldi assembled the defenders of Rome in the great square before St. Peter's and called for volunteers to escape with him from the fortifications and continue the fight against Italy's enemies elsewhere, though he could offer them nothing but 'hunger, thirst, forced marches, battles and death'. Nevertheless, 3000 men responded to his call. He led them through the encircling French army and eluded the pursuing Austrian forces to reach the Adriatic and safety. Many of his followers had died on the way, and so had his South American wife. He himself, after being imprisoned in Piedmont, eventually reached New York. He had already made himself both an outstanding soldier and a patriotic legend, and his greatest achievements were yet to come.

(d) The Failure of the Risings

When the French occupied Rome on 3 July 1849, they dissolved the Assembly and sent the keys of the city to Pius IX, who appointed three cardinals to rule until he returned in April of the next year. His return was welcomed by many Romans, who had long found the ceremonies and pilgrimages of the Church profitable to themselves, while the old beliefs and festivals appealed to the conservative peasants more than the ideas of liberalism and nationalism. The Pope himself had now abandoned all his readiness to be identified with liberalism; he imprisoned hundreds of his subjects and drove thousands more into exile; and he maintained an elaborate system of policing and censorship. His authority over his territory was maintained by a French garrison which was established in Rome and was to be stationed there in the Castle of St. Angelo for over 20 years.

The revolutions were now extinguished throughout the peninsula. Ferdinand II had reasserted his absolutism in Naples and reconquered Sicily with Swiss mercenaries by May 1849 after a series of bombardments which earned him henceforward the name of 'King Bomba'. Austrian troops suppressed the republic in Tuscany and restored the Grand Duke to his throne at the end of July. The Venetian Republic was the last to fall. After the Battle of Novara, the Austrians blockaded the city. Epidemics of cholera and typhus broke out, and the Austrians bombarded the city, but also, for the first time in history, dropped bombs from balloons. Thousands of its inhabitants died, and finally food became so scarce that on 24 August it had to surrender after a siege of nearly four months. Manin was allowed to leave and went to live in exile in Paris.

The failure of the Italian risings of 1848–49 was partly due to the limitations and divisions displayed by the insurgents themselves. Even the radicals among them, though they rose to power as the result of popular discontent, had no real social policy and possessed neither understanding of the common people nor sympathy with their aspirations. In particular, they ignored the peasants. This was to be seen in both Milan and Venice during the spring of 1848, after the apparent defeat of the Austrians. When peasants from the Lombardy countryside tried to enter Milan to join the newly-established civic guard, the provisional government refused to allow them through the city gates and ordered them to return to their villages, and Garibaldi saw with dismay how they welcomed the return of the Austrians to the province in 1849. Similarly, Manin ignored the provincial people of Venetia and concerned himself with establishing such political reforms as open justice and religious toleration in the city of Venice itself. As Denis Mack Smith has written, 'The *Risorgimento* was a civil war between the old and new ruling classes, in which the peasants were neutral except insofar as their own perennial social war became accidentally involved.' The result was that the Italian risings were mostly centred upon individual cities, which could be subdued one by one. And their prospects of success were further undermined by the divisions between moderates and radicals and the local rivalries and suspicions which soon appeared and were clearly seen, for instance, in the reluctant support given to Charles Albert from other Italian states and his attitude towards it. Even the prospect of the suppression of the liberal regimes by the Austrians could not overcome this disunity.

It is unlikely, however, that the defeat of the nationalist movement in Italy was due entirely or even mainly to political disarray among groups of liberals and failure to seek co-operation by the urban insurgents from the peasants of the surrounding rural areas. Above these internal factors were two external reasons which would probably have led to the failure of the revolutions whatever their own weaknesses. The first was the effect of Pius IX's refusal to give his support to the liberation movement. No pope could become involved in hostilities against the Habsburgs. Once, therefore, Piedmont declared war on Austria, the possibility of any success for Gioberti's idea of a federated Italy under the Papacy disappeared immediately. And it became unlikely that there could be a solution to the Italian question which would gain the support of the Roman Catholic powers of Europe. Rather they were now bound to uphold his temporal power and independence. The spiritual aspect of the Pope's position was seen, therefore, to be now a hindrance instead of an advantage to the cause of Italian unity. And the second was that events proved both Mazzini and Charles Albert to be wrong in asserting that Italy could free itself without foreign aid. Once Radetzky had established himself in the Quadrilateral, there was no force in the peninsula capable of dislodging him and preventing him gaining sufficient strength to effect Austria's suppression of the risings. Cavour was shown to be right.

(e) Piedmont and Cavour

'The Pope,' wrote Mazzini in 1849, 'clutches the soul of the Italian nation; Austria the body whenever it shows signs of life; and on every member of that body is enthroned an absolute prince, viceroy in turn under one or other of those powers.' The defeat of the *Risorgimento* did, indeed, seem to be complete by then. There was, however, one place where the risings had gained a measure of victory. This was in the

Kingdom of Piedmont, which symbolized this by continuing to fly the Italian tricolour flag.

Victor Emmanuel II, after succeeding his father, resisted Austrian pressure to withdraw the constitution which Charles Albert had granted to the state. This was not because he was a convinced liberal. He would have preferred to have ruled autocratically, but he thought that any attempt to do so would bring about revolution. He therefore accepted a liberal form of government through expediency rather than principle, but this was a permanent gain for the revolution. It provided for a Legislature with two houses—a Senate nominated by the King and an elected Chamber of Deputies. This shared the making of laws with the King, but the ministers were responsible to it. Roman Catholicism was the official religion of the state, but there was toleration and freedom of the press.

Radetzky granted Piedmont moderate peace terms and annexed none of her territory because he wished to guard against French intervention and support the King against his radicals. In return Victor Emmanuel agreed to deprive the radicals of their control of the Chamber of Deputies, and this was a promise which accorded with his own inclinations. He ignored their majority in the Chamber by appointing a conservative general as Prime Minister, ordered the bombardment of radical Genoa into submission and ratified the Treaty with Austria though the Legislature wanted to renew the war. He warned the voters to endorse his policy because he was resolved 'to save the nation from the tyranny of parties,' but he had twice to dissolve the Legislature and hold elections before getting a moderate liberal majority in the Chamber by the autumn of 1849. He succeeded in gaining popular support for the monarchy as much as was posible after the loss of prestige it had suffered at Custozza and Novara. Though he sometimes governed and raised taxes by royal decree, the constitution remained in existence and, as a practical example of the aims of the *Risorgimento*, was to make it possible for Piedmont later to take the leadership in achieving Italian unity.

While not liking the idea of sharing power with the liberals, Victor Emmanuel was able to make use of their anti-clericalism to strengthen the authority of the monarchy at the expense of the Roman Catholic Church. This was the most extensive legislative accomplishment of the early years of his reign. It brought about the abolition of the favoured position possessed by the Church in Piedmont as the result of a Concordat made with the Papacy as recently as 1841. The liberals wanted this to be done because they considered that the extensive privileges enjoyed by the Church were incompatible with the principle of the equality of all citizens before the law which was contained in the constitution. In 1850, therefore, the Legislature passed a series of laws which abolished the ecclesiastical courts, limited the number of recognized holy days, deprived churches of the right of sanctuary for criminals, required the government's assent for religious institutions to inherit property and instituted civil marriage. Pius IX protested against these laws, and the Archbishop of Turin forbade his clergy to comply with them and tried to compel the government to withdraw by denying absolution and religious burial to the families of those responsible; but the events of 1848–49 had shown that the Papacy was not now in a position to assert itself outside the Papal States. Piedmont was the first Italian state to establish its relations with the Papacy without negotiating a concordat.

These ecclesiastical laws were vigorously supported by Cavour, who had been a member of the Legislature ever since it had been set up under the constitution of 1848. At first he was temporarily unpopular through his opposition to the wish of the Legislature that Piedmont should renew the war on her own against Austria in 1849, but he quickly made himself known as a clever debater and clear thinker. Victor Emmanuel made him Minister of Commerce and Agriculture in 1850, Minister of the Navy in 1851 and Prime Minister in 1852, a position that, by retaining the leadership of a coalition of moderate liberal parties, he was able to hold until his death in 1861.

Cavour came to power with two deeply-held political aims. First, he wanted to continue the development of Piedmont into a strong modern state. Constitutionally this included the reform of the civil code and local administration and the extension of the ecclesiastical laws to bring about the abolition of all religious orders except those engaged in preaching, teaching or caring for the sick. Economically it involved the promotion of industrialization and communications. He encouraged trade by making commercial treaties with Britain, France, Belgium, Holland and the *Zollverein*, and he supported commercial enterprise with government grants, particularly for the construction of railways which he regarded as vitally important for the progress of the state (*see page 117*). By 1860 Piedmont had 818 kilometres of railway line compared with 324 in Lombardy and 280 in the whole of the rest of the peninsula. Piedmont's economic growth under Cavour was, nevertheless, not rapid, and indeed she remained largely an agricultural state with only the very small beginnings of an iron and steel industry in Genoa and Turin. She had, however, assumed the lead in Italy and overtaken Lombardy, the previously most advanced part of the peninsula.

This policy of modernization was essentially a preliminary to the achievement of Cavour's second aim, which was the extension of Piedmont's territory and influence in Italy. He did not, at this time, think of Piedmont as being able to bring about complete Italian unity. He doubted whether the Papal States and the Kingdom of Naples could be brought into a single Italian state. What he believed was possible was the replacement of Austrian predominance in the peninsula by truly independent states with an enlarged, progressive Piedmont as the strongest and most influential among them.

To make Piedmont more powerful, he increased the size and efficiency of the Piedmontese army and navy, but he did not think that his state or any combination of Italian states would be able to wage an effective war against Austria. He opposed and despised the 'shameful, hateful prejudices' of the Mazzinians, who continued to believe that the Italian people could still hope to liberate themselves in the same way that had been attempted in the past and failed so completely. When Mazzini planned a rising in Milan in 1853, Cavour ordered the imprisonment of his followers in Piedmont and may even have warned the Austrian government of the plot in advance. He thought that it was inevitable that Austria would not be dislodged from Italy without war, but he was sure that could only be done with military help from some great power, and he was always certain that the most obvious ally likely to do this was France with her ancient hostility towards the Habsburgs and her newly-established ruler, who was sympathetic towards Italian nationalism and ready to undo the Vienna Settlement.

Bibliography
In addition to the books already mentioned (*see page 120*), events in Italy during this period are treated in detail in G.F.H. Berkeley, *Italy in the Making, June 1846 to January 1848* (CUP, 1936) and *Italy in the Making, January 1848 to November 1848* (CUP, 1940).

Exercises
Additional exercises on aspects of this section will be found on page 194, where aspects of the 1848 revolutions as a whole are examined, and on page 274, where the movement for Italian Unification as a whole is examined.

A *This section consists of questions that might be used for discussion (or written answers) as a way of expanding on the chapter and testing your understanding of it.*

1 What was the European significance of the revolts in Milan and Palermo?
2 What effects did the European revolutions of 1848 have on the Italian states?
3 Who was 'King Wobble', and why was he called this?
4 Why was Charles Albert given only limited support by other Italian states against Austria?
5 Account for the failure of Charles Albert's expedition against Radetzky, and explain what effects it had on other Italian states.
6 Why did Charles Albert abdicate?
7 Why did Pope Pius IX abdicate?
8 Why was it possible for radicals to come to power in Rome but not elsewhere in Europe?
9 Why was the Roman Republic 'the great hope of the united Italy' that radicals wanted?
10 Why was Garibaldi prepared to abandon Mazzini in favour of Charles Albert?
11 Why didn't other European powers object to the French attack on Rome?
12 Why was the return of Pius IX welcomed?
13 Explain why the peasants and their interests were ignored by the Italian revolutionaries of 1848–9.

14 Why did Mack Smith refer to the Italian risings as a 'civil war between the old and the new ruling classes'?
15 What was the one permanent gain from the revolutions?
16 How did Victor Emmanuel II alter the position of the Church in Piedmont?
17 What steps did Cavour take to develop Piedmont?
18 What territorial ambitions did Cavour have for Piedmont?

B *Essay questions (see also page 274)*
1 What were the lessons of 1848–49 for those interested in Italian liberation and unification? How well were the lessons learned? (Cambridge, 1982)
2 'My life has been dedicated to the cause of Italy.' (Charles Albert). Does a study of his reign support this claim? (Welsh, 1981)
3 'The largest obstacle to Italian unity.' Is this a fitting description of Piedmont during the earlier Risorgimento 1815–49? (Welsh, 1983)

C *Debates*
Either by discussion or prepared answers, defend or attack each of the following:
(*i*)   Charles Albert's delay in sending troops against the Austrians.
(*ii*) The radical measures of the Roman Republic.
(*iii*) Louis Napoleon's sending of troops to restore the Pope (*see also page 147*).
(*iv*) The repressive policies of Pius IX in 1849.
(*v*)   The policies of Victor Emmanuel in Piedmont.

D *The revolutions of 1848–49: an overview*
Having examined the various risings in four countries of Europe, this exercise asks you briefly to take an overview of the events you have studied. It is followed by a number of past questions that refer to at least two of the revolutions.

There are perhaps five questions that arise in comparing and contrasting the experience of the different countries in 1848–49, viz.:
(*i*)   Why did the revolutions start at that time and in those places?
(*ii*) In what way or ways did the revolutions succeed?
(*iii*) In what way or ways did they fail?
(*iv*) Why were the revolutions, for the most part, successful in their early stages?
(*v*)   Why did the revolutions, again for the most part, ultimately fail?

On the chart below, a number of answers to each of these questions have been suggested. You should (a) add to these suggested explanations further answers of your own and (b) see how applicable each answer is to each country that you have studied. This could be done simply by ticking or crossing in appropriate places, or, more fully, by explaining how each factor operated in each country. (If you choose to draw out and complete the chart in detail, you will have to enlarge it.)

	France	Austria-Hungary	Germany	Italy
1) *Reasons for outbreak:* a) economic conditions b) inept monarchs c) influence of events elsewhere d) strength of liberal influence e) f)				
2) *Revolutions successful in:* a) overthrowing monarch b) winning liberal constitution c) improving socio-economic conditions d) winning political power for middle-class e) f)				
3) *Revolutions failed in:* a) loss of liberal constitution b) restoration of autocracy c) punishment of leaders d) removal of any socio-economic reforms e) f)				
4) *Reasons for early success:* a) apparent strength of liberalism b) monarchical fear of radicalism c) monarchical sympathy d) e)				
5) *Reasons for later failure:* a) monarchical resolution b) divisions among liberals c) foreign aid against rebels d) failure to use peasants e) failure of revolutionaries to govern effectively when in power f) g)				

Past questions

1 To what extent were the European revolutions of 1848–9 the result of the grievances of the urban and rural lower classes? (Cambridge, 1983)

2 Did weaknesses in the economy or incompetent government do more to explain the revolutions of 1848? (You may, if you wish, confine your answer to any two countries.) (Oxford, 1982)

3 What part did ideology play in the revolutionary movement of 1848–9? (Welsh, 1981)

4 Discuss the comment that the revolutions of 1848–9 in central and eastern Europe revealed the divergence between liberalism and nationalism. (Welsh, 1983)

5 'Apart from their timing, the 1848 Revolutions had very little in common.' Discuss. (Oxford and Cambridge, 1981)

6 'Economic considerations must predominate in any explanation of the revolutions of 1848.' Discuss. (Oxford and Cambridge, 1983)

IV The Dissolution of the Settlement 1852-71

1 Russia and the Crimean War

(a) The Background to War

Contemporary British figures were not enthusiastic about the Crimean War. John Bright, the Liberal politician, when asked by his son the meaning of 'Crimea', replied with an anagram, 'A Crime'. Queen Victoria declared at the outset of hostilities, 'My heart is not in this unsatisfactory war,' though she told King Leopold of Belgium that it was 'incredibly popular' with her subjects. Benjamin Disraeli asserted that it was 'a just but unnecessary war', but another Conservative, the future Lord Salisbury, who had just entered Parliament, thought that 'England put her money on the wrong horse.' Indeed, this war that broke the European peace, which had lasted for nearly 40 years from 1815, came about amid deep uncertainties and disagreements and largely through accidental circumstances. Both sides drifted into war. The events leading up to the beginning of hostilities were confused, the diplomacy was uncertain, and none of the participating governments wished to fight.

The revolutions of 1848, though all suppressed, seriously affected the European diplomatic situation. Many former rulers were replaced by new ones, and the relative strength and influence of the powers was changed. This was particularly serious from the viewpoint of British policy. Metternich's downfall ended the 33 years of the Metternich System and particularly the agreement between Austria and the German states, which had been unpopular in Britain because of its despotic basis. Nevertheless, it had preserved Central Europe from both French and Russian domination and had secured a balance of power on the Continent which had given her a sense of external security and freed her from the need to enter into European commitments. The replacement of Louis Philippe by Louis Napoleon seemed to make France stronger and potentially more aggressive. Most significantly, however, the revolutions of 1848 weakened both Austria and Prussia and considerably increased Russian power and influence. Russia herself had not been troubled by any revolt in Poland during that time. She had been able to prevent foreign help being given to any of the insurgents and to make possible the suppression of the revolutions in Germany, Italy and Hungary; the Hungarian rebels, indeed, were only defeated with Russian military aid. By 1850, therefore, Austria and Prussia seemed equally likely to be condemned to subservience to Russia, who would consequently be able to assert a powerful control over Central Europe during the coming years.

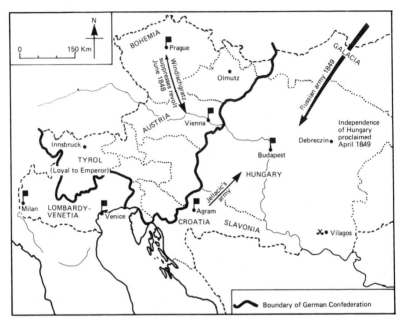

Map 9 Revolutions in the Austrian Empire, 1848–9

Russia's behaviour during the revolutions of 1848 affected British public opinion profoundly. For some years Britain had suspected Russian designs on Constantinople and the route to India; it was believed that they aimed at destroying British influence in the Near East and even invading India (*see Map 10*). At the same time, the Russian government's acts of oppression, particularly in Poland, had become increasingly disliked by liberal-minded people in Britain and stories of Russian brutality in Hungary in 1849 intensified this. Russia was now suspected of tyrannical and aggressive designs in Europe as well. France had long been the most feared country. British naval bases continued to be maintained in the Channel for a war against her. Indeed, the rise of Louis Napoleon to power revived this feeling, and in January 1852 Prince Albert told Prince William of Prussia that people were 'occupied and bothered by the idea of a possible French invasion.' Nevertheless, Russophobia grew in the 1830s and 1840s, encouraged by radical politicians and foreign refugees. The new mistrust of Russia after 1848 made it take on a hysterical tone and became ever more bellicose as events took their course.

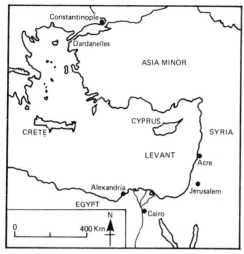

Map 10 The Near East

Unfortunately these circumstances coincided with Palmerston's exclusion from the Foreign Office. Palmerston had not shared the dislike of most British people for Louis Napoleon. He thought that the new ruler of France was friendly towards Britain and in December 1851 expressed his 'entire approbation' of the establishment of the Second Empire in France—a statement made without consulting the Queen or the cabinet. Victoria was indignant and insisted upon his immediate dismissal, which had serious consequences during the following years. His wide knowledge of the European situation and his vigorous, definite ideas about foreign policy might well have averted the uncertainties and misunderstanding which developed during the next three years; but from 1852 Lord John Russell was Foreign Secretary under Lord Aberdeen as Prime Minister, while Palmerston was given the post of Home Secretary.

Russell's outlook on foreign policy was that of a radical Whig. He hated Russian imperialism as much as he hated papal supremacy. He believed that the Tsar Nicholas would only be checked by firmness and by a determination not to make any concession to him. Lord Aberdeen himself, however, took a different view. Believing as an old-fashioned Tory that France was still the greatest threat to Britain, he did not share the radical hostility towards Russia and did not consider that her foreign policy in Europe was dangerous. He was as ready as Palmerston had been between 1832 and 1842 to negotiate with her and was alarmed by the mounting warlike anti-Russian feeling in the country. 'No doubt,' he wrote to the Queen, 'it may be very agreeable to humiliate

199

the Emperor of Russia; but Lord Aberdeen thinks it is paying a little too dear for this pleasure, to check the progress and prosperity of this happy country and to cover Europe with confusion, misery and blood.' But Victoria thought, 'He hopes for more from the Emperor of Russia than he is justified in hoping.'

Unfortunately, Aberdeen's government was a coalition of politicians with varying ideas. Contemporaries called it 'a tessalated pavement' and 'a clique of doctrinaires existing by court favour.' The members of the cabinet were likely to be in disagreement over almost any aspect of foreign policy, but they were particularly divided by the Eastern Question, 'this sad Oriental question' as the Queen called it, which again endangered European peace as it had done in the past (*see page 28*). In addition to the opposing views of Aberdeen and Russell, Palmerston wanted Britain and France to act together to prevent Russia extending her power in the Turkish Empire; but W.E. Gladstone, the Chancellor of the Exchequer, would not agree to this because he did not wish Britain to support the Sultan and so perpetuate the rule of a Muslim despot over his Christian subjects. The British government was thus divided and did not follow a consistent policy. Conciliation might have averted war and so might firmness, but the government failed to persist in one or the other. Instead, it veered between them in a way which neither placated nor deterred the Russian government. In the words of A.J.P. Taylor, they brought about war 'by failing to shout anything'.

(b) The Occasion for War

Though the European situation produced the mistrust between Britain and Russia, it was to be expected that the Eastern Question should provide the occasion for war. Tsar Nicholas naturally wished to take advantage of Austrian and Prussian weakness to increase Russian power in the Balkans. The failure of the European revolutions had increased his self-confidence, and he did not expect the British government to oppose any action he took. During the Egyptian crisis of 1839, he had set out to secure co-operation with Britain (*see page 130*). He had, in fact, tried then to preserve this and the French separation from Britain (which he equally desired) by proposing to Palmerston a secret alliance 'as a security against any efforts that France might make to awaken revolutionary feelings in Europe.' Palmerston in his refusal told him, 'Changes which foreign nations may choose to make in their internal consitution and form of government . . . are considered in England to be matters of domestic concern, which every nation ought to be allowed to settle as it likes.' He emphasized, however, Britain's intention of continuing 'to watch attentively and to guard with care the maintenance of the balance of power' and stated that 'an attempt of one nation to appropriate to itself territory which belongs to another nation' would constitute 'a derangement of the existing balance'. He also explained that under the British constitution a government could not bind future governments by making 'engagements with reference to cases which have not actually risen.'

But Nicholas either misunderstood or did not heed this caution. By 1842 the signing of the Convention of the States further convinced him that Britain was willing to co-operate with him in dividing the Turkish Empire peaceably (*see page 131*). He made a state visit to England in 1844 and satisfied himself that there was no hostility towards Russia, especially when he was cheered by the crowds on the racecourse at Ascot. He also had a discussion on the future of the Turkish Empire with Lord Aberdeen, the then Foreign Secretary, which led to further misunderstanding. He thought this conversation was so important that he had it written in the form of a memorandum, which he sent to Aberdeen, who approved it as an accurate account of their meeting. It declared that both Britain and Russia would maintain the Turkish Empire for as long as possible, but if 'we foresee that it must crumble to pieces, to enter into previous concert as to everything relating to the establishment of a new order of things' in a way that would uphold the security and treaty rights of Russia and Britain and the European balance of power. Aberdeen thought that this declaration of an intention to undertake a joint, friendly settlement of Turkish affairs, if the Empire should collapse, was merely a 'mutual expression of opinion', but Nicholas felt still more confident now that when a suitable opportunity arose Britain would be ready to share with Russia in a distribution of Turkish territory.

He continued to hold this belief. He did not realize, however, the extent to which British public opinion had become more hostile towards Russia after 1848. Still more, he never understood that no British government was likely to accept large Russian gains of Turkish territory. Nor did he realize that British co-operation with Russia in 1840 to frustrate France in Egypt and Syria did not mean that she would now accept Russian control of the Balkans, even if granted a free hand in Egypt in return, which he considered offering her. So, early in 1853 he proposed to act with Britain over Turkey 'lest the sick man should suddenly die on our hands, and his heritage fall into chaos and dissolution.' He suggested that Britain should annex Egypt, Crete and Cyprus, that Serbia, Bulgaria, Moldavia and Wallachia should become Russian-protected states, and that Russia, during the crisis of the dissolution of the Turkish Empire, should occupy Constantinople, which would ultimately be a free city. Lord Aberdeen simply replied with an assurance that, while he did not think that Turkey's end was as near as the Tsar supposed, Britain would only consider the disposal of Turkish territory with Russia's consent. This was so carefully uncertain that the Tsar believed he had Britain's support for such action. And Aberdeen, in his turn, misjudged the Tsar. He told the Queen, 'There is nothing new in this demonstration by the Emperor. It is essentially the same language as he has held for some years.'

In making this approach to the British government, Nicholas again hoped to separate Britain from France. He had now found an opportunity for Russian intervention in Turkish affairs, and France was involved in it. The issue was 'a quarrel of monks' in Palestine. Guardianship of the Holy Places there had long been disputed between the Roman Catholic and Eastern Orthodox Churches. By a treaty of 1740 France had been recognized as the guardian of the rights of the Roman Catholics in the Christian shrines of Jerusalem and Bethlehem at the presumed sites of Christ's birth, crucifixion and burial. There always had been, however, many more Russian than French pilgrims to these places, and the Russian government supported them with generous grants of money. The Orthodox clergy (often with the permission of the Sultan) were able to enlarge their buildings and extend their influence, while Roman Catholics received no assistance from the godless France of the Revolution. With the revival of religion in France after 1815, however, Roman Catholic religious orders became more active, received help for political reasons from the French government after the fall of Mehemet Ali in 1841 and were able, therefore, to begin to oppose the influence of their rivals.

By 1850 the clergy of the two creeds had become involved in a dispute over the Church of the Holy Nativity in Bethlehem, the custody of which they shared. Both groups possessed keys of the church, but the Greeks held the key of the great door, which the Roman Catholics, who had the key of the side door only, also wanted to possess it for the sake of maintaining equality of right. Though this might appear to be a trivial matter, the Tsar could not ignore it. If he did, it would greatly damage the credibility of Russia's claims to be the protector of the religious rights of the Orthodox Christians in the Turkish Empire (*see page 28*). Moreover, this was a situation which he could exploit in the interests of his policy towards Turkey. He not only supported the Orthodox claims in Bethlehem, but also, in March 1853, demanded that the Sultan should recognize Russia as the general and not merely the religious protector of the 15 million Orthodox subjects of the Turkish Empire.

Britain was not involved in the religious dispute. Most of the cabinet were indifferent to the rival claims of the clergy and equally suspicious of Russia and France. Aberdeen, whose control of his ministers was ever decreasing, was known to be still anxious to avoid war and have peace at almost any price. The Sultan was determined to reject the Tsar's demands, considering them humiliating and dangerous to his empire since they would give Russia the right to interfere at any time on behalf of two-fifths of his subjects. The British Ambassador in Constantinople, Lord Stratford de Redcliffe, sympathized with Turkey; but whether he acted independently of Aberdeen's divided government is uncertain. Diplomatic archives do not support contemporary suggestions that he tried to bring about war by personally encouraging the Sultan to resist the Tsar.

France, on the other hand, was inevitably and immediately involved in the dispute. Napoleon III had to decide whether he wished to support the Roman Catholic monks at Bethlehem or not, but there was only one choice he could really make. He was bound to oppose Russia. The Tsar's demands challenged France, who would be humiliated if she did not protect against them. Anti-Russian feeling was mounting in France as well as in Britain. The French press was even writing about avenging the retreat from Moscow even though this was now 40 years in the past. Moreover, the clerical party expected Napoleon to uphold the Roman Catholic cause, and their support was still important for him. Nevertheless, his responsibility for the development of the religious crisis into the outbreak of war was comparatively slight. He liked the idea of hostilities between Britain and Russia, the former allies who had defeated France in 1815. This would disrupt the existing European situation and prepare the way for the establishment of French supremacy on the Continent. He wished to upset the Vienna Settlement, and he had various vague schemes in mind for re-arranging the boundaries of Europe, but typically he wished to do this without war. If there was to be a war, he did not think of it as likely to arise from this episode, but rather as still lying in the unascertainable future. Accordingly, he did not choose at first to consider the Russian attitude provocative.

Another reason for his caution was that French interests did not seem to be as deeply involved in the future of the Turkish Empire as were British, and there could be no enthusiasm in France for a war waged mainly to strengthen Britain's interests in the Near East. He was determined, however, to keep in step with Britain. He thought that his uncle's fatal mistake had been to quarrel with Britain, and he was not going to repeat this. On the contrary, he wanted an alliance with Britain to strengthen his regime and believed that he might now get this. Such a belief led him to action which he would not otherwise have taken. The British government remained as divided as ever. Aberdeen still suspected France more than he did Russia, and a majority of the cabinet were able to convince him that Napoleon should not be allowed to strengthen his position by acting first. So Aberdeen was persuaded to send a British fleet in June to cruise outside the Dardanelles to prevent any Russian naval action against Turkey. Napoleon's hand was forced. He had neither contemplated nor desired such an action, but he felt bound to support Britain by sending a French fleet there also. Not to do so would have deprived him of the British alliance he wanted.

(c) The Coming of War

In 49 BC Julius Ceasar crossed the Rubicon, which meant that he invaded Italy and so began irretrievably his rebellion against the Roman government. Palmerston described the Franco-British naval action of 1853 as 'the passing of the Rubicon'. This is true in that, in the way it was undertaken, it probably made war inevitable, but Palmerston had wanted more vigorous action which he believed would have preserved peace even at that stage. He proposed that the British fleet should enter the Straits and the Sea of Marmora and then sail through the Bosphorus and into the Black Sea, where it could join the Sultan's warships which were protecting the Turkish coast. This, he thought, would have discouraged the Tsar from taking any action at all against Turkey. But Aberdeen would not agree, and the fleet remained in Besika Bay, on the north-west coast of Asia Minor (*see Map 14*).

As it was, the presence of the fleets outside the Dardanelles surprised Nicholas, but did not deter him. He still could not believe that Britain would seriously support Turkey, and he was sure that France would not go to war on her own. He reckoned, therefore, that he could still impose upon the Sultan his demand that Russia should be recognized as the protector of all Orthodox Christians in Turkey, which would humiliate Napoleon III. The Tsar resented Napoleon's adoption of the imperial title and was disturbed by his talk of favouring nationalist causes, such as Poland. He had now become over-confident to the extent of carelessness.

The Anglo-French naval action was sufficient to encourage the Sultan to resist. He finally rejected the Russian proposals. In July Nicholas decided upon military action to force the Sultan to come to terms. He sent his troops into the Danubian Principalities of Moldavia and Wallachia (*see Map 4, page 29*). The division of opinion in the cabinet was still too great to permit the British government to take action. The fleets remained in Besika Bay. The Austrian government intervened in an attempt at mediation. It invited the signatory powers of the Convention of the Straits of 1841 to meet in Vienna, which they did, though Palmerston and Russell were opposed to the idea. The Tsar, beginning now to appreciate the likelihood of a general war, was prepared to be more conciliatory, but the Sultan, confident of British support, prevented the conference arriving at a settlement. As the tension increased, he asked for protection from the British and French fleets. This request came at an opportune time. The autumn gales would soon make it impossible for the ships to remain at their exposed anchorage, and this provided some sort of justification for breaking the Convention of the Straits when they now passed through the Dardanelles.

The fleets anchored at Constantinople. The Sultan felt freed from all restraint. On 23 October he declared war on Russia, and Turkish troops crossed the Danube into the occupied Principalities. In November, thinking that the Turkish navy would be reinforced unless he acted quickly, Nicholas ordered the Russian fleet to attack a Turkish squadron at Sinope on the Black Sea. The Russian ironclads with their new shell-firing guns had no difficulty in sinking the entire Turkish collection of wooden sailing ships, drowning 4000 Turkish sailors.

In Britain, the news of the 'massacre of Sinope', as the press called it, aroused a wave of popular indignation. Aberdeen was accused of cowardice and of betraying Turkey by failing to send the British fleet on into the Black Sea to protect the Turkish ships. Most of the members of the cabinet feared that Napoleon might act first if the British government did nothing. They compelled Aberdeen to take another step towards war. On 3 January the two fleets sailed for the Black Sea. Still the two countries did not declare war on Russia, but the clamour for war, which had been growing in Britain since the autumn, now became intense. The press aroused public opinion against Russia, reminding their readers of the already-known horrors of the Siberian prisons, repeating the allegation that the Russians had fired grapeshot at the floating timbers of the wrecked Turkish ships at Sinope to prevent the survivors swimming ashore and retailing the latest news that Polish women had been publicly flogged for sending Christmas greetings to their husbands who were refugees abroad. Kossuth and the leading Polish exiles addressed crowded meetings all over the country, and ministers were subjected to angry questioning in Parliament.

Napoleon still hoped for a peaceful outcome to the crisis and did not want further action to be taken immediately, but the British government could not withstand popular pressure upon it any longer. On 27 February he had to join with Britain in sending an ultimatum to Russia requiring the withdrawal of her forces from the Principalities within one month. The Tsar did not reply. Even had he been prepared to abandon now his policy towards Turkey, his prestige would not allow him to accept an ultimatum. On 28 March Britain and France declared war on Russia.

The Crimean War followed a series of wars that had been fought between Russia and Turkey for nearly two centuries, but this was a wider war. Now Turkey was supported by Britain and France. Their attitude encouraged the Sultan to resist the Tsar's demands, and they were prepared to take their support to the extent of war. The fundamental reason for this was, as L.C.B. Seaman has said, that 'the Crimean War was as much a war about the European balance of power as it was about the Eastern Question,' to which A.J.P. Taylor has added, 'It was fought against Russia, not in favour of Turkey.' Relations between Russia and Turkey had become a matter for European concern. Particularly after the events of 1848–49, it was impossible for the other interested powers to permit Russia to act towards Turkey as she chose and so gain supremacy in the Balkans and Asia Minor (*see Map 11*). Nicholas acted as he did because he did not realize this. Britain went to war because she believed that her interests there were threatened. France joined her because Napoleon wanted a British alliance, and once hostilities became certain he did not wish Britain alone to gather the fruits of victory. What part was played in the development of events by Aberdeen's inability to pursue unhindered a policy of conciliation and Palmerston's absence from the Foreign Office, a divided cabinet and bellicose public opinion, the vacillations of Napoleon III and the sheer length of time the crisis endured, must be matters for discussion. As it was, the protagonists slid reluctantly into a war which they believed in the end could not be avoided without sacrifice of interests and loss of prestige.

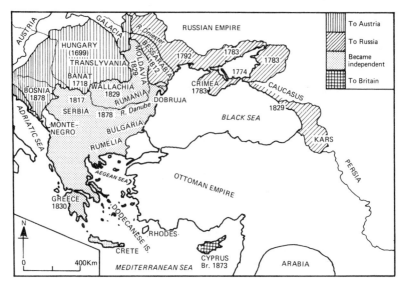

Map 11 The Turkish Empire

At the same time, another power, whose interests were clearly implicated in the situation, persisted in abstention from the conflict. Austria also was concerned about the future of the Turkish Empire. She regarded the Balkans as her sphere of influence and did not want Russia to approach the Danube. Several Austrian ministers, including Count Buol, who became Foreign Minister on the death of Schwarzenberg in April 1852, favoured co-operation with Britain and France in the belief that this might gain the Danubian Principalities for the Austrian Empire and also secure her position in Italy; but the Austrian generals, having learnt the value of Russian assistance in 1849, wished to retain her friendship and feared that a defeated Russia would be replaced by a dominant, hostile France. They knew also that if Austria supported Turkey, her position would mean that she would be subjected to a concerted Russian attack, and that the war for her would be a fight, not for limited aims, but for her very existence against a power at least as strong as herself. Only if Prussia entered the war, they argued, and fought Russia in the East, would it be a war in which Austria could safely take part. Buol tried to reach agreement with Prussia, but Frederick William IV refused to consider entering into a contest where his kingdom also would have to face a Russian onslaught over an issue in which its interests were not involved. The Austrian government, therefore, did not want war to occur and tried to prevent it by mediation. When it came, Francis Joseph, torn between his ministerial and military advisers, remained neutral. The result was that Austria lost Russia's friendship without receiving any compensatory gain from the other side. Her weakness had placed her in a dangerous condition of diplomatic isolation.

1853	March	Russian demand for the right to protect Turkish Orthodox Christians
	June	Franco-British fleet sent to the Dardanelles
	July	Russian troops invade the Danubian Principalities
	October	Declaration of war on Russia by Turkey
		Turkish troops enter the Danubian Principalities
	November	Turkish fleet destroyed at Sinope
1854	January	Allied fleet enters the Black Sea
	February	Franco-British ultimatum to Russia
	March	Franco-British declaration of war on Russia
	July	Austrian ultimatum to Russia
	August	Austrian replace Russian troops in the Principalities
		Four Points issued by Austria
	September	Allied forces land in the Crimea
	October	Siege of Sebastopol begins
		Battle of Balaclava
	November	Battle of Inkerman
		Russian acceptance of Four Points
1855	January	Piedmont joins the Allies
		Fall of Lord Aberdeen's government
	February	Lord Palmerston forms his government
	March	Death of Tsar Nicholas I; succession of Alexander II
	September	Fall of Sebastopol
1856	February	Paris Peace Conference opens
	March	Treaty of Paris signed

Table 10. Date chart of the Crimean War (1853–56)

(d) The Crimean War (1854–56)

Though Austria did not participate in the War, Buol persuaded Francis Joseph to send an ultimatum to Russia, demanding that she sh ild evacuate the Danubian Principalities (*see Map 4, page 29*). Russia was vulnerable to Austrian attack all the way from southern Poland to Bessarabia, and Austria massed several armies on her frontiers. Nicholas was not to know that Francis Joseph had promised his generals that he would never act upon his ultimatum. He did not want to face Austria as an additional opponent in the Balkans. he was likely to have to relinquish the Principalities anyway because of difficulties of supply and pressure from the Turkish army. In August 1854, Russian troops were accordingly withdrawn from the Principalities and replaced by several Austrian regiments, for Austria had signed a convention with Turkey which allowed her to station them there for the duration of hostilities.

The withdrawal of Russian troops from the Principalities deprived Britain and France of their original aim in making war, since Turkish territory was no longer threatened. Moreover, Buol made another attempt at mediation. In August 1854 he suggested Four Points which should be accepted as terms for peace. These were (1) the Russian protectorate of the Principalities to be replaced by a general guarantee of the powers; (2) the navigation of the Danube to be free; (3) the Straits Convention of 1842 to be revised; (4) Russia to renounce her rights as protector of the Orthodox Christians in the Turkish Empire. The allies, still hoping to gain Austria as a co-belligerent, accepted these. Since Russia by her actions had now tacitly agreed to all these points except the third, the only matter at issue was really Russian naval strength in the Black Sea. In November, Nicholas, afraid that Austria might join the allied side, accepted the terms.

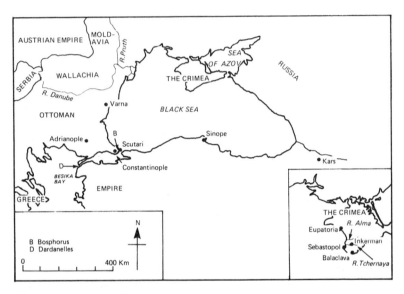

Map 12   The Crimean War

Though fighting had by then begun, peace might thus still have been made, but public opinion in Britain and France had been aroused, and their governments considered themselves bound to pursue hostilities. As long as Russia was powerful in the Black Sea, the threat of renewed aggression by her in the future seemed to remain, and somehow it must be countered. This would have been militarily straightforward if the Central Powers had not been neutral. Prince Albert had foreseen this when he commented, 'If Prussia and Austria go with us, matters are different, and the war becomes impossible for Russia.' But now it was the allies who were faced with serious difficulties. The defection of those strategically-placed countries deprived them of their most likely theatre of war. French and British armies had already been sent to Varna, a Bulgarian port on the Black Sea, to help the Turks (*see Map 12*). There was no use for them there. The allies had to solve the problem of finding somewhere else where they might strike at Russia and inflict on her a defeat which would curb her ambitions.

208

After an ineffective naval raid in the Baltic, the British and French governments decided that their armies should be transferred to make an attack upon Sebastopol, the great fortified naval base in the Crimea to which the Russian Black Sea fleet had withdrawn. Their decision was governed by political rather than strategic considerations. They hoped that the destruction of this stronghold and the elimination of Russian naval power in this sea would safeguard Constantinople and ensure the continued independence of Turkey. Six months of the war had passed before the Franco-British forces landed there in September 1854, and they were already ravaged by cholera brought by the French troops from Marseilles.

Though the neutrality of Austria and Prussia avoided the outbreak of a European conflagration and made the Crimean War a limited conflict, it still involved heavier casualties than any other European war between the end of the Napoleonic War and the beginning of the First World War. It was the first war for almost 40 years which threatened decisively to change national boundaries and the existing balance of power. It was also the first war, after the same period, in which the regular armies and navies of the nations fought against each other. Previous experience of fighting against native forces in Afghanistan or Algeria, insurgents in Poland or Hungary, rioters in the streets of Paris or Ukrainian villages —none of these were any preparation for the conditions of this war. Both sides lacked adequate commanders, training, organization, arms and supplies for this experience. The undertaking of such a distant war was a triumph for the British navy, but the British army probably did the least well in the War, largely because it had been protected from change since its victories in the Peninsula and at Waterloo by its reputation and the Duke of Wellington, who died in 1852.

The two most famous battles of the War, Balaclava and Inkerman, were fought within the first two months of the Crimean campaign, but the allies failed to exploit them, and they had to settle down to a long-drawn-out siege of Sebastopol under terrible conditions (*see Map 12, page 208*). Both sides had to endure the consequences of being improperly prepared to fight such a war. The problems of communication and supply were formidable. The allies were separated by 4000 kilometres of sea-routes from home, while the Russians did not possess a single railway line south of Moscow and had to transport everything by horse and waggon over hundreds of kilometres of mud-bound, unmade roads. The total number of deaths in the War cannot be known with certainty, but it had been estimated that the French lost 95 000 men, the British 20 000, the Russians 110 000 and the Turks 30 000. About one man in five was killed in battle; the other four died from the effects of disease and the bitterly cold weather. The Russians displayed their usual corruption, but no government or army proved itself competent. The consequences of this for the British were exalted in poetry by Lord Tennyson, exposed to the public by William Russell, correspondent of *The Times*, and relieved by Florence Nightingale and her nurses. The political result was the defeat of the Aberdeen government in Parliament. Much against the will of herself and Prince Albert, the Queen sent for Palmerston, who became Prime Minister in February 1855, informing her that he was confident that he could 'effectually conduct public affairs in the present momentous crisis'.

In the previous month Piedmont had joined the allies and sent troops to the Crimea (*see page 265*). Nicholas I died in March and was succeeded by his inexperienced son, Alexander II. The allies, after besieging Sebastopol for nearly a year, at last brought the deadlock in the war to an end. The French captured Malakoff, the fort of the port, and soon afterwards the shattered city itself surrendered. Napoleon III wanted to continue the war until Russia was deprived of Poland and other European territory which she had conquered during the eighteenth century. He was opposed by Palmerston, who would have liked to go on to inflict a more decisive defeat upon Russia, but did not want to antagonize Austria by supporting the Polish cause nor to replace Russian by French supremacy on the Continent. Napoleon's attitude, combined with the economic and financial strain suffered by Russia and signs of discontent among her peasants, made the new Tsar anxious to end the War, while Austria was bringing pressure upon him to come to terms with the allies. So in 1856 a peace conference of the great European powers was held in Paris.

(e) The Treaty of Paris (1856)
The location of the Congress signified the renewed renown and influence gained by France through participation in the War, but its scope was limited compared with that of the Congress of Vienna. Britain and Austria agreed beforehand that they would seek no territorial annexations for themselves and so frustrated Napoleon's wish to initiate a general review of European boundaries. Cavour, who had a place at the Conference as Piedmont's representative, failed in his suggestion that his country should receive the Duchies of Parma and Modena, whose rulers would be given Moldavia and Wallachia in compensation, but he was able to speak at the Conference about the situation in Italy and had the satisfaction of hearing Palmerston denounce Austria's rule over her subject peoples, though he was over-optimistic enough to believe that this meant that Britain would help the Italian cause.

The terms of the Treaty of Paris were based upon the Four Points previously put forward by Austria and were, therefore, concerned mainly with the area of the Black Sea (*see Map 13*). These were imposed upon both Turkey and Russia, though one was a victorious ally and the other a defeated enemy. Sebastopol was not to be refortified. The Dardanelles were to be closed to the warships and open to the merchant vessels of all nations. Neither Russia nor Turkey was to have a naval fleet in the Black Sea. The navigation of the Danube was also to be free, and an international commission was to regulate traffic on it and make it navigable to the sea. Moldavia and Wallachia were to be self-governing under Turkish suzerainty, and Serbia was given the same position —this was at the insistence of Napoleon, who wished to put into effect his genuinely-held belief in the principle of nationality. He opposed Austria's wish to gain the Principalities, saying that he would only agree if she gave up her position in Italy in return, a condition which was quite unacceptable to her. She had also to withdraw her troops from the Danubian territory. In addition, Moldavia was enlarged by the addition of a part of Bessarabia, which was taken from Russia, thus depriving her of access to the Danube. The powers gave up any right to interfere in Turkish affairs, which meant that Russia renounced the Treaty of Kutchuk-Kainardji (*see page 28*); and in return the Sultan promised to grant his Christian subjects equality with the Moslems.

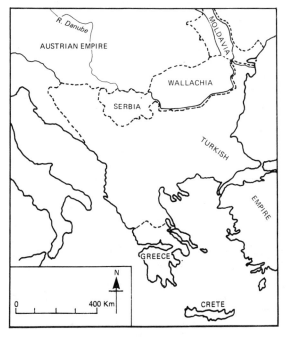

Map 13   The Treaty of Paris, 1856

Much of the Treaty of Paris was as indecisive as the Crimean War itself. This was because, as is common after peace settlements, the victorious powers secured the acceptance of their wishes on paper, but afterwards showed themselves not prepared to enforce those treaty provisions by intervention and possible war.

This applied especially to the neutralization of the Black Sea, which the victors had regarded first as the most important aim of their war and then as the most valuable part of the peace treaty. By depriving both

Russia and Turkey of the right to maintain a navy in the Black Sea, it gave Britain and France, which both had Mediterranean fleets, the ability to send at will warships through the Dardanelles, despite the restrictions imposed upon them, and gain control of this sea. But in 1870, when Russia took advantage of the Franco-Prussian War to repudiate these Black Sea clauses of the Treaty, Gladstone's government was not ready to consider military action to stop her.

Similarly, because the allies had abandoned any idea of intervening to make the Sultan observe his promise of equal treatment for Christians and Moslems in his dominions, the Christians were, in fact, left without toleration or protection. Not only did the Turkish government itself follow a policy of discrimination and persecution, but its corruption and maladministration made it possible for fanatical Moslems to massacre Christians at times of religious excitement. Two years after the Treaty of Paris, the Christian inhabitants of Jedda, the port of Mecca in Arabia, were slaughtered together with the British and French consuls and their families. A British warship bombarded the town, the ringleaders were executed, and the indemnity was paid to the two powers. This was not sufficient, however, to prevent further outbreaks, which were to produce more serious international crises.

Nevertheless, the Crimean War and the Treaty of Paris had important consequences, though these were largely, as so often in such circumstances, unintended and unforeseen by the peacemakers. One of these was to encourage the growth of Balkan nationalism. The Congress would not allow either Austria or Russia to take the place of the failing Turkish Empire in Europe. This enabled the subject races of the Balkans to gain their freedom and divide the peninsula into independent states. This 'Balkanization' later threatened the existence of the Austrian Empire, encouraged Russian intervention in pursuance of her pro-Slav policy and provided the occasion for the outbreak of the First World War.

Russia was not destroyed as a great power, but her influence in Europe was diminished. Alexander II embarked upon a programme of social reform and was neither inclined nor able to undertake such foreign adventures as his father had engaged in. Moreover, Russian foreign policy now turned away from Europe and concentrated upon expanding through Central Asia and supporting the cause of the Slavs and Orthodox Christians beyond her Empire. To safeguard her position in Europe, she began to look for an ally in France and later in Prussia. Austria was isolated and left helpless against nationalism and revolution, as Metternich had long feared she might be. Palmerston's resentment at Prussian neutrality led to her exclusion from the Congress at Paris, except that as a signatory of the Convention of the Straits in 1841, she had to be present later to acquiese in its revision.

The change in the relationships of these three powers brought about the final demise of the Holy Alliance, which had been able to preserve its aims hitherto through their co-operation. The power most to benefit from this situation was Prussia. Though she appeared to have been humiliated at Paris, she had actually scored a considerable diplomatic success. She had preserved her neutrality during the Crimean War without estranging any Continental power, and the ensuing lack of international harmony favoured her policy of expansion in the 1860s. Britain also benefited substantially from the situation. The discord on the Continent was not to be serious enough to involve her in a European war for two generations.

France's regained prestige did not bring her European domination, nor, indeed, many tangible advantages. British fear of Napoleon III's new position, soon to be increased by his subsequent actions, cost him the alliance which he valued so much. This ultimately deprived him of such international influence as he possessed. He wished to destroy the Vienna Settlement, and he thought he would be able to refashion Italy and Germany to suit his plans. In fact, nationalism in these two countries was able to achieve its own ends once Austrian and Russian opposition to them had been eliminated. As has been said, 'Bismarck and Cavour were the chief benefactors of the Crimean War.'

(f) Reform in Russia

Though the Crimean War had not inflicted an overwhelming defeat upon Russia, it was a bitter setback for the Imperial government which had entered upon the conflict with great confidence and hope. For the first time since Peter the Great had been defeated by the Turks on the River Pruth (which flows into the Danube) in 1712, the Tsar's ministers attended a peace conference as the representatives of a defeated power, and the loss of Bessarabian territory, which had been taken by Alexander I in the victorious year of 1812, was a harsh blow to national prestige. The lesson of the war for the country was clear. The allies, fighting from a great distance and relying upon only part of their resources, had conducted a local offensive upon a strongly-fortified place which Russia, despite her own vast size and strategic advantages and the weaknesses and miscalculations of the allies, had not been able to repulse. The modern steamships of the allies had transported supplies more effectively than the primitive, two-wheeled carts of the Russians; their heavy siege guns and new percussion rifles with telescopic sights had outfought the Russian muzzle-loading cannon and smooth-bore muskets. Western European efficiency and industrialization were seen to have overcome the Russian Empire.

This situation compelled the Russian government to think of reforms. Alexander II had been brought up to adhere to his father's ideal of military autocracy, but he was prepared to undertake changes if the national interest required them. Social reform was needed to prevent revolution by the peasantry, which had been made more likely by the loss of confidence in the government brought about by defeat in war; and political reform was needed to modernize the administrative machinery and make it possible for Russia to hold her place among the great powers of Europe.

Most of the landowning nobility and gentry and the Orthodox Church were indifferent to reform, and the peasantry, though restive and embittered, were in no way capable of giving Alexander any active, constructive support. He had to turn to the liberal minority among the nobility and to the intellectual class, composed largely of university teachers and students and writers, who were inspired by the ideals of their foreign counterparts. The Tsar's early measures in the later 1850s, which were designed to gain their support, included a relaxation of the censorship of the press, less government control of the universities and more freedom for Russians to travel abroad. Yet, though these reforms were such as were generally demanded by western liberals, he was determined not to move towards any form of constitutional government. Later he came to be known as the 'Tsar Liberator', but he showed that whatever changes he made would not diminish the authority of the Tsardom in any way.

(g) The Emancipation of the Serfs (1861)

The greater liberty of discussion permitted by Alexander soon produced demands for the emancipation of the privately-owned serfs. Liberals wanted this for humanitarian reasons. Most landowners still opposed it, but a growing number were favourable. Some were alarmed by the local riots, which had become more frequent since the 1840s (*see page 128*). Others were beginning to realize that serf labour was inefficient, unreliable and a hindrance to effective capitalist farming. Traders and manufacturers found that serfdom was even less suitable for their enterprises. The government had now begun a policy of encouraging industrialization by chartering exploitation companies on favourable terms, but as long as peasants were bound to the soil and unable to move from the villages to the towns, the factories and mines could not secure an adequate mobile labour force.

The Crimean War had convinced Alexander of the need for emancipation. The Russian peasant soldiers had fought bravely, even though only a twenty-fifth of them were armed with the new percussion rifles compared with a third of the French and a half of the British. Sometimes a quarter of the troops were cut down by enemy fire as soon as they came into range, but the rest had continued to advance. The Russian army would still have to rely upon the peasants to fill its regiments and fight its wars, but their loyalty could not be depended upon if serfdom lasted. Alexander's attitude towards emancipation was shown in his famous words addressed on 30 March 1856 (the same day as the signing of the Treaty of Paris) to an assembly of the nobility of Moscow: 'It is better to abolish serfdom from above than wait until it begins to abolish itself from below.'

Not until five years later, however, did he issue the Edict of Emancipation, declaring, 'Some twenty million Russian serfs are now not only free, but they may have land in proportion to their deserts. The state will recompense the landowners. The serfs will pay the state in instalments.' The peasants were granted their legal liberty and received in all about half the landowners' estates and were made responsible for an annual levy to repay the compensation awarded by the government to their former landlords. The land, however, did not belong to the peasants individually, but collectively to each *mir*, the organized village community which was medieval in origin. This arranged what crops were to be planted and could regulate the buying and selling of land by peasants.

Compared with the freeing of the American slaves, which took place a few years later, the emancipation of the Russian serfs was carried out peacefully and did not leave the peasants landless, but it had to be based upon a compromise in order to avoid ruining the landowners and dislocating the national economy. The peasants were made free personally, but not economically, and they deeply resented several aspects of the settlement. The division of the estates gave them only four-fifths of the land they had actually been able to farm for themselves as serfs before 1861. The annual 'redemption payments', which they had to make to the government for the next 49 years, were a burden to them, and they disliked having to pay for land which they had always considered was rightly theirs. Moreover, freedom from the landlord had been replaced by dependence upon the *mir*, which in medieval fashion controlled the cultivation of their scattered holdings. Because they did not own the land themselves, they did not try to improve it so that the productivity of the Russian grain fields declined even further. And the peasants retained a hunger for the land that was eventually to contribute to the downfall of the Empire.

Nor did the abolition of serfdom involve only these arrangements in the distribution of the land. Since the peasants were no longer subject to the authority and jurisdiction of the landlords, changes had to be made in local government and the judiciary. In January 1864, *zemstvos* or local elected councils were instituted for districts and provinces. They dealt with such matters as the maintenance of roads, the care of the sick and poor and primary education under the supervision of the autocratic central government, and they were elected through a system of indirect voting by noblemen, townspeople. To compensate them for their loss of control over the serfs, the nobility had a predominant influence. In 1870 a similar system of local government was established separately for the towns. The *zemstvos* achieved important practical results in the establishment of such institutions as hospitals, asylums and particularly primary schools, the number of which was increased from 8000 to 23 000 between 1856 and 1880.

Similarly, since the abolition of serfdom deprived the landlords of their right to settle disputes among the peasants and impose punishments for many offences, it was essential to reform the system of justice. Speranski had codified the law; now new courts and procedures had to be established. In December 1864 changes were introduced which gave expression to western principles of the independence of the law-courts and equal justice for all. Trials were to be held in public. A jury system was introduced. Judges were to be irremovable, professionally-trained and paid a fixed salary. These reforms were not entirely successful. Abuses and corruption remained, and many judges continued to impose the harsh, traditional punishments upon peasants. Flogging, though forbidden in 1863, even increased, the number of cases in which it was inflicted in one district rising from 5452 during 1866–68 to 10 884 during 1872–74. And the idea of the rule of law contained in these reforms was often set aside by arbitrary police action and censorship of the press. Nevertheless, the people (including the peasants) did generally secure a measure of protection against official and autocratic actions which they had not known before.

A further reform required by the abolition of serfdom was in the army. At the time of the Crimean War, Russia still had a vast standing army such as had defeated Frederick the Great and Napoleon. Its officers were noblemen, and its recruits, who served for 25 years, were obtained by quotas from each *mir* and were almost entirely serfs since others could generally secure exemption. This was now changed by General Dimitri Milyutin, who wished to establish a smaller army with a large trained reserve. He sought to follow the principle of the reforms first adopted by the Prussian army in the 1860s (*see page 244*), but he was not able to get his way until 1874 when the lesson of Prussia's victories over Austria and France had been learnt. His system provided for the conscription of all able-bodied men to serve for six years and spend nine years in the reserve, but the actual selection was by ballot, and educational qualifications secured considerable reductions in the length of service. Though Milyutin's purpose was to promote greater military efficiency, it proved to be also an important democratic development. Not only were the nobility compelled to serve in the ranks, but conscription was accompanied by such an effective educational programme that soon literacy in the ranks was five times greater than among the adult male population as a whole.

(h) Revolt and Reaction

The changes of this period encouraged the radical reformers to expect more of the way of western liberalism in Russia than Alexander was prepared to consider. In particular, his refusal to grant a constitution and a parliament provoked disappointment and resentment among them. Their secret societies gained strength. The censorship could not completely suppress their underground literature, but the police were able to put down the several minor, amateurish plots and conspiracies in which they engaged.

In Poland, however, the resistance was again more serious. Alexander introduced several conciliatory measures and reforms there, including a general amnesty, the recognition of Polish as the official language, the establishment of new schools and the emancipation of the Jews. These were quite inadequate for the radical nationalists, who scorned co-operation with the Imperial government and regarded the Tsar's actions as a sign of weakness. Led by students and middle-class townspeople, they agitated for complete Polish independence and the recovery of the lost Lithuanian provinces. The government sought to deprive the revolutionary movement of its leaders in January 1863 by issuing a decree which conscripted young Poles into the army. The plan miscarried. The nationalist leaders at once proclaimed a general insurrection. This did not prove to be as widespread as in 1830. No large-scale battle took place between armies, and the Poles held no cities. They fought in the countryside scattered among groups which numbered altogether some 10 000 against 30 000 Russians, and the same factors as in 1830 contributed to their failure. The landowners mostly sided with them, but few of the peasants, some of whom supported the Russians. They were still divided among 'Reds' and 'Whites', and the western powers did no more than protest, while Prussia deliberately supported Russia (*see page 247*). The revolt was suppressed in about a year, and executions and deportations, confiscations and heavy fines followed.

When his authority had been restored in Poland, Alexander adopted a two fold policy. First, the peasants were emancipated on better terms than they could have expected from a Polish victory. Unlike the Russian serfs, they received full title to their holdings, which amounted to about a third of the land. Redemption payments were lower than in Russia and were financed by a general tax upon all landowners including the nobility. Second, he intensified the policy of Russification. Russian was declared to be the official language of the country. Instruction in all places of education was to be given in Russian, and in 1869 the Polish University of Warsaw was replaced by a completely Russian university. Secular primary schools were founded, and restrictions were placed upon the work of the Roman Catholic clergy. And in 1866 the Kingdom of Poland was renamed the Vistula Region of the Russian Empire.

The policy, however, was largely a failure. The peasants were not converted, as had been intended, into a conservative class, loyal to the Tsarist government which had given them their land. Rather, now that the abolition of serfdom had removed the grievance that had divided them from the landlords, they joined them in opposition to the policy of Russification which offended all classes of Poles.

The Polish rising and an attempt upon his life in St. Petersburg during 1866 turned Alexander towards reaction and repression. This had an important effect upon the Russian intellectuals. Previously important writing and social political thought had been confined almost exclusively to the nobility. From them had come the radical reformers with their secret societies and conspiracies. Now the movement had gained members from the middle class, and in the ferment of opinion during the years following the Crimean War, much discussion was stimulated by the differences between the two broad philosophical attitudes, conventionally described as Westernism and Slavophilism (*see page 328*). But Alexander made the radical intellectuals increasingly dissatisfied with such abstract debate. They took to practical politics and began to form revolutionary terrorist societies.

The earliest of these societies was that of the Nihilists, who accepted this name invented by the novelist Ivan Turgenev in *Fathers and Sons* (1861) for the outlook of Bazarov, its chief character and 'a hero of our time', who recognizes no authority, doubts every general principle and value and accepts only scientifically demonstrable facts and utilitarian ideas. In giving it a political direction, the Nihilists aimed at the reconstruction of society on a communistic basis. They contended that all existing political, social and religious institutions that were not based upon reason must be destroyed before a new organization of society could be set up. They declared war on all the traditions of Russia, particularly the Tsardom and the Orthodox Church and advocated violence to bring about their overthrow, proclaiming a 'terrible, total, universal and merciless destruction of society' as the essential way of securing 'the entire emancipation and happiness of the people'.

Another group were the Populists, whose slogan was 'To the People!' They believed that the peasants were ready to rise against the government and landlords, and that the *mir* could be the basis of a socialist revolution throughout Russia. Populism was particularly strong in the 1870s when hundreds of students went into the countryside to preach their ideas; they met with little success and were easily arrested by the police. The Populists too believed in terror as the only effective means of securing their ends.

There were frequent attempts, successful and unsuccessful, on the lives of high officials by pistol, knife or bomb. Mines and death-traps were constantly laid for Alexander. The government resorted to ever-more severe measures. The censorship of the press was tightened up, the universities were closely supervised, and the powers of the *zemstvos* were reduced. The secret police extended their activities, and when juries acquitted accused terrorists, they deported them to Siberia under their powers of 'administrative exile'. During the first 20 years of Alexander's reign, over a quarter of a million people were sent there.

Bibliography
R.L.V. ffrench Blake, *The Crimean War* (Leo Cooper, 1971) gives a straightforward account of the war. Christopher Hibbert, *The Destruction of Lord Raglan* (Longmans, 1961) and J.S. Curtiss, *The Russian Army under Nicholas I* (Durham, N.C., 1965) deal with its military aspects. Besides the general histories of Russia and Poland already mentioned (*see page 134*), there are W.E. Mosse, *Alexander II and the Modernisation of Russia* (English UP, 1969), G.T. Robinson, *Rural Russia under the Old Regime* (New York, 1932) and R.F. Leslie, *Reform and Insurrection in Russian Poland, 1856–1865* (Athlone Press, 1963).

Exercises

A *This section consists of questions that might be used for discussion (or written answers) as a way of expanding on the chapter and testing your understanding of it:*

1 Why was it that the Crimean War was so unpopular with many British ministers and yet so popular with ordinary people?

2 (a) How had the 1848 Revolutions altered the relative power of Russia, Austria and France?
(b) What effect did these changes have on (i) British public opinion and (ii) British policies?

3 Comment on the view that an inconsistent policy is more likely to bring about war, applying the generalization to other wars as well as the Crimean.

4 What did the Tsar expect Britain's policy to be towards the division of Turkey, and why did he believe this?

5 Why did Nicholas I demand that Russia should become protector of all Orthodox subjects of the Turkish Empire?

6 How do you explain Britain's decision to send a fleet to the Dardanelles in June 1853?

7 Why did the Austrian government mediate in the crisis?

8 Why were Britain and France prepared to respond to the Sultan's request for protection in the summer of 1853?

9 Assess the importance of the British press in bringing about the actual hostilities in 1854.

10 How 'reluctantly' did 'the protaganists slide . . . into a war'?

11 Why did the war continue after the agreement of all parties to Buol's Four Points in November 1854?

12 Why did the Allies decide to attack Sebastopol?

13 Why did no government or army 'prove itself competent'?

14 Why did the war come to an end after the fall of Sebastopol?

15 Outline (a) the terms of the Treaty of Paris and (b) the extent to which each of the terms was actually implemented.

16 What were the most important 'unforeseen consequences' of the Treaty of Paris?

17 Why was Alexander II both enthusiastic but also reluctant to introduce reforms?

18 Why did the Crimean War decide Alexander II on the need for the emancipation of the serfs?

19 Which aspects of emancipation were unsatisfactory for the peasants?

20 What governmental, judicial and military reforms did Alexander introduce?

21 Why did the Poles revolt in 1863?

22 Compare the plans and policies of the Nihilists and the Populists.

B *Essay questions*

(a) The Crimean War

1 'The Eastern Question was essentially about the balance of power.' Consider the crises between 1821 and 1856 in the light of this claim. (Cambridge, 1981)

2 'It was a fumbling, futile war yet rich in unintended consequences.' Discuss this comment on the Crimean War. (Oxford, 1982)

3   What chiefly was at stake in the 'Eastern Question' either (a) in the period 1821–41 or (b) in the period 1841–56? (Welsh, 1981)

4   'Never was so great an effort made for so worthless an object.' (*The Times*, 1861) How accurate was this assessment of the Crimean War? (Welsh, 1983) & (AEB, 1981)

5   Do you agree that the Crimean War 'began by accident and settled nothing'? (Oxford and Cambridge, 1981)

6   'A colourful episode, but not one which contributed significantly to the solution of the Eastern Question'; discuss this view of the Crimean War and its outcome. (London, 1982)

7   Discuss the view that the Crimean War was unnecessary but nevertheless highly significant. (JMB, 1982)

(b)   Russia

1   Describe and account for the continuing opposition to Alexander II in Russia despite his major reforms. (Cambridge, 1981)

2   Comment on the view that Alexander II's domestic policy was 'compassionate but ineffective'. (Cambridge, 1982)

3   'To go back on reforms that have been conceded is a fatal flaw in political judgement.' Discuss this assertion in relation to Alexander II of Russia. (Cambridge, 1983)

4   Examine the growth of opposition to Tsarist autocracy before the accession of Alexander III (1881). (Oxford, 1982)

5   Why, and with what consequences, were attempts made to change the social and administrative structure in Russia following the accession of Alexander II in 1855? (Oxford, 1983)

6   To what extent did the domestic and foreign policies of Alexander II of Russia entitle him to be known as 'the Tsar Liberator'? (SUJB, 1982)

7   What internal problems faced Alexander II on his accession? How far did his reforms solve them? (SUJB, 1983)

8   What were the objectives of the domestic reforms under Alexander II? (Oxford and Cambridge, 1981)

9   'Mere window dressing.' 'Far reaching and ultimately subversive.' Compare these views of the reforms in Russia under Alexander II. (Oxford and Cambridge, 1982)

10   How successful were the reforms of Alexander II in solving the problems of Russian government and society in the nineteenth century? (Oxford and Cambridge, 1983)

11   Why, and to what extent, did Alexander II depart from the conservative policies of his predecessors? (AEB, 1983)

12   For what reasons, when he inherited the throne, did Alexander II think there was a need for reform in Russia? How far-reaching were the reforms he enacted? (London, 1983)

13   Why, and with what consequences during his reign, did Alexander II emancipate the serfs in Russia? (JMB, 1981)

C   *The Treaty of Paris and the consequences of the Crimean War*
In this section, you will be studying extracts from two secondary sources illustrating their authors' views on the peace treaty and the international significance of the Crimean War. Before you study them, remind yourself of the views expressed in this book, by re-reading pages 210 to 213, which,

for the purposes of this exercise, you should regard as Extract C. Then study the additional extracts before answering these questions:

1 List the criticisms, if any, that each author makes of the Treaty of Paris.
2 If the treaty is so open to criticism, why did the peacemakers draw up such terms?
3 List the consequences of the Crimean War that each extract identifies.
4 Which of the authors regards the Crimean War as highly significant, and which plays down its importance? Explain both your decisions and in what way(s) each author sees it as significant.
5 Is it possible to construct an argument to show that the apparent consequences of the war (as identified in 3) would have happened in any case?
6 In what respects do the consequences of the Crimean War appear to be an issue for debate between historians? (You can add to this exercise by studying additional sources from the bibliography on page 218.)

Extract A. from *From Vienna to Versailles* by L.C.B. Seaman (pages 29–31)

'The results of the war, like its causes, are both Turkish and European; but in the main the European consequences are the more important. As far as the Near East was concerned, the Treaty of Paris was merely an elaborate pretence that the Allies had achieved aims which the limited character of the war had prevented them from achieving in reality. To assert that Turkey was a fully sovereign state which was capable of reform, and in whose affairs no other state had a right to interfere, was to pretend that fiction was fact. The Black Sea clauses could not be maintained unless England and France were prepared to renew war the moment Russia felt strong enough to ignore them. These clauses constituted an intolerable affront to Russia, and may be said to have added to the meaningless assertion that Turkey was a fully sovereign power the untenable assertion that Russia was not.

The Treaty of Paris looked like a defeat of Russia by Europe. But by 1856 Europe in the sense of a comity of nations had ceased to exist (which adds piquancy to the fact that it was at this precise moment that Turkey was ceremoniously admitted to it). Austria was on bad terms with England and France because of her equivocal behaviour during the war, and at the Congress found herself gratuitously insulted by the presence of Sardinia and by the patronage of that anti-Austrian state by Austria's presumed allies. And the Anglo-French alliance which had started the war, and which alone could have kept the peace treaty, had ceased to exist before the Congress of Paris had dispersed.

The temporary elimination of Russia elevated Napoleon III to a position of primacy in Europe, and that in itself endangered his alliance with England since the English had certainly not gone to war for the greater glory of Napoleon III. Worse still, the Emperor had already begun overtures to the new Czar, since he now decided that Russia was the only remaining European power worth wooing should he feel inclined at any time to take steps to remould the Italian peninsula. Accordingly he joined forces with the Russians as a patron of the movement for an independent Roumania, a step which the English regarded with the utmost hostility. From the French point of view the Crimean War first secured, but then broke, the Anglo-French alliance on which Napoleon III's international influence ultimately depended. The war raised Napoleon III to a height from which, since he could never sit still, he could only henceforth decline.

If England and Fance were at variance with each other and both were hostile to Austria, the old Holy Alliance was in ruins. Austria was now alone. The old unity-in-inaction with Russia over the Eastern Question having been ended, the situation Metternich had foreseen had at last arrived. Revolution was to break out in the West in new and menacing forms. In Italy a new and more resolute nationalism now arose, armed by Napoleon III and given intelligence by Cavour; and in Germany, Prussia, at long last, after two generations of coma, grasped the opportunities for conquest she had ignored since 1815. Against all this, an isolated Austria could do nothing but blunder from disaster to disaster, while Alexander II stood aside, determined not to repeat the follies of John Sobieski or Nicholas I, both of whom had saved Vienna and gained nothing but ingratitude in return.

The most important clauses of the Treaty of Paris were thus secret ones, unguessed at by the signatories. They provided free and unfettered opportunity for the destruction of Austrian power in Germany and Italy to those who had the courage to act upon them. Bismarck and Cavour were the chief beneficiaries of the Crimean War, and without it there might have been neither a Kingdom of Italy nor a German Empire. Not 1848, but the Peace of Paris, ends the Metternich era, for only with the Crimean War do those political upheavals become possible which Metternich had so long hoped to postpone.'

Extract B. from *Success in European History 1815–1941* by Jack Watson (page 135)

'The most important clause of the Treaty was perhaps that neutralizing the Black Sea. It was repudiated by Alexander II when Europe was occupied with the Franco-Prussian War in 1870. Other parts of the Treaty crumbled rapidly too. In 1862 Wallachia and Moldavia united to become Roumania, and fifteen years later they shook off the last remaining authority of the Sultan. The Sultan for his part showed very little "solicitude for the welfare of his subjects" and, by 1875, there was a new explosion in his Empire. It was a fundamental weakness of the Treaty of Paris that no one had been left with the right to protect Turkey's Christians, the very issue on which the war had begun. Indeed, the peacemakers had specifically rejected the right to interfere in Turkey's internal affairs. The Crimean War and the Treaty of Paris were therefore merely milestones along the dreary road to the settlement of the Eastern Question. Almost nothing had been settled. The Western powers were satisfied that a setback had been administered to the ambitions of the Russians, but the biggest setback was that which had been administered, unwittingly, to the unfortunate subjects of the Ottoman Empire. Even if the intentions of Abdul Mejid were good, a new Sultan came to power in 1861, Abdul Aziz, who combined great extravagance with the traditional Turkish inability to control brutal regional officials.'

2 The Second Empire in France

(a) The Establishment of the Empire
When the Second Empire was proclaimed by Louis Napoleon in December 1852, it inherited the constitution which he had drawn up earlier in the year (*see page 150*), and this was now retained when he

became Emperor instead of President. Its purpose was to give expression in political terms to the Napoleonic Legend (*see page 79*). Though this had played little part in his rise to power, it had always exercised a strong influence upon him since he heard about it from his mother, and he believed that he must remain faithful to it. He never doubted the Legend, and his writings showed how completely he was dominated by it. Now that he had obtained political power, he felt himself bound to put into effect its political ideas, which were essentially those of eighteenth-century rationalism.

The First Empire, as Geoffrey Bruun has shown in *Europe and the French Imperium 1799–1814*, was justified by the Bonapartists in these terms. Its ruler was represented as the supreme, beneficent lawgiver, who sought to give the state stability and, therefore, liberty as well, since liberty was dependent upon order. In his official propaganda, while he was Emperor and later in the *Mémorial de Sainte-Hélène*, Napoleon himself had wished to be represented, not as a military dictator, who had been brought into power by war and reaction, but rather as an outstanding example of the eighteenth-century conception of the Enlightened Despot, whose absolute authority was justified by his concern for the welfare of his subjects and his rational use of government to uphold their true freedom and happiness (*see page 44*). His attempt to put this into effect had unfortunately been interrupted by his defeat and downfall (so he and the Bonapartists asserted). Now the Bonapartists put forward the political system of the Consulate and First Empire as the most desirable form of government for France where there was no tradition (as in Britain) of parliamentary supremacy, but rather the general acceptance of the need for a strong executive acting independently of the legislature.

The July Revolution of 1830 in France had convinced Louis Napoleon that this was the true solution for the country's political problems. It showed that the country was still caught in the vicious circle of revolution and reaction which had begun in the time of Louis XVI. Violent revolutions and changes of regimes had not brought about political progress, but merely created new difficulties and prepared the way for confusion and uncertainty. 'There can be no doubt', he wrote in 1832, 'that what is now wanted are immutable laws which shall ensure the permanent well-being and liberty of the country'; and he asserted that the accomplishment of this 'requires a strong hand'. It demanded gradual reform, moving forward from order to liberty and from a representative form of government to full democracy.

The only aspects of French life where there had been stability since 1815 were, he insisted, where his uncle's administrative institutions had survived, and he argued that France could only hope to gain complete national stability by adopting also the Napoleonic system of government. 'Since France has only maintained herself in the past 50 years by means of the administrative, military, judicial, religious and financial organization provided by the Consulate and Empire, why should we not adopt the political institutions of that period?' he asked. And although the constitution of 1852 opened with an unhesitating guarantee of the principles of 1789, it really expressed the ideas of the Consulate and First Empire. Napoleon III could control the armed forces, make war and treaties, appoint ministers and important officials, initiate legislation and issue the decrees for its execution. The separation of powers, which had marked the Second Republic, was reversed. The executive, headed by the Emperor, was made supreme, and he claimed that this was 'the only structure capable later of supporting a wise and beneficent liberty.'

As in the First Empire, constitutional supremacy depended upon centralized administration. He relied very much upon the prefects, the officials first appointed in 1800 by Napoleon I to control all public administrators and district authorities in the local departments. Under the Second Empire, their powers were increased more than ever before, and they were paid better salaries. They were expected to be not merely administrative officials but political agents as well. They joined with the parish priests in assisting the peasants to vote for Bonapartist candidates in the elections for the Legislative Chamber; they held official banquets and balls for the nobility; and they plied the middle classes with jobs and contracts. In fact, they helped the Emperor to succeed in achieving the popular support which he considered vital when he wrote, 'When one bears our name and when one is at the head of the government, there are two things one must do: satisfy the interests of the most numerous classes and attach oneself to the upper classes.' It was largely through the activities of the prefects that the Second Empire was later recalled in popular memory as the wonderful time when people played games with golden coins.

That Napoleon immediately succeeded in his aim was shown in the first elections for the Legislative Chamber held in 1852. Five-sixths of the official candidates were returned and only six opposition candidates of whom four were Republicans. There were no further risings against him, and of those who had been imprisoned or deported in 1852, all who were prepared to accept the existing government were released by 1856. He did not have to destroy his opponents; he had won over most of them at the outset.

(b) The Splendid Years

For the first ten years of its existence, indeed, the Second Empire gained wide and growing acceptance in France. In the first elections to the Legislative Chamber just more than 84 per cent of the over 6 million voters had supported the government, and this remained almost the same in the next elections in 1857. The republican movement, though retaining working-class support in the towns and industrial areas, was crippled because its leaders were either in exile or silenced. The royalist opposition was divided between Bourbons and Orleanists, and while many of the nobility despised the new, upstart regime, others came to welcome its strength and stability and were ready to come to the Imperial court. The Church was favoured by the Emperor, who shared his uncle's estimation of the social and political influence of religion — the French garrison, sent to protect the Pope in 1849, was maintained in Rome (*see page 147*), and the religious orders were allowed to take a greater part in education. The army was also favoured—its pay was increased, it enjoyed the prestige of military ceremonies and reviews, and, still more, it was engaged in frequent colonial campaigns and two foreign wars in the Crimea and Italy which brought promotion and decorations (*see pages, 208, 230, 231*). The middle class enjoyed the prosperity of these years without fear of social agitation. Above all, the most numerous part of the population, the peasants, were (as Louis Napoleon said) indifferent to politics, not caring whether there were one or two parliaments in Paris or none at all, but ready to support the government which provided roads and wells, schools and hospitals, for the countryside. This was a practical reason why he insisted upon universal suffrage in the elections and plebiscites held during his reign. 'In this system,' he said, 'the conservative rural population can vote down the liberals in the cities.'

In *Des Idées Napoléoniennes*, Louis Napoleon had asserted that the Napoleonic idea was a social, commercial, industrial and humanitarian ideal, and his policy has been associated with the beliefs of Saint-Simon (*see page 83*). A contemporary called him 'Saint-Simon on horseback,' and there were Saint-Simonians who accepted him as one of their number, but it is doubtful whether he had really studied Saint-Simon's teaching. His notions did not include any extensive planning or re-organization of the economy on socialist or other lines. He accepted the liberal laissez-faire outlook which was widely adopted at the time (*see page 380*). He supported, for instance, the general movement in favour of free trade and negotiated a commercial treaty with Britain in 1860, which was followed by similar treaties with ten other European states; these all arranged for the reciprocal reduction of tariffs. Generally, however, he did not think beyond programmes of public works, which would encourage public support for his rule. And here again he believed that this policy was in accordance with the Napoleonic legend. He wrote of his uncle, 'The public works, which the Emperor put into operation into such a large scale, were not only one of the principal causes of domestic prosperity, they even promoted great social progress.'

His aim was essentially to secure sufficient employment and prosperity to make the people content. This did not mean that he was particularly concerned with the promotion of French industrialization; and the economic condition of the country did not greatly change under Napoleon. It remained very much as it had been in the days of the July Monarchy (*see page 81*). The proportion of the population engaged in agriculture only fell from three-quarters to two-thirds between 1848 and 1870. French industry continued to be organized in small family

225

businesses and the land to be divided mainly between peasant landowners. The prosperity of the period still largely came about because the population ceased to grow so rapidly. The comparatively modest increase in industrial production was sufficient to raise the national standard of living.

Napoleon III's most important public works were in connection with the promotion of railways. In Louis Philippe's reign, railway development had been inadequate and haphazard and interrupted by a financial collapse which had been one of the causes of the depression in the winter of 1847–48 (*see page 8*). The political disturbances during the Second Republic prevented any recovery, and in 1850 France had a small length of railway track compared with both Britain and Germany (*see Table 6, page 82*). Napoleon intervened to promote more rapid expansion, amalgamating the several undertakings into six great companies, granting land concessions to them for building new lines and facilitating the provision of capital by financiers and bankers. These measures were so successful that France nearly trebled her railway construction between 1851 and 1859 and increased her total length of track by nearly sixfold in 1870 (*see Table 6, page 82*). The development of the railways stimulated the production of coal, iron and steel, and these industries, though not as flourishing as those of Britain and Germany, began to increase their production more rapidly than before (*see Table 7, page 82*). Napoleon naturally wished his regime to get the credit for the policy, and during the first years of his reign it was said that he never visited a town without ceremonially opening a railway station there.

The most striking of his public undertakings was the continuation of Napoleon I's work in the rebuilding of a large part of Paris under the direction of Baron Haussmann, the financier and planner of German descent, who was appointed Prefect of the Seine in 1853 to accomplish this task. The old medieval city was replaced by that of today. Some 20 000 houses were demolished, and the twisting narrow streets, across which revolutionaries in 1830 and 1848 had erected barricades and defiantly flung paving-stones to defend themselves, were replaced by 135 kilometres of wide, straight, tarmac-surfaced boulevards lined with impressive buildings and trees. A new lavish and luxurious Opera House was built. The old project of joining the palaces of the Louvre and the Tuilleries was revived. More building was done on them in five years than in the previous seven centuries, and the grand design, conceived in the sixteenth century, was completed in a rich baroque style. It is true that behind the rebuilt city the poor still lived in the slums of the decaying suburbs without adequate sanitation or transport; but the changes had the political result of providing work for those evicted from the National Workshops, facilitating the repression of disorder and, above all, making the city a wealthy and splendid capital for the Second Empire.

The Emperor wished the new Paris to be a centre of European

fashion and culture and also of the pleasures for which he himself had acquired a taste during his years of exile. And he succeeded, though within the limitations of the taste and outlook of himself and the upper classes. The great shopping centres offered stylish clothes, magnificent jewellery and other expensive luxuries. The opera was splendid, yet musically old-fashioned, and the originality of Berlioz was over-shadowed by the facile, sentimental Gounod and the light-handed Bizet. The annual art exhibitions displayed the works of the popular, orthodox painters, but not those of the controversial Impressionists. Perhaps the greatest attractions were the can-can, the Folies Bergère and Offenbach's *La Vie Parisienne* (1866) and other light-hearted operettas. Crowds came also, however, to the exhibitions held in 1855 and 1867 to emphasize the claims of the Empire and its capital to excel in the social and economic activities of the century.

Upon becoming Emperor, Louis Napoleon realized that he must have an Empress and a suitable heir to perpetuate his dynasty. The existing heir presumptive was his cousin, Jerome Napoleon (*see Diagram 5, page 146*), who was a republican and an atheist. But none of the old royal families of Europe wished to be united with Napoleon III, who was descended from the minor Corsican nobility. While the marriage negotiations were proceeding unsuccessfully, he fell in love with Eugénie de Montijo, the daughter of a Spanish nobleman, and married her in January 1853. After several miscarriages, she eventually bore him a son in 1856, when the peace conference was meeting in Paris at the end of the Crimean War. The young Prince Imperial was baptized in Notre Dame, and the continuity of the Bonapartist line seemed assured.

Nor was this Eugénie's only contribution to the stability of the imperial regime. She was neither intelligent nor politically well-informed, and later she gained a strong personal influence over her husband which she always exercised in favour of firm absolutism and the claims of Roman Catholicism at home and abroad. But she was strikingly good-looking—tall, elegant with a marvellous complexion —and had perfect taste in dress. In the early days of the Empire she embellished the brilliant court in Paris with her beauty and gave it a dignity which the Emperor lacked. When the Imperial couple visited Queen Victoria in 1855, she brought the first crinoline to England, and there were those who wished that the less exciting English court were more like the French court, but Bagehot understood that Napoleon realized that his court did not perform the same purpose as its counterpart across the Channel. Bagehot pointed out that the Emperor represented a different idea from the Queen. Victoria was 'but the head of an unequal, competing, aristocratic society,' and her 'guarded and retired' court discouraged and mitigated the desire for social distinction and ostentation among her subjects. Napoleon, however, embodied the French principle of equality, and the more magnificent his court be-came, the more equal his subjects were made to appear—'he is magnified that others may be dwarfed.' It was not always easy for the revived court at the Tuilleries to be made splendid. The royal gold and silver plate had disappeared in 1848, and Napoleon was compelled by reasons of cost to replace most of it by the new system of electro-plating; but between them the Emperor and the Empress were able to establish it as a symbol of the splendour and elegance of the era which was welcome to Frenchmen after the middle-class dullness of Louis Philippe's household.

(c) The Failure of Foreign Policy

During the years when Napoleon III was consolidating his position in France in such a spectacular manner, his foreign policy was marked by some success, but mainly by frustration and disappointment. As might be expected, he was hostile to the Vienna Settlement, which had re-arranged his uncle's plans for Europe, but he lacked Napoleon I's military ardour and ruthlessness to attempt to undo the Treaty by war and conquest. He proclaimed, *'L'Empire, c'est la paix,'* and he wished to change the international situation peacefully by diplomatic means, often expressing the hope that there could be 'a general congress of the great powers of Europe' to do this. He had a sincere sympathy with contemporary nationalism and appreciated its increasing importance. His uncle had written in St. Helena that 'the first ruler who calls upon the peoples of Europe will be able to accomplish anything he wishes,' and he thought that somehow support for the growing strength of European nationalism would favour French interests and restore the nation's leadership on the Continent. Particularly he envisaged the creation of states in northern Italy and southern Germany dependent for their existence upon France. At the same time, he considered that Napoleon I's greatest mistake had been to antagonize Britain, so he intended to achieve his aims without arousing British hostility and risking perilous international incidents. Yet his foreign policy was dangerously inconsistent. His idealism conflicted with his de-termination to forward French interests. He was subjected to opposing advice from his ministers and personal hesitations and vacillations. His desire for European conferences was undermined by his liking for conspiracy and secret diplomacy. All this meant, as A.J.P. Taylor has observed, that despite his pacific nature, his policies contributed to the outbreak of the wars of the 1850s and 1860s.

Within two years of the proclamation of the Second Empire, Napoleon III was involved in the Crimean War (*see page 207*). At first it seemed as if this were a successful venture for him. The war was fought jointly with Britain and brought France much diplomatic prestige, but in the end it did not make her dominant in Europe and cost her the valued British alliance. However, at the time he was pleased with the outcome of the war because he believed that it was now possible for him to proceed with his plans to revise the Vienna Settlement, promote European nationalism and extend French influence. This was to be the essential factor in the momentous changes which took place in Europe during the third quarter of the nineteenth century, but events did not turn out as he planned, and others reaped the benefit of his revolutionary foreign policy.

He made his first move in Italy. He had probably thought of intervening there from the time he became President in 1848. His uncle had conducted his first victorious campaign in the peninsula, and he himself had enlisted in the rebel forces fighting in the Papal States in 1831 (*see page 145*). An Italian adventure involved a combination of idealism and plotting that appealed to him. Assisting Italian nationalism against Austrian predominance in the peninsula would reverse an important part of the Vienna Settlement and bring him increased prestige and influence at little risk. British public opinion was sympathetic towards Italian nationalism, while Austria was isolated through her neutrality during the Crimean War.

The impulse for the venture came when a bomb was thrown at the carriage of Napoleon and Eugénie as they drove to the Opera House in Paris in January 1858. Neither of them was hurt, but several bystanders were killed. The assassin, Felice Orsini, was an Italian republican follower of Mazzini. Napoleon interpreted the incident as destiny and exploited it to suit his policy. Orsini was executed, but the French press was allowed to publish his last letter, which was an appeal to Napoleon to help in the liberation of Italy.

The next step was to arrange a secret conference at the spa of Plombières-les-Bains in the Vosges, where he was taking the waters, in July 1858 with Cavour, who was ready to take advantage of the Emperor's ambitions (*see page 265*). The two conspirators did not sign any agreement there, but made definite plans. They proposed that France and Piedmont should fight Austria to secure Lombardy and Venetia and the northern Duchies for Piedmont, who would in return cede to France the French-speaking areas of Savoy and Nice, which the French Republic had claimed in 1792 and the First Treaty of Paris had assigned to France in 1814. Napoleon also secured the marriage of Victor Emmanuel's daughter, Clothilde, to his cousin, Jerome Napoleon.

He did not intend to promote Italian unification by helping Piedmont to gain the whole of the peninsula. This would have abolished the temporal power of the Papacy, so alienating Roman Catholic sympathy in France and inaugurating a dangerously strong state on France's border. Rather, mindful of his uncle's policy, he intended that the influence of an enlarged Piedmont would be balanced by the continued existence of Tuscany, the Papal States and the Kingdom of Naples, and he hoped that all four might be united in a confederation presided over by the Pope. His plan, besides bringing France territory, would put her in Austria's position in Italy and help her to become supreme in the Mediterranean, while he secured for the Bonapartist family a marriage alliance with one of the oldest reigning houses in Europe and could pose as the liberator of the Italians from the Habsburgs and the champion of European nationalism.

By massing troops near the border with Lombardy, Cavour provoked Austria into declaring war against Piedmont, and Napoleon came to his assistance in 1859. He went with his army to the plains of Lombardy, where his uncle had established his military reputation in 1796, but his staff officers were dismayed to find that he could not read a map. As in the Crimea, the superiority of the new French artillery prevailed. After six weeks of fighting, the Austrians were defeated at Magenta and Solferino and driven from Lombardy. The French and Piedmontese armies were about to invade Venetia when Napoleon suddenly made an armistice with Austria and began peace negotiations.

Events had alarmed him. Successful revolutionary movements in the smaller Italian states were now demanding union with Piedmont (*see page 226*). A revolt in the Papal province of the Romagna alarmed the French clericals. Prussia was assembling troops on the Rhine, and the limited trained military reserves at Napoleon's disposal (no more than 74 000 men) made it risky to face the possibility of another war there at the same time as the campaign in northern Italy, particularly as the Austrian forces had safely withdrawn to the redoubtable fortresses of the Quadrilateral (*see Map 8, page 113*). In addition, the bloodshed at Magenta and Solferino had been greater than he expected. The railways were inadequate for military needs. The Piedmontese army was lacking in both armaments and fighting ability. Indeed, the French had done all the fighting and suffered all the casualties at Magenta because the Piedmontese had arrived too late for the battle. Altogether the French had supplied twice as many troops for the campaign and lost twice as many dead or injured as the Piedmontese. There was little chance of the Piedmontese raising a sufficient force to attack the Quadrilateral. A long and costly war might ensue for France, which would probably not be acceptable to French public opinion. Napoleon judged it advisable to end hostilities quickly.

By the Treaty of Villafranca, signed between Napoleon and Francis Joseph in July 1859, Austria ceded Lombardy to Piedmont, but kept Venetia. The rulers were restored to those Italian states which had revolted, but within little more than a year Piedmont obtained the rest of the peninsula except the city of Rome, where the French garrison continued to uphold papal authority (*see page 269*). In return for recognizing these territorial changes, Napoleon after all secured Savoy and Nice for France in March 1860, and the wedding between Prince Jerome and Princess Clothilde had already taken place in the Chapel Royal in Turin.

The French army, when it returned from Italy and marched into Paris after the campaign, received an overwhelming reception. Napoleon's effigy on French coins was now crowned with laurels, and he proclaimed in celebration a general amnesty to all political exiles. Not only had France and the dynasty made gains, but he had, though more extensively than he intended, finally overthrown the Vienna Settlement in Italy. Austrian power had been eliminated over most of the peninsula, and the frail princely states which had depended upon it for their existence were merged into a Kingdom of Italy. But the gains were made at a high cost. Napoleon was the real maker of Italian unification, but his unwitting promotion of the cause had not brought him the gratitude of the new kingdom, which resented being deprived of both Venetia and Rome. France had lost and not gained influence in Italy. Britain's mistrust of him had increased, even though the British government welcomed the formation of the Italian state, hoping to have it as an ally in the Mediterranean. The French liberals were further alienated by Napoleon's desertion of Italian nationalism, while the continuance of the garrison in Rome did not compensate the clerical party for the disappearance of the Papal States. The Italian adventure had not strengthened the French Empire either at home or abroad. Napoleon had avoided another costly conflict, but again he had not achieved the purpose of his plan.

He had at least been able to choose the time for his Italian venture, but the outbreak of the Polish revolt in 1863 came at an awkward moment for him and placed him in a very difficult situation. He wanted Russian acquiescence in his European schemes, but he would have liked to have supported the cause of Polish nationalism and so have conciliated both liberal and clerical opinion in France. He alienated Alexander II by protesting against the suppression of the Poles. He received some British support, but both he and Palmerston knew that they could not fight for the Poles, while Prussia, which had many Polish subjects, massed troops on the Polish frontier and supported the Tsar (*see page 247*). The episode gained him Russian hostility, and British opinion suspected him of wishing to set up a French-dominated Polish state.

Meanwhile, he had at first enjoyed considerable success overseas. The conquest of Algeria was completed, and by 1860 some 290 000 Europeans had settled there. Further south, the coast of Guinea and Dahomey was occupied, and the port of Dakar was founded in 1857 to open up the interior of Senegal. In the Far East, Saigon was captured in 1859, and Cambodia was declared a protectorate in 1862 (*see pages 357, 359, 364*). Most spectacular was the opening by the Empress in 1869 of the Suez Canal, which had been constructed by a French company under Ferdinand de Lesseps and involved the first large-scale use of 10 000 horsepower mechanical excavators and other machines.

Unfortunately for Napoleon, these achievements aroused little interest in France and were all overshadowed by his grandiose and disastrous Mexican adventure. In 1861 the Mexican Republic ceased to pay the interest on its foreign loans. Britain, France and Spain sent a joint expedition there, which secured a resumption of the defaulted payments. Britain and Spain then withdrew their troops, but Napoleon kept the French contingent in the country, and in 1863 he persuaded the Archduke Maximilian, a brother of the Emperor of Austria, to come there with the title of Emperor of Mexico. Napoleon's imagination was stirred by the idea of establishing a powerful centre of Latin culture in this part of the New World; he hoped also to please the French clericals since the Mexican republicans were secularists. And as he was not alone in thinking that the Civil War, then distracting the United States, would result in the permanent dissolution of the Union, he was confident that French influence could now prevail in Central and South America. The French troops in Mexico found it more difficult than had been expected to assert their authority, and in 1865, when the Civil War ended, the victorious United States government declared the French intervention to be an infringement of the Monroe Doctrine (see page 232). Nevertheless, Napoleon maintained his troops there until February 1867, when the growing military strength of Prussia compelled their withdrawal. Maximilian stayed on to be shot by the Mexicans later that year, and his Empress lost her reason. Once again Napoleon's ambitious scheming had proved disastrously inadequate to the situation. His reputation never recovered from the episode.

(d) The Liberal Empire
In 1859 and 1860 Napoleon began to move towards the establishment of the Liberal Empire by which he intended to 'crown order with liberty' and reconcile 'men of good will' to his regime. He had always said that the time would come when he would relinquish some of his authority and seek the widest possible support for his rule from Frenchmen. By then the omens for doing this were not entirely good. He was losing popularity with some groups in the country, particularly the clericals (who mistrusted his foreign policy) and businessmen (who suffered from his free-trade treaties). Yet the elections of 1857 returned to the Legislative Chamber, amid the irresistible number of government supporters, only five Republicans, and they acted constitutionally in opposition and whole-heartedly supported the Italian campaign of 1859. Napoleon, therefore, felt strong enough on the whole to modify his autocratic position. Also, as a result of his advancing age and illness, he wished to provide the Empire with constitutional institutions that would enable it to continue under his son when his personal rule ended with his death.

Having issued the general amnesty of 1859, the next year he took the first step towards liberalizing the Empire by allowing the Senate and the Legislative Chamber to criticize the government by being able to vote a reply to the Emperor's address at the beginning of each session and to publish the record of their debates. This measure increased the influence of the opposition, but in the elections of 1863, though the Republicans increased their representation in Paris and a few large towns where industrial expansion had added to the number of working-class voters, the government still gained an overwhelming majority in the Legislative Chamber. The opposition never had any chance of overthrowing the regime, which was, indeed, so stable that it passed through the disasters of its foreign policy without losing the support of the French people.

Napoleon was encouraged to continue with his reforms. In 1864 the working class were given the right to strike. In 1867 both Houses were allowed to question ministers, and the Senate was given a suspensive veto over laws passed by the Legislative Chamber. And in 1868 the censorship of the press was abolished. The elections of 1869 gave the Republicans many of the larger cities, and they now had 30 members in the Legislative Chamber. Nevertheless, the government was still completely in control, and Napoleon continued his reforms.

Later that year, the Legislative Chamber was given the right to initiate legislation and control the government's policy by granting or refusing taxes. In May 1870 all the changes that had been introduced since 1860 were submitted to a plebiscite and approved by almost as many votes as had been cast for the original constitution 18 years previously. In London, *Punch* published a cartoon which showed France granting the Emperor and his son a new lease as tenants of the throne; and the Republican leaders admitted tht the Empire was still secure. 'More than ever before,' said Napoleon that month, 'we can look forward to the future without fear.'

1860	Senate and Legislative Chamber to reply to the Emperor's address and to publish their debates.
1864	Strikes made legal.
1867	Senate able to suspend laws passed by the Legislative Chamber.
1868	Censorship of the press abolished.
1869	Legislative Chamber to initiate laws and grant or refuse taxes to the government.

Table 11. The Liberal Empire (1860–1870)

Yet already the liberalizing of the Empire had begun to contribute towards its downfall which took place so soon after its hour of triumph. Greater freedom of expression made French opinion more vocal. The removal of the censorship of the press, for instance, led to the publication of 150 more newspapers, and many of them were hostile to the government. Napoleon had to take notice of this development, but since his physical strength was now being sapped by an increasingly painful kidney disease, his ability to take an independent stand and his control over political events were seriously weakened. This concerned most notably the grave issue of national defence.

During the 1860s some of his advisers warned him of the weakness of the French army. This went back to its re-establishment after the Bourbon restoration. Liberals then wanted conscription for reasons of democracy and equality, but conservative, middle-class opinion opposed total conscription of the Prussian model of 1814, while military ideas generally favoured a long-term, professional army. The system adopted provided for conscription to the extent of supplementing recruitment by voluntary enlistment. Each year the required number of conscripts was obtained by ballot, but anyone selected could pay for another man to serve instead of him. The Italian campaign of 1859 showed that the system did not provide a sufficient reserve of trained manpower (*see page 230*), and in the 1860s the disparity between the reserves of the French and Prussian armies steadily increased. Napoleon wished to remedy this, but his efforts were frustrated by widespread opposition in France. At the same time, national indignation against Prussia drove him in 1870 into a war, which he did not think necessary and did not want, and into defeat made inevitable by Prussian military supremacy at the outset of hostilities.

(e) The End of the Empire
In the early 1860s, Napoleon was sympathetic towards Prussia. He welcomed the idea of a Prussian dominated northern Germany. He hoped to have her as a strong ally and did not see any reason to fear her. Her power would be balanced by the Austrian Empire and the southern German states with whom he wished to establish the same French connection as with Piedmont in northern Italy. He displayed his sympathy for Prussia during the Schleswig-Holstein crisis of 1864 (*see page 247*). Bismarck's resort to force here angered and alarmed Britain, but only the French army could have intervened on behalf of Denmark, and Napoleon had no intention of taking such action. Bismarck urged a war of national liberation, and he could not oppose that. He particularly wanted Prussian friendship then. Britain and Russia were estranged from him. He was involved in his Mexican adventure and wished somehow to obtain Venetia peacefully for Italy from Austria. If he aroused Prussian hostility, he would be alone in Europe.

When Prussia and Austria quarrelled after the Danish War, Napoleon thought it was 'a stroke of luck which it seemed would never arise.' It might result in the elimination of Habsburg influence in Germany, which French policy had long wished to achieve. In October 1865 Napoleon met Bismarck at Biarritz (*see page 249*). Since Napoleon kept no record of the conversation, and Bismarck's report is brief and vague, what took place there has inevitably been a matter for conjecture. It is likely, however, that both men wished to keep the future open rather than to make any commitments. If any idea was expressed that France might receive territory on the Rhine or in Belgium in return for her neutrality during a war between Austria and Prussia, it must have been in indefinite terms. What Napoleon was interested in was that Italy should have Venetia; and Bismarck readily agreed to this to be sure of French neutrality. Napoleon expected (as did many others) that a war between Austria and Prussia would be protracted and likely to end in a stalemate, enabling a neutral France to mediate on her own terms.

When the war came in 1866, the rapid, overwhelming Prussian victory over Austria deprived Napoleon of any opportunity to influence its outcome (*see page 248*). He offered to arbitrate, but Bismarck was by then already making peace; and yet he considered that the Treaty of Prague benefited France. A friendly Prussia had destroyed Austrian supremacy in Germany, and the southern German states were left free to strengthen their traditional links with France. Moreover, he considered that the establishment of the North German Confederation and the liberation of Venetia were both to be welcomed as triumphs for the principle of neutrality. His devotion to the Napoleonic Legend had by now brought an air of dangerous unreality into his policy.

The Prussian victory did, however, underline the need for reforming the French army which he had already wanted to undertake. After the Battle of Sadowa, Prussia called up about 100 000 conscripts each year, while France drafted only 56 000. Napoleon wished to abolish the considerable exemptions in the French system to enable the army to receive 160 000 men a year. There was an immediate outcry in the press, and the prefects reported on the unpopularity of the plan. Liberals and republicans held that a larger army would strengthen the Imperial regime; the professional officers did not want such a dilution of their regiments; and the Legislative Chamber did not like having to find money for it. Most French people believed that their army was strong enough without making such unwelcome changes. Nothing was done until, after nearly two years of acrimonious discussion, an army law in 1868 proposed to increase the size of the reserve and set up a new, part-time militia. The only satisfactory step taken to make the army more effective was the adoption of the *chassepot* rifle in imitation of the Prussian breechloading 'needle-gun', which had been so deadly at Sadowa. Public opinion trusted that this would suffice, but even the Legislative Chamber did not vote enough money to enable the army to be equipped properly with it. And Napoleon himself had to finance the *mitrailleuse*, an early version of the machine-gun, when he attempted to introduce it into the army.

Meanwhile, most Frenchmen did not agree with Napoleon's optimistic assessment of Prussia's triumph over Austria. The news of the Battle of Sadowa astonished and alarmed them. They saw it as a vivid revelation of the military strength and aggressive intentions of Prussia, which went on to annex several territories in northern Germany and add 4 million to her population, while France gained nothing and was faced across the Rhine with a serious rival to her position in Europe. National pride was humiliated; the clericals were outraged by the triumph of a Protestant power; and even some generals were alarmed. The opposition politicians were able to exploit the situation in order to discredit Napoleon. He was driven reluctantly to make diplomatic efforts to secure territorial compensation for France. Bismarck not only refused to accept his demands, scorning them as a 'hotel-keeper's bill', but he was able to turn them to good account. When Napoleon sought to get parts of Belgium, Britain was informed. When he sought the Palatinate on the Upper Rhine, the southern German states were informed, and they entered into an alliance with Prussia. Bismarck even denied him Luxemburg. He had placed his greatest hopes upon obtaining this, now that the German Confederation was dissolved, but Bismarck would only agree to the evacuation of the Prussian garrison from the city of Luxemburg in return for its neutralization.

This was the situation in 1870 when the Hohenzollern crisis arose and hurried France into the Franco-Prussian War (*see page 252*). This time Napoleon was driven into war by his own supporters, who wanted to take advantage of the national feeling against Prussia. The Imperialists, resenting the concessions made to liberalism and the criticisims of the opposition, were determined that the regime's prestige should be asserted abroad. Napoleon was unable to resist the war-fever that seized his Empress and his court, his ministers and his majority in the Legislative Chamber. They had no doubt of a French triumph. France had been victorious in every European campaign in which it had taken part since 1815. They expected Prussia to be as soundly defeated as she had been at Jena by Napoleon I in 1806. So the Empire was hurried to its destruction by a final, fatal outburst of unreality. France entered the war with no allies and an ill-prepared army. Within two months, French resistance evaporated, and Napoleon himself was taken prisoner by the Prussians after the Battle of Sedan. Paris endured four months of siege and bombardment, hunger and cold, before capitulating in 1871. An armistice followed, and the Treaty of Frankfurt compelled France to cede Alsace and eastern Lorraine to Germany, pay an indemnity of 5000 million gold francs and support a German army of occupation until this was paid. The Empress Eugénie and her son had already fled to England; they were now joined by Napoleon, who died there in 1873 (*see Map 14, page 254*).

The Franco-Prussian War brought the Second Empire to an end. Other regimes have survived the defeat of a sovereign in battle, but for Napoleon III, whose popularity had been upheld earlier in the year by the plebiscite, downfall was immediate. The main reason for this probably lay in the nature of the Empire itself. A single man created it and directed it almost alone. There were no great figures among his ministers. His conspiratorial nature and devotion to the Napoleonic Legend made him unwilling to share power with others. As long as most Frenchmen were satisfied with the Empire, he enjoyed the full credit for it, but when it went down in military defeat, he suffered immediate condemnation for the disaster.

Napoleon's reputation suffered beyond his lifetime. Marx said that the comparison between the First and Second Empires showed that history repeats itself, first as a tragedy and then as a farce. And Victor Hugo's description of him in 1852 as '*Napoléon le Petit*' was long accepted as accurate by historians. He was a pale imitation of his great uncle. His rule was regarded as a period of disastrous tyranny for

France. Nowadays, however, it is being realized that, despite his weaknesses, he does not deserve such wholesale condemnation. The nature of the Liberal Empire is being better understood. J.A.S. Grenville has called it 'one of the more hopeful and successful periods of French history.' It is seen as an enlightened attempt to solve the political problems which had troubled France since the fall of the *ancien régime*. If he had not been drawn into conflict with Bismarck, he might have been, as Theodore Zeldin has suggested, equally as successful in politics as his uncle was in war and administration.

1808	Birth of Louis Napoleon in Paris.
1811	Birth of the Duke of Reichstadt (Napoleon II).
1815	Defeat of Napoleon I. Hortense and her children exiled.
1817–30	Louis Napoleon educated at Augsburg and Thun.
1821	Death of Napoleon I.
1831	Louis Napoleon joins Italian rising. Death of his elder brother.
1832	Death of the Duke of Reichstadt.
1836	The Strasbourg plot.
1837	Death of Hortense.
1837–40	Louis Napoleon in America and London.
1839	Wrote *Des Idées Napoliennes*.
1840	The Boulogne landing. Louis Napoleon imprisoned at Ham.
1846	Escape from Ham. Settles in London.
1848	President of the French Republic.
1851	*Coup d'état*.
1852	Proclamation of the Empire.
1853	Marriage to Eugénie de Montijo.
1854–56	Crimean War.
1855	The Paris Exhibition.
1856	Congress of Paris. Birth of Prince Imperial.
1858	Orsini's attempt at assassination.
1859	Italian campaign.
1860	Annexation of Nice and Savoy. Commercial treaty with Britain.
1860–70	The Liberal Empire.
1861–67	Mexican adventure.
1867	Second Paris Exhibition.
1870	Franco-Prussian War. End of the Second Empire.
1873	Death of Napoleon III in England.

Table 12. Chronology of Louis Napoleon (1808–1873)

Bibliography
In addition to the general biographies of Louis Napoleon already mentioned (*see page 151*), there are F.A. Simpson, *Louis Napoleon and the Recovery of France, 1848–56* (3rd. edn. Longman, 1951), J.M. Thompson, *Louis Napoleon and the Second Empire* (OUP, 1954), T. Zeldin, *The Political System of Napoleon III* (Macmillan, 1958), Theo Aronson, *The Fall of the Third Napoleon* (Cassell, 1970) and Michael Howard, *The Franco-Prussian War* (Fontana, 1967).

Exercises

A *This section consists of questions that might be used for discussion (or written answers) as a way of expanding on the chapter and testing your understanding of it:*

1 What do you understand by the 'Napoleonic Legend'?
2 What principles underlay Napoleon III's new constitution of 1851?
3 In what way was the 'separation of powers reversed'?
4 Why was Napoleon III so popular in the elections of 1852 and 1857?
5 How is it possible to argue that Napoleon III's economic achievements were extremely limited?
6 Comment on Napoleon III's revival and rebuilding of Paris.
7 Explain Bagehot's distinction between the French and English courts.
8 What guidelines underlay Napoleon III's foreign policy, and why might they be regarded as dangerous?
9 Why did the CrimeanWar cost France an alliance with Britain?
10 What did Napoleon III hope to gain from his involvement in Italy?
11 Why did Napoleon III begin peace negotiations with Austria rather than invade Venetia?
12 Draw up a balance sheet of gains and losses resulting from France's intervention in Italy.
13 Why did Napoleon III not take a more active role in the Polish revolt of 1863?
14 Write a defence of Napoleon's apparently outrageous policy in Mexico.
15 How might it be argued that Napoleon's policy of liberalization was ill-timed?
16 Why was the French army so weak by the late 1860s?
17 Comment on Napoleon's policy towards Bismarck during the Danish and Austrian wars.
18 Why was there such extensive opposition to Napoleon's planned army reforms in the 1860s?
19 Given this opposition to military reforms, explain the extensive support for war against Prussia in 1870.
20 Why did Napoleon flee after France's defeat?

B *Essay questions*

1 'A desperate remedy for a desperate condition.' How fair is this comment on Napoleon III's liberalization of his Empire? (Cambridge, 1981)
2 Napoleon III claimed that the Empire stood for peace. Why then did he involve France in several wars? (SUJB, 1982)
3 Explain the rise of Louis Napoleon to supreme power. Discuss the opinion that until 1860 his policies were mainly successful. (SUJB, 1983)
4 How effectively did Napoleon III solve the problems that had brought about the downfall of the July Monarchy? (Welsh, 1981)
5 How effective a dictator was Napoleon III? (Welsh, 1983)
6 What were Napoleon III's strengths and weaknesses as a statesman? (Oxford and Cambridge, 1983)
7 With what justification may it be argued that the Second French Empire deserved its fate? (AEB, 1982)
8 To what extent can it be argued that, during the Second Empire, France was the most advanced state in continental Europe? (London, 1983)
9 Account for the growth of internal opposition in the last decade of the Second French Empire. (JMB, 1982)

C *Essay writing 6—Balance, Range and Depth*

Having been introduced to the major aspects of essay writing skills in earlier sections, your main task now is to refine and improve upon those skills. Three of the qualities that your writing will most need can be summarised by the terms 'balance', 'range' and 'depth'. To illustrate these qualities, examples have been taken from the last two sections you have studied—the Crimean War and the Second Empire in France.

A balanced essay is one that considers both (or all) sides of an argument or question. Balance is especially important in discussion essays, as a way of ensuring that both 'yes' and 'no' arguments are considered, and in significance essays, to check that the importance of both the aspect(s) highlighted and of other aspects are covered. This seems a very obvious and simple point to make, yet it is surprising how often students ignore it. For example, faced by the question (on a sixteenth century paper): '"Reasonably successful as ruler of Spain and the Netherlands, but a failure as Holy Roman Emperor." Discuss this verdict on Charles V.', one candidate was criticized by the examiners as follows:

'... a good attempt to show that, despite difficulties, Charles' rule in Spain and the Netherlands could be seen as a qualified success. However, there was very little on the Empire (half a sentence on protestantism). ... Thus the candidate had no chance to make the contrast implied in the quotation and the answer was effectively incomplete.'

Study the examples below, and in each case write down the constituent parts that each essay should break down into (the first is done for you as an example).

1 'A desperate remedy for a desperate condition.' How fair is this comment on Napoleon III's liberalization of his Empire?
   This might break down into:
   (a) Consideration of the phrase 'liberalization of his Empire'.
   (b) Arguments to show that the condition of the Empire (i) *was* desperate by 1860 and (ii) was *not* desperate.
   (c) Arguments to show that the remedy of liberalization (i) *was* desperate and (ii) was *not* desperate.
   (d) A conclusion drawing together an answer.
   (Note how, once a title is broken down in this way, it becomes easy to construct an essay plan, as only one or two paragraphs are required on each constituent element.)

2 Discuss the view that the Crimean War was 'unnecessary but nevertheless highly significant'.

3 'He tried hard to emulate the successes and avoid the mistakes of those who had ruled France since 1799.' How far does this explain both the achievements and the failures of Napoleon III?

4 'It was a fumbling, futile war yet rich in unintended consequences.' Discuss this comment on the Crimean War.

As well as balance, it is also important that your essays contain a number, or 'range' of arguments. This is especially true of list essays. It is insufficient to explain three or four reasons why an event took place, or three or four effects that it had. Examiners are looking for candidates who can think of more than that, thereby showing that they have read beyond the basic texts and/or are capable of independent thought. Generally, it is advisable to devise some seven or eight arguments in answer to any question. Thinking through this number of arguments in outline is extremely useful as a revision exercise, and could be rehearsed on the titles below:

5　How were relations between the great powers affected by the Crimean War?
6　Who gained from the Crimean War?
7　Account for the growth of internal opposition in the last decade of the Second French Empire.
8　Why was France easily defeated in the war of 1870–71?
9　How effectively did Napoleon III solve the problems which had brought about the fall of the July Monarchy?

A failure to get sufficient range of arguments into their essays often leads students into the 'narrative trap'. For example, in answer to question 7 above, a student may begin his first three paragraphs as follows (substantiating each opening sentence adequately):

(a) Napoleon III's policy of liberalization in the 1860s facilitated opposition to his regime. . . .
(b) The failure of Napoleon's foreign adventures, culminating in the Mexican fiasco, opened his regime to considerable criticism. . . .
(c) Critics could also point to the skin-deep nature of much of Napoleon's economic programme. . . .

These three paragraphs would have presented perfectly valid answers to the question asked. However, at this point the writer ran out of ideas, having written just over a side in some 20 minutes. What now? In an exam, at least another side to write; at least another 20 minutes to write it in—but what about? At this point, many candidates feel obliged to write something —anything?—as long as it is about Imperial France. So our mythical student may write a political history of France 1852–1870, or an outline of the international crises of the period. If an examiner was to read it, he would write 'not relevant to the question asked' in the margin, and mark it down accordingly. This is the 'narrative trap'—failing to think of sufficient reasons or effects with which to answer a list question, candidates make the second half (or more) of their essays purely narrative, and suffer as a result. A range of *arguments* that relevantly answer the question is therefore essential.

If range provides the horizontal axis of essay success, then 'depth' is the vertical axis. Arguments must be substantiated by reference to detailed factual knowledge that is used to prove the points made in each opening sentence. It is in this respect—and this only—that accurate, detailed factual knowledge is needed for advanced history. Those students and exam candidates who are able to refer to people, dates, events and historians to back up their arguments stand well above those that merely put forward a few tenuous claims or simply write a narrative. The best way to illustrate this quality of depth is by example. Study and discuss the three paragraphs below, each written as a 'mid-essay' paragraph (putting forward the same argument) in answer to the question. 'Who gained from the Crimean War?' Place them in rank order on the basis of their depth alone, although note that the facts included must be relevant to the argument put forward.

240

A Napoleon III gained from the Crimean War. Despite his initial reluctance to join the war, France found herself on the winning side. As a result, Napoleon was able to locate the peace conference in Paris and, through it, humiliate Russia. Consequently, France could be seen once more as a leading European power and in the period following the Treaty of Paris was able to exert influence in Italy—at the expense of Austria, herself weakened by her vacillation during the war—and in other parts of the world. Therefore it can be seen that France gained from the Crimean War.

B The Second Empire of France was one victor of the Crimean War. Napoleon III had joined Britain in sending a fleet to the Dardanelles in 1853, had helped in the siege of Sebastopol and had lost over 30 000 men. As a result of the Treaty of Paris, the Dardanelles were closed to warships, no fleets were to be kept in the Black Sea and the Danube became an international waterway. The Balkan Principalities were returned to Turkey, though they were soon to break away. France played a part in drawing up these terms and therefore gained from her part as a victor in the war.

C France can be said to have gained from the Crimean War. Not only was she on the winning side, but also she gained prestige from the peace conference being held in her capital. The actual terms of the treaty of Paris were to her advantage—with Britain, her fleet could now dominate the Eastern Mediterranean and enter the Dardanelles. Russia's claim to protect Christian subjects in the Turkish Empire had been rebuffed and the settlement of the Danubian principalities was to Napoleon's liking. In addition, the diplomatic consequences of the war also benefited France. Russia had suffered a diplomatic check and Austria had been isolated—France could step into the gap. The advantages given to the nationalities of both Italy and the Balkans suited Napoleon's ideological preferences. In the changed circumstances of post-Crimean Europe, Napoleon III was able to exert considerable influence, most notably in Italy, even though it might be argued that he did not make the most of his new position.

D *A defence of Napoleon III*
As you will have discovered, most contemporaries and modern historians have been critical of Napoleon III, comparing him unfavourably with his namesake and almost mocking some aspects of his rule. In this section, therefore, you are going to write a defence of Napoleon. At the same time, you should develop the ideas on depth considered in Section C above.

Using each of the sentences below as introductions, write a series of paragraphs defending the policies of Napoleon III. In each paragraph, ensure that you both explain the introductory idea and support it by reference to factual evidence.

(i)   Unlike other autocrats, Napoleon made a genuine and heartfelt attempt to liberalize his rule.

(ii) Napoleon was an equally ardent supporter of nationalism, and did his best to support nationalist movements in central and southern Europe.

(iii) It may also be argued that Napoleon's constitutional changes were the first serious attempt to put an end to the circle of revolution followed by reaction that France had experienced since 1815.

241

(iv) Equally, Napoleon III may be regarded as more successful than his predecessors in restoring France's prestige in Europe, at least in the 1850s.

(v) France's economy made considerable advances during the Second Empire.

(vi) Moreover, Napoleon himself cannot alone be held responsible for France's entry into the war of 1870, nor for her defeat in it.

Having completed your defence of the Emperor, you should consider the validity of what you have written in the light of counter-arguments that you have read (or written), thus drawing your own conclusions in a final evaluation of the Second Empire.

3 The Unification of Germany

(a) The German Problem

After the Treaty of Olmütz in 1850, the German problem was still unsolved, and the obstacles to unity seemed as insurmountable as ever. Germany remained a Central European country with largely indefinable and indefensible frontiers and was surrounded by great powers. Since the Middle Ages these powers, especially Austria and France had intervened to prevent German unity and deny the Holy Roman Empire any effective authority. In the years after the Vienna Settlement, Germany still did not show any sign of becoming an established political reality. The Holy Roman Empire had gone, but the Habsburgs were its inheritors, and their interests remained only partly German. Less than a third of the Austrian Empire was within the German Confederation, and of her 12 million subjects so included in it, almost a half were Slavs. Moreover, though Austria was opposed to both German and Italian unification, she was involved in Germany, as the constitutional leader of the Confederation, in a way that she was not in Italy. Unification would mean a reversal of her historic position in Germany entitling her to control the political life of the country and exclude other powers from participating in it.

Austria's position in Germany made it difficult for the nationalists to find a rallying-point for their cause which would give it the possibility of success. So also did the fact that though the German people shared a common language and culture, the political divisions were numerous, and there were religious differences as well. Countries such as Britain and France had emerged from the religious disputes of the sixteenth and seventeenth centuries with their national unity finally strengthened, but the Thirty Years' War (1618–48) preserved and intensified German disunity. Never in their history had the Germans formed a single state, and they had no glorious past like the legends of the Roman Empire and the achievements of the Renaissance which inspired the Italians. The conflicting interests of the numerous German princes and their determination not to give up their own authority in their states had done much to bring about the failure of the constitutional movement at Frankfurt in 1848.

There were, however, two factors which assisted the cause of German unification and made the situation more favourable than in Italy. Prussia played much the same part in Germany as Piedmont in Italy; but Piedmont was only one among other Italian states and by no means the most powerful. Prussia, on the other hand, had achieved for herself the position of a leading European power during the eighteenth century and in territorial extent, after the exclusion of the Habsburgs, comprised two-thirds of Germany in 1848. The consequence of this was that, while Cavour came to realize that Piedmont could never hope to expand in Italy without active foreign assistance, Prussia in the last resort could act on her own if she could ensure the neutrality of the foreign powers. Having achieved this, she was to show that, though her population was only a third of that of Austria or France, she could defeat each in turn.

Again, the economic factor played a greater part in the development of German than Italian unity. Before political action was possible, the *Zollverein*, which was contrary to Austria's protectionist needs, largely excluded her from Germany's economic organization and promoted its leadership by Prussia (*see page 47*). Moreover, the *Zollverein* made Prussia an important country commercially as well as politically. Bismarck strongly favoured the Franco-Prussian trade treaty of 1862, one of the commercial agreements inititated by Napoleon III, which brought Prussia more closely into the economic life of western Europe and increased her international power and prestige.

(b) William I of Prussia

There was, nevertheless, little to indicate during the decade after the revolutions of 1848, that Prussia was to be the centre of German nationalist hopes. Frederick William IV had granted the state a not very liberal constitution (*see page 173*). He dared not repeal it, but proceeded to reduce its effect by such actions as curbing the freedom of the press, forbidding public meetings and imprisoning political opponents without trial. In this he was supported by conservative ministers, who wished to lessen the growth of parliamentary influence and recover as much power for the crown as possible. During these last ten years of Frederick William's reign, therefore, Prussia seemed to be under a government determined to preserved the old order and maintain its position as a separate German kingdom.

In 1858, however, the situation changed in a way that was to lead to the establishment of German unity by Prussia, though not as the liberal nationalists had hoped and expected. In that year, because Frederick William was incapacitated by a stroke and died three years later, his brother William, became Regent and then, in 1861, King as William I. He was more resolute, though less intelligent, than his brother. He had fought in the War of Liberation (1813) against Napoleon and served ever since in the Prussian army to which he was devoted. He felt it deeply humiliating for the army that it had been judged inadequate to fight Austria during the crisis of Olmütz, and he wanted, now that he was in power, to undertake the military reforms which Frederick William had neglected.

The Prussian army still depended upon the measures which had been put into effect to bring about the military recovery of the state after its disastrous defeat at Jena in 1806. These had established a system of conscription by which men served for three years in the army and two in the reserve and then passed into the *Landwehr* or militia. Despite Prussia's rising population, however, the number of recruits enrolled annually remained fixed, and money and influence enabled young men to avoid being called up. Thus, though the country's population had now doubled, the intake of conscripts remained at the original number of 40 000. Some 23 000 men a year did no military service at all, and for the rest the three years' active service was in practice no more than two.

When Prussia mobilized in the Rhineland during Napoleon III's Italian campaign of 1859, the defects of the army were made apparent and stimulated William's determination to bring about changes. He appointed Count von Roon as Minister of War and Field Marshal von Moltke as Chief of the General Staff, both of whom were anti-liberal and anti-Austrian in their outlook. They proposed to create 49 new regiments with their barracks, so as to make it possible for every man to serve in the army for three years, and to reduce the *Landwehr* drastically in size because it was considered to be of little military value.

These measures would raise the size of the regular army from 500 000 to 750 000 and involved considerable additional expenditure. The King asked the Diet to sanction the necessary taxation, but the lower chamber opposed his demand. There was no general objection to an increased army. 'If we are attacked, we defend ourselves,' Engels wrote in 1859. The radically liberal *Fortschrittspartei* or Progressive Party, which had obtained a large majority in the chamber at the elections of 1860, did not question the size of the army, but wished to assert their right to control the government. They also objected to the diminution of the *Landwehr* since it had middle-class officers while those of the regular army were almost exclusively Junkers. They voted the additional cost in 1861 for one year only, but refused to do this again next year. The result was a serious constitutional crisis.

(c) Prince Otto von Bismarck (1815–98)

At this juncture, however, Von Roon persuaded William to appoint Count von Bismarck to be his chief minister. Bismarck came from an impoverished but ancient Junker family of Brandenburg (*see page 310*). Bismarck once said they were 'not only older than the Hohenzollerns, but in no way inferior to them.' Outwardly he seemed to be a typical Junker, and he shared their conservative social outlook which had recently been strengthened by fears of liberal designs upon their lands, but he did not share their political conservatism. The strongest influence upon him came from his middle-class mother, and A.J.P. Taylor has described him as 'a clever sophisticated son of a clever sophisticated mother masquerading all his life as his heavy earthen father'.

After attending university, Bismarck passed the examinations qualifying for admission into the diplomatic service, but (like many Junkers) he was poor and had to spend some years assisting with the management of the family estates. In 1847, however, he entered politics by being elected to the Prussian Diet in Berlin by landowning voters—'I am a Junker,' he said, 'and intend to profit from it.' He made himself known as a fervent anti-liberal, attacking his opponents with offensive sarcasm in powerful speeches.

When the German Confederation was revived in 1851, Frederick William sent him as a Prussian representative to the Diet at Frankfurt (*see page 178*), and this was a turning-point in his life. There he saw the industrial development taking place in the Prussian Rhineland, which he had not known about in Brandenburg or Berlin. He saw that Prussia must adopt an economic policy to assist this and broke with the Junkers who wanted to retain the guilds, apprenticeship rules and other relics of the medieval system. He saw also there that the nationalist movement, despite the failure of 1848, was bound to succeed and threatened to sweep the Prussian kingdom away.

When William came into power, however, Bismarck suffered a temporary set-back to his career. William thought he was too extreme and violent and likely to cause disharmony in Prussia. 'He smells of blood,' he said of Bismarck, 'and can only be employed when the bayonet rules.' He sent Bismarck to be Prussian Ambassador at St. Petersburg from 1859 to 1862 and at Paris in 1862. Bismarck resented this exile, saying he was in 'cold storage'.

The constitutional crisis of 1862, however, made William realize that Bismarck's conservative reputation and unfailing determination made him the man he needed as his minister to deal with the situation. So in that year, at the age of 47, Bismarck became the head of the Prussian government. It has commonly been supposed that when he came to power he had a clearly formulated design in his mind, which he proceeded ruthlessly to put into effect through a series of cleverly-conceived stages, and that the results were always what he intended to achieve in advance. This, however, has been questioned recently and is seen to have been based rather upon a legend fostered by Bismarck himself in his memoirs to promote his own renown. It was also assisted by his gift for striking phrases, such as, 'A war with France lay in the logic of history.'

Recently more importance has been placed upon the weaknesses and mistakes of Bismarck's rivals and opponents, both within and outside Germany, on his basically emotional temperament (which he inherited from his mother) and on his extraordinary political good fortune which he was able to exploit to his advantage. He himself wrote, 'Politics is neither arithmetic nor mathematics. To be sure one has to reckon with given and unknown factors, but there are no rules and formulae with which to sum up the results in advance. Only professors can create scientific laws.' And again he said, 'Politics is not in itself an exact and logical science, but it is the capacity to choose in each fleeting moment of the situation that which is least harmful or most opportune.' He thought of himself as 'the helpless child of time' and confessed that he had rarely been in a situation where he could take independent action or himself determine the course of events. In fact, Bismarck's success in politics came about, not because he sought to follow an inflexible plan, but because he was resourceful enough to take advantage of circumstances, to change his designs in the face of developments and to gain such short-term advantages as he could from them. He wrote, 'By himself the individual can create nothing; he can only wait until he hears God's footsteps resounding through events and then spring forward to seize the hem of His garment—that is all.' In any political situation, therefore, he liked to leave his options open and to have several possible courses of action, one of which might be the best to undertake as events unfolded themselves.

When Bismarck became William's chief minister during the crisis of 1862, he persuaded the King to defy the Diet and levy the military taxes without its consent, while at the same time the press was closely censored, and liberals were dismissed from the civil service. Bismarck rightly calculated that this could be done with little fear of trouble. German nationalists had hitherto been liberal because, following the examples of Britain and France (the only ones available), they thought that a great national state must have a liberal, parliamentary constitution. But middle-class influence was weak in Prussia, and the ruling military and landowning classes hated liberalism. Moreover, the failure of the liberals in 1848 had seriously weakened their position. Prussians (and other Germans too) now growingly felt that the national cause must be achieved, even at the cost of freedom. This was to remain the national outlook, and German liberals could not resist it. The impotence of the Diet in the face of Bismarck's determination was but the beginning of the story.

At the same time, Bismarck proposed to overwhelm all opposition to himself in Prussia by achieving a successful policy in Germany. His policy was in the Hohenzollern tradition, as followed by Frederick William the Great Elector (1640–88) and Frederick the Great (1740–86), who had both sought to outstrip other German states and assert Prussian power over them. In particular, this governed his attitude towards German unity. Since attending the Diet at Frankfurt, he had realized that some sort of unity was inevitable in the future; but the question still was how would it come? He remained firm in his determination that it should not be under the liberals, who would destroy Prussia as it existed. He saw that their great handicap, which had led to their failure in 1848, was that they had no organized force at their command. Hence his speech to the Diet in 1862 in which he said, 'Germany does not look to Prussia's liberalism, but to her strength,' and then, in his best-known words, 'The great questions of the day will not be decided by speeches and resolutions of majorities—that was the great mistake from 1848 to 1849—but by blood and iron.'

So he set out to achieve German unity by the Prussian conquest of the country, which he did by a series of improvisations. He showed himself a supreme opportunist, prepared to use any movement, liberal or anti-liberal, when it suited his immediate objective, and as readily discard it as soon as it had served his purpose. And all the time, his policy was backed up by the remodelled Prussian army and von Moltke's strategic abilities.

(d) The Danish War (1864)

Bismarck did not have to wait long to begin to put his policy into effect. In 1863 he was presented with three developments which made this possible. He did not bring them about, but he made them serve his own purposes with typical opportunism.

After the Treaty of Olmütz, Austria had made efforts to increase her power in Germany. When Bismarck was a member of the Diet at Frankfurt, she tried to dissolve the *Zollverein*, and Bismarck defeated her by gaining support from the smaller German states. Now, in order to gain compensation for her defeat in Italy, she attempted to remodel the constitution of the German Confederation to her advantage. The plan was for a central authority of six states (Austria, Prussia and three others) under Austrian presidency and an assembly consisting of representatives chosen by the diets of the individual German states. Francis Joseph invited the German princes to meet at Frankfurt to discuss the scheme. William thought that he should attend, but Bismarck knew that by now Austria's diplomatic and military position was weak. He persuaded William not to go, and the princes were not prepared to accept the arrangement without Prussia. Bismarck had shown that Austria could no longer make herself stronger in Germany against Prussian opposition.

At the same time as Bismarck was contending with this matter in Germany, the Polish revolt broke out (*see page 216*). Bismarck had long believed that Prussia needed Russian friendship if she were to succeed in fashioning Germany as she wished. He had whole-heartedly supported Prussian neutrality during the Crimean War. Now he took action to support the Tsar and preserve Prussian Poland (*see page 217*). And Alexander II, while wishing to avoid any possibility of war with the European powers, wanted to abrogate the Russian clauses of the Treaty of Paris and was, therefore, glad to have Prussian support. The Polish revolt also divided France from Russia and aroused British suspicions of Napoleon III (*see page 234*). In any event, the French ruler, after his experience in Italy, was shown to be less ready for European adventures than he had been, particularly that he was now physically in decline and preoccupied with his Mexican plan. Moreover, he still favoured German nationalism and desired to see the remnants of the Vienna Settlement destroyed. It was clear that Prussia was now in a better position than at any time since 1815 to establish the position of the German Confederation without the likelihood of united European action against her.

The consequences of this situation became apparent during the third development in 1863 when the Schleswig-Holstein question again became acute (*see page 175*). This time Palmerston said that only three persons knew the answer to it—he himself, who had forgotten; the Prince Consort, who was dead; and God, who would not tell. Whether or not he had suffered from such a complete loss of memory, Palmerston was indeed to show as the crisis unfolded that he completely failed to understand the situation. In 1863 the Danish government proposed to incorporate the Duchies with Denmark, which roused German opinion indignantly as had happened in 1848. Bismarck wished to avenge the national humiliation Prussia had suffered then; and already through this territory ran the Kiel Canal (which was to be reconstructed by 1895) linking the Baltic with the North Sea and thus of immense strategic and commercial importance to Prussia (*see Map 15, page 255*).

Bismarck was no more ready than Frederick William had been in 1848 to consider anything but Prussia's interests. The other German states proposed that the Duchies should be occupied by an army of the Confederation, but this would have meant that Prussia would have been acting in consort with German liberalism, and the Duchies would have been absorbed into Germany. To prevent this, Bismarck proposed an alliance with Austria to make war on Denmark and take the Duchies from her. The Austrian government could not refuse to do this because she could hardly hope to maintain her position in Germany if she remained aloof from a settlement of the question. Denmark was easily defeated in the summer of 1864 and, contrary to her expectations, received no help from the great powers. Palmerston had not believed that Prussia would really act against Denmark, and when she did, he protested vigorously, but had to admit that there was nothing that Britain could do to support the Danish government. Moreover, British isolationism had been growing since the Crimean War and had become strongly opposed to interference on the Continent.

Palmerston's death the next year came at the end of an era. Though militarily insignificant, the Danish War of 1864 was of great political importance. It showed that Prussia was now able to ignore the German Confederation and compel Austria to fall into line with her wishes.

At the end of the war, the Duchies, instead of gaining their independence, were placed under joint Austro-Prussian occupation. Bismarck wished to secure them for Prussia; but Austria, still asserting herself more than her position justified, tried to bargain with Prussia. She declared that she would only agree to annexation of them by Prussia in return for the cession to her of a part of Silesia, a province which Frederick the Great had taken from her (*see Map 6, page 46*), and a guarantee of her possession of Venetia. Bismarck could not accept these terms, but he did not want war against Austria. The war against Denmark and the occupation of the Duchies had gained him national support in Prussia, but had revived fears of Prussian aggression among the other states and turned German opinion against him. He was also uncertain of Napoleon III. After long discussion, he succeeded in persuading Austria to accept the Convention of Gastein, a temporary agreement which in his own words 'papered over the cracks'. Holstein was to be administered by Austria and Schleswig by Prussia until they could arrive at a lasting arrangement. It was the Austrian government which insisted that this partition of the Duchies should be provisional; it was still determined not to recognize Prussia as an equal in Germany. Bismarck was content to accept this arrangement. It gave him time to decide what policy to follow in the circumstances.

(e) The Austro-Prussian War (1866)

Bismarck still wanted Holstein for Prussia and hoped also to exclude Austria from northern Germany. He would have preferred to do this peacefully by offering Austria in exchange a guarantee of her position in Italy and the Balkans, but this proved to be impossible. Francis Joseph was prepared to negotiate with Prussia, but not to relinquish the Austrian presidency of the German Confederation. Bismarck, therefore, had to consider war, which he always wanted to use only as a last resort because he feared it might be dangerous and get out of hand. He prepared for this possibility by ensuring the isolation of Austria. He was convinced by the conduct of Britain and Russia during the Danish War that they would not intervene in a conflict between Austria and Prussia. He also thought it likely that Italy could be persuaded to become an ally of Prussia. His most important step, therefore, had to be to secure the benevolent neutrality of France.

His opportunity came when he met Napoleon III at Biarritz in 1865 and found that French impartiality could be gained by securing Venetia for Italy (*see page 234*). He then immediately opened negotiations with Italy. He discovered that Victor Emmanuel, being suspicious that he might merely use Italy to obtain Prussia's aims in Germany, wanted a promise that he would take action against Austria to deprive her of Venetia within a definite time. Accordingly, the treaty signed between Prussia and Italy in April 1866 stipulated that Italy would follow Prussia in attacking Austria within three months of the signing of the agreement. Bismarck was ready to accept this arrangement because he feared that Austria might try to secure Italian neutrality by surrendering Venetia to her without a war. Victor Emmanuel wanted to fight, but the decision to begin an Italo-Prussian offensive lay with Bismarck, and he regarded war as inevitable. He now had to act quickly, and he wished to provoke Austria into involving Prussia in what he could claim as a defensive war.

He was assisted in doing this by Victor Emmanuel's bellicosity and by the slowness of the Austrians in mobilizing, which took six weeks to complete, twice as long as the Prussian army required. This meant that when Austria became alarmed by Bismarck's diplomatic man-oeuvering, she had to undertake the seemingly aggressive step of be-ginning to mobilize before Prussia; and the pace of her mobilization had to be increased when, as Victor Emmanuel was resolved to have war as soon as possible, the Italian army mobilized. The expense of a lengthy Austrian mobilization would be unendurable, so early in June the Austrian government formally asked the Diet of the Confederation to consider the Schleswig-Holstein question, an action which Bismarck declared to be a breach of the Convention of Gastein.

Even while Prussian mobilization proceeded, Bismarck was able to send troops into Holstein immediately. Austria appealed to the Diet, which agreed to the mobilization of the German states against Prussia. Bismarck's reply was to declare the Confederation dissolved and order the northern states of Saxony, Hanover and Hesse-Cassel to side with Prussia (*see Map 6, page 46*). When they refused, they were invaded by a Prussian army and soon collapsed. Meanwhile, the main Prussian forces converged upon Bohemia, where early in July the armies of Austria and Saxony were defeated at the Battle of Sadowa, at which Prussia intro-duced the double military innovation of directing her troops by telegraph and using trains to achieve a strategic junction of separate armies. The way to Vienna now lay open to the Prussian forces, and Francis Joseph obtained an armistice. The war was over in seven weeks.

Bismarck has always been praised for the statesmanlike moderation of the peace treaty he made with Austria at the end of the war. He has been represented as wishing to avoid unnecessarily humiliating and weakening Austria, particularly by not compelling her to cede any territory to Prussia, so as to gain her revived friendship later. Realistically, however, the terms of the settlement gave Prussia all that Bismarck wanted to obtain from the war, and he did not consider Austria in a position to resume hostilities anyway. Moreover, he wanted a quick settlement with Austria. He was still uncertain whether France and Russia might not yet intervene, and he knew that they both did not want the Austrian Empire to be seriously weakened because they believed that it would act as a counter-weight to Prussia's increasing power. Bismarck himself did not think that this could be so, but he had his own reasons for not wishing to threaten Austria's existence. 'I could not visualize for the countries comprising the Austrian monarchy,' he wrote in 1866, 'any future that would be acceptable to us if that monarchy were destroyed. What could one set up instead in that part of Europe which is today occupied by the Austrian state from the Tyrol to the Bukovina? In that geographic area, any newly-formed creations would only be of a permanently revolutionary nature.' And he was bound to think that the time might come when Austria would be a suitable ally for Prussia. 'We need Austria's strength in future for ourselves,' he said.

The Treaty of Prague between Austria and Prussia was signed in August 1866. Austria had to consent to the dissolution of the German Confederation and her exclusion from any future German organization. She had also to recognize Prussian absorption of Hanover, Hesse-Cassel, Nassau and the Free City of Frankfurt, together with Prussian annexation of Schleswig and Holstein (*see Map 15, page 255*). Prussian troops were to withdraw from Habsburg territory, but Venetia was to be ceded to Italy.

The German Confederation of the Vienna Settlement was partly replaced by a new North German Confederation, consisting of a union of Prussia and all the German states north of the River Main. Its President was the King of Prussia, who controlled foreign policy, could declare war and make peace and had the power to appoint and dismiss the Federal Chancellor, the first (and only) holder of this office being Bismarck. The component states kept their own rulers and governments, but their armies were placed under federal control. Legislation was shared by a Federal Council or Bundesrat, consisting of representatives of the state governments in proportion to their size and in practice dominated by Prussia, and the Reichstag, which was elected by universal male suffrage. Though it lasted only a short time, the main features of the constitution of the North German Confederation were to be preserved in the constitution of the German Empire.

An important consequence of defeat for Austria was that she was compelled to concede Hungarian demands and to change the character of her Empire by means of the *Ausgleich* (*see page 322*). Moreover, having now lost her old place in both Germany and Italy, she turned her attention towards strengthening her influence in the south and east with important international consequences that were to destroy the peace of Europe in the next century.

Austria was not alone in suffering defeat at the hands of Bismarck. Prussian liberalism and consitutionalism also were overwhelmed and never recovered. On the very same day as the Battle of Sadowa, elections to the Prussian Diet increased the number of conservative members from 38 to 142 in the lower chamber. And when, in September, Bismarck introduced into the new chamber an indemnity bill legalizing the action of the government in having raised taxes without a constitutional budget since 1862, only seven members voted against it. Bismarck's success in excluding Austria from Germany and uniting Northern Germany made it impossible for his former opponents to resist the popular tide of Prussian opinion which rose in his favour despite his authoritarian and monarchical outlook. The liberals were demoralized and split into two parties—the Progressives and the National Liberals (*see page 312*).

The territories gained by Prussia after the War increased her population by over 4 million inhabitants. These included Hanoverians and other Germans historically hostile to Prussia as well as Poles and Danes. The old Protestant predominance of Brandenburg-Prussia was further weakened, and political problems were raised which were later to face Bismarck in the German Empire. Nevertheless, the victory over Austria and the formation of the North German Confederation not only gave Prussia undisputed supremacy in Germany, but also made her one of the leading European powers.

(f) The Franco-Prussian War (1870–71)

When the victory of 1866 fulfilled Prussia's traditional policy of seeking supremacy in northern Germany, Bismarck had no further definite aims in foreign policy. He was content that the southern German states should retain their 'international, independent existence' and that the Germans in the Austrian Empire should remain under Habsburg rule. 'For German Austria we have no use, either wholly or in part,' he insisted. And after the formation of the North German Confederation, he said repeatedly, 'We have done enough for our generation,' and he meant it. He certainly did not want to fight France. Nor did Napoleon III want to fight Prussia; but French opinion after 1866 drove him to make demands for territorial compensation, and Bismarck took appropriate yet peaceful steps to protect himself against the aggressive mood which this displayed (*see page 235*).

Of course Bismarck had to consider the possibility of war against France, but if it should come, he did not want it soon because each year's postponement of hostilities added another 100 000 trained soldiers to the Prussian army. There is no evidence to support the usual assumption (afterwards asserted by Bismarck himself) that he deliberately intervened in the Spanish marriage question in order to provoke France into war. This would suppose that he planned such a war over a period of years, which is very unlikely. Indeed, there is no certainty about the time when he began to accept the idea of war nor about what results he expected to achieve from it.

The Spanish episode began in September 1868 when there was a revolution in that country. Queen Isabella II, the ruling monarch, was expelled, and the revolutionary party decided upon the establishment of a constitutional government with a new sovereign. This at once presented it with a difficult problem. 'Finding a democratic king in Europe,' said the leader of the insurgents, 'is like looking for an atheist in Heaven.' Eventually they offered the throne to Prince Leopold, a member of the Roman Catholic branch of the Hohenzollern family and a relative of the King of Prussia.

Bismarck had nothing to do with the Spanish approach to the Prince, but he certainly encouraged him to accept the offer when it had been made. This was no doubt another example of his opportunism. The incident gave him the chance to consider the pursuit of alternative courses, which he always like to do. He must certainly have seen that there was a possibility that it might bring about war between France and Prussia. He probably also believed that if France did peacefully accept the accession of Leopold to the Spanish throne, it would promote Prussian prestige and security and act as a possible check upon French aggression.

Leopold allowed himself to be persuaded to accept the offer, though he was reluctant to be a constitutional monarch in Spain, and King William of Prussia, who did not wish his family to become involved in Spanish politics, also was unwilling for him to go. Then, owing to the blunder of a cipher clerk in the German legation at Madrid, Bismarck's plans were ruined because the fact of the candidature unexpectedly became public before Leopold was formally announced as King by the Spanish government. If France had not known anything until this had taken place, she would have found it difficult to oppose a decision already made in Spain. Napoleon would probably have been compelled, as in 1866, to accept what had already happened. As it was, this was seen in France as an example of Prussian scheming which must be thwarted. Popular reaction to the news was indignant and violent. Reckless speeches about 'French honour' were made in the Legislative Chamber, and the press spoke fearfully about the danger of encirclement by the Hohenzollerns. This greatly upset William. It seemed to confirm his worst fears about the episode. He secured the withdrawal by Leopold of his candidature.

This was a diplomatic triumph for France. It raised the prestige and morale of the Napoleonic regime. Bismarck's reputation was publicly and profoundly threatened, but he was saved by a grave mistake on the part of the French government, which threw away its moral advantage by over-reaching itself. A group at the French court, headed by the Empress, persuaded Napoleon to agree to the exploitation of the situation by the mounting of a diplomatic counter-offensive against Prussia. In July 1870 the French ambassador in Berlin was instructed to obtain personally from William an 'assurance that he will not authorize a renewal of the candidature' of Leopold for the Spanish throne. He met William in the public gardens at Ems, where the King was taking the waters, and put his request to him. William replied, in a perfectly polite manner, that he could not give an assurance in such a form.

Bismarck had become increasingly alarmed. Prussia had been humiliated by a France in which the spirit of aggression seemed to have become stronger than ever. It was probably now that he decided that war was preferable to such a situation; and he took occasion by a piece of improvisation to place responsibility for it upon France. William sent a report of his conversation with the French ambassador by wire to Bismarck in Berlin, who drew up his own version of it. He said later, 'The difference in the impression of the shortened text of the Ems telegram, compared with the one the original would have produced, was not the result of stronger words but of the form, which made the pronouncement appear as final, while in the original it would have seemed only like part of a pending negotiation to be continued in Berlin.' Bismarck's version of the telegram, which was published in Berlin, ended, 'His Majesty the King has refused to receive the French ambassador again and has told him through the adjutant on duty that His Majesty has nothing further to convey to the ambassador.'

The Ems telegram was an immediate cause of hostilities, but not the only one. Once the French government had failed to secure the guarantee required from William the war party were determined to have no more negotiations. Moreover, French public opinion was aroused as Bismarck had intended it should be. His action served to stimulate popular war-fever in Paris and make it impossible for Napoleon and the peace party in the French government to oppose the declaration of war upon Prussia. Bismarck had succeeded in his stratagem. Attention in Prussia was now diverted from the mistake in the opportunity given to France to humiliate the country. He could now represent Prussia as engaged in a war of national defence against French hostility to the whole of Germany; and he could hope to redeem everything by victory.

France fought without allies, while Prussia was supported both by the other states of the North German Confederation and by those in the south, so strong was the feeling against France throughout Germany. From the beginning the French army was inferior in numbers, armaments and leadership. During August it suffered a series of severe defeats along the eastern frontier. When Napoleon himself marched with inferior forces to the relief of the beleaguered garrison at Metz, he was trapped at Sedan. He surrendered in September, and the Treaty of Frankfurt followed (*see page 236*).

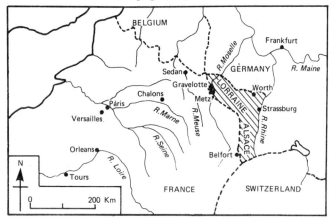

Map 14 The Franco-Prussian War, 1870–71

In comparison with his treatment of Austria in 1866, Bismarck deprived France of territory at the end of this war. In later years, he said that he annexed Alsace and Lorraine on military advice for reasons of national security, but there is no evidence for this. In fact, at the beginning of the war, in order to stimulate the support of the southern German states, he had announced that Germany would claim this territory. Moreover, he had always insisted that the war was waged in defence of Germany against French aggression. Now France had to be punished for her misdeeds and German nationalism rewarded for its patriotism. He was not troubled by the thought of French resentment at the loss of these provinces. He said that the fact of defeat alone would make France resentful whether or not she were deprived of territory.

Anti-French feeling had brought all the German states into the war, and now that victory was won, popular opinion wanted the union to be preserved permanently. The time had come to establish the German Empire. Bismarck was determined that it should not have a liberal constitution and that Prussian should retain in it the power she had in the North German Confederation. William was as determined as his brother had been in 1848 that he would only accept the imperial crown from the German princes and not the people. Bismarck negotiated with representatives of the four southern German states, who came to the Prussian military headquarters at Versailles. By playing upon their fears and jealousies of each other he had no difficulty in getting Baden, Württemberg and Hesse to accept his conditions, and Ludwig II, who had become King of Bavaria in 1864, was won over by the promise of a secret annual grant of £20 000, paid from the confiscated fortune of the deposed King of Hanover, to enable him to continue his passion for castle-building.

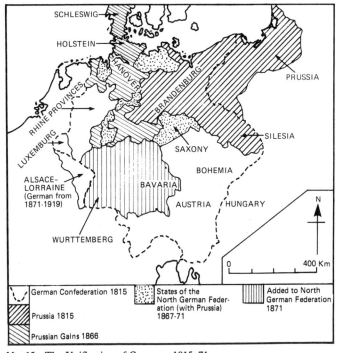

Map15 The Unification of Germany 1815–71.

255

The German princes then offered the imperial crown to William I of Prussia. He accepted it and now became also the Emperor William I of Germany. In January 1871, before Paris had fallen, the new Empire was proclaimed in the great Hall of Mirrors of the Palace of Versailles, which Louis XIV had built as a symbol of the pre-eminence of France in the triumphs of war and the arts of peace. William appointed Bismarck as the Imperial Chancellor. The German Empire claimed to be the legal successor to the Holy Roman Empire, and though the German people had not been consulted about its creation, the proclamation spoke of their 'unanimous desire to renew and continue the German imperial dignity, dormant for more than 60 years.' As L.C.B. Seaman has observed, however, this new German Empire was in reality a Prussian Empire. German unity had been brought about by bringing all the separate states within Prussian control. Though the Empire did not include the Germans within the Austrian Empire, it was now the strongest power on the Continent and was inevitably to be the centre of European politics during the coming years.

1815		German Confederation established
1817	October	Wartburg Festival
1818		Zollverein formed by Prussia
1819	March	Murder of Kotzebue
	October	Carlsbad Decrees
1832	May	Demonstrations at Hambach
	June	Carlsbad Decrees strengthened
1835		First steam railway in Germany
1840		Death of Frederick William III of Prussia; succession of Frederick William IV
1844–5		Revolts in Silesia
1847–8		Unrest in Bavaria
1848	March	Grand Duke of Baden grants reforms
	March	Rioting in Berlin
	March	*Vorparlament* meets in Frankfurt-on-Main
	May	Constituent Assembly meets in Berlin
	May	Frankfurt Assembly meets
	December	Constituent Assembly dissolved
1849	March	German constitution drawn up by Frankfurt Assembly
	April	Constitution rejected by Frederick William IV
	December	Collapse of Frankfurt Assembly
1850	February	Prussian constitution established by Frederick William IV
	March	Erfurt Union
	November	Treaty of Ölmutz; dissolution of Erfurt Union
1858		Frederick William IV incapacitated; William becomes Regent
1861		Death of Frederick William IV; William I King of Prussia
1862		Prussian Diet refuses to vote military budget
		Bismarck made chief minister in Prussia
1863		Austrian attempt to remodel German Confederation
		Polish Revolt
		Schleswig-Holstein crisis

1864		Danish War
		Convention of Gastein
1866	April	Italo-Prussian Alliance
	June-July	Austro-Prussian War
	August	Treaty of Prague
1867		North German Confederation established
1870	July	Outbreak of Franco-Prussian War
	September	Surrender of Napoleon III
1871	January	Proclamation of German Empire
	May	Treaty of Frankfurt

Table 13. Chronology of German Unification (1815–1871)

Bibliography

E. Eyck, *Bismarck and the German Empire* (Allen & Unwin, 1950), O. Pflanze, *Bismarck and the Development of Germany, 1815–71* (Princeton, 1963), R.R. Sellman, *Bismarck and the Unification of Germany* (Methuen, 1974) and A.J.P. Taylor, *Bismarck: The Man and the Statesman* (Hamish Hamilton, 1955).

Exercises

A   *This section consists of questions that are intended for discussion (or written answers) as a way of expanding on the chapter and testing your understanding of it:*

1   What do you understand by 'the German problem'?
2   What were the major obstacles to German unification in 1860?
3   How did the Regency and subsequent succession of William I alter Prussian policy?
4   Why did the Progressive Party provoke a constitutional crisis in 1862?
5   Comment on Bismarck's background, political ability and ideas.
6   Why did Prussians feel 'that the national cause must be achieved, even at the cost of freedom'?
7   Why did Bismarck think that German unity would be achieved by 'blood and iron' rather than by 'speeches and resolutions'?
8   Do you agree that Bismarck was fortunate that the rest of Europe was too weak or divided to oppose his plans in the 1860s?
9   In what ways was Bismarck's opportunism illustrated by the Schleswig-Holstein dispute and its settlement?
10 How and why did Austrian actions help Bismarck's plans in 1866?
11 Why did Prussia succeed so easily in the war of 1866?
12 Do you accept the view that the terms of the treaty of Prague were generous?
13 Why did the other states accept the constitutional terms of the new North German Confederation?
14 Why was there so little opposition in Prussia to Bismarck's policies and curbing of liberalism?
15 Comment on the relative roles of Bismarck and Napoleon III in bringing about the Franco-Prussian War.
16 To what extent was the Franco-Prussian War brought about by chance and blunder?

17 Why did the Ems telegram lead to war?
18 Given her military inferiority, why was France so keen to have a war with Prussia? (*See also page 236.*)
19 Did Bismarck make a mistake in taking Alsace-Lorraine in the treaty of Frankfurt?
20 Why did the other German states accept Prussian domination in 1871?

B *Essay questions*
1 In what ways was either Italy or Germany still not fully unified by 1871? (Cambridge, 1981)
2 To what extent was the political unification of Germany due to (a) the growth of the Prussian *Zollverein* (b) Bismarck's diplomacy and wars? (SUJB, 1981)
3 Analyse the causes and the consequences of the Franco-Prussian War. (SUJB, 1983)
4 Consider the view that Germany united was no more than Prussia enlarged. (Welsh, 1981)
5 Were Bismarck's intentions embodied in the Germany of 1871? (Welsh, 1983)
6 Why did Austria lose her primacy in either Germany or Italy? (Oxford and Cambridge, 1981)
7 'Nationalism was probably the least important of the causes of unification.' Discuss with reference to either Italy or Germany. (Oxford and Cambridge, 1982)
8 Why had Prussia, rather than Austria, achieved dominance in Germany by 1866? (Oxford and Cambridge, 1983)
9 Why was Prussia able so decisively in the 1860s to oust the Habsburgs from the leadership of Germany? (London, 1981)
10 Discuss the suggestion that, from 1862 to 1871, Bismarck was little more than an unscrupulous opportunist. (London, 1983)
11 'It was the policies of Napoleon III rather than those of Bismarck which led to the Franco-Prussian War of 1870.' Discuss this statement. (JMB, 1981)
12 'Anyone who has ever looked into the glazed eyes of a soldier dying on the battlefield will think hard before starting a war.' (Bismarck, 1867) Why, then, despite this sentiment, did Bismarck resort to war on three occasions between 1862 and 1870? (JMB, 1982)

C *German Unification: a guide to the areas of debate*
(a) Introduction
The unification of Germany is regarded as one of the most significant events of the nineteenth century. It ended centuries of disunity and division, and led to the creation of a new Central European power, larger, more populous and more prosperous than almost all its West European rivals. This in turn led to a complete change in the European 'balance of power' and to an upheaval in international relations that can be seen to have resulted in the Great War of 1914–18. Indeed, most Europeans in the first half of the twentieth century saw the newly created Germany as responsible for both that war and the Second World War. At its simplest, therefore, it has been argued that 'a powerful, united Germany causes international tensions and wars.' In the last quarter of the twentieth century, this argument has not lost its force, and talk of German

reunification still creates international disquiet. Consequently, the events that led to German unity have been a major area of study, and have led to a variety of arguments and different interpretations. It is essential that you widen your reading on this subject; as you do so, you should find the guidelines below helpful, as they point to some of the aspects that have been debated by historians.

(b) The Bismarckian view of events

Several authors point out that Bismarck was an expert at making the well-chosen phrase that was intended not only for his audience but also, in part at least, for posterity. These phrases have often been seen as indications of his true intent and as explanations of what subsequently happened. For example, his famous 'blood and iron' speech of 1862 has been taken to mean both that he planned, deliberately and intentionally, to use war as the means to German unification and, from this, that war and diplomacy were more important factors in bringing about unification than any others. Both these assertions have since been challenged. After his resignation in 1890, Bismarck wrote his Memoirs, in which he interpreted the events of his chancellorship—from 1862 to 1890—in a favourable light. Of them, Seaman has written, '. . . their chief purpose was to prove that all his predecessors and all his successors were fools, that he alone was the Man . . .' It is therefore important to guard against seeing the events that led to German unification only in the way that Bismarck wished them to be seen, while at the same time not wholly discounting the views and recollections of such a key character.

(c) The extent of German unification

There are two aspects to this discussion. Firstly, it has been argued that Bismarck did not unify all of Germany, but only a part of it. His Germany was the 'Kleindeutschland' (Little Germany) that did not include those Germans who lived under Habsburg control, chiefly in the Austrian and Bohemian parts of the Austro-Hungarian Empire. These Germans—some 10 million of them by the end of the century—remained outside Germany until the late 1930s, when they were brought into the Third Reich by Hitler's annexation of Austria and parts of Czechoslovakia. Only then was the 'Grossdeutschland' (Large Germany) created. The Reich of 1871 can therefore be seen as *a* German Empire rather than *the* German Empire. From this, most authors have concluded that Bismarck's plans were comparatively limited and unambitious.

Secondly, the new state has been seen by many historians as an enlarged Prussia rather than a united Germany. They argue that Bismarck took the lead in bringing about the unification, often acting in the interests of Prussia rather than the German states as a whole, as in the case of the Schleswig-Holstein question in 1864. The smaller states were often bullied into accepting Prussian control: for example, in 1863, Francis Joseph's plans for reconstructing the German Confederation (*see page 247*) were destroyed by Prussia's refusal to co-operate. When the new state *was* reorganised, firstly through the North German Confederation of July 1867 and then by the constitution of the German Empire of 1871, it provided for Prussian leadership, both through the pre-eminence of the Prussian King as Emperor and through Prussian domination of such democratic forms as existed—the Bundesrat and the Reichstag (*see page 310*). Furthermore, the new Empire proved to be, throughout the period 1871–1914, a Prussian creation that continued to serve Prussian interests, as Chapters V, 2 and VI, 3 illustrate.

(d) The reasons for German unification in the 1860s

You have already studied the hopes and failures of a number of groups seeking greater unity in Germany in the nineteenth century (see page 170). Why, therefore, was unification achieved at last in the 1860s? And why was it achieved in the way it was—through Prussian leadership and three successful wars? The traditional and simple answers to these questions were much influenced by the Bismarckian view of events—until the 1860s those that sought unification were well-intentioned liberals who tried to use persuasion and peaceful means: all very reasonable and optimistic, but ineffectual. Enter Bismarck, the man of action and will, to put an end to their shilly-shallying and show how the job should really be done—a clear plan, political ability and a preparedness to use force. Thus Bismarck provided the missing ingredients and the problem was solved.

Bismarck's personal role and talents are further examined in section e) below. So far as the factors that led to unification are concerned, historians have recently placed less emphasis both on his personal contribution and on the need for the wars of the 1860s as a means to unification. It has been argued instead that Prussia fought Denmark in 1864 only to ensure that Schleswig and Holstein came under Prussian control rather than fell to the German Confederation. This war was thus against the interests of German unity, rather than for it. Equally, it has been argued that the war with Austria was undertaken to please Napoleon III of France, since he would no longer accept continued Austrian control of Venetia in North Italy (see page 234). In this view, Bismarck overestimated Napoleon and regarded the Seven Weeks War as extremely hazardous. So far as the Franco-Prussian War is concerned, some historians regard it as a senseless war brought about by jingoism and by error. Seaman expresses this view as follows: 'Nothing is more frightening than the contrast between the dreadful and irrevocable consequences of this war and the triviality and irrationality of those on both sides who made it.' The war was certainly not essential to bring the South German states under Prussian control—given the political, economic and military domination of the North German Confederation (under Prussia's leadership) after 1866, the Southern States could not have remained effectively independent of it for long. Consequently, the view of the united Germany being forged 'by blood and iron' has undergone considerable revision.

Instead, a number of other factors have been stressed. Much greater emphasis has been placed on the economic development of Germany, and especially Prussia, in the period between 1815 and 1860. The changes made to the Prussian economy after her defeat at Jena in 1806, her territorial gains made at the Congress of Vienna and the development of the Zollverein after 1834 all helped the Prussian economy. Lee argues that these factors led to a take-off in the Prussian economy in the 1850s and 1860s, and he cites a threefold increase in both railway mileage and coal production to support his view. In turn, this expansion combined with the contraction of the Austrian economy to give Prussia domination over the economies of the smaller German states that would eventually lead to political changes. J.M. Keynes, in The Economic Consequences of the Peace

(1919), turned Bismarck's famous phrase to argue that 'The German Empire was created more by coal and iron than by blood and iron.' More stress has also been placed on the role of other European powers in bringing about German unification. As a result of the crises and wars of the previous 30 years, there was little agreement between these great powers. France and Russia had fallen out over the Polish Revolt of 1863 (*see page 231*), and neither wished to see Austria's position and power enhanced, especially after the Crimean War. Equally, Britain had little desire to support France against Prussia, nor did she possess the naval and military strength to do so. As Lee has written, 'more than at any other time in the nineteenth century there was a power vacuum in Europe, and Bismarck was able to pursue his own designs, unimpeded by the gravitational pull of international diplomacy.'

As well as being divided between themselves, the other Powers had their own interests and priorities. In Russia, Tsar Alexander attempted to solve the weaknesses revealed by the Crimean War (*see page 213*). Austria faced problems in North Italy, as well as the renewed opposition of the Magyars to her domination—an opposition that resulted in the new constitutional arrangements of 1867. It was not therefore surprising that she was unable to provide much opposition to Prussia in 1866. Neither Britain nor newly united Italy had any desire to involve themselves in the affairs of Central Europe, while Napoleon III had as many internal concerns as the others, but still chose to challenge Prussia. By their divisions and by their preoccupations, then, it can be argued that the other European powers unwittingly contributed to Prussia's successes in the 1860s.

(e) The role of Bismarck
In the light of these other factors, Bismarck's role as the 'unifier' of Germany may now be considered. It was traditionally held that he achieved the unification of Germany by embarking on a set plan of war and diplomacy that deliberately set out to hoodwink or subdue the other powers. In this scheme, he created a war with Denmark in 1864 in order to provide the excuse for a subsequent war with Austria, he made Napoleon III believe France would benefit from Prussia's defeat of Austria, won Austria to his side by the generous terms of the Treaty of Prague and then connived with the Spanish to bring about a war in which he could humiliate France. In this scheme of things, Bismarck was the master diplomat, manipulating the other powers of Europe with consummate ease.

This view, created at least in part by Bismarck himself, is now regarded more as a pattern imposed on events after they took place rather than before. Instead, Bismarck is seen as a talented politician and expert opportunist, who took advantage of situations as they arose and who was, in a number of cases, downright lucky in the way in which others behaved and events turned out. It has also been argued that in most cases he had a number of alternative possible courses of action and that he reacted to the actions of others as much as he determined events himself. For example, there is no doubt that he aimed to at least reduce and if possible remove Austrian influence from at least Northern and if possible all of Germany. The aim itself thus had a number of stages; so too did the means. Austria could be an ally against others, as she was in 1864, and might even agree to a division of influence in Germany. This was how events transpired in 1864–5. Thereafter, the Gastein agreement *could* provide the basis for further agreements or, if desired, an occasion for dispute. At the same time, Bismarck ensured that Russia, through Prussian support against the Polish rising, and France, through the Biarritz meeting with Napoleon III, remained friendly. In this instance, as, arguably, in others, Bismarck's success was in creating circumstances that gave Prussia a framework within which diplomatic success was likely, but other means were also available.

This line of argument is not intended to take all credit away from Bismarck. Rather, it is to see his role in a more complex light, and to stress the part played by others. It is a line that is still being explored and has yet to fully take account of Bismarck's famous statement to Disraeli, made in 1862: 'When the army has been brought to such a state as to command respect, then I shall take the first opportunity to declare war with Austria, burst asunder the German Confederation, bring the middle and smaller states into subjection, and give Germany a national union under the leadership of Prussia.' Disraeli reported that he also told him of his plans for war with Denmark and the defeat of France. The 'Bismarck debate' is far from over yet.

(f) Conclusion

In this section, most of the interpretative aspects of Bismarck and German unification have been outlined. They should be used to help you in your further reading, in the course of which you should attempt to identify the standpoint of other authors. In particular, as you read, try to answer each of the following questions with regard to each author:

(i)   Does he comment on Bismarck's own writings and speeches as an influence on how German unification is viewed? If so, how? If not, has he been influenced by the Bismarckian view?

(ii) Does he comment on the *Kleindeutschland/Grossdeutschland* issue? or on Prussia's domination of the new German Empire?

(iii) What does he see as the main reasons for the unification of Germany in the 1860s?

(iv) What view does he take of Bismarck's personal role?

(v)   Does he comment on the significance of the unification of Germany? If so, in what ways?

It is impossible to draw your attention to all the possible sources on this subject. However, you should find some of the following helpful:

E. Eyck — *Bismarck and the German Empire*
S.J. Lee — *Aspects of European History 1789–1980*, pp 84–93
E.J. Passant — *A Short History of Germany 1815–1945*
J.G. Rohl — *From Bismarck to Hitler*
L.C.B. Seaman — *From Vienna to Versailles*, pp 96–129
D. Thomson — *Europe since Napoleon*, pp 307–320
Anthony Wood — *Europe 1815–1945*, pp 207–224 and 238–239
See also an article in *History Today*, September 1984, by D.G. Williamson.

4 The Italian Kingdom

(a) Italian Unification

In 1852, when Cavour became Prime Minister of Piedmont, no one expected that within ten years Italian unification would largely be achieved. The obstacles against it seemed as formidable as ever. The risings of 1848–49 had all failed. The peninsula was still divided into ten separate Italian states (*see Map 8, page 113*), every one of which wished to retain its independent existence. There seemed to be no possibility of reviving even the partial measure of Italian unity initiated by Napoleon I more than 50 years previously.

The nationalists could claim in favour of their cause that Italy possessed good natural boundaries and that the people had a common religion and shared the memories of ancient Rome and Renaissance Italy. There was, however, no strong communal feeling throughout the peninsula, and the attempts of the *Risorgimento* to establish a national Italian language made slow progress. To the territorial divisions were added, therefore, many other regional differences of dialect and outlook, customs and traditions. People from the north and south, from towns and countryside, might be as foreigners to each other when they met.

Moreover, events since 1815 had shown that the great majority of the people had no interest in either self-government or national unification. About 90 per cent of the Italian population were peasants, who had probably never heard of the word 'Italy'. They had no political ideas and were moved only by animosity towards their landlords. Many of them looked to the state governments for protection against the new middle-class landowners, who in parts of Italy were purchasing estates from the old nobility and proving themselves more exacting in their demands upon tenants and labourers. Many Italians, indeed, wanted, above all else, fair, efficient government from wherever it came. After the revolts of 1820 and 1830, there were those who went so far as to petition Metternich to annex more territory in the peninsula, which he declined to do. There were also Italians who served in the Austrian army and fought against other Italians during the wars of the *Risorgimento*.

Nor were the nationalists themselves united. There was disagreement and jealousy between the leaders in the comparatively rich and advanced northern part of the country and those in the southern part which was poor. There was also friction between the Piedmontese, who were monarchists, and the Mazzinians, who were republicans (*see page 115*). There were also disagreements between papalists and anti-clericalists. The failure of the risings of 1848–49, with their aftermath of disillusionment and resentment, had brought inevitable mistrust and recriminations and increased the dissensions within the movement.

Neither the secret societies nor the nationalist uprisings had gained the widespread support necessary for their success. Those who wanted Italian unification were a small minority, and during the revolts of 1848–49 they had made no effort to gain wider support for their cause (*see page 189*). In 1860, however, Garibaldi was to be able to conquer Sicily because a simultaneous peasant rising, inspired by social and economic motives, had broken out on the island when he landed there (*see page 267*).

Even more serious were the external obstacles to Italian unification. The international position of the Papacy brought prestige to Italy, and some writers liked to recall how the medieval popes had once fought for Italian independence against foreign invaders. Gioberti had hoped that a federation of Italian states might have been achieved under the Pope; and Pius IX for a brief period from 1846 seemed about to accept the moral leadership of Italian nationalism, but he soon showed himself as determined as his predecessors to maintain his temporal power (*see pages 115, 185*). The mere existence of the Papal States, stretching from coast to coast right across Central Italy, was bound to bring the nationalist movement into conflict with the Roman Catholic Church. Events had shown also that the great Roman Catholic powers, especially France and Austria, were ready to uphold the Pope's sovereign rights and anxious to retain the territorial integrity of the Papal States.

Austria, indeed, was bound to wish to preserve her domination of the peninsula (*see Map 8, page 113*). She still held Lombardy and Venetia, controlled the centre through her client, Habsburg-related princes in Parma, Modena and Tuscany, and in 1820, 1831 and 1848–49 had shown herself ready to uphold the authority of any despotic Italian rulers and quell insurrections in their territory, and these rulers themselves had sided with Austria in order to retain their power. Similarly, the creation of some sort of a permanent union of the Italian states (like the German Confederation of 1815) would certainly be contrary to the interests of Austria, since Italian weakness was necessary for her to maintain her position in Europe.

By 1852 Italian nationalists were looking more and more to Piedmont to achieve their aims. She had taken an important part in opposing Austria during the risings of 1848–49, and since then Cavour had set out to make her a strong, modern state and wished to extend her influence and territory in the peninsula (*see pages 192, 210*). But she was still small in both area and resources. None could be certain that she was likely to possess the will and display the ability to overcome the obstacles in the way of Italian unification and take the lead in achieving it.

(b) Cavour and Napoleon III

Cavour was a realist in politics. He wished to set Piedmont at the head of a movement which would exclude Austria from Italy, but he understood the situation in the peninsula. He had nothing but contempt for the Mazzinians, who still thought that this could be achieved in the way that had been attempted and had failed in the past (*see page 193*). He believed that they would never gain the support of the one class likely to bring about the liberation of Italy. He believed that the main hope for the success of such a movement lay not in a universal feeling of Italian patriotism, but rather in the individual aspirations and grievances of the small but important intellectual and official class. It was they who protested in the separate states against taxes and conscription and clerical and aristocratic privileges. They were the opponents of misgovernment and unenlightenment, but at the same time wished to avoid widespread, radical change in political and social matters.

Cavour believed also that the obstacles in the way of any immediate accomplishment of his aim were insurmountable. Like Bismarck, he adapted his policy and objectives to changing circumstances, though he had fewer resources than Bismarck and was not as ruthless. The only real advances, he used to say, were those which were slow and wisely ordered. Since he was not supported, like Bismarck, by military strength, he had to rely upon diplomacy to bring these about. Though he did not think of Italian unification, but of the extension of Piedmont to include all the northern part of the peninsula (*see page 192*), he realized that even such a limited extension of territory by her would arouse Austrian opposition and would not be accomplished without foreign help. His Italian policy, therefore, involved European negotiation and understanding to achieve success.

It used to be thought that Cavour deliberately involved Piedmont in the Crimean War (in which she had no direct interest) in order to secure for her more definite recognition among the powers of Europe. It was, however, King Victor Emmanuel who wanted to enter the war in the hope of gaining military glory for himself and increasing his power in the state. Cavour had to accept the King's decision, but he then did his best to exploit it to Piedmont's advantage; and he was disappointed in the outcome. The Italian question was brought to the attention of the Congress of Paris in 1856, but he was not as successful there as he had hoped he might be (*see page 210*). Piedmont gained neither territory nor an immediate ally. He had British sympathy, but no more; public opinion there, once the war was over, did not favour further European adventures. He had to accept this, but he learnt something at the Congress that was to be of great advantage in the longer run. He realized that Napoleon III was interested in Italian nationalism and might be induced to support Piedmont.

From this time onwards, he was determined to secure Napoleon as an ally, and the Orsini plot gave him the opportunity (*see page 229*). Within two years of the signing of the Treaty of Paris, he was able to get such an alliance at Plombières. Like Napoleon, his ideas of territorial expansion for Piedmont were limited to the north, and he showed his realism by his willingness to cede Savoy and Nice to France in return for her help in gaining Lombardy and Venetia by war against Austria. He agreed also at Plombières to Napoleon's plan for arranging Italy, after victory had been won against Austria, into a federation of four kingdoms under the presidency of the Pope (*see page 229*). No doubt he considered the scheme unworkable and unlikely to be put into practice, but he was prepared to accept it in order to have Napoleon's support for Piedmont. Finally, he managed to persuade Victor Emmanuel to agree to the marriage of his 15-year-old daughter, Clothilde, to Napoleon's disreputable cousin, Jerome, who was 36.

It was decided at Plombières that Cavour was to bring the war about in such a way as to make Austria appear the aggressor. He therefore mobilized Piedmontese troops on the border with Lombardy, and Austria allowed herself to be provoked into starting hostilities in April 1859, but then delayed further movements of her troops, and Napoleon had plenty of time to intervene. Then, after the battles of Magenta and Solferino had been won, Napoleon suddenly decided in July to put an end to the fighting though only Lombardy had been conquered. Cavour expressed shock and surprise and claimed that he had been betrayed, but he must have been sufficiently realistic to appreciate that the deficiencies of the Piedmontese army alone gave Napoleon adequate military reasons for his action (*see page 230*). Nevertheless, he resigned his post as Prime Minister when Victor Emmanuel refused to continue the war alone.

Meanwhile, in May 1859, Cavour's supporters had organized peaceful revolutions in the Duchies of Parma, Modena and Tuscany and that part of the Papal States known as the Romagna. Since they controlled the new governments that were set up in these territories, they were able to get them to demand union with Piedmont. Moreover, they refused to accept the return of their old rulers as ordered by the Treaty of Villafranca signed by Napoleon III and Francis Joseph in July 1859.

It was clear that these rulers could only be restored by force; and Austria, after her defeats at Magenta and Solferino, was unlikely to be able to assert herself in Central Italy again. Yet Piedmont could do nothing unless she had foreign support. Cavour, however, was able to break the deadlock by getting British and French support. In Britain, a general election in 1859 had brought back Palmerston as Prime Minister with Lord John Russell as Foreign Secretary. These 'two dreadful old men', as Queen Victoria called them, were in favour of Italian unification. So Palmerston warned both France and Austria that the British government would oppose any intervention by them in the Duchies, while Russell proposed that their inhabitants should vote on the question of annexation by Piedmont. And Napoleon now decided that he did not wish British influence to be established in Italy and that he would support Piedmont so that he would gain Savoy and Nice after all.

Accordingly, in January 1860, Cavour was made Prime Minister again by Victor Emmanuel, who had become increasingly sympathetic towards his policies. Cavour made an agreement with Napoleon by which the Duchies and the Romagna were to be free to join Piedmont in return for the cession of Savoy and Nice to France. The inhabitants of all these territories voted in plebiscites, which confirmed both sides of the transaction. So within only ten months of the Treaty of Villafranca, Victor Emmanuel had become the ruler of all northern Italy except Venetia (*see Map 8, page 113*). His kingdom had more than doubled in population and now included almost half Italy's population.

(c) Cavour and Garibaldi

Mazzini and the republicans disliked Piedmont's success. They feared that it seriously threatened their dream of an Italian state being established by a popular revolution sweeping through the peninsula. They decided upon a counter-stroke to establish themselves in the south. Mazzini's agents had no difficulty in stimulating the nationalists in Sicily to initiate a revolt in April 1860. Since 1848 'King Bomba' had acquired a notorious reputation for his treatment of political opponents. Some 20 000 nationalists were in prison and another 50 000 under house-arrest. Gladstone had, while holidaying in Naples in 1852, described the regime as 'the negation of God erected into a system of government'. 'Bomba' had died in 1859 and been succeeded by his son, Francis II, nicknamed 'Bombino', who continued his father's despotic government. As in 1848, the leaders of the revolt gained popular support for their revolt because of the hatred of Sicilians for Neapolitans and the resentment of the peasants against the landowners (*see page 183*).

'Bombino's' army would probably have been able to suppress the revolt, but Garibaldi saw this as his opportunity to assist the struggle with his followers as he had done at Rome in 1849 (*see page 188*). During the war against Austria in 1859, he had assisted Piedmont by waging a guerrilla campaign around Lake Como, alarming Cavour by the revolutionary fervour he inspired by his speeches in the Lombard towns, and Napoleon by the fear that he would go on to invade the Papal States. Now the revolt in Sicily appealed to his imagination. He disliked Cavour's reliance upon Napoleon, and the loss of his native city to France infuriated him. He decided to force Cavour's hand by intervening in Sicily with the hope of spreading a revolution up the peninsula which would merge the two Sicilies, Rome and Venetia into a single Italian state. He was sure that the undisciplined and insufficient forces of the Mazzinians would never do this.

Garibaldi asked the Piedmontese government for arms and other help, but Cavour was opposed to the idea of his expedition. This was partly because he was jealous of Garibaldi, whom he saw as a more popular rival in the Italian cause, but also because he was fearful of the expedition. Internationally, he thought it might lead to European intervention, particularly if Garibaldi threatened Rome. Nationally, he feared it might become a radical, republican crusade, which would not only conquer southern Italy, but even irresistibly gain support in the newly-enlarged Kingdom of Piedmont and cause instability and anarchy. It is true that Garibaldi had now broken with Mazzini and spoke of Victor Emmanuel as the 'King of Italy', but he remained a republican at heart, and Cavour did not trust him. He would have liked to have been able to stop the expedition, but he could not act openly because he sensed that Italian nationalist opinion everywhere would support Garibaldi. He had, therefore, to oppose secretly Garibaldi's operation, and when these still went ahead, he hoped that Garibaldi would fail and ruin his cause, which he saw as republican and anti-Piedmontese.

By May 1860 Garibaldi had gathered nearly 1500 redshirts (who were to become known as the Thousand) and sailed with them and his mistress in two paddle-steamers from Genoa. They steamed into Marsala, a small port on the western coast of Sicily. In the harbour were two small British cruisers, and when a Neapolitan battleship arrived, the captain held his fire, and it has been suggested that he thought the redshirts were British redcoats on board military transports which had a naval escort. Garibaldi landed his men unopposed and took possession of the town. Over it he hoisted the Italian tricolour in the name of Victor Emmanuel. And, contrary to general expectations, his success continued unabated. Though there were 25 000 Neapolitan troops on the island, their generalship was poor and unable to counter the guerrilla tactics of the redshirts, who were helped by ruthless bands of local peasant fighters. In two months Sicily was conquered.

Cavour called upon Garibaldi to hand over the island to Victor Emmanuel, but he refused. He knew that Piedmontese control would prevent him carrying his campaign to the mainland and on to Rome, which was his intention. There was now nothing to stop him doing this. Both Palmerston and Napoleon, though public opinion in their countries supported the picturesque figure of Garibaldi, viewed his plans with apprehension; but they suspected each other of wishing to benefit from the situation, and this mutual mistrust made joint Anglo-French naval action to check him impossible. Garibaldi crossed unhindered to Naples, where he was again aided by a peasant revolt. Military opposition to him collapsed, and Francis II fled.

Mazzini now arrived in Naples, but remained in obscurity. He had no influence over Garibaldi and was resigned to the failure of his dream for Italy. But Cavour shared the common misapprehension that Mazzini and Garibaldi were working together as they had during the Roman Republic of 1849. He feared that Italy might become divided between a monarchical north and a republican south, with disruption as the result. He feared also that when Garibaldi made his advance on Rome, he would become involved in fighting with the French garrison in the city, and Austria too might be drawn in if he persisted in his determination to conquer Venetia. And even if he were successful and agreed to put Victor Emmanuel on the throne of a united Italy, the concord of the new kingdom would be threatened by the radicals who supported him.

Cavour now had to accept the inevitability of a united Italy. The only way to ensure that it took place under Piedmontese control was to send an army southwards down the peninsula. Since Napoleon shared his fears, he was able to secure French agreement for this move. So Piedmontese troops invaded the Papal States 'to save them from the revolution.' They received little welcome from the inhabitants, and those who resisted the invaders were shot. Ten days after Garibaldi's entry into the city of Naples in October, the Piedmontese defeated the small Papal army at Castelfidardo. The Piedmontese could now occupy the whole of the Pope's territory, but to satisfy Napoleon's wishes, Rome and the Patrimony of St. Peter were left unconquered.

The Piedmontese continued their southward advance. This raised the threat of civil war in the peninsula, but Garibaldi was glad that they were coming. The remnants of the Neopolitan army had established themselves in prepared, fortified positions from which he could not dislodge them without the help of regular troops. Moreover, he had no ambition for political power and, despite the frustration of his own plans, he was prepared to accept a united Italian kingdom under Victor Emmanuel. He made no objection when the Piedmontese troops entered the territory he had conquered. Cavour organized plebiscites in the Two Sicilies and the Papal States which produced (since there was really no alternative) the expected overwhelming majority in favour of union with Piedmont. Towards the end of 1860, Victor Emmanuel arrived in Naples and met Garibaldi, who greeted him dramatically with the words, 'I salute the first King of Italy.' The King made a state entry into Naples, received the territory from Garibaldi and ordered the disbandment of the Thousand. The Kingdom of Italy was now proclaimed with Victor Emmanuel as its ruler 'by the grace of God and the rule of the people.' The first parliament met at Turin, the Piedmontese capital, in March 1861. Later that year Cavour died.

(d) Venetia and Rome
When the Kingdom of Italy had been established, Lord John Russell issued a dispatch to the British ambassador at Turin in which he praised 'the gratifying spectacle of a people building up the edifice of their liberties and consolidating the work of their independence.' He wanted also to express the hope that Rome and Venetia might 'share in the freedom and good government of the rest of Italy,' but Queen Victoria, who considered that Garibaldi had made England 'half-crazed', rightly insisted that such language would be resented by Austria. Nevertheless, until this was accomplished, the Italian question was not at an end. And, in the event, the way in which both these territories were incorporated into the Kingdom emphasized the continuing reliance of the *Risorgimento* upon foreign support and made Italians feel that they had not secured the prestige which they wanted as a great European nation.

The war of 1866 against Austria was a military catastrophe for Italy and a humiliating blow to her national pride. Victor Emmanuel was as determined to have a conflict on this occasion as he had been to intervene in the Crimean War. He again saw military victory as a means of enhancing his prestige and authority. During the negotiations with

Bismarck and the events leading up to the war, he made this clear (*see page 249*). He did not want Austria to be able to relinquish Venetia peacefully in order to save herself from a war on two fronts; such a cession would have thwarted his wish to gain the province by conquest. When the war came, however, the Italian armed forces were found to be badly equipped, trained and led. Victor Emmanuel assumed supreme command, but did nothing effective. Napoleon III, though his qualifications to speak in this way were doubtful, mockingly remarked that the King would never understand the first thing about war. Despite her superior numbers, Italy was defeated by the Austrians at Custozza and also suffered a crushing naval disaster at Lissa (where most of the sailors in the Austrian warships were Italians). Italy ingloriously received Venetia only because of Prussia's overwhelming victory over Austria. To add to her humiliation, not one Venetian town had risen during the war against its Austrian garrison, and no peasants in the Venetian countryside had volunteered to fight. However, once Italian troops occupied the province, their presence ensured that the usual plebiscite produced a majority of 647 246 votes to 69 for union with the Kingdom.

When Victor Emmanuel heard this news, he said, 'This is the finest day of my life; Italy is made,' and then he added, 'but it is not complete.' From 1861 the Italian parliament had claimed Rome as the capital of the Kingdom, and the *Risorgimento* could not be regarded as fulfilled until this was so. The setbacks of 1866 made the King anxious to restore his reputation by securing the city, but the French garrison continued to preserve it for the Papacy. Garibaldi made two attempts with private expeditions to capture it, but neither Victor Emmanuel nor Napoleon was prepared to allow him to do this. He was humiliatingly checked by a Piedmontese force in 1862 and again by the French garrison in 1867. On neither occasion did the Romans show any sign of wishing to be liberated.

Pius IX had, indeed, meanwhile emphasized in a succession of impressive ceremonies the unique religious importance of the city. In 1862 he called all the bishops of the Roman Catholic Church to Rome to attend the canonization of the 26 missionaries to Japan who had been put to death there in 1597, and four years later he again called them to the city for the eighteenth centenary of the martyrdom of the apostles Peter and Paul. Soon afterwards he announced that he would convoke the Vatican Council, which would open in 1869, the fifteenth anniversary of his proclamation of the dogma of the Immaculate Conception of the Virgin Mary (*see page 390*), and conclude with festivities in 1871 to celebrate the twenty-fifth anniversary of his election as Pope.

The bishops came to the Council, but its meetings were brought to a sudden end in 1870 when the Italian army marched into the city after the outbreak of the Franco-Prussian War had compelled Napoleon to withdraw his troops. The Italian government and parliament was transferred to Rome, and the King took up residence in the Quirinal Palace.

The event brought no protest from the Roman Catholic rulers of Europe. They had not been pleased by the proclamation of Papal Infallibility at the Council (*see page 390*). It did, however, result in an estrangement between the Papacy and the Italian state. The Italian parliament passed the Law of Guarantees, which recognized the Pope's religious authority in Rome and declared him immune from arrest and protected by the same treason laws as the King. Pius, however, rejected this and excommunicated the King and his government. He and his successors now voluntarily confined themselves to the Vatican Palace. This inevitably increased the anti-clericalism of the Italian liberals, which had already been stimulated by the Syllabus of Errors issued by Pius in 1864. In this he had condemned almost every political principle of the age, including rationalism, liberalism, socialism, universal suffrage, secular education, religious toleration and the subordination of the Church to the State (*see page 390*). The confrontation between the Italian government and the Papacy proved to be divisive in the Kingdom since the anti-clerical laws of Piedmont were extended to the rest of the country, which offended most of the population.

(e) The Kingdom of Italy

Bad relations with the Papacy were not the only troubles faced by the Italian kingdom from its beginning. Unification did not bring about unity. The divisive factors, such as the weakness of Italian as a common language, continued. Cavour had spoken bad Italian, and Victor Emmanuel never liked using it at all. French long remained the normal language of all classes in Piedmont. At the end of the nineteenth century, only about two per cent of Italians spoke literary Italian.

Unification was immediately followed by administrative 'Piedmontization'. The King always surrounded himself with Piedmontese advisers. The old local boundaries were obliterated and the centralized Piedmontese constitution was extended to the whole peninsula, to the indignation of many of the newly-annexed states. They wished to keep their own traditions and institutions and felt as if they were being treated as conquered territories. The Sicilians, who had revolted to free themselves from Naples, particularly resented having a fresh domination imposed upon them. The new kingdom was a constitutional monarchy, but the franchise for the Italian parliament was as restricted as it had been for the Piedmontese parliament. Half a million of the population of 22 million had the vote, and only 300 000 ever used it in any election.

In fact, the typically liberal aims of Cavour and his supporters — democratic institutions, free trade and opportunities for the middle classes meant nothing to the peasants who formed the overwhelming majority of the population. Their troubles, especially in the south, were not political but social and economic—they suffered from poverty and illiteracy, shortage of land and unemployment. In some places they had supported the revolts against the old rulers hoping to obtain land and economic security, but the new government supported the classes which oppressed them. Again, the manufacturers of the northern provinces benefited from the extension of low tariffs from Piedmont to the rest of the country, but the primitive local industries of the south suffered severely by being deprived of protection.

The economic and social problems were made worse by the government's financial policy. Cavour's modernization of Piedmont had been achieved at the cost of failure to balance the state's budget for ten successive years. This created a large national debt, which was inherited by the new kingdom, and the deficit had been increased by the cost of the war of 1859. The situation was made worse by continuing heavy military expenditure. The nationalists were determined that Italy should have a large, well-equipped army and navy, not only because Venetia and Rome had to be gained as soon as possible, but also she had to have such forces as a sign that she was a great power. So the average annual expenditure of the government on this was always more than a quarter and sometimes more than a third of the Kingdom's revenue.

This was too great a burden for the country, which was poor in relation to other European lands and was becoming, with the spread of industrialization on the Continent, still poorer because of its lack of iron, coal and oil. Soon the total expenditure of the government amounted to twice as much as that of all the former states together had been, and its revenue brought in less than half of this sum.

Successive ministers of finance tried to check the growing national deficit by proposing to reduce military expenditure, but were always defeated in the parliament. To raise money the government adopted various expedients. The currency was devalued. Loans were issued, which paid eight per cent interest and yet were offered at 70 per cent or less than their value. In 1866, after the war against Austria, 2382 monasteries and convents were closed and their property confiscated and sold by the government. Such devices, however, did not prevent higher taxation, but the upper and middle classes who controlled the parliament, were unwilling to bear the burden themselves. Income and personal property was taxed only lightly and consumption in almost all forms heavily, though Italy had almost the lowest wages in Europe. Among the increased taxes imposed during the 1860s were those on salt, tobacco and the grinding of wheat and corn. These indirect taxes caused peasant revolts, one of the most serious being in January 1869, when the first collection of the grinding tax led to a fortnight of disturbances in which some 250 people were killed, 1000 injured and 4000 imprisoned.

Much more serious was the 'Brigands' War', as the government called it, which lasted for years in the south. Those Neapolitans who wanted the restoration of the Bourbons were able to exploit the wish for local autonomy, support for the Roman Catholic Church and resentment against the government and the landlords among the southern peasantry. Half the Italian army had to be stationed permanently in the south. Martial law was frequently applied over large districts where bands of resisters held out in the hills and forests, and the extension of conscription to the whole Kingdom resulted in large numbers of young men joining them to avoid military service. In 1866 armed insurgents were able to take over the town of Palermo for a week. The casualties in this almost continuous guerrilla civil war probably amounted to more than those of all the three wars fought against Austria in 1848–49, 1859 and 1866.

The political, economic and social circumstances prevailing in Italy during these years combined to prevent parliamentary government functioning properly. The limited franchise tended to distance the politicians from reality. Instead of the development of large, powerful political parties, each with defined, practical aims and able to form stable governments, short-lived coalitions of small, disunited groups, patronage, corruption and the manipulation of men and parties prevailed. The large majority of the population, unrepresented in parliament, regarded the successive governments with indifference or hostility. These were to be the permanent features of Italian politics for the rest of the century and beyond.

Cavour died six months after the establishment of a united Italy which he had not wanted to take place at that time. The *Risorgimento* finally triumphed not through a national movement of moral regeneration as Mazzini had urged and Garibaldi still believed possible, but by fighting and annexation. The new kingdom lacked political traditions and experience, and the circumstances of its formation resulted in a regime which itself created fresh problems. Garibaldi became in popular memory the great hero of Italian nationalism, but perhaps Cavour was right in not wishing to hurry forward the creation of a single Italian state.

1815		Formation of the Carbonari
1820	July	Outbreak of revolt in Naples
1821	March	Revolt in Naples suppressed by Austria
	March	Revolt in Piedmont; abdication of Victor Emmanuel I
	March	Piedmontese revolt defeated at Novara
1830		Risings in Central Italy
1831	March	Young Italy founded by Mazzini
1838		Failure of Mazzini's invasion of Savoy
1843		Gioberti's *On the Moral and Civil Primacy of the Italians*
1846		Pope Pius IX
1848	January	Tobacco riots in Milan
	January	Rising in Palermo
	February	Grand Duke of Tuscany grants constitution
	March	Charles Albert of Piedmont and Pius IX grant constitutions
	March	Risings in Milan and Venice
	March	Charles Albert declares war on Austria
	May	Charles Albert defeats Austrians at Goito
	July	Venice, Parma, Piacenza and Modena seek union with Piedmont
	November	Revolt in Rome

1849	March	Austrians defeat Charles Albert at Novara
	March	Abdication of Charles Albert; succession of Victor Emmanuel II
	May	Neapolitan reconquest of Sicily
	July	French troops occupy Rome
	August	Austrians capture Venice
1850		Ecclesiastical laws in Piedmont
1851		Cavour becomes Prime Minister of Piedmont
1855	January	Piedmont intervenes in Crimean War
1856	March	Treaty of Paris
1858	July	Napoleon III and Cavour meet at Plombières
1859	April	France and Piedmont declare war on Austria
	May	Revolts in Modena, Parma, Tuscany and the Romagna
	July	Treaty of Villafranca; resignation of Cavour
1860	January	Cavour returns to office
	March	Savoy and Nice ceded to France, Lombardy to Piedmont
	April	Revolt in Sicily
	May	Garibaldi lands at Marsala
	August	Garibaldi invades Naples
	September	Piedmontese troops occupy Papal States
	October	Piedmontese invasion of Naples
1861	March	Kingdom of Italy proclaimed
1866	June	Italy and Prussia declare war on Austria
	August	Treaty of Prague; Venetia ceded to Italy
1870	September	Italian army enters Rome

Table 15. Date chart of Italian unification (1815–1870)

Bibliography

In addition to the books already mentioned (*see page 120*), there are four by D. Mack Smith, *Cavour and Garibaldi in 1860* (CUP, 1954), *Garibaldi* (Hutchinson, 1957), *Italy, 1860–1960* (Michigan, 1959) and *Victor Emmanuel, Cavour and the Risorgimento* (OUP, 1971).

Exercises

A   *This section consists of questions that might be used for discussion (or written answers) as a way of expanding on the chapter and testing your understanding of it:*

1   Why did any form of Italian unification seem so unlikely in the early 1850s?

2   Why did Cavour oppose the Mazzinians and look rather to the middle-class?

3   What did Piedmont gain from her participation in the Crimean War?

4   What was the significance of the Plombières meeting?

5   Why did Napoleon III withdraw from the war against Austria after the conquest of Lombardy?

6   How did British and French policies help Cavour in 1859–60?

7   Account in outline for Piedmont's success, 1858–60.

8   Why were 'Bomba' and 'Bombino' so called?

9   Why did Cavour fear Garibaldi's planned expedition, but nonetheless not prevent it?

10   Explain Garibaldi's success in conquering Sicily.

11   Why did Garibaldi refuse to hand Sicily over to the Piedmontese?

12 What does 'Cavour now had to accept the inevitability of a united Italy' (*page 268*) tell you about Cavour's plans and qualities of leadership?
13 Why did Garibaldi accept the Piedmontese army's arrival in Naples?
14 How could Victor Emmanuel claim to be ruler 'by the grace of God and the rule of the people' (*page 269*), and why did he do so?
15 Comment on the Piedmontese acquisition of Venetia.
16 Explain why the Piedmontese and French stopped Garibaldi's attacks on Rome in the 1860s, yet an Italian army occupied it in 1871.
17 What did Pope Pius IX do to try to restore the prestige of the Papacy in the late 1869s?
18 What was the significance for the new Kingdom of the split between the King and the Pope?
19 What other problems did the new Kingdom face?
20 Why were taxes on incomes kept low while those on consumption remained high?
21 Why was there revolt in the Southern part of the new Kingdom?
22 What advantages and what disadvantages did unification appear to bring to Italians?

B *Essay questions*
1 Why was so much of the progress towards Italian unification achieved in the years 1859–61? (Cambridge, 1983)
2 Why was the Kingdom of Piedmont-Sardinia able to secure political control over so much of Italy so quickly in the years 1859–1861? (Oxford, 1981)
3 Compare the difficulties faced by Cavour and Bismarck in unifying their countries. (Oxford, 1982)
4 Why was Italy eventually united as a monarchy, rather than as a republic or as a federation under the Papacy? (Oxford, 1983)
5 Assess the contributions of (a) Cavour, (b) Napoleon III to the liberation and unification of Italy. (SUJB, 1981)
6 How and why was Italy united as a constitutional monarchy rather than as a democratic republic or as a federation headed by the Pope? (SUJB, 1982)
7 In what ways did (a) Pius IX, (b) Mazzini, (c) Garibaldi assist or obstruct the liberation and unification of Italy? (SUJB, 1983)
8 'Italy owed her unity more to external aid than to her own endeavours.' Examine critically this judgement upon the movement for Italian unification in the period 1859–70. (Welsh, 1981)
9 What interests benefited, and what interests suffered, by the unification of Italy? (Welsh, 1981)
10 When, and in what ways, did Cavour and Garibaldi promote or hinder the unification of Italy? (Welsh, 1982)
11 Has Garibaldi's contribution to the achievement of Italian Unification been undervalued? (Welsh, 1983)
12 'Cavour was a late, and a reluctant, convert to the idea of Italian unification.' Do you agree? (Oxford and Cambridge, 1983)
13 Is it true to say that Cavour was 'a Piedmontese expansionist, not an Italian nationalist'? (AEB, 1981)
14 Assess the relative contributions to the unification of Italy of Cavour, Garibaldi and Napoleon III. (AEB, 1982)
15 Why, in the period 1848–61, did the movement for republicanism in Italy fail? (AEB, 1983)

16 'The strength of Italian nationalism is largely a myth; it was the support of the major powers rather than the efforts of Italians themselves which secured the ultimate success of the *Risorgimento* between 1852 and 1870.' Discuss this statement (JMB, 1980)

17 How important to the cause of Italian unification was the contribution of Garibaldi? (JMB, 1981)

18 'By exploiting Italian nationalism Cavour brought about the Piedmontese conquest of Italy.' Discuss this statement. (JMB, 1982)

C *Documents on the unification of Italy*
This is a long and detailed exercise, and it may be advisable to divide a group up to tackle different parts of it.

Document A. The Historiography of Italian Unification from the Introduction to *The Risorgimento and the Unification of Italy* by Derek Beales (Longman, 1981) pages 13 and 14.

'On the face of it, the unification of Italy happened very quickly, owed much to good fortune, and was largely an affair of war and diplomacy. At the beginning of the year 1859 Italy was divided politically into seven main parts. Six of these were sovereign states in themselves; the seventh, consisting of Lombardy and Venetia, was included within the Austrian Empire. In the previous three centuries, dynasties had been shuffled and boundaries adjusted, but the map of the peninsula had not altered fundamentally—except briefly during two periods of French domination between 1796 and 1815. The country had never been united politically since the sixth century. Yet in less than two years, between April 1859 and November 1860, almost the whole of Italy was brought under one ruler, King Victor Emmanuel II of Sardinia. . . .

Most Italians and Italian historians, however, see unification differently. To them it was not the sudden and accidental upshot of war and diplomacy. It was a result or a stage of their national revival, known as the Risorgimento, which originated in the eighteenth century and has lasted, according to many writers, into the twentieth. This is how Giorgio Candeloro puts it in the most notable recent history of modern Italy by an Italian: "In commom usage the word Risorgimento refers to the movement which led to the formation of the Italian national unitary state."

This formulation begs the very question which is my chief concern to try to resolve. Certainly there was an Italian national revival, but it seems to me that the precise relationship between Risorgimento and unification is exceedingly hard to determine.

Merely by posing this problem I separate myself from the main tradition of Italian historical writing. This is of course dangerous and might be though presumptuous, since the enormous majority of works on this subject belong to that tradition. But an English historian, especially one born in the twentieth century, could scarcely find it possible to enter into the spirit of Italian historiography of the Risorgimento. He cannot, in the first place, fully share the patriotic feelings of Italians. And, more serious, his philosophical presuppositions will be different from those of most Italian historians.

English readers ought to know something, however sketchy, of Italian historiography, not only because its tendencies have a long history and themselves help to explain the Risorgimento, but also because it has

276

inevitably guided English historians of Italy. Even before unification, men who wished to make Italians more conscious of their nationality sought their justification in history. Of these Vincenzo Gioberti had fantastic but particularly influential views. Since unification, historians and publicists have glorified all who played a part in it, and tried to fit into the story many who have little claim to belong there. Differences among Italians have been played down, the role of Italian soldiers magnified, and the origins of the development pushed further and further back in time. No doubt some such campaign was necessary to the strengthening of Italian feelings of nationhood.'

1   What factors does Beales emphasise in his view of the causes of uni-fication?
2   How does his view differ from that of most Italian writers?
3   What do you understand by the term '*Risorgimento*'? What does this tell you about the title of Beales's book?

Document B. Memoirs by Mazzini (1845), quoted in *Europe in the Nineteenth Century* by E. Lipson (A. & C. Black, 1960) pp 162–3.

We are a people of from one-and-twenty to two-and-twenty millions of men, known from time immemorial by the same name, as the people of Italy; enclosed by natural limits the clearest ever marked out by the Deity—the sea and the highest mountains in Europe; speaking the same language, modified by dialects varying from each other less than do the Scotch and the English; having the same creeds, the same manners, the same habits . . . proud of the noblest tradition in politics, science and art, that adorns European history; having twice given to Humanity a tie, a watchword of Unity—once, in the Rome of the Emperors, again, ere they had betrayed their mission, in the Rome of the Popes; gifted with active, ready and brilliant faculties . . . rich in every source of material well-being that, fraternally and liberally worked, could make ourselves happy, and open to sister nations the brightest prospect in the world.

We have no flag, no political name, no rank, among European nations. We have no common centre, no common fact, no common market. We are dismembered into eight States—Lombardy, Parma, Tuscany, Modena, Lucca, the Popedom, Piedmont, the kingdom of Naples—all independent of one another, without alliance, without unity of aim, without organized connexion between them. Eight lines of custom-houses, without counting the impediments appertaining to the internal administration of each State, sever our material interests, oppose our advancement, and forbid us large manufactures, large commercial activity, and all those encouragements to our capabilities that a centre of impulse would afford. Prohibitions or enormous duties check the import and export of articles of the first necessity in each State of Italy. Territorial and industrial products abound in one province that are deficient in another; and we may not freely sell the superfluities or exchange among ourselves the necessities. Eight different systems of currency, of weights and measures, of civil, commercial and penal legislation, of administrative organization, and of police restriction, divide us, and render us as much as possible strangers to each other. And *all* these States among which we are partitioned are ruled by *despotic* Governments, in whose working the country has no agency whatever. There exists not in any of these States, either liberty of the press, or of united action, or of speech, or of collective petition, or of the introduction of foreign books, or of education, or of anything. One of these States, comprising nearly a fourth of the Italian population, belongs to the foreigner—to Austria; the others, some from family ties, some from a conscious feebleness, tamely submit to her influence.'

4 What do you understand by each of the following terms and phrases used by Mazzini:
   (a) 'a watchword of Unity'
   (b) 'oppose our advancement'
   (c) 'despotic Government'
   (d) 'collective petition'
5 What lines of argument does Mazzini use to put the case for a united Italy?
6 What forms of government did Mazzini have in mind for his united Italy?
7 How important an influence on unification would Beales (in Document A) regard Mazzini?
8 What would Mazzini have thought of the united Italy that emerged in the 1860s?

Document C. Cavour's report on his meeting with Napoleon III at Plombières, 20th July 1858 from *The Making of Italy* by D. Mack Smith pp 238–247 (Macmillan, 1968) (Only extracts from the text of Cavour's report are included here; a fuller account is provided in Beales, op.cit. page 155 ff.)

'As soon as I entered the Emperor's study, he raised the question which was the purpose of my journey. He began by saying that he had decided to support Piedmont with all his power in a war against Austria, provided that the war was undertaken for a non-revolutionary end which could be justified in the eyes of diplomatic circles—and still more in the eyes of French and European public opinion.

Since the search for a plausible excuse presented our main problem before we could agree, I felt obliged to treat that question before any others. First I suggested that we could use the grievances occasioned by Austria's bad faith in not carrying out her commercial treaty. To this the Emperor answered that a petty commercial question could not be made the occasion for a great war designed to change the map of Europe. Then I proposed to revive the objections we had made at the Congress of Paris against the illegitimate extension of Austrian power in Italy: for instance, the treaty of 1847 between Austria and the Dukes of Parma and Modena; the prolonged Austrian occupation of the Romagna and the Legations; the new fortifications at Piacenza.

The Emperor did not like these pretexts. He observed that the grievances we had put forward in 1856 had not been to make France and England intervene in our favour, and they would still not appear to justify an appeal to arms. "Besides," he added, "inasmuch as French troops are in Rome, I can hardly demand that Austria withdraw hers from Ancona and Bologna." This was a reasonable objection, and I therefore had to give up my second proposition; this was a pity, for it had a frankness and boldness which went perfectly with the noble and generous character of Your Majesty and the people you govern.

My position now became embarrassing because I had no other precise proposal to make. The Emperor came to my aid, and together we set ourselves to discussing each state in Italy, seeking grounds for war. It was very hard to find any. After we had gone over the whole peninsula without success, we arrived at Massa and Carrara, and there we discovered what we had been so ardently seeking. After I had given the Emperor a description of that unhappy country, of which he already had a clear enough idea anyway, we agreed on instigating the inhabitants to petition Your Majesty, asking protection and even demanding the annexation of the Duchies to Piedmont. This Your Majesty would decline, but you would take note of the Duke of Modena's oppressive policy and would address him a haughty and menacing note. The Duke, confident of Austrian support, would reply impertinently. Thereupon Your Majesty would occupy Massa, and the war could begin.

As it would be the Duke of Modena who would look responsible, the Emperor believes the war would be popular not only in France, but in England and the rest of Europe, because the Duke is considered, rightly or wrongly, the scapegoat of despotism. Besides, since he has not recognized any sovereign who has ruled in France since 1830, the Emperor need have less regard toward him than any other ruler.

Once we had settled this first question, the Emperor said: "Before going further we must consider two grave difficulties in Italy: the Pope and the King of Naples. I must treat both of them with some circumspection: the first, so as not to stir up French Catholics against me, the second so as to keep the sympathies of Russia, who makes it a point of honour to protect King Ferdinand."

I answered that, as for the Pope, it would be easy to keep him in possession of Rome by means of the French garrison there, while letting the provinces of the Romagna revolt. Since the Pope had been unwilling to follow advice over the Romagna, he could not complain if these provinces took the first occasion to free themselves from a detestable form of government which the Pope had stubbornly refused to reform. As for the King of Naples, there was no need to worry about him unless he took up the cause of Austria; but his subjects would be free to get rid of his paternal rule if the occasion offered.

This reply satisfied the Emperor, and we went on to the main question: what would be the objective of the war?

The Emperor readily agreed that it was necessary to drive the Austrians out of Italy once and for all, and to leave them without an inch of territory south of the Alps or west of the Isonzo. But how was Italy to be organized after that? After a long discussion, which I spare Your Majesty, we agreed more or less to the following principles, recognizing that they were subject to modification as the course of the war might determine. The valley of the Po, the Romagna, and the Legations would form a kingdom of Upper Italy under the House of Savoy. Rome and its immediate surroundings would be left to the Pope. The rest of the Papal States, together with Tuscany, would form a kingdom of central Italy. The Neapolitan frontier would be left unchanged. These four Italian states would form a confederation on the pattern of the German Bund, the presidency of which would be given to the Pope to console him for losing the best part of his States.

This arrangement seems to me fully acceptable. Your Majesty would be legal sovereign of the richest and most powerful half of Italy, and hence would in practice dominate the whole peninsula . . .

After we had settled the fate of Italy, the Emperor asked me what France would get, and whether your Majesty would cede Savoy and the County of Nice. I answered that Your Majesty believed in the principle of nationalities and realized accordingly that Savoy ought to be reunited with France; and that consequently you were ready to make this sacrifice, even though it would be extremely painful to renounce the country which had been the cradle of your family and whose people had given your ancestors so many proofs of affection and devotion. The question of Nice was different because the people of Nice by origin, language and customs, were closer to Piedmont than France, and consequently their incorporation into the Empire would be contrary to that very principle for which we were taking up arms. The Emperor stroked his moustache several times, and merely remarked that these were for him quite secondary questions which we could discuss later.

Then we proceeded to examine how the war could be won, and the Emperor observed that we would have to isolate Austria so that she would be our sole opponent. That was why he deemed it so important that the grounds for war be such as would not alarm the other continental powers. Better still if they were also popular in England. He seemed convinced that what we had decided would fulfil this double purpose. The Emperor counts positively on England's neutrality; he advised me to make every effort to influence opinion in that country to compel the government (which is a slave to public opinion) not to side with Austria. He counts, too, on the antipathy of the Prince of Prussia toward the Austrians to keep Prussia from deciding against us. As for Russia, Alexander has repeatedly promised not to oppose Napoleon's Italian projects. Unless the Emperor is deluding himself, which I am not inclined to believe after all he told me, it would simply be a matter of a war between France and ourselves on one side and Austria on the other.

The Emperor nevertheless believes that, even reduced to these proportions, there remain formidable difficulties. There is no denying that Austria is very strong. The wars of the first Empire were proof of that. Napoleon Bonaparte had to fight her for fifteen years in Italy and Germany; he had to destroy many of her armies, take away provinces and subject her to crushing indemnities. But always he found her back on the battlefield ready to take up the fight. And one is bound to recognize that, in the last wars of the Empire, at the terrible battle of Leipzig, it was the Austrian battalions which contributed most to the defeat of the French army. It will therefore take more than two or three victorious battles in the valleys of the Po or Tagliamento before Austria will evacuate Italy. We will have to penetrate to the heart of the Empire and threaten Vienna itself before Austria will make peace on our terms.

Success will thus require very considerable forces. . . .

The Emperor did not make the marriage of Princess Clothilde with his cousin a *sine qua non* condition, but he showed clearly that it was of the greatest importance to him. If the marriage does not take place, if you reject the Emperor's proposal without good reason, what will happen? Will the alliance be broken? That is possible, but I do not believe it. The alliance will be made. But the Emperor will bring to it a quite different spirit from the one which he would have brought if, in exchange for the crown of Italy which he offers Your Majesty, you had granted him your daughter's hand for his nearest relative. If there is one quality which characterizes the Emperor, it is the permanence of his likes and his dislikes. He never forgets a service, just as he never forgives an injury. The rejection to which he has now laid himself open would be a blood insult, let there be no mistake about it. Refusal would have another disadvantage. We should then have an implacable enemy in the inner counsels of the Emperor. Prince Napoleon, even more Corsican than his cousin, would mortally hate us; the position he occupies, to say nothing of that to which he may aspire, as well as the affection and I would almost say the weakness the Emperor has for him, all this would give him many ways of satisfying his hatred. . . .'

9   To provide you with a factual basis, outline briefly the major topics discussed by Cavour and Napoleon III.
10 What difficulties would Cavour have in undertaking a war '. . . for a non-revolutionary end which could be justified in the eyes of diplomatic circles—and still more in the eyes of the French and European public opinions'?
    How did Cavour hope to overcome these difficulties?
11 Why did the Pope and the King of Naples pose 'grave difficulties'?
12 Why did Cavour regard the planned arrangements for the future division of Italy as 'fully acceptable'?
13 How realistic did the plans for the war against Austria turn out to be?
14 Who was it planned that Princess Clothilde should marry, and why was this likely to raise difficulties?
15 What does this Document reveal about the personalities of Cavour and Napoleon III?

Document D. The Sardinian Proclamation of War with Austria, 29th April, 1859, reproduced in *European Diplomatic History 1815–1914*, edited by H. N. Weill (Exposition Press, New York, 1972)

'PEOPLE OF THE KINGDOM!

Austria attacks us with a powerful army, which, while professing a love of peace, she has assembled to assault us in the unhappy provinces subject to her domination.

Unable to support the example of our civil order, and unwilling to submit to the judgement of an European Congress, on the evils and dangers of which she alone is the cause in Italy, Austria violates her promise to England, and makes a case of War out of a law of honour.

Austria dares to demand the diminution of our troops; that that brave youth, which from all parts of Italy has thronged to her standard of national independence, be disarmed, and handed over to her.

A jealous guardian of the ancestral common patrimony of honour and glory, I have handed over to my beloved cousin Prince Eugène the Government of the State, while I myself again draw the sword.

The brave soldiers of the Emperor Napoleon, my generous Ally, will fight the fight of liberty and justice with my soldiers.

PEOPLE OF ITALY!

Austria attacks Piedmont because I have advocated the cause of our common country in the Councils of Europe, and because I have not been insensible to your cry of anguish. Thus she has violently broken those Treaties which she never respected; thus now all right is on the side of the nation, and I can conscientiously perform the vow made on the tomb of my illustrious parent. Taking up Arms in the defence of my Throne, of the liberty of my people, and of the honour of the Italian name, I fight for the rights of the whole nation.

We trust in God and in our concord; in the valour of the soldiers of Italy, and in the alliance of the noble French nation, and we trust in the justice of public opinion.

My only ambition is to be the first soldier of Italian Independence.
Turin, 29th April, 1859.

Viva l'Italia!

VICTOR EMMANUEL.'

16 Note and comment on the King's dual appeal—'People of the Kingdom' and 'People of Italy'.

17 What arguments does Victor Emmanuel put forward to justify the declaration of war, and how valid do you consider these to be? (Refer back to the opening section of Document C. and comment on whether this document sheds any light on the influence of Risorgimento writers.)

Document E. A British Observer on Garibaldi's exploits in 1860, from *The Campaign of Garibaldi in the Two Sicilies: A Personal Narrative* by Commander Charles Stuart Forbes (Edinburgh & London, 1861), reproduced in Weill op.cit. p.138 ff.

'On the 14th [of April, 1860], thirteen insurgents, taken with arms in their hands at the Guancia Convent, were shot by sentence of court-martial at Palermo. By this act the Neapolitan Government blew away every prospect of reconciliation, for it determined Garibaldi to come to the rescue. With difficulty restrained by his friends from a last visit to his Nizzard home, which might have been attended with untoward results, he now decided upon organising a Southern expedition; for, though he had never counselled the insurrection in Sicily, he had promised to help all Italians that would assist themselves; and no longer able to remain a passive spectator of their sacrifices, he summoned his followers of the old Cacciatori once more; at the same time sending word to the Sicilians to confine themselves to the mountainous portions of the island until his arrival.

To Italians he appealed in the following

PROCLAMATION.

Italians!—The Sicilians are fighting against the enemies of Italy and for Italy. To help them with money, arms, and especially men, is the duty of every Italian.

The chief cause of the misfortunes of Italy has been disunion, and the indifference one province showed for the fate of another.

The salvation of Italy dates from the day when the sons of the same soil hastened to the support of their brothers in danger.

If we abandon the brave sons of Sicily to themselves, they will have to fight the mercenaries of the Bourbon, as well as those of Austria and of the priest who rules at Rome.

Let the people of the free provinces raise their voices in favour of their brethren who are fighting—let them send their generous youth to where men are fighting for their country.

Let the Marches, Umbria, Sabine, the Roman Campagna, and the Neapolitan territory rise, so as to divide the enemy's forces.

If the cities do not offer a sufficient basis for insurrection, let the more resolute throw themselves into the open country.

A brave man can always find a weapon. In the name of Heaven, harken not to the voice of those who cram themselves at well-served tables.

Let us arm. Let us fight for our brothers; to-morrow we can fight for ourselves.

A handful of brave men, who have followed me in battles for our country, are advancing with me to the rescue. Italy knows them; they always appear at the hour of danger. Brave and generous companions, they have devoted their lives to their country; they will shed their last drop of blood for it, seeking no other reward than that of a pure conscience.

"Italy and Victor Emmanuel!" that was our battle cry when we crossed the Ticino; it will resound into the very depths of Ætna.

As this prophetic battle-cry re-echoes from the hills of Italy to the Tarpeian Mount, the tottering throne of tyranny will fall to pieces, and the whole country will rise like one man.

To arms, then! Let us by one blow put an end to our chronic misfortunes. Let us show the world that this is truly the land once trodden by the great Roman race.

G. GARIBALDI.

It is not wholly impossible but that the bitter cup he had swallowed regarding Savoy and Nice may have influenced him in espousing this most congenial distraction.

No sooner had Garibaldi unpacked his red shirt, than the whole of North Italy responded: it was the one thing needful to give direction to an impulse which was panting for a leader. Subscriptions were opened all over Italy; men came forward by thousands; transport was the only hitch. And it was wisely determined that the first expedition should be composed only of tried men, leaving the others to come after as transport might become available.

. . . As for Garibaldi, he was nearly devoured by the population as he advanced. Salerno was gone mad; its inhabitants could hardly realise the dream. A few short hours before, Afant de Rivera [the commander appointed by the King of Naples] were [was] lording it over them with 12 000 men, and here was their deliverer entering with half-a-dozen of his staff in a couple of open carriages, his nearest troops being sixty or seventy miles behind him.

It is almost impossible to paint with a pen this magic scene, the romantic beauty of the well-known bay, the town illuminated, *à giorno*, throngs of armed men and excited women in the streets; bands in every direction: in short, a population who had been deprived of speech from its infancy, hailing their deliverer; while he who had consecrated a life to the achievement of his sublime task, was with difficulty forcing his way through the dense masses which crowded round to obtain a glimpse of the idol of their country.

. . . . .

From the hour when he dreamt "Italian Unity," he declared war to every obstacle in his path, whether priestly or princely. When he saw a Mastai Ferretti in the Papal Chair, he hailed him from the banks of the Plata; when he saw an Italian prince lead on against the Austrians, he hastened to join him. Though Europe dared not oppose a French occupation of Rome, he did. By his uncompromising hostility to oppressors, whether foreign or domestic, he revivified the nation, and inaugurated that spirit which has emancipated sixteeen millions of his countrymen. Three millions more are yearning in Rome and Venetia, and because he is bold enough to avow his determination to finish his task, haggard diplomacy desires him to be more circumspect. What, in the name of heaven, has diplomacy ever done for Italy, since it condemned her to half a century of misrule at the treaty of Vienna?

Garibaldi has nothing to conceal; he declared himself, twenty-seven years since, at Genoa. He feels the anguish of Venice, and says, "Be patient—I come!"

He sees the Rome of the Popes made the hotbed of intrigue against the rising liberties of his country, and though she is bristling with French bayonets, he declares she shall be the Italian capital.'

18 Compare Garibaldi's appeal to the Italian people with the arguments put forward by Mazzini in Document B.
19 What does the description of Garibaldi's arrival in Salerno tell you about the impact Garibaldi had, both in Italy and in Europe as a whole?
20 Why is the author of this document so full of praise for Garibaldi?
21 At Plombières, Napoleon spoke of the importance of winning over European public opinion: how did Garibaldi influence this?

Document F. A letter from Cavour, from *Cavour e l'Inghilterra* Vol II, Tome II (Bologna, 1933) pp 93–94, reproduced in Beales, *op.cit.* page 169.
'In Sicily, Garibaldi has let himself become intoxicated with his success. Instead of carrying annexation, or allowing it to be carried, he dreams of conquering Naples and delivering Italy. If moderating counsels came to him from England, for which he has great respect, that would be most advantageous. I know the Minister cannot put himself in direct contact with Garibaldi; but he could indoctrinate the Admiral, who seems to me to be a man of much tact and authority.

Annexation would get us out of an embarrassing situation, because it would bring Garibaldi back into a regular position. If annexation is delayed, I foresee the greatest difficulties.

As for Naples, . . . I do not yet know precisely what I shall say. If they would really consent to cede Sicily, and would help us to demolish Rome, I believe that we could come to an agreement, at least for a time. . . .'

22 When, to whom, and for what purpose do you expect this letter to have been written?
23 What do you understand by the term 'annexation' as used here?
24 What 'greatest difficulties' do you think that Cavour foresees?

Summary
25 (a) What different types of historical source are represented by the Documents in this section?

(b) Comment on the value and utility of each of these types, and outline the difficulties presented by each.

26 What light do these documents shed on:

(a) the differing interpretations of unification as presented by Beales in Document A?

(b) the personalities and relative contributions of Mazzini, Cavour and Garibaldi?

D *Italian unification—the role of other powers*

As section B above indicates, one of the factors leading to unification that is frequently discussed is the part played by the other European powers. This section is intended to help you consider this aspect.

1 The other powers may be identified as France, Austria, Russia, Britain and Prussia. These were the powers—especially the first two—which might have been expected to have affected events in Italy, either by direct intervention or by ignoring events there. Before studying what they actually did, write down what attitude you would have expected each of these countries to have taken to

(a) the enlargement of the kingdom of Piedmont

(b) the unification of the Italian state.

In each case, explain why you expected that attitude.

2 Study both this chapter and other sources. As you do so, complete a date chart like that below, entering on to it all the actions that the Powers took in Italy, and any decisions they made *not* to involve themselves.

	France	*Austria*	*Russia*	*Britain*	*Prussia*
1858					
1859					
1860					
1870					
1871					

3 Use the information provided by your chart to answer these questions.

(a) What actions taken by (i) France and (ii) Austria in Italy influenced events there between 1858 and 1871? Did they hasten or slow down the process of unification?

(b) Did *actions* by any of the other three powers in Italy affect the process of unification? If so, how?

(c) Did the *inaction* of any of these three powers affect the process of unification? If so, how?

V The Great Powers 1871–90

1 The Third Republic in France

(a) The National Assembly

In peace-time there had been no revolutionary party strong enough to overthrow the Second Empire. Its end came about through an external event and not an internal development. It was destroyed, not by popular revolution, but by military defeat. It could not survive the Battle of Sedan (*see page 236*). The constitutional changes, following Napoleon III's surrender to the Prussians, were carried out by reluctant politicians. They established a republic, which most Frenchmen did not want.

When the news of the collapse at Sedan reached Paris, crowds gathered in the streets, and the Empress and the Prince Imperial fled to England with the help of an American dentist. A mob, led by members of the opposition, secured the proclamation of a republic (which was to become known as the Third Republic) at the Hôtel de Ville in the way that had now become traditional. The Legislative Chamber, afraid that revolutionaries might seize power, proclaimed the establishment of a provisional Government of National Defence composed solely of the deputies representing Paris. The important ministries were held by Republicans, who were determined to continue the war against Prussia. They believed that, as in 1792, the Republic would expel the invaders from French soil and gain overwhelming popularity from an outburst of patriotic enthusiasm. The size of the National Guard in Paris was doubled and soon contained 360 000 men. But within three weeks the Prussian forces had cut off Paris from the rest of the country. Léon Gambetta, one of the youngest and most energetic ministers, escaped from the besieged city in a balloon to Tours, where he tried ineffectively to organize the unwilling peasantry into new armies to resist the enemy on the Loire.

After the fall of Paris, Bismarck made it clear that he would only make peace with a representative and undisputed French government, and he agreed to an armistice in January 1871 to permit the election of a National Assembly the next month. This met at Bordeaux, and it consisted of 396 Monarchists (214 Orleanists and 182 Legitimists), 20 Bonapartists and 228 Republicans, mostly from Paris and other large towns. The Republicans remained in a minority, partly because they were identified with anti-clericalism and hostility to private property, and also they were associated with the continuance of the war, and the peasants wanted peace. The Assembly, therefore, immediately accepted the Prussian peace-terms, which inflicted severe losses in population and economic strength upon France (*see page 236*).

To the monarchical majority in the Assembly, such a time of national humiliation did not seem suitable for the restoration of the monarchy. They preferred to postpone this to a more favourable occasion and to identify the Republicans with the discredit of defeat. So they appointed a Republican, Jules Grévy, as President of the National Assembly, while the veteran Thiers, who had been returned by 26 departments (as was allowed in the elections), was their inevitable choice to form a government, and they gave him the vague title of Head of the Executive Power. He undertook, by what came to be known as the Pact of Bordeaux, to remain impartial between the different political parties, and he formed a coalition government from among them. The Assembly now moved to Versailles. It had to go there because the deputies from the provinces distrusted radical Paris so deeply that they refused to meet within the capital itself.

(b) The Paris Commune (1871)
Feeling in Paris was equally hostile towards the Assembly. Patriotic anger at the peace treaty, republican fears of the government, metropolitan suspicion of the provinces and the sufferings of the poorer classes after the siege, all contributed towards this embitterment. The Assembly, which had property-owners and financiers among its members, made the situation worse by ordering the immediate payment of all rents and commercial debts, which had been postponed during the war. It went on to stop the pay of the National Guard, which now included a majority of the poorer Parisians, and order the taking over of its 400 guns, but the regular troops sent in March to do this fraternized with the National Guardsmen, who seized and hanged the two generals commanding them.

Thiers withdrew all government departments and forces from Paris. The only organized body left in the city was the Central Committee of the National Guard, mainly composed of working-class and lower middle-class delegates from almost all its battalions. This held elections to create a municipal government called the Commune, a name which recalled the days from 1792 to 1794, when the Paris mob had controlled the government and France. Some 229 000 Parisians voted, which was about 70 per cent of the electorate. The international Socialist movement was later to claim the Paris Commune as part of its history, but Karl Marx wrote, 'The Commune was in no way socialist, nor could it be.' In fact, the Socialists, though providing many of its most active leaders, formed only a minority of its members. It had considerable support from the middle-class, many of whom had been ruined by the Assembly's decision about rents and debts. The political outlook of the Commune was reformist rather than socialist. Most of the Communards were inspired by the events and spirit of the Revolution of 1789. They were liberal and anticlerical, and among their objectives were free education and the fixing of working-hours and wages.

To the Versailles government, however, the Commune appeared as a dangerous revolutionary movement set to defy it and destroy its authority before the state had recovered from war and defeat. The red flags now flying over the 20 town halls of Paris seemed to be a defiant challenge to national unity and stability. It was determined not to negotiate with the Commune, but to end it.

Thiers reorganized his forces at Versailles, doubling their numbers to 80 000 by successfully negotiating with Bismarck for the release of French prisoners of war. While the German occupation forces remained inactive in the suburbs, the second siege of Paris began in April. This time it was by a French army under Marshal MacMahon, who had fought in Algeria and the Crimea and been wounded and taken prisoner at Sedan. His troops shot prisoners taken in clashes, and the Commune retaliated by seizing hostages in the city. After a bombardment lasting six weeks, his forces broke into the city and took it after a week of merciless street-fighting. Paris suffered more damage than in any war, and more people were killed than during the twelve months of the Terror in 1793–94. Prisoners were massacred on both sides, and the Communards shot many hostages, including the Archbishop of Paris. As the defenders fell back after the steady capture of their barricades, they burned some of the most famous buildings in the centre of the city, among them the Tuilleries and the Hôtel de Ville. The Versailles troops lost about a thousand dead in the fighting, and more than 20 000 Parisians were probably killed; and afterwards 13 450 received terms of imprisonment and 7500 were transported to convict settlements in tropical colonies overseas.

The Commune represented the last attempt by Paris to dictate the form of French government to the provinces. This was a process that had begun in the seventeenth century and had led Louis XIV to transfer the court and government to his newly-built palace at Versailles in an effort to defeat it; and since the Revolution of 1789 Paris had dominated France and determined the nature of her successive political regimes. The June Days of 1848 had not destroyed that situation, but the more terrible events of 1871 did. The influence of Paris in national affairs was never now to be as it had been before. Symbolic of this was the abolition of the National Guard by the Assembly in August 1871, after it had played an important part in French history since its establishment in the days after the fall of the Bastille in 1789.

The Versailles government had not regarded the Commune as a simple desire to defend republicanism, but rather as a threat to the very social and political order of the state. It could represent it as an attempt by the extremists in the capital to impose a socialist dictatorship upon

288

the rest of the country. This also was held to justify the severity with which its supporters were treated after its 72 days of defiant existence. The result was that the French socialist movement, through the loss of its leaders, was eliminated from national politics for nearly ten years; but the Third Republic gained the support of the peasants and property-owners and all who wanted stability and order in the state. This did much to enable it to develop in a peaceful and constitutional manner and survive the hostility of its opponents during its first uncertain years.

(c) The Survival of the Republic

Since it was now clear that the Republic would not threaten property or privilege, Thiers could be certain that he had the confidence of the most powerful classes in the state. The elections of February 1871 had shown that the country desperately wanted peace, and he himself believed that France needed a period of conservative stability to ensure her national recovery.

It was essential to pay off as soon as possible the indemnity imposed upon France under the Treaty of Frankfurt so as to end the German occupation of the 43 eastern departments. The necessary amount of money for this was raised by government loans, and the last German troops left France in September 1873, which was a much earlier date than had been expected, and it caused Bismarck some concern.

Bismarck distrusted also the reorganization of the French army and the introduction of conscription in 1872, which was another achievement of Thiers. The period of service in the regular army was fixed at five years, but numerous exemptions on family and educational grounds were allowed to remain. Nevertheless, France was brought closer to the adoption of a system of universal military service than at any time since the end of the First Empire. In addition, plans were made for the used of the French railways in time of war (to remedy a serious weakness in 1870), and in 1874 the French general staff was reformed on the Prussian model.

These measures were accompanied by a profound change in the attitude of the French people towards the army. So powerful was this that Marx said that the Third Republic was not based upon 'Liberty, Equality, Fraternity', but rather upon 'Infantry, Cavalry, Artillery'. No longer was there the widespread opposition to providing France with a large, well-equipped army which had frustrated Napoleon III. Now the ideal, adopted in all political circles, was rather that of 'the nation in arms'. Radicals looked back to the 'citizen armies' of the *levée en masse*, which had saved the Republic in the early days of the Revolutionary War, and hoped now that its spirit would be revived in a system of democratic equality for national defence. Conservatives hoped that it would be the instrument of unity and revival in which universal service would heal class divisions and discipline the nation in the cause of patriotism. At the same time, the middle classes and peasants now accepted the army as the safeguard of social order and peace. And the professional officers, as a result of their experiences in 1870, no longer preferred a large reserve and militia to a regular army of trained conscripts.

Now that the immediate political problems had been faced, the need to provide France with a permanent form of government had to be considered, and it cost Thiers the support of the National Assembly. His personal preference was for a constitutional monarchy on British lines, but he had come to the conclusion that France would have to remain republican, and in November 1872 he expressed this belief. 'It is the republic which divides us least,' he said, and again, 'To wish for anything else would mean revolution, the most formidable of all revolutions.' Such a deliberate violation of the Pact of Bordeaux angered the Monarchists in the Assembly, who forced him to resign in May 1873.

Since the Monarchists did not want the successor of Thiers to possess the same powers and perhaps thwart the restoration of the monarchy, they separated the leadership of the government from that of the state. The victor over the Commune, Marshal MacMahon, who was a conservative Roman Catholic and the descendant of an Irish Jacobite who had gone into exile with James II, was made President of the Republic, and he appointed the Duke of Broglie, an Orleanist, as prime minister. In doing this, the Monarchists did in fact promote a republican form of government since they replaced the practically absolute authority, which Thiers possessed, by a parliamentary government, but this was unintentional. They still wanted to bring back the monarchy.

The monarchical movement was closely associated with the continuing religious revival in the country, and the Roman Catholic Church sympathized with its aims and accepted its protection. While the peasantry had remained constant to the faith, now the wealthier classes were particularly attracted to it as a powerful influence in favour of social stability. Many people believed that the disasters of the war were due to the widespread laxity of thought and morals under the Second Empire. With such encouragement, religious orders multiplied, and so did their schools, orphanages and hospitals. Among the most prominent of these orders were the Assumptionists, founded at Nîmes in 1843, who sought to popularize devotion to the cult of the Sacred Heart of Jesus to gain pity for the sorrows of France. The symbol of this in Paris was the great new Church of the Sacré-Coeur, on the dominating heights of Montmartre, which was built in 1873 by public subscription on the authority of the National Assembly, by way of expiation for the nation's sins; and thousands of pilgrims were carried by the railways to visit Lourdes and other shrines as an act of penitence. The Government supported the Church in its activities and gave it privileges, particularly in finance and education, which were greater even than those it had enjoyed during the Second Empire. The result was to increase the anticlericalism of the Republicans.

The Monarchists, however, failed to secure the speedy restoration of the monarchy, which their majority in the Assembly and the support of the Church and many of the people would have seemed to have made inevitable. One difficulty was their division between Legitimists and Orleanists, but they did come to an agreement. The Orleanists, though more numerous, were ready to support the Bourbon claimant, the elderly Count of Chambord (a grandson of Charles X), who was childless, on condition that when he died he would be succeeded by their claimant, the Count of Paris (the grandson of Louis Philippe). But the Count of Chambord, though ready to promote universal suffrage and constitutional liberties, refused to abandon the white flag and fleur de lis of the Bourbons—'I will not let the standard of Henry IV, of Francis I, of Joan of Arc, be torn from my hands,' he said. The Monarchists knew that only the tricolour would be acceptable to French people of all classes. They realized that they could do nothing but wait until the Count of Chambord's death made it possible for them to put forward the Count of Paris, who was as ready as his grandfather had been to accept the flag of the Revolution. They sought the necessary delay by fixing MacMahon's term of office at seven years.

(d) The Constitution of the Republic (1875)
The Count of Chambord, however, lived on and persisted in maintaining his position over the flag, which he believed was vital to mark him as a true King of France—'Without my principle,' he declared, 'I am but a fat man with a limp.' Though an improvisation without a constitution, the Republic survived, and republican enthusiasm increased under Gambetta, who was now the active, forceful leader of the movement. The Republicans began to win by-elections to the Assembly. Between 1871 and 1874, 126 Republicans were elected, but only 23 Monarchists and 10 Bonapartists. The Monarchist majority was steadily threatened, but they were able to preserve it. In January 1875, however, the Assembly managed to pass by one vote a law providing for the election of future presidents. Since this changed the presidency from a temporary expedient to a permanent institution, it indirectly committed France to a republican form of government.

This was not followed, however, by the construction of a formal, planned constitution. The Monarchists in the Assembly were not prepared to do this, but they were ready to compromise so as to avoid a deadlock and a general election in which they were certain to suffer heavy losses. The Assembly, therefore, merely passed a number of laws dealing with various aspects of government. The Republicans under Gambetta were willing to compromise with the Monarchists and to retain several conservative features. There was to be a Legislature, consisting of a Chamber of Deputies, elected every four years by universal male suffrage, and a Senate, consisting of 75 life members nominated by the Assembly and 225 elected for nine years by a special electoral college in each department and arranged to favour rural

France. The Chamber of Deputies and the Senate together were to appoint the President for seven years. He was to choose the ministers, who were to be responsible to the Legislature, and he could dissolve the Chamber on the advice of the Senate. The Council of Ministers was to be the executive body, and its President was to become popularly known as 'Prime Minister', the traditional title originating in the *ancien régime*.

The Monarchists succeeded in gaining for the Senate, which was likely to be conservative, equal legislative powers with the Chamber of Deputies. Also the relationship between the President, Senate and Chamber was left uncertain, and the procedure for revising the constitution was simple. The Monarchists hoped that the time would come when the presidency could easily be taken over by a king and the republic converted into a monarchy. In fact, however, this constitution was to last, practically unchanged, until the collapse of the Third Republic when France was defeated in 1940.

(e) The Consolidation of the Republic

The National Assembly, after an existence of nearly five years, now dissolved itself, and a general election was held early in 1876. The Monarchists retained their control of the Senate, but the Republicans gained 360 seats in the Chamber of Deputies against 78 Monarchists and 75 Bonapartists (who were more popular now that Napoleon III's death had made the Young Prince Imperial their claimant). Many voters were prepared to support the Republic once it had been legally established, and the question of war and peace was no longer an issue. Also, Gambetta and other prominent Republicans were more able than the leading Monarchists, who had become discredited by their clericalism and failure to establish a monarchy.

With the President and the Senate opposed to the Chamber, the Constitution was unworkable. Two Prime Ministers, appointed by MacMahon, followed each other after only a few months. In May 1877 MacMahon took advantage of the situation to dismiss the existing ministry, recall the Duke of Broglie to the premiership and obtain the consent of the Senate to a dissolution of the Chamber and another general election. MacMahon and Broglie both tried hard by propaganda, intimidation of the press and promises to voters to win over the electorate. They were supported by the Church and the landowners, but the peasants were beginning to abandon their traditional respect for these two rural authorities. The Republicans lost only 36 seats and retained their majority in the Chamber. For a few months, MacMahon tried to keep in power conservative ministers of his own choice, most of whom were not members of the Legislature, but the Chamber refused to pass the budget. In November he had to give way and appoint a Republican ministry acceptable to the Chamber. A partial renewal of its members brought a Republican majority in the Senate as well in January 1879, and MacMahon soon afterwards resigned and was replaced as President by Grévy. In that year also the Legislature returned to Paris from Versailles.

The events of these years not only finally established the Third Republic, but also made sure that it was to be governed by the Assembly and not by the President. The Prime Minister now effectively chose his colleagues in the Council of Ministers, who had to have the support of the Chamber. Though the President retained his constitutional right to dissolve the Chamber, he never again exercised it. Since there could now only be a general election every four years, the organization of large, disciplined political parties, on British lines, became impossible. A ministry could not preserve itself by threatening to obtain a dissolution of the Chamber if deputies defeated it, and the parties found it impossible to enforce the allegiance of their own members. Both the Republicans and the Monarchists were really coalitions of small groups of deputies, each member of which preserved his liberty of action, including voting against ministries they had agreed to support and so condemning them to brief periods of office. The Third Republic was to have a hundred different ministries during its life of less than 70 years. And the President's right to appoint a new Prime Minister was, indeed, the only important function he actually performed in the government of the Republic.

Though the Republican success was very much due to Gambetta's vigorous campaigning in the elections of 1876 and 1877, Grévy, as a moderate Republican, mistrusted his radical reforming ideas, and he was not to become Prime Minister until a few months before his death in 1882. The most influential politician of the period was Jules Ferry, a former member of the Government of National Defence, who was Prime Minister from 1880 to 1881 and again from 1883 to 1885. During the 1880s, and particularly during the years when he was in power, government policy was aimed at establishing the Republic as a liberal, constitutional state. In 1881, for instance, the press was finally freed from restriction, and public meetings no longer required official authorization, while the Communards were granted a full amnesty. Although itself far from revolutionary, the Republic adopted the revolutionary song, *La Marseillaise*, as the national anthem, and the Fourteenth of July, the anniversary of the storming of the Bastille, was made a public holiday. Steps were also taken to protect the Republic further against any monarchical revival. These included laws passed in 1884 prohibiting any revision of the republican form of government or the election to the presidency of any member of a former reigning royal family in France, and in 1886 all members of such families were expelled from France. Ferry also embarked, not without opposition, on a policy of colonial expansion, which was eventually to give France an overseas empire second only to the British Empire (*see page 358*).

(f) Clericalism

The Republicans believed, however, that the most important task immediately before them was to limit the power of the Church. During the election campaign of 1878, Gambetta conducted a vigorous attack on clericalism, the influence of the clergy in politics. 'Clericalism, that is the danger,' he declared, and he knew that it was a slogan which would gain him support from Republicans, most of whom were now even more anticlerical than ever. The issue was a divisive legacy from the Revolution of 1789. Ever since its sufferings at the hands of the revolutionaries, who had sought to abolish religion in France, the Church had largely been on the side of conservatism and monarchism, and since 1870 this connection had become even closer. When the Republicans considered the Church's means of propaganda and the part it had played in influencing elections, they were ready to believe that the strengthened Church of the religious revival represented the most serious threat to the future of the Republic.

Not that it was entirely a political question. France had taken the leading part in the development of the rationalism of eighteenth-century Europe, and the tradition of Voltaire and other writers, who had set out to 'cite the Divinity itself at the bar of reason,' remained strong in French intellectual circles. This was now reinforced by belief in the certainty of unending human progress presented by the discoveries and inventions of the Industrial Revolution. In such a new world, religion had no place; it was seen as an outworn superstition which impeded the attainment of that universal happiness now offered to mankind. Faith must give place to science and reason. Many Republicans unhesitatingly accepted these ideas. They believed, indeed, that the Republic should identify itself with them and seek to put them into effect; but the Syllabus of Errors and the Dogma of Papal Infallibility seemed to make it clear that the Papacy was on the side of reaction and obscurantism (*see page 63*), and the Ultramontanism of the French Church was as powerful as ever. Many Republicans thought, therefore, that for political and intellectual reasons the influence of the Church in France should be drastically reduced.

The area in which it seemed most urgent to do this was education. Napoleon I, in order to prevent the Church regaining the control over education which it had possessed under the *ancien régime*, had conceived a scheme for national, government controlled education at all ages and levels, but it was very imperfectly put into practice, and since then little had been done to extend it. Primary education, though the responsibility of the towns and rural districts, was often undertaken almost entirely by the teaching orders of the Church. Secondary education for boys was provided by the state *lycées*, but many parents disliked their military emphasis, which Napoleon had thought important, and preferred to send their sons to schools managed by priests. Napoleon had been content to leave secondary education for girls in the hands of the Church—'Religion is an important affair in a public institution for the instruction of young ladies,' he wrote. 'Let them be brought up to believe and not to reason'—and convent schools still provided almost the only secondary education available for girls.

Moreover, though most boys and nearly all girls attended religious schools, they amounted to only two-fifths of all French children, and there were still not enough state schools to supplement them so that everyone had even an elementary education. A Republican estimate in 1879 put illiteracy at 15 per cent of the population.

Republican deununciation of the Church's part in education was twofold. They asserted that children taught in religious schools received conservative and anti-republican instruction which influenced them for the rest of their lives. From 1849 the introduction of universal suffrage had brought Monarchist or Bonapartist majorities in the elections, and the Republicans saw the effect of the religious schools in this. Again, the Republicans had their rival legend to explain France's defeat in 1870. They did not believe that it had been brought about by the sins of the nation. They held that it was due to the inferiority of French education compared with that of Prussia. They alleged that, while Prussian schools provided instruction in the sciences and modern languages, French education was largely religious and classical as it had been in the seventeenth century.

Ferry was a determined opponent of clerical control in education and was Minister of Education before he became Prime Minister. Under his leadership a number of anticlerical laws were passed. In 1880 the Jesuits and several other religious orders were dissolved, and their members were forbidden to teach in state schools. More state secondary schools were established for girls and boys. In 1882 religious instruction was removed from all state schools. These measures were accompanied by the abolition of chaplains in the armed forces and the removal of nursing nuns from hospitals. Since France was still mainly a Roman Catholic country, the enforcement of this policy met with much opposition. Some 400 magistrates and officials resigned rather than enforce the laws, and troops had sometimes to be called to clear monasteries (though convents were left unmolested). This legislation was the prelude to the separation of Church and State, which was to be enacted early the next century, and the beginning of a bitter political dispute which lasted almost as long as the Third Republic.

(g) Boulangism

The years between 1879 and 1882 saw the real foundation of the Third Republic, and since the elections of 1881 had given the Republicans 467 seats in the Assembly, its future seemed assured. Yet during the 1880s, at the same time as the government was liberalizing the state, its stability was threatened. The Republicans hoped to maintain their political power by relying upon the lower middle classes, and in 1884 they sought their continued support by ending the system of life-membership of the Senate and giving more power to local government by allowing all mayors, except those in Paris, to be elected by local councils. By now, however, Republican unity was threatened by the growth of the Radicals, who claimed to represent the industrial working-class and were opposed to the social conservatism and the colonial policy of the Republicans. The Radicals had a formidable leader in Georges Clemenceau, whose ruthlessness and biting tongue had already gained him the nickname of 'the Tiger'. At the same time the death of the Prince Imperial in 1879 and of the Count of Chambord in 1883 left the Count of Paris as the only claimant to the throne, and the Monarchists seemed to be less divided than usual. The result was that the elections of 1885 reduced the number of Republican seats in the Assembly to 383, of whom 180 were Radicals.

A government including Radical ministers had to be formed, and it took office at the beginning of a period of serious economic crisis. This was part of a general European depression, which had begun in 1873, and France was particularly slow in recovering from it because of her shortage of cheap, easily-mined coal, which made her industries internationally uncompetitive, and the steadily decreasing growth of the population, which deprived her of the possibility of establishing expanding production and home markets. In addition, a disastrous blight ('phylloxera vastata') ravaged the French vineyards at this time with economic effects that have been calculated as being twice as severe as those of the War of 1870–71. All classes in France suffered from this situation. It was one of the reasons for the growth of the Radicals, but since no party seemed to be able to deal with the crisis, it also caused a general disenchantment with the politics of the state and a widespread anti- parliamentarian movement, which posed a serious threat to the Republic.

This threat became apparent when Clemenceau secured the appointment of General George Boulanger as Minister of War in 1886. Boulanger was born in 1837, the son of a Breton father and a Welsh mother. He served in the army in Algeria and Italy and fought in the Franco-Prussian War in which he was wounded seriously enough not to be involved in the affair of the Commune. During the 1880s he expressed strong Radical views and so won Clemenceau's support. As Minister of War, he showed concern for the welfare of the army by improving the conditions of service for both officers and men and also that he was a sound Republican by removing prominent Monarchists from military posts and by having the sentry-boxes painted red, white and blue. Whenever he took his place at the head of regiments during military reviews, as a martial, blond-bearded figure, mounted on a magnificent black horse, he was acclaimed by Parisians as a symbol of the new place of the army in the Republic. And his popularity grew when he made anti-German speeches, which drew him a rebuke from Bismarck.

The conservative Republicans became alarmed and deprived him his ministerial post and had him sent away to a command in the provinces in May 1887. Crowds of Parisians gathered at the railway station as he departed, cheering him and making an effort to prevent his train leaving. Clemenceau now disowned him—'General Boulanger's popularity,' he declared in the Chamber, 'has come too soon to one who likes noise too much.' The Republic, however, was not safe. It was to face a further crisis which gave Boulanger another opportunity to seek popularity.

In the autumn of 1887, the news was revealed of a scandal involving the President's son-in-law, Daniel Wilson, the son of a Scottish engineer who had made a fortune by providing Paris with gas-lighting. Daniel Wilson had abused his position by selling decorations and honours in the presidential gift. Grévy unwillingly resigned in December. The Radicals refused to have Ferry as his successor, and in the end the office went to a moderate Republican, Sadi Carnot, a grandson of the 'organizer of victory' Revolutionary War.

Meanwhile, Boulanger had followed his rejection at the hands of the Radical leaders by approaching the Monarchists, who were ready to use his popularity to overthrow the discredited Republic. He promised them that when he was a minister again, he would set in motion a royalist *coup d'état*. The government compelled him to retire from the army in March 1888. He took advantage of this to stand for election to the Chamber. Though he was supplied with money by prominent Monarchists, he kept this a secret. He stood for a programme of constitutional reform, particularly the abolition of the Senate, which he accused of being the chief obstacle to constitutional reform. He had the support, not only of the army and the Church, but also of many of the workers and unemployed. He gained overwhelming majorities in a series of by-elections in a number of constituencies, including the Nord and the Seine, the two largest and most industrialized departments in France.

At the beginning of 1889, many people expected Boulanger to seize power, but he hesitated. He probably realized that his support was, in fact, so diverse and indeterminate that he had no real basis for power and a policy. At any rate, the government took the opportunity to bring legal proceedings against him for treasonably threatening the state. He fled to Brussels, where, two years later, he shot himself over the grave of his mistress. Clemenceau said, 'He died as he had lived—like a subaltern.'

By then Boulangism was discredited. In the general election of 1889 the Republicans kept their majority, the Monarchists lost some seats, and only about 40 Boulangists were elected, mainly in the previously Radical districts of Paris; but it showed that over a third of the voters were opposed to the existence of the Republic. The threat from the Monarchists was over—their cause had now lost all popular appeal, and Boulangism revealed their futility. Nevertheless, the Church and the army persisted in their hostility and now many of the working-class, despairing of the conservative policies of the Republicans, had deserted them in favour of antiparliamentary action, an ominous development for the future.

The centenary of the Revolution of 1789 was commemorated with impressive celebrations in France, including a great exhibition in Paris which bequeathed the Eiffel Tower to the city, but the underlying weakness of the Republic went back to the Revolution. It had failed to secure for France a means of giving dignity to the governmental system and of obtaining that respect for the form of the state which is essential for national unity. In Britain this was provided by the awe felt for the Crown and in the United States of America by the reverence accorded to the text of the Constitution; but France had now no such great unifying institution accepted by all her people. The result was that the Third Republic was to face further dangerous crises during the 1890s.

Bibliography

In addition to the general histories of France (*see page 55*), the first part of this period is covered by Alistair Horne, *The Fall of Paris: The Siege and the Commune, 1870–1871* (Macmillan, 1967) and Stewart Edwards, *The Paris Commune, 1871* (Eyre & Spottiswoode, 1971). There are also F.H. Brabant, *The Beginnings of the Third Republic in France* (Macmillan, 1940) J. Hampden Jackson, *Clemenceau and the Third Republic* (EUP, 1946) and D. Thomson, *Democracy in France* (3rd. edn. OUP, 1938).

Exercises

A   *This section consists of questions that might be used for discussion (or written answers) as a way of expanding on the chapter and testing your understanding of it:*

1   Why were the Republicans' hopes of 'an upsurge of patriotism to expel the invaders' not fulfilled?
2   Refer back to page 000. Explain the differences between Orleanists and Legitimists (Bourbons).
3   Why did not the Monarchists take the opportunity to restore the monarchy in 1871?
4   Why were the provincial deputies of the Assembly reluctant to move to Paris?
5   The Assembly appears to have undertaken a number of measures likely to provoke a reaction in Paris: why therefore did they approve them?
6   What do you understand by 'The political outlook of the Commune was reformist rather than socialist' (*page 288*)?
7   Why was there such a bloody battle for Paris in 1871?
8   Refer back to the earlier sections on France in the nineteenth century. In the light of these, examine the claim that 'Paris had dominated France and determined the nature of her successive political regimes' (*page 288*).
9   What effects did the defeat of the Commune have on support for the Third Republic?
10   Why was Bismarck concerned by developments in France 1871–73?
11   (a) Comment on Thiers' view that 'It is the republic which divides us least' (*page 290*).
   (b) Why did this statement break the Pact of Bordeaux?
12   Explain the revival of militarism and Roman Catholicism in the early years of the Third Republic.
13   What factors led to the failure of the Monarchists to restore the monarchy in the 1870s?
14   Why was no formal, written Constitution drawn up?
15   Were the constitutional arrangements for the Third Republic a compromise, reasonably acceptable to all political parties?
16   Why was the constitution unworkable after the 1876 election?
17   How and why had the powers of the Presidency altered by 1880?
18   How did Ferry's reforms of the 1880s change France?

19 Why were the Republicans so eager to restrict the powers and influence of the Catholic Church?
20 What do you understand by 'the Ultramontanism of the Church in France' (page 294)?
21 Why did the Republicans move first against the Church's influence in education, and why did their proposals arouse such hostility?
22 Explain the differences between the Radicals and the Republicans.
23 Why was the Republic threatened in the 1880s?
24 Why was Boulanger so popular, and why therefore was he dismissed from the government?
25 Why did Boulanger fail to seize power in 1889?
26 Assess the strengths and weaknesses of the Republic in 1890.

B *Essay questions*
1 Was the Third Republic in serious danger between 1875 and 1886? (Cambridge, 1982)
2 'It is a republic which divided us least.' Was this the main reason why the Third Republic survived to 1890? (Oxford, 1981)
3 What was the importance of the Paris Commune, 1870–1? (Oxford, 1982)
4 Why, in the 1870s, did France successively reject imperial rule, the Paris Commune and the restoration of the monarchy? (Oxford, 1983)
5 Illustrate and explain the instability of the Third French Republic during the years 1870–1907. (SUJB, 1982)
6 To what extent did the constitutional stability of the Third Republic before 1914 mask deep social and political divisions among French people? (Welsh, 1981)
7 'The surprise of the 1870s was not so much that Bonapartism reappeared on the French political scene, but that its resurgence was so limited after Sedan.' How far do you agree with this judgement? (Welsh, 1981)
8 'It was unstable, but it endured.' How do you explain this apparent contradiction in the Third French Republic? (Welsh, 1982)
9 What light does the career of either Gambetta or Ferry throw on the problems facing the Third French Republic? (Welsh, 1982)
10 'The Third French Republic survived only because every alternative was discredited.' Discuss with reference to 1870–1914. (Oxford and Cambridge, 1982)
11 What did France owe to either Jules Ferry or Adolphe Thiers? (AEB, 1981)
12 Explain the resilience of the French Third Republic in the period 1875–1914. (AEB, 1983)
13 Why did the Empire of Napoleon III come to an end in 1870, and what political difficulties had the French to overcome during the next ten years? (London, 1981)
14 'Born in defeat, the Third French Republic had by 1904 not only overcome internal opposition but had regained for France the status of a major power.' Discuss this statement. (JMB, 1982)

C *Documentary extracts on the Third Republic*
Note that in this section the extracts are followed not by questions, but by open-ended statements; you are expected to complete each statement as fully as possible for yourself, referring, where relevant, to the document.

Document A. Boulanger's Appeal to the Voters of Paris, January, 1889, from *Le Général Boulanger* by Charles Chincholle (Paris, 1889) quoted in Derfler op.cit. p.132

'Voters of the Seine,

The Parliamentarians, who once did everything to make me eligible, are now maddened by the idea of seeing me elected. My sword worried them. They took it from me. And now they are more worried than at the time when I still wore it.

Actually, it is not me they are afraid of; it is universal suffrage, whose repeated verdicts bear witness to the disgust aroused in the country by their degeneracy, incapacity, base intrigues, and irksome discussions which have all belittled the Republic.

It is more convenient for them, as a matter of fact, to hold me responsible for the disrepute into which they have fallen, than to ascribe it to their egoism and to their indifference to the interests and griefs of the people.

In order not to be forced to blame themselves, they blame me, in attributing to me the most improbable dictatorial designs. Just as I was overthrown as minister under the pretext that I stood for war, I am being opposed as candidate under the pretext that I stand for dictatorship.

Dictatorship! Is it not we who have endured it under all its forms? Does not one propose every day to invent laws of exception for my electors and myself? If the idea of playing dictator could ever come to me, it seems to me it should have come when, as Minister of War, I held control of the entire army. Did I at that time behave in any way such as to merit this injurious suspicion?

No! I have accepted the good wishes of all without dreaming of "stealing the popularity" of anyone. What is there that is dictatorial in a program which calls for constitutional revision by the most democratic system, by means of a constituent assembly, where each deputy will have every opportunity to state and defend his opinions?

The chiefs of the republican party were sufficiently assured of my republicanism to open ministerial gates to me. In what way, since then, have I forfeited the esteem of the Republic? Let someone tell me of a single act, a single declaration in which I have not openly affirmed it? But I seek, as does France, a Republic comprised of something other than a collection of ambitions and cupidities. What can we hope from people who, according to their own admission, after having been mistaken for fifteen years, dare to present themselves to you again and once more ask for your confidence?

Voters of the Seine,

France today thirsts for justice, righteousness, and disinterestedness.

To try with you to uproot the squandering which exhausts and the rivalries which degrade her, gives me the opportunity to serve her again.

The country is the patrimony of all. You will prevent it from becoming the spoils of a few.

Long live France. Long live the Republic.

General Boulanger'

1 Boulanger could support his claim that the Parliamentarians were degenerate and incapable by. . . .

2 He dismisses the accusation that he stands for dictatorship by. . . .

Document B. Cardinal Lavigerie's toast to the monarchist officers of a Mediterranean squadron, November 12th, 1890, cited in *Les Catholiques républicaines; Histoires et souvenirs* (Paris, 1905) pp 277–278, quoted in Derfler op. cit. p.135.

'. . . Unity, in view of the still-bleeding past and of the ever-threatening future, constitutes our supreme need at this time. It also constitutes the prime wish of the Church, throughout all the ranks in its hierarchy. She does not, of course, ask us to renounce either the memory of past glories or the sentiments of fidelity and gratitude which are honored by all. But when the will of a people is clearly affirmed; when the form of a government, as Leo XIII recently proclaimed, contains nothing inherently contrary to the principles which alone can allow Christians and civilized nations to endure, when it is necessary to pull one's country back from the abyss which threatens it, unqualified support must be given. The time has come, in short, to state that the trial has been won. . . .

It would be foolish to hope to support the columns of a building without entering the structure itself; would not only this prevent those who wish to destroy it from accomplishing their work of madness. . . .'

3 Cardinal Lavigerie argues that members of the Church should now support the Republic because. . . .

4 This speech may be regarded as surprising because . . .; on the other hand. . . .

D *Essay writing skills 7—an essay marking exercise*

One of the most valuable ways of learning how best to write essays is to read other people's. This process also helps you to see what standard you are seeking to attain, and what faults to avoid. In the exercise that follows, you will find four essays written by A level students under exam conditions. For purposes of veracity, expression and spelling have been left unaltered. The question they tackled was:

'It is a Republic which divides us least': was this the main reason why the French Third Republic survived? (Note that dates were *not* attached to the title, but that it was taken to cover the period 1871–1914.)

You may choose to mark the essays in one (or both) of two ways:

(a) Impression marking—simply read the essays and decide by your impression what grade, if any, it is worth, from A to E. Write down the grade you give each, and explain why you have given that grade.

(b) Point marking—by this system, you are awarding points or marks thus:

  i) Give one mark for each significant and relevant fact or explanation included.

  ii) Give a half-mark for any demonstration of knowledge that has not been made relevant, nor explained.

  iii) Having totalled these marks, you may add or subtract up to 2 marks for the overall understanding shown.

  iv) You should now have a total mark, out of a maximum of 25. A level grades correspond approximately to: 18 and over—A; 15–17—B; 13–14—C; 12—D; 10–11—E; less than 10—0 or F.

You should then be able to place the four essays in what you consider their order of excellence, and discuss what grade you consider each is worth. In a group, you may then find it helpful to discuss the relative importance of a number of factors, such as clarity of argument, depth of factual knowledge, range and variety of arguments, ability to answer the question set, the importance of spelling and expression and the value of introductions and conclusions.

Clearly, this exercise can be readily applied to any set of essays that you are able to put together, and may be repeated regularly.

A The republic had been established almost as a breathing space for France before a different form of Government could be decided upon. For many years the republic encountered problems difficulties and opposition but still it stumbled on. On the surface the survival of the republic is almost astonishing when considering that in the first meeting of the National Assembly there was an antirepublican majority. However if this is examined in more depth the results do not appear as surprising.

Opposition to the republic was divieded into three separate factions. While the monarchists numbere 400 out of the 630 Deputies they could not agree on what form of government would take its place. The three factions were the Legitimists, the Orleanists and Bonapartists. The Legitimists took a similar stance to that of Charles X against the 1789 Revolution in trying to decrease its political and socail effects. The Orleanists however favoured a more liberal limited monarchy, while the Bonarpartists favoured the Imperial tradition and a distinct strong dictatorial executive deriving its source of authority through plebicites. There were massive rifts between these groups which were later to be shown as inreconcilable. The 1871–3 Tricoleur controversy did not help the Legitimists candidate to the throne, the Comte de Chambourd said he would not take power unless the national flag was changed to the old white standard of the Bourbons. This was something neither the Orleanists or Bonapartists would stand for. The only two groups who would agree to the reintroduction of a monarchy, the Legitimists and Orleanists but were still united in opposing an Empire favoured by the Bonapartists. There were also religious differences between the groups. The Orleanists and Bonapartists did not like the Ultramontane Legitimists but could not agree and present a coherant alternative over the role religion should play. The anti-republicans lost the initiative with their internal disagreements and indicivness which meant many deserted their ranks, such as Thiers, saying: 'There is only one throne, three men cannot sit on it.'

Support for the Republic could be united together when a threat occured. Despite the fact those who supported the republic were made up of many diverse and often conflicting groups, they could all swallow their differences and close ranks. When Macmahon secured an agreement with the Senate to dissolve the House of Deputies and call an election, or when General Boulanger looked liked holding a coup d'eta the republicans would unite under their saying 'No enemies on the left'.

The urgency for a change from the republic and its possibility was gradually removed. Constitutional changes through the 1875 Wallon Amendment Act and other changes, secured a seven year Presidency and an Upper Chamber both of which could be later easily adjusted to a monarchy. This took the bitter taste of the republic away from the monarchists mouths and as the Comte de Paris commented 'If we cannot make a monarchy we must make something as like it as possible'. By election victories for the republicans, and defections by many prominent politicians and their supporters such as Thiers or the Comte de Chambourd (because he was refused a change in the tricoleur), and an increasing support amoung the electorate for the republicans meant the anti-republican majority was gradually eaten away until it no longer existed. Thus making it necessary for any threat to the republic to be outside the constitution and thus more difficult.

The republic began to gain support on its own merit and achievements. It had successfully fended off various challenges from Macmahon and Boulanger which in itself gave the republic more prestige. There had been a toning down of attitude by some Radicals such as Gambetta who said 'We shall be prudent' and Grevey promised a safe republic both of which showed the republic as more acceptable and viable. Gradually reforms were made such as the Workmen's Compensation Act of 1898, the 10 hours factory Act of 1906 and the Old Age Pensions law of 1911. This secured more support amoung people while centres of opposition were being stiffled. Combes, the Prime Minister 1902–5, following the Dreyfus Affair took a tough line and passed reforms stopping the Church and army from taking any active part in politics.

The rapid national recovery following the Franco-Prussian war, the reconstruction programme and almost instantaneous reforms such as 1872 army acts all showed virtually from its beginning the republic and its leaders were working. Opposition to the Republic was divided whereas its support was not. Despite the other factors over the survival of the republic such as the gradual display of competance and increase in support there is one underlying reason for its continuation. Because there was an initial republican majority that was unable to decide on an alternative and that the republicans would always unite, the most obvious conclusion would be to agree with Thiers opinion that 'It is a republic that divides us least.'

B   Since the defeat of Napoleon in 1815 France had been in a political turmoil. Governments led by monarchists and republics did very little. The French people could not decide on a satisfactory type of Leadership. The leaders that did evolve were often unenspiring and weak so consequently both domestic and foreign policies suffered. By the 1870s France was finally ready to explode. The Monarchists in power suffered a revolution. The Republicans, who caused the revolution, turned Paris into a commune which lasted for two months and only fell to the might of an army. By 1875 a new constitution had been set up on a Republican basis with a President at the head. Thus the 3rd Republic had started a reign of over fifty years. The reasons for its apparant success were varied, and although it was 'the Republic that divides us least' there were many other reasons for its success.

The Third Republic survived for so long because it united in the face of opposition, it also gained the support of much of france, meaning that the internal opposition was weak. The main opposition to the Republic came from the Right of the political scale, the Monarchists, Orleananists and Bonapartists all attacked its structure. However whenever the Right attacked the Republic the left united and defeated the Right who could not pull together as the left could 'No enemies on the Left'. Every time opposition rose the left would unite and fight. The Republicans also stood firm and united against external problems, not caused through Political reasons. The Boulanger problem, Dreyfus affair and Panama scandal all hit at the supports of the Republic, but because there was so much strength in the united Republicans the Republic did not fall or even loose face.

The only chance for the Right to destroy the Republic came in the first years when they still held the majority of power in France. However they could not join together and defeat the Republic. They disagreed on points of importance ie the new leader or the shape of the constitution, so consequently they remained divided and as the Left was united were quickly defeated. As time passed more and more people started to support the Republic, so the chances of its downfall became less and less. The Right wing support dwindled as the Left wing support grew. Consequently the Republic went from strength to strength. After a short period of time the left had the support of just under half of the deputies.

Although the governments in the Third Republic seemed unstable infact they were fairly strong. Although there were fifty governments in fourty years the polititians came back time and time again meaning that they became more aware of the problems facing polititians. Out of 561 polititians 120 served in five or more governments. This meant that the polititians who did come back were very often stronger and more efficient. Men like Delcasse and Thiers gave the Governments of the Third Republic extra support.

The Third Republic also had much external support from outside Parliment, increasing its chances of survival. The Beauracracy which was very strong and influencial supported the Republic and gave it additional strength. Guerard said 'As long as the Beaurocrat is at his desk France survives.' This shows that although the Governments fell with amazing regularity the Beaurocrats kept the country moving. The Republic also had the support of the media. The press stood behind the Republic almost totally. The Left controlled most of the national papers. This was something that the Right wing did not have. Infact the Right did not even control one national paper. The Delegation de Gauches also helped to keep the French third Republic from falling as its propeganda drew support away from the Right Wing to the left wing, capitalizing on the inefficiency of the Right Wing support.

Although the Third Republic was 'a republic that divides us least' this was not the main reason for in the beginning there was more support against it than for however after a time this did become the main reason. There were also other reasons though. Firstly the Left wing Republic supporters stood united against all opposition both politically and non-politicaly. As time went on the opposition fell and the support grew as the Republican influence spread like a disease through France. The only factions which could have brought down the Republic did not act quickly enough. When the Right wing did attack the Republic it was usually in small divided doses that did not pose a threat to the united left. As the left gained support the likelyhood of its failure dwindled. The French Third Republic survived where others would have fell due to the fact that rather than dividing in the face of opposition it pulled closer, uniting its support. 'United we stand, divided we fall.' The Republic saw this and survived against all major opposition. This meant a seemingly week and unstable governmental system survived for over fifty years where others would have failed.

C   'The recognition and consolidation of the Republic, the only form of government compatible with popular rights.' So claimed the Commune Manifesto in 1871. Indeed at this time of internal unrest with the Paris 'Bloody Week' (1871) and international humiliation at the loss of Alsace Lorraine in 1871, all other alternatives seem to have failed. The Republic (1871–1914) appeared to be the only alternative, its belief in ideas of Liberty and Rights of Man seemed to guarantee the support and unity of the mases. But just how far it united the French electorate is another question.

The Third Republic's internal stability and unity was one of the chief factors in its survival. Although over forty years the Republic had fifty different governments it remained stable and unified. Although there was a frequent change in ministries the same politicians were in them, it was only the type of office which changed. Delcasse was one such politician who was minister of foreign affairs six times between 1898–1905. The Republic therefore gained from this as many of the ministers became very experienced. The stability of the bureaucratic structure was also an advantage. It was based upon the Napoleonic idea of 'conseil d'etat'. This administation was the stabilizing force, being immune from political quarrels. As Guerard said:

'So long as the bureaucrat sits at his desk France survives.'

The firmness with which the Republic supressed the opposition was also significant in its survival. During the 1905 CGT attack on the republic resulted in stern reprisals, also in 1910 during the great railway strike the strikers were put in the army by the Government. The major threat to the Republic, the Church, was dealt with just as harshly. Ferry's secular policies reduced the power of the Church, in 1882 the State took over responsibility for primary education. Acts such as this and the nationalizing of Church lands in 1904 successful reduced the power the Church held, politically. It reduced the force with which the Church could oppose the Republic as the Church became a part of the Empire and not a seperate political entity.

The weak and divided opposition of the Right wing further meant that the Republic was virtually unopposed during its 'reign'. The Right already had natural divisions between them, being divided into three main groups: The Orleanists, Bonapartists and Legitimists. These three hostile groups seriously harmed the force of the opposition to the Republic as they divided the support of the opposition, and so weakened it. In 1871 the Right wing split was highlighted over the question of a future candidate. The serious divisons between the groups were widened further, weakening them still more. Certain crises, such as the Dreyfus Affair (1894–1906), discredited the Right Wing, loosing a lot of their support among the masses. Without such support the opposition was virtually impotent against the Third Republic, which was gaining popular support quickly. The result of deciding popularity and internal divisions meant that the Right became frustrated, and many defected to the Chamber of Deputies, such as Thiers in 1872. Again this served only to weakened the Right further and strengthen the Republic.

The popular legislative programme of the Third Republic united middle and working class support of the Republic. The middle classes supported the Republic for its cautious, moderate policies as Gambetta claimed in 1871: 'We shall be prudent.' In 1880 the Republic appealed to the middle classes through allowing the remaining exiled veterans of the Commune to return. But it was Ferry's colonial policy which gained middle-class favour, particularly the traders and financiers. In 1881 French occupation of Tunis provide an area for middle class investment. Further middle classes' quest for raw materials for their expanding industries were satisfied by French expansion into Morocco. French foreign policy was also policy with the middle classes, expanding their commerical interests through alliances, such as the 1898 Commercial treaty with Italy. The middle classes were vital for the Republic's survival as they held a great deal of political and economic power.

Working class support was also united in favour of the Republic. Ferry's social reforms, such as the 1881 full rights of public meetings. Also in 1910 old age pensions were introduced and in 1909 there was the Ten Hours Factory Act. The Republic's colonial policy was particularly popular. Expansion in Africa, such as gaining in 1893 French Guinea and the Ivory Coast satisfied the masses demand for national prestige.

The Republic unified the masses, more so than any monarchy or dictatorship would as it was based upon a constitution. Although the Republic was discredited in certain affairs such as the Panama Scandel, 1894 it still managed to keep control, this was perhaps due to powerful propaganda machines such as the newspapers for example 'Siecle'. But perhaps its real power lay in the fact that there was really no other alternative. As Thiers said:

'All governments, what ever their names, are now essentially republican in character.'

D   When Thiers made his now famous pronouncement, he could not have had in mind France's turbulent history since the Revolution. Indeed, among the various forms of government during and since 1789, the two Republics (1792–99 and 1848–52) had been among the shortest lived and least acceptable. Monarchy and Bonapartism had 'divided Frenchmen least.' However, this troubled history did in one way contribute to the longevity of the Third Republic—given the frequent past changes of government, Frenchmen were increasingly reluctant to support the overthrow of their government.

In the circumstances of the 1870s, Thiers was correct in his analysis of his people's attitudes. Offered the choice of anything BUT a Republic, most Frenchmen would have fallen into one of three camps. Firstly, there were the Legitimists, who supported the Bourbon claimant to the throne, the Comte de Chambord, the heir to Charles X's France and adamant in his determination to restore the legitimate French monarchy in its traditional form, even to the extent of the white flag of pre-Revolutionary days. The other Monarchist group were the Orleanists, supporters of the Comte de Paris, heir to Louis Philippe and the July Monarchy, and thus more prepared to accept a form of limited, constitutional monarchy.

Thirdly, there were the Bonapartists who hoped to restore a form of strong executive such as the two Napoleons had enjoyed. These three groups were all opposed to the Republic, but could not agree on a single candidate—and as Thiers said, three men could not sit on one throne—and differed so much over constitutional and religious matters that there was no chance of them forming a united, coherent opposition.

In contrast, the variety of Radicals, Republicans and Socialists that supported the Republic hid their differences well and closed ranks in times of crisis. Also, the Republic was comparatively moderate. In its early days, Gambetta had said, 'We shall be prudent'. This moderation both enabled a wide range of people to support it and made it more acceptable to less extreme opponents.

However, there were other factors that also contributed to the survival of the Republic. Most importantly, its policies in the first thirty years of its life won it support. In 1889, over 200 Right wing deputies had been elected—in 1906, they could muster barely a hundred. Politically, the constitutional acts of the 1870s, such as the provision for a seven year presidency, were prudent, while later legislation, such as Ferry's tariffs and the social welfare measures of the 1900s, won the support of a variety of classes. While the French economy did not grow at the rate of the German or Russian, it did recover from the defeat of 1871 and subsequent indemnity, and overcame the phylloxera devastation of the 1880s. It is interesting to reflect what might have happened had there been a major economic crisis in, say, the 1890s—given the later experiences of Italy and Germany, it is arguable whether the Republic would have survived. The Republic's foreign policy also appeared creditable. Admittedly, 'les provinces perdues' of the 1870 war were not recovered, but an empire had been consolidated, an alliance with Russia secured and Germany had been made sufficiently anxious to have huffed and puffed more than once. Despite their early doubts, Frenchmen could be increasingly confident in the ability of their Republican government to lead them.

Again in contrast, the record of the Right was increasingly tarnished. Admittedly, the Wilson and Panama Scandals had enbled monarchists to point to 'the wrong kind of people' in government, but for the most part it was the Right who was to look foolish. Boulanger, its darling of 1888, made his ludicrous exit, while every twist of the Dreyfus Affair seemed to reveal yet further the ineptitude and prejudice of those twin bastions of anti-Republicanism, the Church and the army. Victory for the principles of Republicanism, freedom, justice, the rights of man against the rights of the state, in the outcome of the Dreyfus Affair was perhaps a turning point for the fortunes of the Third Republic.

It may also be argued that the Republic was fortunate in having talented leaders to guide it through difficulties. In its early years, Gambetta and then Thiers were the architects of post-war recovery, while Ferry introduced the anti-clerical, educational and imperial policies of the 1880s. By the end of the century, a second generation of such men, led by Clemenceau and Briand, was emerging, and were to play a major part in the Republic's survival to 1940.

Equally, the Third Republic was, despite appearances, a remarkably stable ship of state. Although governments tended to be short-lived, the same men—Grevy, Delcasse, Freycinet, Dupuy—appeared in government after government, providing a wealth of personal knowledge and experience. The civil service too has been praised, based as it was upon Napoleonic principles, and cited as an aspect of stability.

Finally, the control of the emerging media helped the survival of the Republic. 'L'Aurore' and 'Siecle' in the towns, and 'La Republique Francaise' in the countryside were mass circulation newspapers that supported the Republic. As late twentieth centuries British Tories have seen only too well, the popular press can be a powerful ally.

It is difficult to disagree with Thiers implied view that the Third Republic survived because of the divisions among its opponents. Nonetheless, it was critical to the Republic's survival that it was relatively successful while its opponents were increasingly embarassed. Had the Republic followed less moderate policies, or suffered an economic whirlwind, or launched a fruitless attack on Alsace and Lorraine, the story might well have been different.

2 The German Empire

(a) The Imperial Constitution

The constitution of the German Empire, proclaimed at Versailles in January 1871, was really an enlargement of the North German Confederation of 1867. It consisted of four kingdoms (Prussia, Bavaria, Württemberg and Saxony), six grand duchies, five duchies, seven principalities, three free cities (Hamburg, Bremen and Lübeck) and the Imperial provinces of Alsace and Lorraine (*see Map 6, page 46*). These 26 units varied greatly in area and influence. Bavaria was almost as large as Scotland, Württemberg was larger than Wales, and Saxony was smaller than Yorkshire. Each of the states retained its own royal, princely or ducal family and its own separate government for local affairs. Saxony, Württemberg and Bavaria retained their own army. Bavaria had special 'reserved rights,' which permitted her to have her own diplomatic service and control her postal, telegraphic and railway systems. But the Empire was really a federation only in form; in practice Prussia dominated all the other states.

Prussia was greater in area and population than all the rest of the German Empire together, and the Prussian capital, Berlin, was also the Imperial capital. The Imperial government dealt with defence, foreign affairs, trade, coinage, customs and (except for Bavaria) railways, posts and telegraphs, and was under the control of the King of Prussia (as German Emperor), who delegated his civil power to the Imperial Chancellor and his military power to the General Staff.

There was an Imperial Legislature consisting of two houses, the Bundesrat and the Reichstag. The Bundesrat had 58 members, one from each of the 26 states, except for the larger ones which had more. Prussia had 17, Bavaria six and Württemberg four each. Thus Prussia was in a minority of the membership of the house, but since a vote of 14 against a motion meant its rejection, she had in fact a decisive veto. The members were nominated annually by the legislatures of the states, which themselves had varying systems of voting. Prussia retained her restrictive system under the constitution of 1850 (*see page 173*). The Bundesrat's agreement was required before bills were passed by the Reichstag, and it had to be consulted on all important matters of foreign policy, including a declaration of war; but it steadily lost influence from 1871 and was not to meet in 1914 until Germany was already at war.

The members of the Reichstag were elected every three years by all men over the age of 25, but it was, in a German Socialist's words, 'the fig-leaf of absolutism'. It could reject laws, but not initiate them. Its consent was needed to levy new taxes, but not to continue existing ones. The Emperor could and did dissolve it with the consent of the Bundesrat. Above all, the Chancellor and other Imperial ministers were appointed and dismissed by the Emperor, and the Reichstag had no control over them. Nor could members of the Reichstag be appointed ministers.

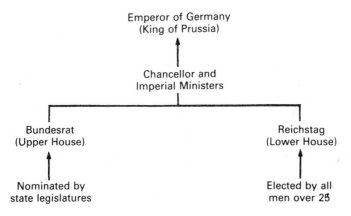

Diagram 7. Organization of German Constitution (1871)

Bismarck adapted the constitution of the North German Confederation because circumstances in 1871 required the same compromise between unification and federation, between monarchical power and popular democracy, which he had to effect in 1867. So Prussian power was masked, concessions were made to the rulers of the states in order to secure their co-operation, and the Reichstag could keep the Imperial government informed about public opinion and enable it to take any necessary action. Succeeding years, however, largely destroyed this compromise. The Empire never grew out of its warlike origins. The entrenched Prussian military and bureaucratic classes extended their power over Germany with Bismarck's assistance, and the Imperial government increasingly undermined or destroyed opposition to its authority. It was able to do this without great difficulty because the tide of opinion turned strongly against federalism and democracy in Germany. National sentiment came to require a firmly-governed state and to regard the separate kingdoms and princedoms within it as empty symbols.

(b) Political Parties

Though the Imperial constitution prevented the Reichstag from achieving such political power as the House of Commons in Britain or the Chamber of Deputies in France, it had some important functions, particularly the rejection of laws and the initiation of taxes. There was, therefore, sufficient scope for political parties to operate in the government of Germany. Owing to the importance of Prussia in the Empire, most of these were in their origin Prussian parties which expanded into German parties in the 1870s and continued their role in Imperial politics. The result was a plurality of parties with exclusive and conflicting interests and aims, which made co-operation between them difficult, whether in support of the Imperial administration or in opposition to it.

The Conservatives were divided into two main parties. The old Prussian Conservatives drew their support almost entirely from the agrarian lands east of the Elbe and their leaders from the Junkers. They had opposed Bismarck's policy of unification and Prussia's entry into the Empire, and they only expanded from a Prussian into a German party in 1876. German industrialization threatened their economic and social position, but they were able to retain a good deal of power. They were strongly placed not only at court and in the army, but also in the higher ranks of the bureaucracy, and the Prussian system of voting meant that they were always in control of the Prussian Diet. The other, smaller Conservative party, the Free Conservatives, had been founded in Prussia in 1866. They drew their membership wider territorially and socially, particularly from the wealthy commercial, industrial and professional classes. Their outlook was very similar to that which Bismarck had adopted since 1848 (*see page 245*), and they steadily supported him.

In addition to the small German People's Party, which was confined to southern Germany, there were also two main Liberal parties in Germany. These were the Progressives and the National Liberals, both now German parties, but originating as Prussian parties which had separated from each other in 1866 (*see page 251*). The Progressives remained opposed to Bismarck's policy of despotic nationalism, which had brought the Empire into being, and refused to sacrifice liberal principles to German interests. They continued to uphold the liberal ideals of personal freedom and limitation of governmental power. Being essentially individualists and men of principle, they tended to be weakened by disagreements and divisions among themselves, and they knew that they were unlikely to achieve their aims in the Empire. The National Liberals, on the other hand, continued to support Bismarck, as they had done in 1866, in the interests of German unification. They had abandoned their desire for a constitutional German state, but still wished to establish as much as possible of the traditional features of liberal belief the government and laws of the Empire. They had the largest number of seats of any single party in the Reichstag in 1871 (*see Table 15, page 321*).

Another Prussian party which expanded into a German party in 1871 was the Centre Party. This had been founded in Prussia to protect the interests of the Roman Catholic minority in the state, and now it adopted the same policy in Germany since Roman Catholics (following the exclusion of Austria) were also in a minority in the Empire as a whole. Owing its existence to the religious disunity brought about by the Reformation in Germany, there was no political party like it in any other European country. It was, in fact, hardly a political party. It had no defined political principles, but was prepared to co-operate with any other politician or party as long as the rights of the Roman Catholic Church in Germany was upheld, and its religious unity made it the best disciplined of the German parties. It was, of course, strongest in the Roman Catholic parts of Germany, of which the Rhineland and Bavaria were the most important. It also, however, received support from Alsatians, Poles, Hanoverians and others who opposed the new Empire, even though some of them were Protestants. It wanted a truly federal Germany, in which the Roman Catholic states would be free from Imperial interference, and so they opposed any extension of Imperial authority.

Working-class politicians, who considered themselves abandoned by the Liberals, had founded the Social Democratic Party in 1869. This adopted Marxism as its 'official position' and expected to wage 'an ever more bitter class struggle' against capitalism and the state. It had only two members in the Reichstag in 1871, but thereafter it made steady progress, especially after 1875 when it succeeded in uniting the various socialist groups within its membership and establishing contacts with trade unions. It was not destroyed by the serious restrictions placed upon it by Bismarck's anti-Socialist legislation (*see page 316*), and by 1890 it had 35 members in the Reichstag. This was due, above all, to the rapid economic progress of Germany after 1871 towards becoming an urban industrial country, a development that brought demands from the workers which were steadily resisted by the Imperial government. The party was able to attract a steadily growing number of new recruits. More and more it drew its support from the lowest classes, who left the countryside for the factory towns and were successfully encouraged to make use of their right to vote for the first time. It was more successful in its propaganda than the other parties and its contacts with its members, largely through co-operation with the trade unions, were closer.

(c) The Kulturkampf

In the first Reichstag, elected in 1871, Bismarck had to rely mainly upon the votes of the National Liberals and the Free Conservatives and usually managed to secure a slight majority among the 382 members. In order to promote German strength, unity and prosperity, he hurried through in a decade such measures as modernization of federal administration, an Imperial coinage, a postal and telegraph system, control of the railways, a common code of criminal and civil law and regulations for industrial undertakings and trade combinations. These were very like reforms which Gladstone's ministry was undertaking at the same time in Britain, but they were more extensive and effective. Bismarck's measures were opposed by the Centre Party, but the National Liberals, though he allowed them no share in the government of the Empire, supported them. Like Liberals everywhere, they failed to recognize that such reforms increased the authority of the State in a way potentially dangerous to democracy and liberalism.

Bismarck concerned himself also with education, and this brought him into conflict with the Roman Catholic Church and the Centre Party in the grandiosely named *Kulturkampf* ('conflict of civilizations'). The situation in Germany was fundamentally the same as in other nineteenth-century European countries, where education was an issue involving governments and arousing religious conflict. This conflict was sharper in Germany than elsewhere, partly because past history had given the Roman Catholics in Germany a keenly defensive attitude, which made them now determined to protect their position against the Imperial government, and partly because Bismarck considered that the political expression of their attitude, the Centre Party, which was hostile to the Imperial constitution and ready to seek support from Austria and France, was a dangerous rallying point of discontent in the Empire. He therefore welcomed the conflict and enlarged its scope because it gained him further support from the anti-clerical Liberals and offered him a means of destroying the Centre Party. He said the Roman Catholics could be made into 'something to hate for unity'. As in international diplomacy, so he was very ready in domestic politics to achieve his end by playing off his opponents against each other.

The *Kulturkampf* began after the proclamation of the doctrine of Papal Infallibility (*see page 390*). A number of German priests and laypeople, particularly those who were professors and teachers in universities and schools, refused to accept this pronouncement and formed themselves into a separate body, the Old Catholics. The bishops excommunicated them and demanded their removal from their teaching posts, but Bismarck saw this as an opportunity to intervene in the education question and take action against the Roman Catholic Church. He refused to allow the dismissal of the Old Catholics and arranged for a number of churches to be handed over to them. When the Centre Party began a campaign against him, he replied by withdrawing the German envoy from the Vatican in 1872 and during the next three years, with the aid of the Liberals in the Reichstag, secured the passing of measures against the Roman Catholic Church. These were much the same as had been taken by liberal governments in other countries. The Jesuits were expelled from Germany, schools were placed under state inspection, and civil marriage was made obligatory, whether followed by a religious ceremony or not. More severe action was taken in Prussia, where the May Laws of May 1873 subjected ecclesiastical appointments to governmental control and theological colleges to state inspection, besides dissolving or expelling religious orders.

Bismarck, however, did not achieve the success he had expected. A fierce struggle followed the passing of these measures. Pope Pius IX declared the May Laws null and void, and Roman Catholic clergy were not deterred by punishment from resisting them. By 1876 every Prussian bishop was in prison or had left the country, and 1400 parishes were without a priest in charge. The Church gained sympathy and support, and Roman Catholics rallied to the Centre Party, which doubled its seats in the Prussian Diet and increased its numbers in the Reichstag close to those of the National Liberals.

The episode brought Bismarck the first political defeat of his career because he saw that he was in a hopeless position. The Conservatives did not share the wish of the Liberals for state-controlled, secular education and particularly disapproved of the institution of civil marriage. They expressed their anxieties to William I, who shared them, declaring that baptism might be abolished next. Bismarck also feared the possibility of an alliance between the Centre Party and the Socialists against the government and he disliked the growing dependence upon the National Liberals which the *Kulturkampf* compelled him to accept.

He realized that he must extricate himself from the dangerous situation. The death of Pius IX and the election of the more conciliatory Leo XIII to the Papacy in 1878 made this possible for him. He entered into direct negotiations with the new Pope with the result that by 1887 all the restrictions on the Church were removed except for the expulsion of the Jesuits, the state inspection of schools and civil marriage. He had, therefore, made some important gains, but he had failed to bring about the destruction of the Centre Party.

(d) Protection
Bismarck particularly wished to bring to an end his dependence upon the National Liberals because he knew that he would not have their support for policies which he wished to adopt in 1878. He was facing a number of financial and economic problems. The Imperial government's income was largely derived from the profits of the postal and telegraph services and supplemented by contributions from the states and taxes levied by the Legislature. This was now proving inadequate to meet its growing activities. Bismarck became interested in the idea of customs duties, not only to bring the Imperial government an increased revenue, but also to lessen its dependence upon the states and the Legislature, which he was anxious to bring about.

There were also economic reasons why Germany should join the other European countries, which (with the notable exception of Britain) were becoming protectionist. From the early 1850s, Prussia, while enjoying a thriving economy, had followed a policy of relative free trade and had led first the *Zollverein* and then the North German Confederation and the Empire in the same direction. Such a situation benefited the Junkers and other landowners exporting grain (which foreign countries could purchase in return for sending manufactured goods to Germany), the merchants in the ports and western German cities and all others engaged in overseas trade. Some manufacturers in the 1860s, especially the iron and steel producers in the Ruhr and Upper Silesia and the textile manufacturers of southern Germany, did, however, complain of foreign competition and ask for protection. Nevertheless, on the foundation of the Empire, such criticism was stilled. Unification and the French indemnity encouraged an economic boom, while the newly-gained iron ore of Lorraine stimulated the growth of the heavy industries. Prosperity seemed, therefore, to justify a continuance of free trade.

From 1873, however, the Empire was affected by the long-lasting general European economic depression. The first sign of its impact upon Germany was a decline in the expansion of the railways. Since 1850 the length of track had increased rapidly (*see Table 6, page 82*), and the work of construction provided the largest orders for the iron and steel manufacturers, but as the economic depression began, capital was no longer available for their construction. Iron and steel works suffered, and so did German industry as a whole with the decline in trade in Europe.

German industrialists, therefore, began to demand protection, asserting that foreign countries, while protected by tariffs against German imports, could export their own products freely to Germany. Moreover, at this time also, the United States and Russia were beginning to export large quantities of grain which was sold more cheaply in western Germany than the grain grown in East Prussia. So the Junkers and other landowners joined in the campaign for assistance from the government. They were the more ready to do this because economic liberalism had only been adopted for a relatively short period in Germany. There was an older tradition of control, direction and help for industry and agriculture. Frederick the Great, during the last years of his reign from 1763 to 1786, devoted himself to promoting Prussian prosperity by supervising such undertakings as planting woods, draining wasteland, dredging rivers, building roads and financing commercial and industrial undertakings. And in the nineteenth century, the building of the railways, though accomplished by private companies, had been undertaken under close government direction in Germany.

Bismarck's determination to promote German industry gave him an economic reason for favouring the introduction of tariffs. He saw that the western industrial nations were turning away from *laissez-faire* liberalism to economic nationalism. This would prevail in the future, and he did not want Germany to be left behind.

The elections of 1878 to the Reichstag gave Bismarck the opportunity to abandon the acceptance of a liberal free trade policy which he had hitherto maintained. As in other European countries the middle-class supporters of the Liberals were now beginning to align themselves with the ruling classes, and popular sentiment was particularly turning against the party in Germany. Bismarck now had a Reichstag which would be prepared to approve of customes duties. The National Liberals lost some 30 seats in the elections and became inferior in numbers to the combined strength of the two Conservative parties; and the Centre Party maintained its strength (*see Table 15, page 321*). The Conservatives, especially since the Prussian landowners and the great Rhineland industrialists were becoming increasingly allied through intermarriage, favoured protection. The Centre Party was prepared to accept it as a means of hastening the decline of the National Liberals and in return for an end to the attacks upon the Roman Catholic Church.

In 1879 duties were imposed upon imported iron, steel and grain as the beginnings of a protectionist system which was extended in later years. As he intended it should, Bismarck's new economic policy had important political results. He did not intend that the Empire should become a liberal, constitutional state, and he was glad that his dependence upon the National Liberals in the Reichstag was ended. The party was split, in accordance with his declared intention of squeezing them against the wall until they squealed. In 1880 28 of their members broke away to join the Progressives. The rest accepted tariffs and continued to support Bismarck, who now had no need to take account of their views.

On the other hand, the Conservatives were closely bound to the Empire, and the differences between the two Conservative Parties grew less. They needed industrial and agricultural protection to uphold their interests, and they consequently had to support Imperial policy as a whole. The Centre Party, though supporting the introduction of tariffs, deprived Bismarck of using them to bring the Imperial government the financial independence he wanted to gain for it. They were not prepared to allow such a further centralization of the empire. They insisted that the yield from the customs duties, above a fixed amount, was to be shared each year among the states to whom the Imperial government would still have to apply for contributions to secure it an adequate annual income. The Centre Party thus entered upon the role of a negative, balancing power in Imperial politics.

(e) Socialism
By the later 1870s, while he was considering protective tariffs, Bismarck had become alarmed by the growing support for the Social Democratic Party. Like Napoleon III in France, he had wanted universal male suffrage in the German Empire to gain the support of the conservative peasantry, but now the growing urban working class could

315

not be relied upon in this way. Bismarck was determined to take action against the Social Democrats because they opposed protectionism, which would mean dearer food for the poorer classes, but still more because he considered that they were an even greater threat to the constitution of the Empire than the Centre Party. Moreover, such action would be a further embarrassment for the Liberals, who would be placed in a difficult dilemma. They would know that such oppressive measures were wrong, but at the same time would like the activities of the Social Democrats to be restricted. On the other hand, the Conservatives would support him unreservedly, and so also would the Centre Party for the same reasons it supported protectionism and because of the Marxist, anti-religious beliefs of the Socialists.

In 1878 two attempts were made to assassinate the Emperor William I. Though no proof could be established that the Social Democrats were involved in either, Bismarck alleged that they were both the result of a Socialist conspiracy. The elections to the Reichstag that year were fought in this atmosphere, which contributed towards the result. The Social Democrats lost only three of their 12 seats, but Bismarck had a Reichstag favourable towards legislation bringing both protectionism and anti-Socialist measures.

He was able to get the Legislature to pass in 1878 the Exceptional Law 'against the activities of Social Democracy threatening the common welfare.' This made the party illegal and prohibited its clubs, assemblies, publications and agitation. Rather more than 100 people a year were imprisoned for infringing its provisions. Yet the constitution of the Empire made it possible for Social Democrats to stand as candidates at elections and to sit in the Reichstag, where they were protected by parliamentary privilege. Despite the handicaps imposed upon them and attempts to redraw the boundaries of the constituencies, so that each contained as many rural voters as possible, the party was not only able to survive, but to increase its electoral vote. As with the Centre Party, Bismarck's attack upon it served to strengthen its support from the section of the population it represented.

However, he had learnt from the *Kulturkampf*. He was now more subtle and supplemented his repressive measures with a constructive policy as well. He was aware of the social problems of industrialization, and so as to 'take the wind out of the sails' of what he always called 'revolutionary socialism', he introduced a number of measures designed to give workers some protection against the hazards of their life. These were insurance against sickness in 1883, insurance against accidents in 1884 and old-age pensions in 1889. The cost of these was shared between the employer, the worker and the government. Though neither Bismarck nor the Conservatives were willing to have factory acts or provision for the unemployed, this was the first such programme of social security in Europe, and it anticipated by 20 years the introduction of similar benefits by Lloyd George in Britain.

The National Liberals opposed the scheme as 'state socialism', which was contrary to their *laissez-faire* beliefs, and the Progressives also attacked it as giving increased power to a government that was not subject to parliamentary control; but Bismarck was very ready for the Imperial administration to assume these functions.

These social reforms did not, any more than the Exceptional Law, destroy the Social Democrats; but they did bind the working-classes to the Empire, which provided for their security, and largely eliminated the revolutionary element in the Social Democratic Party. Nevertheless, the increasing support given to the Social Democratic Party indicated that the workers still had grievances and wanted changes. Bismarck overstated the situation when he said, 'A man who can look forward to a pension is far more contented and easier to manage than one who cannot. Men are like animals—they are contented as long as they are secure and well-fed.' The Social Democrats and the trade unions had no wish to overthrow the German state, but they did wish to gain for their members improved working conditions, a greater share of the national wealth and more influence in the political system.

(f) Bismarck and William II

William I, the first German Emperor, died in 1888. When Lord Salisbury, the British Prime Minister, heard the news, he said, 'The ship is leaving the harbour. This is the crossing of the bar. I can see the sea covered with white horses.' William I's son, Frederick, was already suffering from cancer and died after being Emperor for only three months. He was succeeded by his son, William II, a young man of 28, who was destined to be the last German Emperor.

His accession inevitably made a difference to Bismarck, who had been able to have his way under his grandfather. 'His majesty is like a horse,' Bismarck had said of William I. 'He takes fright at any unaccustomed object and grows obstinate if driven, but gradually gets used to it.' William I had been primarily a soldier rather than a politician. He was impressed by Bismarck's ability and in the end was influenced by his arguments.

William II, however, was determined to assume personal control of the government. Bismarck remarked that the Emperor seemed to want to be his own Chancellor, and, indeed it was only natural that a new, young ruler should not wish to be directed by an old minister. Moreover, William was in many ways typical of the Germany of the time. He was a young man of the generation that considered that the era of Bismarck was over. He had not known the difficulties and dangers through which the country had struggled to unity and nationhood. He knew only the Empire that had triumphed over its enemies and was growing in strength with limitless and self-justifiable ambitions in Europe and beyond, the Empire that had induced Bismarck to acquire German colonies in 1884 (*see page 361*). This inevitably influenced the new Emperor's attitude towards Bismarck. William I had often mistrusted Bismarck, but ever-mindful of the events which had sent him into exile in 1848 and nearly lost him his throne in 1862, he regarded, in the last resort, the Chancellor as the indispensable upholder of the monarchy. To William II, however, Bismarck was simply an encumbrance and a check who prevented him acting independently as the monarch should and embarking upon a policy more suited to the place Germany had now gained for herself in the world. Bismarck thought that he had achieved a balanced solution to the problems of both home and foreign policy and wished to maintain things as they were. William believed that the time had come for change.

The differences between the two men came to a head in March 1890, when William dismissed Bismarck. William's comment on the occasion was in the same maritime vein as Lord Salisbury's—'The ship's course remains the same. "Full steam ahead" is the order.' The immediate disagreement between them came about through the general election of 1890, when the Social Democrats secured more members than ever before (*see Table 15, page 321*). Bismarck wanted to take further measures against the party; William high-mindedly wanted to unite all Germans behind him and would not consent to such a step. There were other reasons for Bismarck's departure. William wanted to support Austrian control of the Balkans, even if it meant hostility with Russia, and he desired greater German colonial expansion and the building of a large navy. He intended to abandon a policy of carefulness, moderation and limited aims and go 'full steam ahead'. Bismarck was not prepared to compromise at all. As a young man he had said, 'I will play music as I like or not at all.'

(g) Bismarck's Germany

The events of 1890 were not really due to the consequences of a clash of policy and temperament between Emperor and Chancellor. Their cause was rather to be found in the structure of the political system of the Empire set up by Bismarck himself. National unification, so long sought in Germany, was achieved in 1871, but only after the crushing of the liberal revolution of 1848 by the conservative princely and military forces. Not a single representative of the German people was present when the Empire was proclaimed at Versailles. Bismarck was determined that it should not come into being with any suggestion of a democratic process. He made use of the old order to create the German national state by means of a revolution imposed from above.

The Empire was not the liberal-democratic national state, which reformers had aspired to create before 1848, but Prussian domination imposed over the whole of Germany. This inevitably meant that it was an authoritarian, militaristic state. Without her Hohenzollern rulers and her army, Prussia would not have been able to become a great power, and Bismarck's Germany rested upon the Prussian monarchy and army.

The Liberals were unable to oppose this effectively. They had accepted the Imperial constitution, and the Reichstag was not empowered to change this. And the prestige of the army was even greater in 1871 than it had been in 1866, when they had acquiesced in Bismark's unconstitutional military expenditure. A very similar situation was repeated in 1874, when Bismarck proposed that the financing of the army should be removed permanently from the control of the Reichstag. When the National Liberals objected, he threatened them with new elections, and they were very ready to agree to the *Septennat* under which the military budget was voted for seven years at a time. This was a similar triumph for Bismarck as the bill of indemnity had been eight years previously. It was a clear example of the way in which the Prussian administrative and military class could dominate the public life of the Empire; and Thomas Mann, the writer, sarcastically characterized the ideal German citizen as 'General Dr. von Staat'.

The result was that the Reichstag, whose position was so dubious under the Imperial constitution, failed completely to develop a sound parliamentary system and responsible political parties. Politicians knew that authority in the state did not rest with them. The Liberals, the natural opponents of the Prussian regime, failed completely to arrest the course of events. They capitulated to the growing authoritarianism, militarism and prosperity of the Empire; and as elsewhere in Europe, their ideals were ceasing to appeal to the middle-classes who had been the backbone of their support. And the industrialists, growing ever richer and more powerful, did not, as in other countries, support an anti-aristocratic, egalitarian parliamentarianism, but believed that the maintenance of their new position depended upon the existing political and social order.

Nevertheless, the steadily increasing political importance of the Social Democrats showed the greatest weakness of the political system. There was a deep discrepancy between it and the social structure. It took little account of the social changes coming into being through the industrial revolution. Though the Social Democrats were not revolutionary, the demands they put forward, which included the reform of the franchise, heavier taxation upon the wealthy, factory legislation and freedom for trade unions, were unacceptable to the ruling classes. Bismarck tried to destroy the Socialists; William II wished to unite them patriotically under his leadership. Both failed; and after the fall of Bismarck, there was a growing tendency to reduce the threat to the Empire from its unresolved social pressures by a policy of external assertion and aggression.

Bibliography
Further books about Bismarck, as well as those already indicated (*see page 257*), are B.J. Elliott, *Bismarck, the Kaiser and Germany* (Longman, 1972) and W.N. Medlicott, *Bismarck and Modern Germany)* Hodder & Stoughton, 1975). General histories of Germany are W.M. Simon, *Germany in the Age of Bismarck* (Allen & Unwin, 1968), J.C.G.

Röhl, *From Bismarck to Hitler* (Longman, 1970) and Gordon Craig, *German History, 1867–1945*) OUP, 1981).

Exercises

A   *This section consists of questions that are intended for discussion (or written answers) as a way of expanding on the chapter and testing your understanding of it:*

1   Why was the German Empire a federation 'only in form'?
2   What do you understand by the term, 'the fig-leaf of absolutism'?
3   Why was it that the circumstances of 1871 required compromises?
4   Outline the policies and ideas of the main political parties in the German Empire, and explain why they were unable to co-operate with one another.
5   Why were the Imperial reforms of the 1870s a potential threat to democracy?
6   Why was Bismarck so hostile to the Centre Party?
7   Who were the Old Catholics, and why did Bismarck support them?
8   Why was there such widespread opposition to Bismarck's measures against the Catholic Church?
9   Who 'won' the *Kulturkampf*?
10   What is protectionism, and why was Bismarck attracted to it?
11   How did Bismarck use the protection issue to divide the political parties?
12   How can the Centre Party be seen as a 'negative, balancing power'?
13   Why was Bismarck so keen to combat the rise of the Socialist Party?
14   Why was Bismarck increasingly hostile to the National Liberals?
15   Why did Bismarck introduce some of the first social welfare measures in Europe?
16   Why did Bismarck's measures fail to destroy the Social Democrats?
17   Compare Kaiser William I with Kaiser William II.
18   Explain why the German Empire that emerged after 1871 was so different from the Germany that the liberals had hoped for.

B   *Essay questions*

1   How far were Bismarck's domestic problems after 1871 the result of his policies and achievements before that date? (Cambridge, 1982)
2   Was the *Kulturkampf* Bismarck's most serious mistake in domestic policy? (Oxford, 1982)
3   What were the main features of the united German Empire established in 1871? What internal problems faced Bismarck and how did he deal with them in the period 1871–1890? (SUJB, 1982)
4   How far can the German Empire created in 1871 be described as a constitutional monarchy? (Welsh, 1981)
5   Why did Bismarck use war as an instrument of policy before 1871 and not after that year? (Welsh, 1982)
6   How, and how successfully, did Bismarck attempt to consolidate domestic support for the German Empire after 1871? (Oxford and Cambridge, 1981)
7   'Conservative paternalism.' Would you agree with this description of Bismarck's domestic policy after 1871? (Oxford and Cambridge, 1983)
8   'The single, dominating impulse throughout his career was the exercise of power.' How valid is this assessment of Bismarck's objectives in domestic policies? (AEB, 1981)
9   Assess the strengths and weaknesses of Germany at the fall of Bismarck in 1890. (AEB, 1982)

10 'Fundamentally a reactionary.' Consider this comment on Bismarck's domestic policies in the period 1871–90. (AEB, 1983)
11 In what ways, and with what success, did the authorities of the Reich encourage the development of a German national consciousness in the period 1871–1890? (London, 1983)

C *Bismarck and the political parties*
Study the Table of Reichstag Election results below, and answer the questions that follow it.

Party	Number of Deputies							
	1871	*1874*	*1877*	*1878*	*1881*	*1884*	*1887*	*1890*
Conservatives	54	22	40	59	50	78	80	73
Free Conservatives	38	36	38	57	28	28	41	20
National Liberals	150	155	128	99	47	51	99	42
Progressives	47	50	52	39	115	74	32	76
Centre	58	91	93	94	100	99	98	106
Social Democrats	2	9	12	9	12	24	11	35
Others	33	34	34	40	45	43	36	45
Total	382	397	397	397	397	397	397	397

Table 15. Parties in the Reichstag (1871–1890)

1 In order to clarify the trends of these results, construct a line graph using different colours for each of the six major parties.
2 Identify the major overall trends discernible for this graph, and then explain the main reasons for each of these trends.
3 What do these figures tell you about Bismarck's handling of the political parties, both throughout the period as a whole and in particular cases of individual issues, elections etc.?
4 Would you agree or disagree with each of the following statements? Explain your answer by reference both to this charge and to other sources:
  (a) The steady support for the Centre Party indicated a continuing hostility to the federal structure and an effort on the part of voters to uphold the rights of the individual states.
  (b) Bismarck overestimated (and overreacted to) the support for the Social Democrats.

3 The Austro-Hungarian Empire

(a) The End of Absolutism (1848–67)
For a dozen years after the risings of 1848 had been subdued (*see page 161*), Habsburg rule seemed to be re-established firmly in the Austrian Empire. The system adopted by Schwarzenberg was a firm absolutism, based upon armed force, and it was efficient, but it failed to overcome the discontent of the subject races, who still wanted the freedom they had tried to obtain in 1848. Its greatest failure was to meet the increasing costs of the regime. When other European countries were undertaking rapid European expansion, Austria faced mounting financial difficulties. It was clear that the regime could only hope to endure as long as it was at peace and avoided war.

Austrian neutrality was preserved during the Crimean War, but in 1859 came her defeat in northern Italy by France and Piedmont (*see page 230*)—the news of the Battle of Magenta brought about the sudden death of Metternich in his eighty-seventh year. The Imperial government slipped further into debt and suffered a damaging loss of prestige as a result of the failure of the army and its generals. Moreover, as before in Austrian history, the Empire's most dangerous province, Hungary, took advantage of the situation and made her discontent apparent. Troops stationed in Hungary could not safely be removed away to Lombardy; Hungarian regiments were unreliable in action; and Kossuth, the leader of the Magyar revolt of 1848–49, visited Napoleon III's headquarters in Milan, ready to provide him with a Hungarian legion. The Magyars resumed their demands for a separate administration for their part of the Empire, and Francis Joseph thought it advisable to make them some concessions. The Hungarian Diet was restored as before 1848, and the Magyar language once again replaced the German language which Schwarzenberg had made official in Hungary.

The still more disastrous defeat of Austria by Prussia in 1866 could not merely be followed by further conciliatory concessions to Hungary. A settlement was now necessary if the Empire were to hold together. The Magyars demanded a renewal of the rights which Kossuth had obtained by the March Laws of 1848, and the Imperial government had to enter into negotiations with their leaders. The result was the *Ausgleich* or Compromise of 1867 by which the governments of Austria and Hungary were separated. The Austrian Empire became the Austro-Hungarian Empire and was transformed from a centralized, absolutist state into a dualist, constitutional system.

(b) The Dual Monarchy (1867)

The Habsburg dominions were now divided into two areas, the boundary between them being the Leitha, a small tributary of the Danube almost at the gates of Vienna. The Empire of Austria (sometimes called Cisleithania) was composed of the 17 western and north-eastern provinces, among them Bohemia and Moravia, with Vienna as its capital. The Kingdom of Hungary (Transleithania) comprised the historic lands of St. Stephen's Crown, including Croatia and Slavonia, with Budapest as its capital. Each part had its own Diet and administration for internal purposes, and Francis Joseph was now both Emperor of Austria and King of Hungary (*see Map 5, page 39*).

Nevertheless, the arrangement was a true compromise because there was no revival of the virtually complete independence briefly established by Hungary in 1848. The Hungarian connection with the monarchy was not merely to be personal and nominal. The two parts of the Dual Monarchy had their own ministries and parliaments, but the Empire remained a unitary state through institutions common to these two parts. These were the Joint Ministries for War, Foreign Affairs and

Finance, to which Austria contributed 70 per cent and Hungary 30 per cent of the money needed for their operations, and the two Delegations (assemblies each consisting of 60 members from the Austrian or Hungarian parliament), which met alternately every year in the same city—Vienna or Budapest—but always separately, to discuss the work of the Joint Ministries and instruct their parliaments to vote a budget for them (*see Diagrams*). There was a common standing army, based on universal conscription, with separate auxiliary forces. There was free trade between the two parts provided by a customs union, and there was also a common currency controlled by a joint financial institution, the Austro-Hungarian state bank.

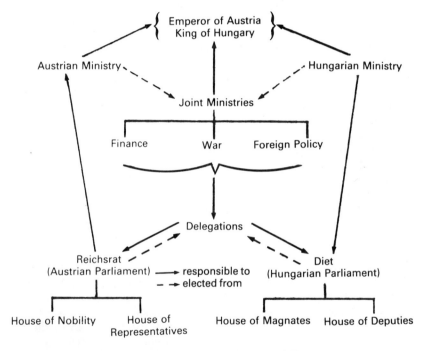

Diagram 8. Organization of Austro-Hungarian Constitution (1867)

The administration of both parts of the Dual Monachy was autocratic. In Austria the House of Representatives of the Reichsrat was elected by a complicated four-class system, which preserved a permanent majority for the wealthy landowners. In addition, the Reichsrat could be overruled by the Emperor and did not sit for long periods; it was not sitting in 1914 when war was declared. In Hungary also the franchise was restricted, and House of Deputies was elected only by Magyar taxpayers. The Dual Monarchy, therefore, hoped to be able to satisfy both the ruling Germans in Austria and the Magyars in Hungary by allowing each group to retain its authority there.

323

(c) The Survival of the Empire

In fact, the Habsburgs probably made the widest gains from the *Ausgleich*. It served them well and secured the survival of their dynasty for half a century longer. An important reason for this was the position of the Emperor himself. He was the most influential common focus of unity in the divided Empire. The aristocracy in both parts of the Dual Monarchy gave their loyalty to Francis Joseph because he was the guaranteeing symbol of their position. In himself he was not a man capable of inspiring popular loyalty to his person or enthusiasm for the Empire. Remote and austere in character, he was a conscientious administrator and depended upon the strength of his army to uphold the dynastic power which he had been taught it was his duty to exercise.

He could rely upon the loyalty of the army, which had to be large to defend the Emperor's exposed frontiers, but had shown itself dependable in the past as an instrument for the defence of the political and social order. It provided a career for its higher officers from the aristocracy and social advancement for its regimental officers, who were for the most part of relatively humble origins. Its conscript recruits came from all over the Empire, but the practice was continued of stationing troops of one nationality in the territory of another.

The civil service was equally dependent upon and attached to the Imperial government and administered the Empire with general efficiency. The common institutions on the whole achieved their purpose, the three Joint Ministers particularly becoming an effective instrument of administration. Much was done to deal with one of the Empire's most serious problems, its economic backwardness. For instance, at this time, when the European network of railways was rapidly expanding, the growth of the Austrian railways was the fastest. A great deal of construction was done by means of French capital, but the state also participated, and by 1884 the principal companies had been nationalized. During the war of 1914–18, it was largely the Austrian railways which provided the Central Powers with the immense military advantage of being able to move troops easily from one front to another.

Moreover, free trade between Austria and Hungary enabled them together to form a very satisfactory economic unit, since Austria rapidly became industrialized, while Hungary remained largely agricultural. Nearly three-quarters of the trade of each of these two parts of the Empire was with the other, but at the same time Austria gained growing markets for her manufactured goods in the Balkans, especially after the main Balkan railway line through Serbia and Bulgaria was finished in 1888.

These developments made Vienna, the Habsburg capital, an important centre of commerce. In addition, it retained its position as a cultural and intellectual centre. It had first achieved this during the second half of the eighteenth century under the Empress Maria Theresa and her son, Joseph II (*see page 40*). The splendour of their court attracted artists and musicians, scholars and architects, to the city.

Many palaces and churches, streets and squares, were built in the sumptuous Baroque style and furnished with art treasures and foreign masterpeices. Court patronage encouraged a theatrical tradition which developed into the German opera and drama. The Congress of Vienna renewed the city's prestige, which continued throughout the nineteenth century. Under Francis Joseph, it became famous also for its university and publishing houses and was a centre of banking and fashion. Possession of this city as the centre of his rule assisted the survival of the power and influence of the Emperor after the establishment of the Dual Monarchy.

The final bulwark of the Habsburgs was still the Roman Catholic Church, to which some 80 per cent of the population of the Empire belonged. In Austria, however, this had to face opposition from the German liberals, who succeeded in getting the Concordat suspended in 1870 and secularized the schools in 1874, but after they lost power in 1879, ecclesiastical control over education was restored some years later.

(d) The Racial Situation

The *Ausgleich* could not remedy the underlying flaw of the Empire, which continued to be its diverse population with its several races, distinct in origin and language and opposed in aims and ambitions (*see Map 5, page 39*). Indeed, the *Ausgleich* made the problem worse because the example of Hungary raised the expectations of these races in a way that was incompatible with the existence of the Dual Monarchy. The Germans formed about 25 per cent of the whole population and the Magyars 16 per cent, so that together they were in a minority. The most numerous race were the Slavs, who formed nearly 42 per cent of the population. They were divided into seven different racial groups—in Austria, the Czechs, Slovaks, Poles and Ruthenians; in Hungary, the Slovenes, Croats and Serbs. All these Slav peoples had migrated from southern Russia and north-eastern Poland betweeen the second and seventh centuries AD.

The situation was complex in Austria and was further complicated by the rapid growth of industry, which brought an influx of Slav peasants into German towns and the accompanying development of Slav middle-classes. By the end of the century, the Slavs outnumbered the Germans by almost two to one. Some Germans, doubtful whether the Habsburg dynasty could continue to preserve their supremacy, began to form political parties which looked towards Germany for their salvation.

This worsened German relations with the Czechs, who were the most important of the Slavs in Austria and numbered nearly a third of the population. There was a rapid growth in Czech nationalism during the second half of the nineteenth century. Czech schools were founded, and in 1882 the University of Prague was divided into Czech and German parts. In the 1880s the Austrian government made many concessions to the Czechs. Their language was given equality with German in the administration of Bohemia and Moravia; they were given posts in the civil service; and later they benefited from the extension of the franchise. Conflict between Czechs and Germans became sharp. It rendered the Diet ineffective and split the rising Social Democratic party. Yet this did not seriously threaten Habsburg rule in Austria. Most Czechs did not want to destroy the monarchy. They feared that their geographical position would place them in danger, if they were independent, from the German Empire. Also, they were becoming industrialized, and the economic unity of the Empire brought them prosperity. Most of their leaders would have been content to wrest more power from the Germans. Francis Joseph gained from the rivalry between the two peoples, which divided any opposition to his position and made his power in the Empire of Austria seem to be firmly established.

Much more serious were the racial difficulties and dangers in the Kingdom of Hungary. At the time of the *Ausgleich*, Francis Joseph had favoured some kind of federal administration for the Empire, centred in Vienna, in which all the nationalities would be represented, but the Magyars would have none of this idea. They had insisted that they should be given control of the whole of the ancient Hungarian kingdom at its greatest extent, though they formed less than half of its population. Count Andrassy, their spokesman, told Francis Joseph, 'You look after your Slavs, and we will look after ours.' In fact, they acted as if they situation did not exist. Of the subject peoples in Hungary, only the Croats, in 1868, secured any measure of self-government, and only in Croatia was Magyar not the official language. Throughout the Kingdom, not only was the franchise restricted to those with a high property qualification, but the elections themselves were held in public and organized in such a way as to leave control of the Diet in Budapest in the hands of the Magyar landed aristocracy. Persistent attempts were made, particularly in the schools, to Magyarize the people. In 1900 the Magyars filled 95 per cent of the state posts and owned 80 per cent of the newspapers.

Here lay the supreme danger of the Dual Monarchy. South of Hungary, on the other side of the Danube, was the independent state of Serbia, which wished to unite all the southern Slavs, inside and outside the Austro-Hungarian Empire, into a great Slav state; and ever since their first national rising against the Turks in 1807–10 the Serbs had shown themselves ready to seek Russian support to gain this end. The Empire's dualist system of government made a unitary treatment of the nationality question impossible, and the situation was to prove beyond solution. The two Balkan provinces of Bosnia and Herzegovina played an acute part in this development. Their occupation by the Imperial government in 1878, followed by their annexation 30 years later, contributed towards the outbreak of the war which was to destroy the Empire (*see page 347*).

Bibliography

To supplement the general histories of Austria (*see page 51*), there is A.J. May, *The Habsburg Monarchy* (OUP, 1951). The racial question is discussed in R.W. Seton-Watson, *The South Slav Question* (Constable, 1911) and *Racial Problems in Hungary* (Constable, 1908).

Exercises

A   *This section consists of questions that might be used for discussion (or written answers) as a way of expanding on the chapter and testing your understanding of it:*

1   Refer back to Section III, Part 2 (*page 154*). Outline the reasons for the discontent of the subject races in the Austrian Empire. What actions had the Hungarians taken in 1848, and how had their demands been ended?

2   Why did Austria's defeat by Prussia in 1866 make further concessions to Hungary necessary?

3   Explain the difference between a 'centralized, absolutist state' and a 'dualist, constitutional system'.

4   In what ways did the new Empire remain a single state?

5   What factors enabled the new Dual Monarchy to survive?

6   Compare the economic development of Austria-Hungary with that of other European powers.

7   Why did the government make concessions to the Czechs in the 1880s, and what effects did these concessions have?

8   How can it be argued that the policy of Magyarization played into the hands of the Serbs?

B   *Essay questions: Essay Writing Skills 8—Identification of Types*
Having checked your understanding of the different essay types already explained, identify what type (or combination of types) of essay each of the following is. From this, go on to explain what the question is asking and how you would go about answering it (e.g. List type question—requires a list of reasons for the establishment of the *Ausgleich*—reasons to be included would be. . . .).

1   'He gave the Habsburg Empire a new lease of life.' 'He made inevitable the collapse of his dynasty.' Which is the more appropriate verdict on the Emperor Franz Josef? (Cambridge, 1982)

2   To what extent was the *Ausgleich* a solution to the problems of the Habsburg Empire? (Cambridge, 1983)

3   'This realm is like a worm-eaten house: if one part is removed, one cannot tell how much will follow.' How far do these words explain the policies of the Habsburg Empire between 1850 and 1890? (Oxford, 1981)

4   'The Habsburg monarchy attempted to maintain its power by exploiting national divisions rather than by fostering a common loyalty within the Empire.' Do you agree with this verdict on the policies of the Dual Monarchy in the nineteenth century? (Oxford, 1982).

5   How and why did the events of 1866–1867 force Austria to give up its position in Germany? To what extent did the reorganization of the Habsburg Empire in 1867 give it stability and ensure its survival? (SUJB, 1982)

6   Account for the rapid recovery of the Habsburg Empire after 1848. (Welsh, 1981)

327

4 The Russian Empire

(a) Slavophilism and Panslavism

By the 1850s, higher education had made considerable progress in Russia, and people from beyond the nobility, including the sons of Orthodox priests, government officials, businessmen and even a few peasants, had joined the ranks of the intellectuals, and the discussion of new ideas among them was to have a considerable influence upon the politics of the country. The most important of these ideas were the two contending intellectual currents of Westernism and Slavophilism (*see page 218*). The differences between Westerners and Slavophils had a largely historical basis and went back to the reign of Peter the Great (1682–1725).

The Westerners thought that Russia should continue along the way initiated by Peter. They believed that the only chance of greatness and even of survival for the country in the future lay in the unbroken adoption of the achievements of western technology and science and the imitation of its political institutions, such as elected parliaments and local officials, responsible ministers and an efficient civil service. They insisted that Russia must recognize herself as belonging to western Europe and accept what they regarded as the most valuable of its ideas. Most Westerners were rationalists and radicals, but not active politicians. They preferred to express their belief in the abstract rather than become involved in campaigns for such reforms as the abolition of serfdom and the autocracy.

The Slavophils, on the other hand, believed that Peter's policy had been disastrous for Russia and should be abandoned completely. They mainly condemned it because it was secularist and materialistic, non-religious and unspiritual. Peter had encouraged the adoption of western techniques and skills and the development of industry and capitalism, which would destroy the older order in the country. They wished to preserve 'Holy Russia' and keep her true to her unique national past. They supported the authority of the Russian Orthodox Church to save the country (as one of them said) from 'the crimes of Europe'. They also upheld the *mir* as the type of economic organization that would enable Russia to avoid the evils of nineteenth-century industrialization. They idealized it as the Russian alternative to the exploitation of factory workers by western manufacturers.

When in the later 1860s, Alexander II adopted a policy of repression and reaction, some of the intellectuals became dissatisfied with the abstract theoretical nature of their discussions and believed that they must take up the Tsar's challenge to their hopes for the future. They established political movements of which the most important were the Nihilists and the Populists (*see page 218*). The Nihilists originated with the Westerners. They were determined to destroy tsarism and create a new society based upon rationalism and science as the culmination of the westernizing process which they believed Russia should follow. And the Populists began as those Slavophils who held that socialism was the only way of refashioning Russia on the basis of the *mir* and that revolution alone would achieve this.

Most of the Slavophils, however, were far from being either socialists or revolutionaries. On the contrary, they upheld the absolutism of the Tsar and the rule of the landed aristocracy over the peasants as essential a part of the true Russia as the Orthodox Church. Though they might criticize some aspects of tsarist policy, they were firm upholders of the regime and the traditions it represented. They received support from Alexander II because they were opposed to western liberalism which he hated and feared.

Nevertheless, despite their conservatism, these Slavophils had a strong sense of mission and destiny. And they thought that this not only meant that Russia should seek her own foreordained goal, but also act as an ethical and religious evangelist in Europe. From this aspect of Slavophilism developed the nationalist, political Panslav movement.

Panslavism had largely originated in the 1820s among the Slavs who were subject peoples of the Habsburg Empire. It stressed their linguistic affinities, common membership of the Orthodox Church and need to secure their independence from their traditional enemies, the Turks and Germans. Now it was seen in Russia as the expression of the country's mission to champion the cause of all peoples of Slav race. Panslav writers described schemes for a great Slav federation under Russian leadership and control with its capital at Constantinople, where the Cross would be placed once more on St. Sophia's Cathedral. It was unlikely, however, that the Slav peoples would in fact be induced to accept such a unity which would transcend their separate nationalisms. It had nothing to offer some Slavs. It had certainly nothing to offer the Poles, who were Roman Catholics, resented their rule by Russia and valued their ties with western Europe. Similarly the Croats, who also were Roman Catholics, had little sympathy with it and, even after their domination by the Magyars, looked to the Habsburgs as their champions. The Slav peoples of south-eastern Europe were ready to accept it as a means of gaining their freedom from Turkish or Habsburg rule, but as the Bulgars particularly showed after 1878, they regarded it as only a temporary expedient to be renounced whenever circumstances made it no longer favourable to them (*see page 349*).

The founding of the Moscow Slavonic Benevolent Committee in 1858 and the holding of the Moscow Slavonic Ethnographic Exhibition in 1867 did much to win support from the Russian ruling classes for the Panslav movement. The Russian government, though more aware of the practical limitations of Panslavism than its writers, recognized its advantages as a means of enabling Russia to recover the European influence she had lost through the Crimean War. It might also bring the longed-for prize of possession of Constantinople and the Straits and thus access to the Mediterranean, which was becoming more desirable now that Russian exports of grain were so important (*see page 334*). Alexander II, who had hitherto looked upon the movement with disfavour, visited the Ethnographic Exhibition and addressed the representatives of the other Slav races as 'brother Slavs'.

(b) Failure in Foreign Policy (1871–87)
Bismarck once said, 'Russia has nothing to do in the West. She only contracts Nihilism and other diseases there. Her mission is in Asia. There she stands for civilization.' For some 15 years after the Crimean War, Russia had concentrated upon expansion eastwards towards both Central Asia and the Far East. By the 1870s, however, she needed to consolidate her successes there, and the time seemed favourable for a renewal of Russian intervention in Europe (*see page 342*).

Accordingly in 1871 the Russian government renounced the Black Sea clauses of the Treaty of Paris (*see page 210*). The next year it induced the Sultan of Turkey to separate the Slavs from the Greek Patriarch of Constantinople and place them under a new Exarch, who was a Bulgar. These first steps towards the revival of Russian interest in her spheres of influence in Europe were accompanied by the beginning of the long-overdue reform of the army in 1874 (*see page 216*).

Nevertheless, for the first half of the decade there was no threat to peace in that part of Europe. She needed and wanted peace. The situation was changed by the revolt in Bosnia and Herzegovina against Turkish rule in July 1875 (*see page 343*). Russian opinion was inflamed by the events in these provinces and still more by the Bulgarian massacres and so readily supported the declaration of war on Turkey in April 1877. But Russia was not yet ready for war. The military reforms were far from complete and effective, and the still unfinished railway system could not supply the Russian forces in the Balkans adequately. The vital fortress of Plevna was not taken until December 1877 when the way was at last open to Constantinople.

Russia imposed upon Turkey the Treaty of San Stefano, which was largely drawn up by General Paul Ignatyev, Russian Ambassador at Constantinople from 1864 to 1877 and a champion of the Panslav movement. She had, however, to accept British and Austrian demands that the settlement should be revised internationally by the Congress of Berlin in 1878 (*see page 347*). The War had revealed some serious problems to the Russian government. As well as Russia's military weaknesses, she had not yet rebuilt her Black Sea fleet, and the short war strained her finances so severely that a billion roubles of new paper currency had to be issued in 1877.

Russian designs in the Balkans suffered a serious set-back at the Congress of Berlin. Turkey was not expelled from Europe, and the Straits were no nearer to Russian possession. Bosnia and Herzegovina came under Austrian occupation. Serbia and Montenegro did not gain a common frontier, and the Bulgars, though they owed their autonomy to Russia, showed no signs of being prepared to accept her domination. Panslavism was judged to have failed (*see page 346*).

(c) The Return of Reaction

The effects of this failure of Russian foreign policy were even more disastrous at home. It caused bitter resentment, especially among those who had suffered from the dislocation of the economy, and stimulated the revolutionary movement. From among the Populists came a new secret terrorist society called 'The Will of the People'. Early in 1878 one of their number, a young woman of noble birth, shot the chief of the St. Petersburg police to avenge the flogging of a fellow-revolutionary on his orders; and the next year they pledged themselves to assassinate Alexander II. In 1880 they blew up the dining-room of the Winter Palace in St. Petersburg with heavy loss of life, but the Tsar escaped.

A number of liberals petitioned him to grant the country a constitution, and he decided to attempt to gain support from the moderates by making some political concessions. He agreed to a scheme, drawn up by Count Louis-Melikov, his Minister of the Interior, by which a number of elected representatives were to be associated in the drafting of certain laws, but this did not satisfy the moderate opposition nor placate the revolutionaries.

In March 1881, as he was returning to the Winter Palace in a carriage, after giving final approval to this scheme, Alexander was fatally wounded by a bomb thrown at him by a terrorist. The assassination did not produce a revolution. The political and social order remained unshaken, and he was succeeded by his son, Alexander III.

The new Tsar was a powerful personality, conscientious in his devotion to duty and astute but narrow-minded. He disliked all forms of liberalism and during his father's reign had opposed ideas of reform. His father's assassination confirmed his conservatism. He believed that the terrorists had been encouraged by the political concessions that had been made since the Crimean War. He was determined to reassert the authority of the tsardom to the full. His reign became one of reaction and repression, an attempt to return to the past.

Alexander III had been and continued to be deeply influenced by his chief tutor, Constantine Pobedonostev, a former Professor of Civil Law at Moscow University and since 1880 the Senior Procurator of the Holy Synod. He virtually controlled the internal politics of Russia during Alexander's reign and is said to have provided the model for the Grand

Inquisitor in Tolstoy's novel, *The Brothers Karamazov* (1879). He mistrusted such western ideas as liberal institutions, civil liberties and particularly parliamentary government, which he called 'the great lie of our time'. To oppose their dangerous influence in the Empire, he stood for the promotion of Russian culture, the strengthening of the autocracy of the tsardom and the upholding of the Orthodox religion. He drafted the accession manifesto of the new Tsar, who proclaimed in it his 'faith in the strength and right of autocratic power' and declared that he would 'introduce order and justice' into the institutions created by his father.

The Louis-Melikov plan of legislative reform approved by Alexander II was immediately abandoned. In its place, the numbers and powers of the secret police were increased, the terrorists were hanged or sentenced to long terms of imprisonment and exile and fourteen newspapers were suppressed. In the countryside, steps were taken to reduce the freedom which the peasants had gained with the abolition of serfdom. This policy reached its climax in 1889 when new officials, known as land captains, were appointed from among local landowners, often former serf-owners, with full powers over the *zemstvos* and local officials; and, at the same time, the franchise for election to *zemstvos* was limited, and their activities were limited. The next year, provincial governors and other officials were given increased powers, particularly to forbid action by the *zemstvos*, and this even hindered local measures of relief during the serious outbreaks of famine and plague in the years 1891 and 1892 because the government was suspicious of provincial initiative but itself was incapable of action.

A deliberate policy was adopted to ensure that education at all stages was conducted in accordance with the outlook of the regime. In the primary schools, Pobedonostev was able to ensure that an important place was given in the curriculum to religious instruction which taught the pupils the duty of unquestioning obedience to the edicts of Church and State. He wished secondary and higher education to be restricted to the children of the governing classes. In 1887 an official circular to provincial officials expressed the desirability of the exclusion from secondary schools of 'children of coachmen, servants, cooks, washerwomen, small shopkeepers and persons of a similar type, whose children, perhaps with the exception of those gifted with unusual abilities, should certainly not be brought out of the social environment to which they belong.' The universities in 1884 were placed completely under the control of the government, which took over the appointment of all principals and important professors and dismissed many liberal teachers.

Pobedonostev's wish to establish the supremacy of Russian culture led Alexander III also to embark upon a policy of Russification with the intention of compelling the peoples of the Empire to accept the Russian language, religion and traditions, though less than half their number were themselves Russian. Russian was made a compulsory subject in schools in Poland and the Baltic provinces. Polish Catholics, Baltic Lutherans and Trans-caucasian Muslims were harrassed and subjected to missions by the Orthodox Church. While provincial governors were provided with funds to assist the building of new Orthodox churches, the adherents of other religions could only build places of worship for themselves with the permission of the Holy Synod.

The harshest measures were directed against Russia's 5 million Jews, partly because there were Jews among the revolutionary leaders, and partly because anti-semitism served as an outlet for popular discontent. Alexander II's murder was followed by immediate violence against Jews and attacks on their houses and shops. These were called 'pogroms' (meaning in Russian devastation or destruction), and the word passed into the English language at this time. They continued periodically, often with police connivance. In addition, numerous anti-Jewish decrees were issued. The Pale, the area on the borderlands of Poland in which Jews were allowed to settle, was reduced in size. Jews were not permitted to acquire land and only a limited number of Jews were accepted as students at secondary schools and universities or admitted into the professions. Anti-semitism became official Russian policy, creating a disastrous impression outside the country and driving thousands of her Jews to migrate to the United States and western Europe from the 1880s onwards.

The police had done much to track down and destroy the terrorist organizations before Alexander II's assassination, and this was completed early in the new reign. There were occasional terrorist plots against Alexander III. Among those hanged in 1887 after one such plot was Alexander Ulyanov, whose younger brother changed his name to Lenin.

The terrorist movement, indeed, declined rapidly after 1881 and by the end of the century had almost ceased to exist. Apart from local peasant unrest, there was no popular rising against the tsarist regime until 1905. There was, in fact, widespread support for the government's measures against terrorists, and the Russian revolutionary movement itself was disillusioned by the political futility of terrorism.

(d) The Economic Situation
The most serious economic problem in Russia during the later part of the nineteenth century was rural overpopulation combined with stagnation in agriculture. The population increased rapidly year by year. In European Russia alone, it grew from some 50 million in the early 1860s to 82 million in 1897. But the output from the land stayed practically the same. The situation which followed the abolition of serfdom did not make for improved agricultural production. The financial burdens on the peasants were heavy, both through the levy paid to the government to compensate the landowners for the loss of estates and through the heavy indirect taxation imposed by the government on everyday necessities which consequently affected the poorest

classes most grievously. And as the population increased, and the land was divided into yet smaller holdings, the *mir* was unable to allocate plots to everyone and prevent the growth of a number of landless labourers. Primitive methods of cultivation were retained, and the desperate need of the peasants to grow as much as they could resulted sometimes in an 'economy of devastation' so that the crops began to yield even less from the exhausted soil. Moreover, foreign indebtedness compelled Russia to sell her grain abroad, and from the 1830s it represented about a half of the total value of her exports and some 15 per cent of her total production of grain. This continued even if there were serious shortages of food at home, as occurred particularly in 1891 and 1892 when famine and an attendant cholera epidemic cost half a million lives.

At the same time, this period was one of rapid industrial progress in Russia. In 1865 there were 1425 factories in the Empire with 392 718 workers with a turnover of 296 million roubles; but by 1880 the number had increased to 16 564 factories with 616 925 workers and a turnover of 731 million roubles. Moreover, industry became increasingly concentrated under large enterprises. In the cotton industry 43 per cent of the workers were engaged in mills employing over 100 people in 1866, 51 per cent in 1879 and 72 per cent in 1894. In the coal industry, the largest mines multiplied their output sevenfold from 1882 to 1894, but the rest hardly increased their output. The old factory system based on serfdom had been replaced by a modern, capitalist organization relying on free wage labour. And this new capitalism made possible the growth of railway construction. By 1880 the total length of track was about 24 000 kilometres, two-thirds of which had been built in the last decade, and by the end of the 1890s it was to be doubled again. Nevertheless, Russia's industry was on a small scale and continued to lag behind that of western Europe. The census of 1897 showed that five-sixths of the population worked in agriculture and only a sixth in industry.

Yet Russia was entering upon a fresh economic phase, and one of its results was the formation of a new industrial working class, which though small was steadily growing and perhaps numbered as many as 3 million by the end of the century. Industry was not short of labour, since rural overpopulation caused peasants to crowd into the towns, seeking employment in the factories. Wages were generally low and working conditions bad. Though some factory laws were passed, the government usually supported the employers and ruthlessly suppressed strikes or other 'mutinous' activities.

At the other end of the social scale, this period also saw the emergence of a class of industrialists and businessmen. Many of these came from the older merchant class, but few had the capital required to develop Russian industry, and much of it was acquired by foreign investment, principally French. In agriculture, many of the nobility could not survive the combined effect of the abolition of serfdom and the agricultural difficulties, and they sold their land outside their class. Others, however, ran their estates profitably, especially in the blackearth region of the southern provinces, which had been opened up by a network of railways linking them with Moscow, St. Petersburg and the Baltic and Black Sea ports. They were joined by the *kulaks*, who were the richer peasants, and together produced the grain available for export abroad with the labour of the low-paid and heavily taxed landless peasants.

This, indeed, was the way in which Russia paid for the modernization of her economy and also for her military power and expansionist foreign policy. Both the government and industry needed foreign loans, and if these were to be secured, interest on the money borrowed had to be paid regularly and fully. This led to heavy taxes and the sale of grain abroad, which reduced the peasants and workers to poverty and even starvation. Imperial policy, therefore, benefited the landowning and capitalist classes, but involved a large part of the people in both political and economic subjection.

Disillusionment with the political futility of terrorism in the face of this situation led to it being gradually supplanted by Marxism as the chief expression of opposition to the regime. During the early 1880s a number of Populists in exile in Switzerland became converted to Marxism. The most important of them was George Plekhanov, who in 1883 founded in Geneva a group known as *Osvobozhdenie Trude* —'Liberation of Labour.' He wrote several pamphlets in which he argued that in Russia socialism could not be based upon the backward peasantry and the out-of-date *mir*, but only upon the industrial working-class, who would inevitably increase in size and importance with the growth of capitalism in Russia. Thus, he argued, the factory could be made the lever to overthrow the existing regime in favour of a new society. Russian socialists, therefore, he insisted, must seek to educate and organize the workers into a mass movement ready to overthrow the tsardom and bring about the socialist revolution.

The first organized Russian Marxist group was formed in St. Petersburg in 1883 and was followed by others in several cities. At first these were secret study and discussion groups among university students and other intellectuals, but by 1894, when Alexander III died, Marxist ideas had begun to spread to the industrial workers, and groups were formed among them. These began to train leaders for the future. A prominent member of the St. Petersburg group was the son of a school inspector, Vladimir Lenin, who was sentenced in 1895 to three years' exile in Siberia for his propagandist activities.

Bibliography
In addition to the books already mentioned (*see pages 134, 218*), there are H. Seton-Watson, *The Decline of Imperial Russia, 1855–1914* (New edn., Methuen, 1952) and *The Russian Empire* (OUP, 1967).

Exercises

A *This section consists of questions that might be used for discussion (or written answers) as a way of expanding on the chapter and testing your understanding of it:*

1 Explain the differences between the Westerners and Slavophils.
2 Why were the Populists exceptional among the Slavophils?
3 What do you understand by Panslavism, and why was it not popular with some of the Slav peoples?
4 How did both the Slav peoples and the Russian government plan to exploit Panslavism to their advantage?
5 What steps did the Russian government take in the 1870s as a preliminary to renewing her activity in Europe?
6 Why did Russia fail in the war against Turkey, and in its aftermath?
7 Why did the Russian government's foreign failure 'stimulate the revolutionary movement'?
8 Why didn't the assassination of Alexander II lead to widespread revolution?
9 Outline the political ideas of Alexander III and Pobiedonostev.
10 In what ways were the reforms of Alexander II undone in the 1880s?
11 Why, and with what effects, were the Jews persecuted in the 1880s?
12 Why was there so little opposition to the Tsarist regime in the later years of Alexander III's reign?
13 Why did Russian agriculture remain so backward in the latter years of the nineteenth century, while industry made rapid progress?
14 What effects did the Russian government's economic policies have on the different sectors of Russian society?
15 Was it inevitable that Marxist groups would develop among the Russian working class in the late nineteenth century?

B *Essay questions*

1 Explain Russia's treatment of her serfs during the period 1815–1914. (Oxford, 1981)
2 Why were the reforms of 1860 introduced into Russia? To what extent did they serve their purpose? (Welsh, 1983)
3 'Alexander II was just as typical a Romanov and reactionary Tsar as was Alexander III.' Is this too harsh a judgement? (London, 1982)
4 Discuss the significance for Poland and for Europe of the Polish Revolutions of 1830 and 1863. (JMB, 1984)

C *The Tsars Alexander*
Alexander II was known as 'The Tsar Liberator'; Alexander III is regarded as the epitome of Tsarist autocracy. Yet historians have frequently challenged this simple view, and this exercise helps you to examine their debate. Draw out and complete a chart like that below, comparing the policies of the two Tsars under a number of headings. Use not only this chapter, but also section IV:1 and any other sources you have available.

Area of policy	Alexander II	Alexander III
Politics: (a) political beliefs and attitudes (b) political reforms undertaken (c) attitude to opposition groups (d) judicial policies (e) attitudes to minorities		
Religious views and policies		
Foreign policy: (a) Russian army and other forces (b) Central Asia (c) The Far East (d) European and Balkan policies		
Social and economic policies: (a) Educational policy (b) Agriculture and peasantry (c) Industry		

Having completed the comparison chart in as much detail as possible, what view do you take of the two Tsars?

D *Documentary evidence*

In general, the primary sources you have consulted have been of a governmental or diplomatic nature. In this section, you will be examining three extracts from biographical sources; in reading them, you should consider not only what you can learn from them about Tsarist Russia, but also of what value this type of source is.

Source A. from *Spirit to Survive, The Memoirs of Princess Nicholas Galitzine,* published by William Kimber & Co Ltd, 1976.

'When my grandfather got married he settled at an estate at Vorganovo in the province of Smolensk. It was a beautiful estate. It was surrounded by forests, and a calm river ran close by a well-kept park. A large lake lay at some distance from the main house, and beyond it lay stables, the houses for the workmen, cow-sheds and all sorts of household buildings. The park, dark and cool and shady, was very pleasant to sit in on a hot summer day, and surrounding the house was an Italian garden. There were two other houses a short way away and an avenue running down to the lake, where there was a foot-bridge leading to the back-yard buildings . . . .

With the birth of their second child my parents now moved to the "Middle House" at Vorganovo. . . . By the time I was born (1900). . . . We still continued to live in the country with occasional visits to St. Petersburg, spending half the summer months in my Grandmother Narischkine's estate at Stepanovskoye. There the house was a very grand affair and consisted in fact of three very large houses joined together. The centre one was huge, white with a colonnade and large coat of arms right at the top of the roof. (How well I remember it in every detail as it lay on the ground, smashed to bits by the Bolsheviks, when I visited the place in the early twenties. Also pulled down and broken was a stone lion, one of a pair of which we children were especially fond. I was very depressed at seeing this, and I remember thinking, "What is the sense of this sort of destruction?")

Inside, the furniture was expensively upholstered, the pictures rare and often valuable, including some Canalettos, (my great-grandfather had been a collector). Less valuable but more interesting to us were those galleries containing portraits of our ancestors—for instance I remember one life-size painting of our great-grandmother (born a Princess Galitzine) getting ready for the hunt, seated on a horse which was being held by two pages. She was waving goodbye to two young girls, one of them holding a baby in her arms.

Source B. from *What Then Must We do?* (1886) by Leo Tolstoy, translated by Aylmer Maude.

'The work is intense and ceaseless. All work with their utmost strength and during this work eat up not only all their scanty supplies of food but also any reserves they may have had: never too stout, they grow leaner by the end of the harvest work.

Here is a small group engaged on mowing: three peasants, one an old man, another his nephew (a young married lad), and a boot-maker, a sinewy fellow who has been a domestic serf—this hay-harvest decides their fate for the coming winter for them all: whether they can keep a cow and pay the taxes. They have already worked unceasingly and continuously for two weeks. Rain has hindered the work. After the rain, when the wind has dried the grass, they decide to finish the work, and to get on more quickly they decide to each bring two women to it. With the old man comes his wife, a woman of fifty worn out by hard work and eleven childbirths, and deaf but still a good worker, and his thirteen year-old daughter, a small girl but strong and quick. With the nephew comes his wife, a woman as strong and tall as a man, and his sister-in-law the pregnant wife of a soldier. With the bootmaker comes his wife, a good worker, and her mother, an old woman finishing her eighth decade, and who usually goes out begging. They all line up, and work from morning till evening in the sweltering blaze of the June sun. It is steaming and the rain threatens. Every hour of work is precious. They grudge the time to fetch water or kvas.

A tiny boy, the old woman's grandson, fetches some water for them. The old woman, evidently only anxious not to be driven away from the work, does not let the rake out of her hands, though she can hardly, with effort, move along. The lad, all bent up and taking short steps with his bare little feet, brings along the jug of water which is heavier than himself, changing it from hand to hand. The girl shoulders the load of hay which is also heavier than she; she takes a few steps, stops, and throws it down unable to carry it farther. The old woman of fifty rakes unceasingly and, with her kerchief brushed to one side, drags the hay along, breathing heavily and tottering in her walk; the woman of eighty does nothing but rake, but even that is beyond her strength: she slowly drags her feet in their bark shoes and with wrinkled brows looks sombrely before her like one who is seriously ill or is dying. The old man purposely sends her farther away from the others to rake near the hay-cocks so that she should not have to keep up with them, but without pause and with the same death-like, sombre face she works on as long as the others do.

The sun is already setting behind the woods and the hay-cocks are not yet all cleared away and much remains to be done . . . .

But here is the proprietor's house. That same evening when from the village nothing is heard but the clang of the whetstones of the exhausted haymakers returning from the fields, the sound of the hammers straightening out the dents in the scythe blades, the shouts of women and girls who, having just had time to put down their rakes, are already running to drive in the cattle—from the proprietor's house other sounds are heard: drin, drin, drin: goes the piano, and an Hungarian song rings out, and amid those songs occasionally comes the knock of croquet-mallets on the balls. Near the stable stands a carriage to which four well-fed horses are harnessed. . . .

In that house two women hardly manage to wash up all the crockery for the gentlefolk who have just had a meal, and two peasants in dress coats are running up and down stairs serving coffee, tea, wine, and seltzer water. Upstairs a table is spread: they have just finished eating and will soon eat again until midnight, till three o'clock, often till cock-crow.

Some of them sit smoking and playing cards, others sit and smoke and talk liberalism; others move about from place to place, eat, smoke, and not knowing what to do decide to go out for a drive. There are some fifteen healthy men and women there and some thirty able-bodied men and women servants working for them.

Here it is no longer possible to make the excuse that such is the order of things; none of this was prearranged. We ourselves carefully arrange this way of life, taking grain and labour away from the overburdened peasant folk. We live as though we had no connection with the dying washer-woman, the fifteen year-old prostitute, the woman exhausted by cigarette making, and the drained excessive labour of the old women and children around us who lack sufficient food; we live—enjoying ourselves in luxury—as if there were no connection between these things and our life; we do not wish to see that were it not for our idle, luxurious and depraved way of life, there would also not be this excessive toil, and that without this excessive toil such lives as ours would be impossible.

We imagine that their sufferings are one thing and our life another, and that we, living as we do, are as innocent as pure doves.'

Source C. from *Memoirs of a Revolutionist* (1899) by Prince Kropotkin

'Wealth was measured in those times by the number of 'souls' that a landed proprietor owned. So many "souls" meant so many male serfs; women did not count. My father, who owned nearly 1200 souls, in three different provinces, and who had, in addition to his peasants' holdings, large tracts of land which were cultivated by these peasants, was accounted a rich man. He lived up to his reputation, which meant that his house was open to any number of visitors, and that he kept a very large household.

We were a family of eight, occasionally of ten or twelve; our fifty servants at Moscow and half as many more in the country were not considered one too many. Four coachmen to attend a dozen horses, three cooks for the masters and two more for the servants, a dozen men to wait upon at dinner time (one man, plate in hand, to stand behind each person seated at the table), and girls innumerable in the maidservants' room —how could anyone do with less than this? Besides, the ambition of every landed proprietor was that everything required for his household should be made at home, by his own men.

To maintain such numbers of servants as were kept in our house in town would have been simply ruinous, if all provisions had to be bought at Moscow; but in those times of serfdom things were managed very simply. When winter came, father sat at his table and wrote the following to the manager of his estate:

"On receipt of this, and as soon as the winter communication is established in the city of Moscow, twenty-five peasant sledges, drawn by two horses each, one horse from each house, and one sledge and one man from each second house, are to be loaded with (so many) quarters of oats, (so many) of wheat, and (so many) of rye, as also with all the poultry and geese and ducks, well frozen, which have to be killed this winter, well packed and accompanied by a complete list, under the supervision of a well-chosen man";—and so it went on for a couple of pages, till the next full stop was reached. After this there followed an enumeration of the penalties which would be inflicted in case the provisions should not reach the house situated in such a street, number so and so, in due time and in good condition.

Some time before Christmas the twenty-five peasant sledges really entered our gates, and covered the surface of the wide yard. . . .'

Now answer these questions:
1 What new light do these sources throw on life in Tsarist Russia?
2 What do they tell you about the attitudes of their authors? (Having answered this question, research for yourself something about each author.)
3 What are the particular virtues and limitations of biographies as a form of historical evidence?

VI International Rivalry 1871–90

1 The Eastern Question

(a) Russian Advances in Asia

Russian expansion in the nineteenth century, always reaching out for the open seas, showed a general tendency to be concentrated in one particular direction at one time. When an advance seemed impossible in one area, she turned towards another in which resistance to her designs was likely to be less effective. Her defeat in the Crimean War checked her attempts to move south-westwards into the Balkans towards Constantinople for the next 20 years. Consequently, during Alexander II's reign, she turned her attention towards Asia in two directions—eastwards towards the Pacific coast and south-eastwards towards Persia and Afghanistan—and in both these areas she gained considerable success (see Map 19, page 364).

The Russian advance to the Pacific had been prepared under Ivan the Terrible, when in 1582 a force of Cossacks defeated the Tartars on the River Irtysh and annexed western Siberia. Thereafter the Russians moved slowly across the vast Siberian plains and forests and a century later took Kamchatka, a peninsula of eastern Siberia stretching southwards into the Pacific. During the nineteenth century this process continued and brought Russia into contact with the two Far Eastern empires—Japan and China. In the 1850s she annexed the island of Sakhalin and the Kurile Isles, but in 1875 had to cede the Kuriles to Japan in return for Japanese recognition of Russian possession of Sakhalin. China, however, was not able to bargain with Russia. In 1860 the Treaty of Peking settled the border between the two empires, making the Rivers Amur and Assuri the frontier and enabling Russia the next year to begin the construction of the port of Vladivostock. There in 1891 work started on the great Trans-Siberian Railway that was to reach back to Moscow.

By the second half of the nineteenth century, Russia had been expanding south-eastwards to Central Asia, which was inhabited by marauding, half-nomadic Mongol tribes, for 100 years at a rate, it has been calculated, of 142 square kilometres a day. The final penetration, conquest and settlement of the area occupied a period of some 15 years. The subjugation of the Caucasus, began in the first half of the century, was completed between 1859 and 1864. Russian forces entered Samarkand in 1868, and five years later a series of campaigns had given them in quick succession all Turkestan, Bokhara and Khiva. The Russian government continually insisted that it wished only to make a limited advance, but its forces were drawn further and further south by the need to subdue hostile peoples and the difficulty of controlling from St. Petersburg ambitious local administrators and military commanders (*see Map 19, page 364*).

Foreign reaction to the Russian advances in the Far East was comparatively slight. America's dislike of a Russian presence on the Pacific coast was placated in 1867 when Russia agreed to sell her Alaska; it had been Russian since 1796, but was virtually uncolonized and completely defenceless. Britain was probably the power most alarmed by Russia's designs. She had secured a predominant trading position in China (*see page 363*), though she did not wish to secure a monopoly for herself there. She adopted an 'open door' policy towards the country by which any nation could trade there and not seek to impose restrictions upon others. However, Russia, being a land-based military power and not a flourishing commercial country, seemed determined to assert her position in the Far East by gaining territory from China, building strategic ports and linking them with railways. Fear of such Russian designs in the Far East was to lead to the formation of the Anglo-Japanese Alliance in 1902.

Russian progress in Central Asia alarmed Britain much more. She had sought to protect her position in India by maintaining a barrier of neutral states—Persia, Afghanistan and Tibet—running in a crescent round northern India (*see page 353*). Of these the most important was Afghanistan on the North-Western Frontier. The Russian campaigns of the 1860s brought them to the River Oxus, the northern frontier of Afghanistan, and halved the distance between the Russian Empire and the British outposts in India.

The British fear was that Russia might be able to make herself influential in this area and perhaps in eastern Persia as well. From there she might stir up rebellion among the tribesmen in the mountains of the North-West Frontier. These warlike peoples, who provided a large part of the native troops in the Indian army, were mainly Muslims. If Russia were able to inspire the Amir of Afghanistan and the Shar of Persia to accept her leadership in a holy war against the rule of the British infidels, these tribesmen might well join in, and the threat to British rule in India would be as serious as during the Mutiny of 1857–58. Yet there was nothing that Britain could do about it. She had no way of preventing the Russians advancing either eastwards or southwards in Asia.

(b) The Bulgarian Question
By the 1870s, however, at the time when Alexander II had become a supporter of Panslavism, the Russian government began to look again towards south-eastern Europe (*see page 330*). This caused even greater

anxiety in Britain. Her fear of Russian designs upon the Straits of Constantinople and the eastern Mediterranean was as strong as ever. It was a repetition of the situation which had led to the Crimean War. Then Britain had been able to act against Russia because she had the help of an ally. If she were to check Russia this time, she would again need an ally.

The prelude to this change in Russian foreign policy came in 1871. France's defeat in the Franco-Prussian War gave her an irresistible opportunity to renounce the Black Sea clauses of the Treaty of Paris of 1856 (*see page 330*) and announce her intention to refortify Sebastopol and base a fleet there again. Her neutrality during the War brought her Bismarck's support, and Gladstone's government in Britain had no choice but to accept the situation.

Four years later, a new crisis occurred in the Balkans. This had become increasingly likely since the end of the Crimean War. The promises made by the Sultan of Turkey, Abdul Mejid, at Paris had proved completely worthless (*see page 212*). The cruelty, corruption and incompetence of his rule over his Christian subjects continued unabated; and the situation was the same under Abdul Aziz, who succeeded him as Sultan in 1861. Now, following a bad harvest the year before, the serb peasants of the provinces of Bosnia and Herzegovina, where taxation was harsh and serfdom still existed, broke out in revolt against the Turks in July 1875.

In February of that year Benjamin Disraeli had become prime minister at the head of a Conservative government in Britain. He came into office knowing little about foreign affairs, but was determined to reassert Britain's power in Europe, which he accused Gladstone of having neglected. He wished to uphold Britain's strategic interests and to show that she was as great a power as she had been in the time of the Crimean War. He accepted the traditional belief that the preservation of the Turkish Empire was essential for Britain as a protection against Russian designs in the Near East. Indeed, he believed that the opening of the Suez Canal made this region still more important for Britain. He thought that the Canal was vital to the British Empire and dramatically showed this in November 1875 when he arranged for the British government to purchase the bankrupt Khedive of Egypt's foundation shares in the Suez Canal Company. He was bound, therefore, to believe that Britain must support the Turkish government's efforts to suppress this revolt in Bosnia and Herzegovina.

On the other hand, the Russian government, if Panslavism were to mean anything, had to support the rebels. Austria-Hungary, however, did not wish to see Russian influence grow in the Balkans, and Count Andrassy, the Foreign Minister, believed that the maintenance of Turkish rule there was in her best interests. He hoped that the Turks would be able to subdue their rebellious subjects quickly and unaided. Bismarck wanted to prevent a dispute between Russia and Austria. He was anxious to preserve the League of the Three Emperors, which he had persuaded these two countries to join with Germany in forming in 1873 (*see page 370*). He persuaded them, therefore, to join with Germany in presenting the Berlin Memorandum to the Sultan in May 1876. This was a note calling upon him to introduce reforms into the government of his dominions. Disraeli refused to endorse it and sent warships to Besika Bay at the entrance to the Dardanelles as Lord Aberdeen had done in 1853 (*see page 204*).

Disraeli wished to destroy the unity of the League of the Three Emperors. When it had been formed in 1873, he said, 'The balance of power has been entirely destroyed, and the country which suffers most . . . is England.' He now saw the action of the League as a concealed attempt by Russia and Austria to partition Turkey with German support. He was resolved that he would not be placed in such a helpless position as Gladstone had been over the Black Sea clauses (*see page 343*), whose vain appeal for international action over the issue had led Bismarck to call him scornfully 'Professor Gladstone'.

Queen Victoria, however, had misgivings about Disraeli's attitude. She said that his refusal to join with other countries in an approach to the situation in Bosnia and Herzegovina might encourage the Sultan to refuse to consider reforms and to think that he could rely upon British support in his difficulties. Indeed, the immediate effect of the League's action was to arouse national feeling in Turkey. In May, following demonstrations by Muslim students, the Sultan was deposed, as was his successor three months later, and in August Abdul Hamid II finally gained the throne. The new Sultan, however, was unable to suppress the revolt in his Empire, and the semi-independent states of Serbia and Montenegro declared war in support of their fellow-Serbs. Serbia was defeated by Turkey, but the revolt now spread to Bulgaria. The Turks, alarmed by the worsening situation, embarked upon a deliberate policy of terrorism against the Bulgars. Irregular Asian troops committed widespread atrocities and massacred some 12 000 men, women and children.

This seemed a horrifying event even to contemporary Europe. Christians were shocked because their co-religionists had been put to death by Muslims. Others were angered because it undermined the general idea of progress and civilization, toleration and goodwill, accepted as the distinguishing achievement of the age. Gladstone put himself at the head of these protestors. In September he wrote a long pamphlet, *The Bulgarian Horrors and the Question of the East,* in which he denounced the 'Bulgarian atrocities' committed by the Turks and demanded that they should be made to remove themselves 'bag and baggage' with the utmost speed 'from the province they have desolated and profaned'.

Disraeli said that Gladstone was 'inebriated with the exuberance of his own verbosity', but his pamphlet transferred attention from the Russian threat to the plight of the Balkan subject-peoples, and it placed the emphasis upon moral questions rather than national interests. It made sufficient impression in Britain to prevent Disraeli taking any form of direct action. He decided to attempt a peaceful settlement by summoning a conference of the great powers at Constantinople. The conference demanded equality for Muslims and Christians in the Turkish Empire and a guarantee by the Sultan of self-government for Bosnia and Herzegovina. At first it seemed that Disraeli's policy might succeed. Abdul Hamid countered the requirement of the conference by going even further and proclaiming a new parliamentary constitution on western lines for the whole of the Empire. This, however, was only a move to prevent allied action against him, and after several months he dismissed the minister who had drawn up the new constitution and resumed his despotic rule.

(c) Russian Intervention and the Treaty of San Stefano

The vain attempts of the powers at mediation, added to the continuing atrocities in Bulgaria and the failure of a stream of Russian volunteers to save Serbia from Turkish invasion, aroused opinion in Russia. Alexander was determined not to repeat the mistake that had led to the Crimean War by allowing Russia to become isolated again. He did not think, however, that the other nations would now oppose Russian intervention to protect the Bulgarians and to compel Turkey to accept the reforms they had demanded; and he made sure of Austro-Hungarian neutrality by promising to gain Bosnia and Herzegovina for her. He declared war on Turkey in April 1877 and was joined by Romania, Serbia, Montenegro and Bulgaria.

Russian armies advanced through Romania and crossed the Danube into Bulgaria, but then they did not find the campaign as easy as they had expected, and the Turks were able to hold up their progress in the Balkans (*see page 330*). The result of this delay was to make British public opinion forget the Bulgarian atrocities and indulge in both fierce anti- Russian feeling and admiration for the Turkish stand at Plevna, a Bulgarian town which was only 30 kilometres south of the Danube. Disraeli could, therefore, revert to his original policy of supporting Turkey. The Russian armies at last occupied Adrianople in January 1878. Disraeli ordered 7000 troops to be brought from India and moved the naval squadron from Besika Bay to the island of Prinkipo within sight of Constantinople. Supported by an equally apprehensive Austria-Hungary, the British government demanded that Russia should end the war.

The British people succumbed to war fever. Queen Victoria wrote to Disraeli, 'Oh if the Queen were a man, she would like to go and give those horrid Russians, whose word one cannot trust, such a beating.' In London, Gladstone was hooted in the streets, and the windows of his house were broken; in Manchester, an effigy of him, marked 'Gladstone, England's Traitor' was burnt. Nightly the famous music-hall song expressed the wish of the audiences not to fight, but by jingo if they did . . ., and *Rule Britannia* was sung in the public houses. Russia, however, was hardly in a position to continue the war against Turkey, let alone take on fresh opponents as well.

She did not send her troops on to Constantinople, but in March 1878 she imposed upon Turkey the Treaty of San Stefano. This recognized the full sovereignty of Serbia, Montenegro and Romania (formed when Moldavia and Wallachia combined in 1862). Serbia and Montenegro were enlarged, Montenegro doubling her population and gaining two small ports on the Adriatic Sea. Romania was compelled to cede the province of Bessarabia to Russia in exchange for the less valuable Dobrudja. The Treaty also created a large autonomous state of Bulgaria with territory coinciding roughly with the exarchate and stretching from the River Danube to the Aegean Sea and from the Black Sea to within 80 kilometres of the Adriatic (*see Map 16*). This would now become the largest state in the Balkans and cut completely in two the Turkish Empire there. It was to remain under the Sultan's suzerainty, but with a prince nominated by Russia. The effect of the Treaty would be to establish a virtual Russian protectorate over the eastern part of the Balkan peninsula, commanding the route between Serbia and Salonika.

Map 16   The Treaty of San Stefano, 1878

When the news of the Treaty reached London, the *Morning Post* stated, 'By a master-stroke of diplomacy, if not of duplicity, Russia has in three short weeks completely outflanked England and Austria,' and commented, 'The English Parliament danced like marionettes while she pulled the wires.' Andrassy called the Treaty an 'Orthodox Slav sermon,' but Panslavism had made Russia overreach herself. Alexander had brought upon her the very isolation he had wanted to avoid and also provided Britain with the ally she needed to oppose Russian designs. Austrian-Hungary objected as strongly as Britain to the new 'big Bulgaria', which they both feared would be used by Russia to dominate all south-eastern Europe. Disraeli was determined to have the settlement changed. He called out the reserves in Britain and moved the Indian troops through the Suez Canal to Malta. Russia was still unable to contemplate war (*see page 330*); and Bismarck decided that he could no longer stand aside.

(d) The Treaty of Berlin (1878)

Bismarck had hoped to avoid being involved in the Eastern Question at this time, but he did not want a general war to break out in Europe, and he felt bound by Germany's interests to retain Austrian friendship which he feared would be lost if she looked to Britain for support. He called upon the powers to discuss the crisis at an international conference in Berlin. Again Russia had to submit, and the other powers were ready to accept his mediation.

The Congress of Berlin was attended by Russia, Turkey, Austria, Britain, France, Italy and Germany. When it met in June, most of its decisions had already been settled secretly in advance by negotiations between these powers, but they were confirmed by the Treaty of Berlin, which was to be the last important territorial readjustment of the Balkans in the nineteenth century. Russia was allowed to have Bessarabia, but in return she had to agree to the abandonment of the 'big Bulgaria' of the Treaty of San Stefano. This was now divided into three. The northern part became an autonomous 'little Bulgaria'; the central part, Eastern Roumelia, was to remain in the Turkish Empire under a Christian governor; and the southern part, which included Macedonia, was returned to direct Turkish rule. Austria-Hungary was allowed to occupy the provinces of Bosnia and Herzegovina and also the Sanjak of Novibazar, a corridor of territory separating Serbia and Montenegro (*see Map 17*). Austria-Hungary was held to be answerable to the Treaty Powers of 1878 for her administration of these territories, which remained legally within the Turkish Empire. Lord Salisbury, Disraeli's Foreign Secretary, called this arrangement 'left-handed annexation'. Britain gained control of Cyprus as a further base in the Mediterranean. France was encouraged to take Tunis (*see page 358*). Only Italy got nothing.

It was Lord Salisbury's idea that Britain should occupy Cyprus. He was anxious that Turkey should be strengthened against possible future Russian threats, and Cyprus would be a convenient point from which British support could be given to Turkey. Salisbury wanted also the Sultan at last to be compelled effectively to improve the condition of his Christian subjects. He got little support from Disraeli, who said that the Foreign Secretary did not seem aware that his function was 'to keep the Russians out of Turkey, not to create an ideal existence for Turkish Christians.' The Congress did, however, accept Salisbury's proposal that European consuls should be attached to the Turkish government to ensure 'a pure administration of justice' for the Christians. The Sultan gave his usual promise that he would make sure that his Christian subjects were better treated in the future.

347

Map 17 The Treaty of Berlin, 1878

When Disraeli returned from Berlin, he made the well-known claim that he had brought with him 'peace with honour', and he had certainly achieved his purpose to the extent of preventing war, checking Russia and averting the collapse of Turkey; and he believed that he had undermined the effectiveness of the League of the Three Emperors. The settlement did bring the period of peace which the powers desired, but it did not accomplish all it had proposed. There was no marked improvement in the condition of the Sultan's Christian subjects, though this might have been so if Salisbury's plan for consuls in Turkey had not been cancelled by Gladstone when he became Prime Minister in 1880. Still more, the settlement left all the powers dissatisfied and anxious. Bulgaria resented the truncation of her territory. Serbia now regarded both the Habsburgs and the Turks as oppressors of her fellow-countrymen. Among the great powers, though Britain and Austria-Hungary had asserted themselves, neither had achieved their main object of preserving Turkish power intact in the Balkans. Andrassy had been compelled by the continued existence of Bulgaria to agree to Austria's territorial gains in the Balkans to safeguard her influence in the northern part of the peninsula, but as a Hungarian aristocrat he disliked any increase in the Slav population of the Empire and doubted the wisdom of this action. Above all, Russia had fought a costly and ultimately successful war and yet been compelled to relinquish nearly all her gains. Though Bismarck had been reluctant to take the initiative in getting the situation settled peacefully, it was made clear to all the powers that Germany had now become the ultimate arbiter of peace and war in Europe, and the realization increased, rather than reduced, international tension.

Yet for 30 years after the Treaty of Berlin, the Eastern Question was relatively quiet. Russia was still unable, for the remainder of the nineteenth century, to assert herself in the Balkans. Serbia and Montenegro were long alienated from Russia by her sponsorship of the 'big Bulgarian'; and both her impotence and the final failure of Panslavism were shown by the prolonged Bulgarian crisis of 1885–87. In 1885 the people of Eastern Roumelia revolted against Turkish rule and declared their union with Bulgaria. It might have seemed that this would have pleased Russia, but the 'little Bulgaria', set up in 1878, had shown no gratitude for the part played by Russia in the establishment of her autonomy and had insisted upon pursuing an independent policy. It was Russia now which objected to the enlargement of Bulgaria, while Austria-Hungary and Britain, because of Bulgaria's anti-Russian policy, supported it. Bismarck made it clear in the Reinsurance Treaty of 1887 that, if he were compelled to intervene in the matter, it would be on the side of Austria-Hungary (*see page 375*). The Russians were unable, therefore, either to undo the act of unification or to impose a Russian ruler upon Bulgaria, and the crisis eventually ended without war.

Bibliography

For the background to this phase of the Eastern Question, there is W.E. Mosse, *The Rise and Fall of the Crimean System, 1855–1871* (John Murray, 1963) and for the later years B.H. Sumner, *Russia and the Balkans, 1870–1880* (OUP, 1937), R.H. Davison, *Reform in the Ottoman Empire, 1856–1876* (Princeton, 1963) and W.N. Medlicott, *The Congress of Berlin and After* (Methuen, 1938). For British policy, see Robert Blake, *Disraeli* (Methuen, 1969), J.A.S. Grenville, *Lord Salisbury and Foreign Policy* (London University Press, 1964) and R.T. Shannon, *Gladstone and the Bulgarian Agitation, 1876* (Nelson, 1963)

Exercises

A   *This section consists of questions that might be used for discussion (or written answers) as a way of expanding on the chapter and testing your understanding of it:*

1   For what reasons was Russian foreign policy in the nineteenth century broadly expansionist?

2   Why was Russian expansion in the Far East and Central Asia so rapid?

3   Why did both these Russian successes cause such concern to Great Britain?

4   Why did Russian policy look again at South East Europe in the 1870s?

5   How did the Great Powers line up in 1875? And why did they take the sides they did?

6   Why did Disraeli send warships to Besika Bay when the Berlin Memorandum was issued?

7   Were the Bulgarian massacres a turning-point in the history of the Eastern Question? How significant were the 'moral questions' that they raised?

8   Why was British public opinion apparently so fickle in the 1870s?

9   Why did Russia stop fighting in March 1878?

10 What do you understand by 'Panslavism had made Russia overreach herself'?
11 Why did the powers agree to meet in Berlin in 1878?
12 In what ways was the Treaty of Berlin more acceptable to Britain and Austria-Hungary than the Treaty of San Stefano?
13 What problems did the Treaty of Berlin leave unresolved?
14 Why did Russia object to the creation of 'big Bulgaria' in 1885?

B *Essay questions*
1 'The most important turning point in the history of the Eastern Question in the nineteenth century.' Consider this comment on the Treaty of Berlin in 1878. (Cambridge, 1982)
2 In 1856 at Paris and again in 1878 at Berlin the powers had to deal with 'the Eastern Question'. How much had it changed in that period? (Oxford, 1981)
3 'The Treaty of Berlin may have served the peace in 1878, but it sowed the seeds of further friction and war in the course of the next forty years.' Discuss. (SUJB, 1983)
4 Do you agree that the Russo-Turkish War of 1877–8 was essentially a continuation of the Crimean War? (Welsh, 1982)
5 Why did the Balkan Crisis of 1875–8 matter to anyone other than the Turkish or Balkan peoples? (Welsh, 1982)
6 Why did the treaty of Berlin, 1878, fail to solve the Eastern Question? (AEB, 1981)
7 What evidence is there to support the opinion that from 1832 to 1878 the Ottoman Empire survived only because other powers rushed regularly to its rescue? (London, 1983)
8 Discuss the strengths and weaknesses of the settlement reached at the Congress of Berlin (1878). (JMB, 1981)

C *Extract question* (London, 1981)

The problems of the Balkans 1875–1914
Study the extract below and then answer questions (*a*) to (*h*) which follow:
line 'To Her Majesty's Principal Secretary of State.
Sir:
I have the honour to inclose a copy of the Treaty which was signed today *at Berlin* by the seven Signatory Powers of the Treaty of Paris. The Treaty is
5 one of unusual length, and enters fully into *the various questions raised by the Treaty of San Stefano*, so far as they *affect the dispositions of the Treaty of Paris*. The alterations which are made in the Preliminary Treaty are very large, and extend to nearly all the Articles of that instrument. Their general effect has been to restore, with due security for good government,
10 a very large territory to the Government of the Sultan; and they tend powerfully *to secure from external assault the stability and independence of his Empire*. Provisions having for their object to insure *entire equality of all religions before the law* have been applied to all the territories affected by the Treaty.
15 The policy which has received the sanction of the congress of Berlin is generally coincident with that which has been sustained by Her Majesty's Government since the Treaty of San Stefano was published, and which was indicated in the Circular of the 1st April. . . .

The essential contention of the Circular, that the Articles of the Pre-
20 liminary Treaty, as being a departure from the Treaty of Paris, must be
discussed by the Congress as a whole . . . has been admitted to the largest
possible extent. Of the detailed objections made in the Circular of the
Treaty of San Stefano, the first and most important is couched in the
following terms:

25 "The most important consequences to which the Treaty practically leads
are those which result from its action as a whole upon the nations of
South-Eastern Europe. By the articles creating *the new Bulgaria*, a strong
Slav State will be created *under the auspices and control of Russia*, possessing
important harbours upon the shores of the Black Sea and Archipelago, and
30 conferring upon that Power a preponderating influence over both the
political and commercial relations in those seas.

It will be so constituted as to merge in the dominant Slav majority a
considerable mass of population which is Greek in race and sympathy. . . .
The provision by which this new State is to be subjected to a ruler whom
35 Russia will practically choose, its administration framed by a Russian
Commissary, and the first working of its institutions commenced under
the control of a Russian army, sufficiently indicates the political system of
which in future it is to form a part."

It will be seen that all these objections have been removed by the Treaty of
40 Berlin. It has *radically changed the disposition of the vast region to which*, in
the Treaty of San Stefano, *the name of Bulgaria is given.*'
(*A Memorandum from Lord Salisbury, July 1878*)

(Maximum
marks)

(*a*) Name the chairman who presided over the Congress 'at (1)
Berlin' (line 3).

(*b*) (i) What had led to the renewal of Balkan conflict in the (5)
middle years of the 1870s?

(ii) Show how the Treaty of San Stefano could be said to
'affect the dispositions of the Treaty of Paris' (line 6).

(*c*) Explain what international problems (other than those rela- (4)
ting to the internal disposition of territories in the Balkans),
for *either* Britain and France *or* Germany and Austria, were
seen in 1878 to have arisen from 'the various questions
raised by the Treaty of San Stefano' (line 5).

(*d*) Show how the European powers in 1875–77 had failed, (3)
from the Sultan's point of view, 'to secure from external
assault the stability and independence of his Empire' (lines
11–12).

(*e*) Explain how the Congress of Berlin 'radically changed the (3)
disposition of the vast region to which . . . the name of
Bulgaria is given' (lines 40–41).

(*f*) Why did the 'entire equality of all religions before the law' (3)
(line 12) continue to be an important question in the
Balkans after 1878?

(*g*) Show how the events of the decade after 1878 belied the (4)
assertion in this extract that 'the new Bulgaria' would be
'under the auspices and control of Russia' (lines 27–28).

(*h*) Explain the international importance of the growth of   (8)
Balkan national feeling in the period 1890–1913.

D   *Areas of debate*
A number of issues have been debated by historians of the Eastern
Question. To help you to examine these, prepare outline arguments to
either support *or* refute each of the statements below. You should refer not
only to this chapter, but also to section IV:1. In addition, you should
consult the sources referred to in the bibliography on page 349 and
wherever possible identify the attitude that the authors take to each
question.
(i)   Without the aid of foreign governments and their armies, the
Ottoman Empire in Europe would have collapsed well before 1875.
(ii)   Throughout the nineteenth century, the 'Eastern Question' remained
essentially the same—who would win the Balkans: Russia or
Austria-Hungary?
(iii) The development of nationalist movements in the Balkans opened up
a third alternative to the Eastern Question.
(iv)   Britain's involvement in the Eastern Question was the result of her
desire to be seen as a world power, and was not essential to the
defence of her economic or strategic interests.
(v)   The treaty of Berlin posed more problems than it solved.

E   *The Great Powers and the Balkans in the 1870s and 1880s*
The aim of this section is to enable you to consider the aims and role of the
four Great Powers in the Eastern Question in this period by, firstly,
constructing and completing a chart like that below and then summarizing
the position of each of those powers.

	Aims in the Balkans, c. 1870	*Attitude to Treaty of San Stefano, 1878*	*Attitude to Treaty of Berlin, 1878*	*Remaining hopes and concerns*
Russia				
Great Britain				
Germany				
Austria-Hungary				

2 The Expansion of Europe

(a) The Unimportance of Colonies
Though the nineteenth century was to be marked by an unprecedented
outburst of European expansion overseas, it was late in coming. During
the first half of the century all the European states engaged in comparatively little colonial activity and empire-building; and there were
several reasons for this attitude.
Large overseas empires settled by peoples from a European mother-
land were no longer in favour. By 1815 the two greatest of such

empires, which had been established by Britain and Spain, had been shattered by revolts of colonists who wanted their independence. This development long affected European opinion. The value of such colonies of settlement was generally doubted. It was believed that the effort and expense of establishing them was almost certain to be wasted as sooner or later they would want to break away and devote themselves to their own interests.

The British outlook in 1815 was shown by the attitude taken by Castlereagh at the Congress of Vienna towards this question (*see page 14*). Interest in Britain was by then more concerned with commerce rather than with establishing new colonies. It was generally assumed that it was better for the country to have areas of economic influence and exploitation, such as South America (*see page 32*), than to go to the expense and trouble of annexing colonies. 'Why should we marry the lady,' said a Foreign Office official, 'when we can have her without marriage?' The few overseas gains which Britain secured at the Congress of Vienna were designed primarily to promote the defence of the leading maritime routes serving these areas. British policy, as Palmerston remarked later, was 'to secure the roads to trade'.

Moreover, Britain could continue to adopt this attitude for nearly half a century after 1815. Because of her naval and industrial supremacy, the rest of the world had to buy her goods and send her raw materials in exchange. The establishment of the United States of America, for instance, only very slowly altered the pattern of her trade with the new republic as it had existed in colonial times. Britain, therefore, did not have to seek colonial markets with the urgency she had done during the eighteenth century, and she further emphasized her dominant commercial position in the world by adopting free trade between the 1840s and 1860s.

It might appear that the exception to this was the steady British conquest of India. It is true that it later came to be believed that political control of the sub-continent assisted British trade, especially the export of machinery and cotton goods in return for jute and tea; but the contemporary reason for the expansion of India was that the frontiers of 1818 proved insecure and had to be widened to the limits of the peninsula and into Burma and Malaya. Moreover, despite this, every Governor-General who promoted the conquest of India had to do so in the face of considerable official resistance; and once this security had been largely achieved, no further addition to British territory took place in this area during the second half of the nineteenth century, except the conquest of Upper Burma in 1886.

Elsewhere in the world, British expansion came about either from the needs of possessions already held in 1815 or from the initiative of private individuals and companies. For instance, Cape Colony grew because the settlers needed more land; and New Zealand was annexed as a result of the activities of the New Zealand Company, which established the settlement of Wellington.

Among the Continental states, France had possessed a large overseas empire in the seventeenth and eighteenth centuries; but the twofold strain of maintaining her position as both a great colonial and a dominant European power had been too much for her resources, and she lost much of her empire during the series of wars against Britain which culminated in the Napoleonic War. The result was a similar revulsion against empire-building on the part of French opinion. Moreover, the discovery of sugar-beet (promoted by Napoleon as a measure against the British blockade) and the abolition of slavery greatly reduced the value of the French West Indian islands retained by France after 1815. Consequently the establishment of a new French Empire was undertaken only slowly and with hesitation in Algeria, Indo-China and Senegal between the 1830s and 1860s (*see page 364*).

Among the other European states, Holland alone had considerable colonies, but though the Dutch East Indies during this period contributed a considerable surplus to the treasury of Holland, these colonies expanded territorially hardly at all. In fact, the Continental powers were not interested in colonial activity and were at the same time hardly in a position to engage in it. A great deal of their energy had to be concentrated upon establishing their own industrial systems and transport facilities. In addition, these European states were preoccupied with the rise of new powers and the consequences for themselves. Questions of expansion and unification within Europe dominated their attention and policies.

(b) The New Imperialism

Not until the second half of the nineteenth century did the leading European states display a new imperialism, which led them to seek further territory, and it hardly got under way until the early 1870s. Thereafter, however, its progress was rapid, and by the 1880s colonial rivalries between them had become acute. The three main imperialist powers of this period were Britain, France and Russia, and the reasons for their urge to expand in this way were diverse and complex.

It was long assumed by historians that the most important or even the only motive of this imperialist movement was economic. It was believed that colonies were desired by the industrial countries of Europe so that they could find new opportunities of investing the surplus capital gained by the profits of their manufacturing undertakings, obtain fresh markets for their products and secure additional sources of food and raw materials to feed their growing populations and supply the needs of their factories. In fact, however, there is little evidence to support this idea. Britain did invest large amounts of capital abroad in the later nineteenth century, but most of it went, not to the recently-acquired African colonies, but rather to the United States of America, Canada, Argentina, South Africa and Australasia, and these countries also provided her with her imports of food and raw materials as well as markets for her exports. Similarly, French investment went mainly to the Near

East, Russia and South America, and her trade with her colonies was never important for her economy. And, finally, Russia had no surplus capital to invest, and her imperialism took the form of expansion into the contiguous land-mass of Asia, much of which was relatively empty and incapable of providing economic advantages to the new rulers.

In fact, it seems likely that the rise of imperialism came about through national sentiment rather than economic interest. Europeans came to believe that possession of a colonial empire was an essential mark of a great power. A strong country should have colonies, and colonies made a country strong. British patriotism desired for the 'land of hope and glory' that 'wider still and wider shall thy bounds be set' and that 'God, who made thee mightier, make the mightier yet.' And for Continental nations, this feeling was intensified by national resentment and frustration which followed the change in the European balance of power after 1870. States, which could no longer hope to expand in Europe, might yet gain large territories elsewhere. France sought to compensate for her loss of position and prestige through defeat in war by colonial activity in Africa and Asia; and the check to Russian arms in the Near East at the Congress of Berlin contributed to her desire to extend her power in Central Asia and the Far East.

Imperialism itself also led to strained relations and rivalry between states when one took possession of territory which another desired. In this way the British occupation of Egypt in 1882 led to a period of bad Anglo-French relations, when the French dream of control over equatorial Africa clashed with the British wish to secure their communications from Cairo to the Cape. The 'scramble for Africa' particularly had in it a good deal of national competition and considerations of prestige and advantage.

Some of the ideals and psychological needs of the time also supported the new imperialism. The activities of explorers and adventurers, anti-slavery societies and Christian missions, all these gave a powerful impulse to the colonial movements. Among the great missionaries and explorers were David Livingstone, sent out by the London Missionary Society, who from 1849 onwards made three long journeys through the unknown interior of Africa, and Cardinal Charles Lavigerie, who led his group of French White Fathers into East Africa. Such men were followed by evangelists, teachers and doctors, and their reports often urged their governments to annex the territories in which they were working and assist them to combat the slave trade, tribal warfare and other evils. Their entreaties met with a response from those who did not share their zeal to establish Christianity overseas, but accepted the common belief that it was the duty of European peoples to 'take up the White Man's burden' or undertake *la mission civilisatrice* and bring to the backward areas the benefits of contemporary civilization by just and efficient rule.

Finally, the actual taking up of territory during this period of imperialism was carried out by a relatively small number of men who were

355

in a position to act decisively on their own. Communications were not good enough to enable governments to keep a close control over them, and they were able to take the initiative whenever ambition and enthusiasm inspired them. For instance, Frederick Lugard, acting on behalf of the British East Africa Company in 1890, secured control of Uganda, which was annexed by Britain four years later; Joseph Galleni, the French soldier, did much to mould the forward policy which led France to occupy Indo-China by 1885; and Count Muravyie, the Governor-General of Eastern Siberia, encouraged further Russian expansion during the 1850s, which resulted in the occupation of the island of Sakhalin and the Kurile Archipelago.

In the later nineteenth century, the three main European powers of the new imperialism were joined by two others, Germany and Italy, both of which were late in acquiring colonies. For a long time Bismarck insisted that Germany should concentrate on safeguarding her security and developing her resources rather than venturing on overseas schemes. 'I am no man for colonies, which install officials and erect garrisons,' he said. He considered that the paramount need of the new German Empire was to consolidate its position on the Continent. 'My map of Africa lies in Europe,' he said. 'Here lies Russia and here lies France, and we are in the middle. That is my map of Africa.' In the 1880s German national feeling increasingly began to demand overseas possessions, and here also it was not for economic reasons. Again motives of national prestige predominated. The demand was that Germany should gain her rightful 'place in the sun' together with the other colonial powers.

In 1884 Bismarck gave way to this popular demand for colonies. He did this partly to strengthen his standing in the country and weaken the Progressives, who were opposed to colonies, but he was influenced more by European considerations. He thought the move was likely to provoke a quarrel with Britain, which suited his foreign policy (*see page 361*). He hoped that it might lead to an understanding with France based upon opposition to Britain, whose occupation of Egypt had aroused such bitter French resentment. He hoped also that it would discredit the Crown Prince Frederick, and heir to the throne, who was married to Queen Victoria's daughter and was liberal and pro-British in his outlook. Years later Bismarck's son made this motive clear. 'When we entered upon a colonial policy,' he said, 'we had to reckon with a long reign of the Crown Prince. During this reign, English influence would have been dominant. To prevent this, we had to embark upon a colonial policy because it was popular and conveniently adapted to bring us into conflict with England at any given moment.'

The German overseas empire acquired by Bismarck consisted almost entirely of great colonial areas in Africa, but the Germans, once they had obtained them, never developed nor invested in them to the same extent as Britain. By 1914 the colonies contained in all no more than 5000 permanent German inhabitants and received from the Imperial government subsidies which totalled six times as much as the profits made from them. The German people consequently became disillusioned and believed that they had entered the race for colonies too late and lost their chance of valuable possessions. This added to the growing frustration and dismay they felt because their country seemed unable to gain the position of security and strength in Europe which they desired.

Italy was also among the states driven by European considerations of power and prestige to undertake colonial ventures. After unification she still had territorial ambitions towards Trentino in the southern Tyrol and along the Dalmatian coast, and failure to realize these fostered a national wish to gain territory in Africa. The occupation of Algeria by France in 1830 had already caused Italian resentment, which was increased when she occupied Tunisia in 1881. The Italian government retaliated by taking possession of Assab Bay, on the west coast of the Red Sea, the next year and three years later occupied the port of Marsowah on the same coast. Italian forces advanced into the highlands of the interior, and in 1889 the Italian settlements were consolidated into the province of Eritrea, and a protectorate was proclaimed over part of the Somali coast. The Italian dream of a colonial empire in East Africa was to be destroyed, however, when an Italian army was routed by the Abyssinians at Adowa in 1896. Italy had neither the resources nor the tradition to succeed as a colonial power (*see Map 19*).

(c) The Mediterranean and the Middle East

Among the earliest European colonial acquisitions in the post-Napoleonic period was the French occupation of Algeria. The North African coast was still nominally part of the Turkish Empire, but had become virtually a collection of independent states under local rulers, whose piratical activities were a source of trouble to the maritime nations using the Mediterranean. Their raids on French shipping eventually led to the sending of a fleet in 1830 (less than three weeks before the fall of Charles X) to bombard the port of Algiers into submission. This was followed by the landing of an expeditionary force which attempted to establish control of the interior. Though Algeria was formally annexed in 1842, the conquest of the country was only slowly undertaken under Louis Philippe and was directed by officials rather than ministers and without popular enthusiasm. The first scheme to dispossess the tribesmen of their land did not come about until 1871 when the first settlers from Alsace were introduced. This produced a serious uprising, which was suppressed and followed by further confiscations of land which was given to fresh settlers. It was, however, to take 53 years for the whole of Algeria to be subdued and French rule to be effectively established.

French involvement in Algeria inevitably brought them into contact with neighbouring Tunisia, which was ruled in virtual autonomy by its Bey under the nominal suzerainty of the Sultan. French economic penetration of the country proceeded during the Second Empire. Most of the railways, telegraphs and other public works were French-owned, and over five-sixths of the public debt was held in France. The Bey's administration was incompetent, and on several occasions international intervention was necessary to save him from bankruptcy.

In 1878 both Salisbury and Bismarck encouraged France at the Congress of Berlin to occupy Tunisia. Salisbury wanted to gain her support for British policy in the Near East; Bismarck's purpose was not, as its commonly supposed, to estrange Italy from France, but rather to divert French ambitions away from Europe. France, however, did not want to add to her troubles with the Algerian tribesmen by becoming entangled in Tunisia. In 1881, nevertheless, she had to act because of disturbances there. The French settlers in Algeria, fearing that the large Italian community already established in Tunisia would call for action by their government, urged the French government to forestall this.

The French Prime Minister was Jules Ferry (*see page 293*). The army and the foreign office persuaded him that it would be undesirable to have a European power established next to Algeria. Using a raid into Algeria by Tunisian tribes as the pretext, he sent an expeditionary force against the Bey of Tunis and established a French protectorate over his state. This was achieved with little fighting, but French opinion was deeply divided over it. Gambetta wrote approvingly to Ferry that it meant that France was now resuming her rank as a great power, but Clemenceau accused him of 'disloyalty' for engaging the country in an unnecessary war.

French hesitation about embarking upon a policy of colonial expansion was shown soon afterwards by an incident at the eastern end of the Mediterranean, which involved her in a clash with Britain. Disraeli's purchase of the extravagant Khedive of Egypt's shares in the Suez Canal Company in 1875 had not solved his financial difficulties. The next year he suspended payment of his debts, and in 1878 France and Britain, the states to which he was principally endebted, established a joint control over Egyptian finances in order to safeguard their interests. Gladstone accused Disraeli of 'ruinous aggression' in this matter; but when he himself became Prime Minister in 1880 he found that the policy could not be reversed. There was a nationalist rising in 1881. A Franco-British fleet steamed into Alexandria the next year, but the Chamber of Deputies did not want France to run the risk of being involved in a war in Egypt, and the French warships were recalled, leaving the British to bombard the forts and occupy the country. Gladstone hoped the British occupation would be temporary; but concern for the safety of the Canal was to lengthen it to 75 years, and revolt in the Sudan compelled Britain in 1898 to occupy that country as well.

French opinion regarded the British occupation of Egypt in 1881 as a national humiliation, though she had excluded herself from it. French association with the country had begun with Napoleon's unsuccessful campaign there, and a French company owned the Canal. Resentment gave strength to French imperialism and especially to the idea of an aggressive policy in Africa. Pressure was placed upon the government in the Chamber of Deputies by a group led by the Algerian-born deputy, Eugénie Etienne, and in the country by the *Comité d'Afrique Française*. It was not until after 1890, however, that France made important gains south of the Sahara and began the establishment of her empire in equatorial Africa (*see Map 18, page 360*).

(d) The Partition of Africa

To Europeans in the nineteenth century, Africa was known as the Dark Continent, and before the last quarter of the century they had barely penetrated beyond its coastal fringes. The British had the colonies of the Cape and Natal in the south, a number of small commercial settlements from the Gambia to the Niger Delta on the west coast and a controlling treaty with the Sultan of Zanzibar in the east. The French were established in Algeria and Tunisia in the north, in scattered trading posts from Senegal to Gabon in the west and in Madagascar and the Comoro Islands in the east. Portugal had claims, going back to the sixteenth and seventeenth centuries, to Angola and Mozambique, but her rule over both these colonies had largely collapsed during the eighteenth century. And even in these few areas of European penetration, their presence was mainly confined to coastal forts and commercial posts, often engaged in the slave trade. Beyond missionaries and explorers and the Boers in the south, none had moved into the interior of the continent.

But, while in 1875 only a tenth of the area of Africa was governed by Europeans, by 1900 much less than a tenth was ruled by Africans, only Liberia, Morocco, Libya and Abyssinia still retaining their independence. Africa was the last continent to attract European expansion, but when this began, supremacy in technology and organization ensured that it was accomplished rapidly. The power and aggressiveness of the new imperialism were apparent, but the reasons behind it were not so clear. 'I do not exactly know the cause of this sudden revolution, but there it is,' observed Lord Salisbury in 1891 when, as Foreign Secretary and Prime Minister, he had already assisted the extension of British influence over half the continent in a period of six years. Indeed, the movement was inspired by a variety of motives, but probably the most important was a desire on the part of the European countries to preserve, consolidate and develop the African possessions, which they already had, in the face of apparent threats to them.

The first impulse towards the 'scramble for Africa' came from the ruler of a country which possessed neither colonial ambitions nor achievements. King Leopold II of Belgium was a man of dynastic ambition, energy and enthusiasm for which his small European state did not provide him with an outlet. He wished to find satisfaction in overseas schemes, but when he came to the Belgian throne in 1865 he found that his ministers were as opposed to colonial adventures as other

359

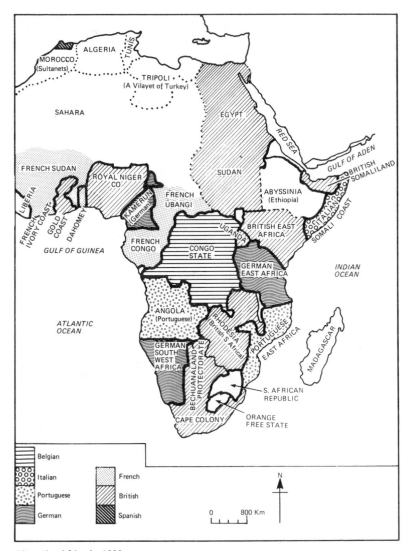

Map 18 Africa in 1890

European statesmen. He believed, therefore, that he must establish and develop a personal empire, and he saw the unclaimed centre of tropical Africa as the place for this. By supporting Sir Henry Stanley in his explorations he was able between 1879 and 1884 to stake his claim to the greater part of the Congo Basin and in 1885 established the Independent State of the Congo with himself as its ruler.

This quickly set off a series of claims and counter-claims from the other powers, who saw themselves menaced by the existence of such a large state in the middle of the continent. The French explorer, Pierre de Brazza, had journeyed along the north bank of the Congo in 1880, and in 1882 the Chamber annexed that area. The Portuguese renewed their interest in their neglected colony of Angola, and in 1884 the British recognized their claim to control the mouth of the Congo with the intention of thwarting both France and Leopold II.

This was the situation which led Bismarck to intervene in the contest for colonies. Within eighteen months, from the end of 1884 to the beginning of 1886, he laid claim to Togoland and the Cameroons in West Africa, German South-West Africa adjacent to Cape Colony and German East Africa in the mainland territory of the Sultan of Zanzibar.

This action did not bring about the hoped-for quarrel with Britain, which was occupied with the situation in Egypt and did not wish to acquire more African territory. France, however, was stirred into action. For years she had thought little of her west coast trading posts because of the 'trivial scale of French interest there,' as a minister wrote in 1874. She abandoned the Ivory Coast and in 1880 considered leaving Dahomey and Gabon. But the effect of Leopold II's claim was to arouse imperialistic ideas and a realization of the advantages of linking these possessions with the upper basin of the Congo. French officials began to make treaties with the native chiefs on the Lower Niger.

These treaties threatened British trade on the coast, and British merchants complained of the lack of support they had from their government. In response the government began to make its treaties in the area of the Niger, and this rivalry with the French added to the ill feeling already aroused by the situation in Egypt.

At this time also, there was another development which led to growing European intervention in Africa. This was the spread of instability in the continent itself. Hitherto the powers had been able to engage in trade in Africa without annexing large areas of territory, but this had depended upon the persistence of a stable native society in these regions. Now, however, this trade was beginning to bring about the break up of African society. Africans were acquiring fresh forms of wealth, and important new classes were coming into being. This, in its turn, caused social unrest and local crises, which hindered trade and made it more necessary for the powers to establish political control there. This development began on the West African coast during the early 1880s.

Bismarck decided to take advantage of this uncertain situation by summoning the Conference of Berlin to define the limits of European expansion in Africa. It met from November 1884 to February 1885 and was attended by the representatives of 15 governments. He intended it to be an anti-British move, but Britain and France were able to settle their differences in Central Africa. The Conference recognized the Congo State and provided it with access to the sea by an exchange of territory with Portugal; and the French agreed to retain only the region around Brazzaville on the north bank. In addition, control of the Lower Niger was accorded to Britain and of the Upper Niger to France. Bismarck was able to insist that the Conference should accept the idea of a formal diplomatic division of the disputed areas of Africa between the powers. He represented it as the best way of avoiding international friction, but since the Conference laid it down that in future territorial claims upon African areas should depend upon 'effective occupation', the reliance upon 'spheres of influence', which Britain had preferred to make rather than engage in annexation, was no longer likely to be successful. The actual result, therefore, would probably be increased rivalry with France.

Though 'effective occupation' was, in fact, a vague and almost meaningless phrase, it did have the effect of spurring both Britain and France to renewed colonial activity in Africa. The French moved southwards from their Mediterranean possessions and eastwards from Senegal, on the west coast of Africa, where they had established a slaving-post during the seventeenth century, until by 1890 they dominated the vast hinterland of West Africa from the Equator to the Mediterranean. On the other side of Africa, they gained a foothold in Somaliland, lying at the southern end of the Red Sea and separated from their main African empire by the Sudan and Abyssinia. French colonial ambition now envisaged a great domain linking up with the new territories in North Africa and stretching from the Atlantic across the Sudan to the Indian Ocean.

This, however, was to bring France into direct conflict with Britain. The British had hardly installed themselves in Egypt in 1881 when they were threatened by a further example of African instability. This occurred further south in the Sudan. Since 1810 Egypt had station-garrisons in the Sudan, but in 1881 the Mahdi, a fanatical Muslim leader, stirred the Sudanese into revolt against the Egyptians. The British government in 1884 sent General Gordon to evacuate the threatened Egyptian garrisons, but he was murdered, and the whole country fell into the power of the Mahdi. Not until 1896 did the British set out to subdue the Sudan, but when they did it was fatal to French ambitions in the region. A British force compelled a French force to withdraw when they met at Fashoda on the White Nile in 1898 (*see page 355*).

On the west coast, the French advanced into Guinea, the Ivory Coast and eventually Dahomey. The British consolidated their hold on Gambia, Sierra Leone and the Gold Coast, which had also been seventeenth-century slaving posts. Now as colonies they provided a further cause of tension with France by cutting off her empire from the Atlantic coast, and in 1886 the British government extended its rule over Nigeria in order to protect this area, in which the Royal Niger Company worked, against French and German encroachment. From the Indian Ocean, Britain also moved westwards, securing part of

Somaliland in 1884 and British East Africa (Kenya) the next year. In 1890 Lugard arrived in Uganda with one maxim gun and supported the Protestants or *wa-ingleza* (the English party) against the *wa-franza* (the French party), who were Roman Catholics converted by Lavigerie's White Fathers. The Imperial British East Africa Company then opened up the country, which was annexed by Britain in 1894.

In southern Africa, the British had possessed the Cape settlement since 1815 (*see page 14*); but she regarded this (as she did also Egypt and Zanzibar) as an outpost for the protection of the route to India. For the greater part of the nineteenth century, British governments were content to retain control of Cape Colony and Natal and allow the Boers to form their two inland republics of the Transvaal and the Orange Free State. However, from the 1870s increasing trade and railway-building and, still more, the discovery of gold and diamonds in the area changed the situation, and the German annexation of South-West Africa compelled Britain to declare that she had a sphere of influence as far north as the Zambezi. Bechuanaland was annexed in 1885, Rhodesia in 1889 and Nyasaland in 1893. This thrust northwards was in accordance with the imperial ambitions of Lord Milner and Cecil Rhodes, who dreamt of a British dominion stretching from the Cape to Cairo, but it was to bring Britain into conflict with the Boers before the end of the century.

(e) Expansion in the Far East

The second important region of European expansion in the nineteenth century was India and the Far East. Britain had established herself so thoroughly in India that its development rested with her alone, but the Far East brought further rivalry between the European powers. The countries bordering the Pacific were more attractive and wealthy than the African territories, and though they were densely populated and highly civilized, they were not able during this period to resist effectively the technological resources employed by the European nations.

The largest area in Asia was China, an empire which for centuries had been virtually closed to Europeans, but in the nineteenth century this determination to exclude foreign trade and penetration could not be maintained. British merchants (mainly through the East India Company) took the lead in opening up commerce with this vast country, which resulted in the so-called Opium War (1839–42). During this, Britain occupied Hong Kong, which she kept under the Treaty of Nanking, and also secured the opening of the five 'Treaty Ports' of Canton, Amoy, Foochow, Nangpo and Shanghai to foreign trade by all Europeans. This settlement, together with a commercial treaty concluded the next year, enabled Britain to gain a predominant trading position in China (*see Map 19, page 364*).

By the time of the Second Empire, France became a rival in securing Chinese markets. French missionaries and traders were prominent in Siam and Indo-China (Vietnam), and both asked their government to

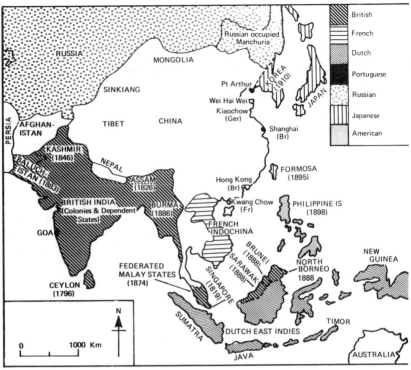

Map 19 The Far East

support their cause. Under Napoleon III a foothold was established in the Mekong Delta, and after the Franco-Prussian War, Ferry was persuaded to take the initiative again here as in Tunisia. The object now was to secure a waterway into China by way of the Red River, running into the Gulf of Tonkin, and so provide an alternative to the trade-routes to the treaty ports. This resulted, however, in a long and costly war with China, which became increasingly unpopular with French opinion which was indifferent to colonial adventures and had bitter memories of Napoleon III's Mexican affair. In 1885, when the French were defeated at Tonkin, Ferry's opponents, led by Clemenceau, shouted him down with cries of 'Tonkin-Ferry' and compelled him to resign from office. The campaign, however, was successfully concluded, and Indo-China was declared a French colony in 1887. Imperialism in Asia was thus more concerned with economic factors than in Africa. The seizure of territory was limited and mainly aimed at securing access to markets.

(f) The Results of Imperialism
During this period there was little popular enthusiasm in the European countries for the colonies they seized. Jules Ferry said that the only

thing that interested most Frenchmen in their new empire was the belly-dance. It is true that Disraeli, during the election campaign of 1874, attacked Gladstone for neglecting the colonies and adopted an imperialistic attitude, saying, 'No minister in this country will do his duty who neglects any opportunity of reconstructing as much as possible our colonial empire.' He took such a stand because he wanted to appeal to working-class voters, whom he reckoned were interested in the British Empire because from them came the majority of the many families who emigrated overseas throughout the century. By 1865 more than seven million people had left the British Isles, and after that date the number was never less than 100 000 a year; but at first half of the emigrants went to the United States of America, and though an increasing number later went to the British Empire, it was to such colonies of settlement as Canada, South Africa, Australia and New Zealand and not to the colonies obtained as the result of the rise of the new imperialism.

National sentiment and prestige continued to play a major part in the European annexation of colonies. Europeans came to feel that, if others possessed colonies, then their country must have them too. Lord Salisbury on one occasion spoke slightingly of the popular British demand for 'some territorial or cartographic consolation', saying, 'It will not be useful, and it will be expensive; but as a matter of pure sentiment, we shall have to do it.' And imperialist questions did exacerbate European relations out of proportion to the value of the colonies to the countries concerned. Perhaps the most striking example of this was the way in which resentment at the British occupation of Egypt obsessed French foreign policy during the later part of this period and gave Bismarck the opportunity to use it to achieve the end of his own policy.

Bibliography

M. Wolfe, *The Economic Causes of Imperialism* (John Wiley, 1972), K. Moore, *Kipling and the White Man's Burden* (Faber, 1968), E. Halladay, *The Emergent Continent: Africa in the Nineteenth Century* (Benn, 1972), M.E. Chamberlain, *The Scramble for Africa* (Longman, 1974), P. Gifford and W.R. Louis (ed.), *Britain and Germany in Africa* (New Haven, 1967) and *France and Britain in Africa* (New Haven, 1971).

Exercises

A *This section consists of questions that might be used for discussion (or written answers) as a way of expanding on the chapter and testing your understanding of it:*

1 Explain Britain's attitude to colonial expansion in the first half of the nineteenth century.

2 Why was there, generally, so little interest in colonial expansion before the last part of the century?

3 What do you understand by the term 'new imperialism'?

4 Why were the European powers so keen to gain colonies after 1870?
5 Why did Germany and Italy join the colonial race a) at all and b) so comparatively late?
6 Why did France extend her Empire and influence in North Africa?
7 What effects did Britain's domination of Egypt have on French policies?
8 Comment on Lord Salisbury's view 'I do not exactly know the cause of this sudden revolution. . . .'
9 Why was Leopold II's claim to the Congo such a decisive step in the Scramble for Africa?
10 How significant was the Conference of Berlin of 1884–5?
11 To outline the process of colonization in Africa, and to show the relationship between different events, draw out and complete a chart like the one below. Having completed it, explain what conclusions you can draw from it.

	Britain	France	Germany	Belgium	Portugal	Italy
Possessed in 1880						
Gained by: 1881						
1882						
1883						
1884						
1885						
1898						
1899						
1900						

12 Why did the European powers seek colonies in Africa and the Far East rather than elsewhere?
13 What were the major effects of the colonization a) on the areas colonized and b) on the European powers and their relations with each other?

B *Essay questions*
1 'The motives for the partition of Africa were diplomatic rather than economic.' Do you agree with this statement? (Cambridge, 1981)
2 'In 1870 the European powers showed little enthusiasm for the acquisition of overseas territory.' Why, then, was Africa partitioned before the end of the century? (Cambridge, 1982)
3 'They partitioned Africa to secure peace in Europe.' Is this a valid comment on the aims of late nineteenth-century European diplomats? (Oxford, 1982)
4 What were the causes, and the consequences for international relations, of the 'Scramble for Africa'? (SUJB, 1981)
5 Would you agree with the statement that 'the imperial expansion of the European powers, 1870–1914, was the result of rivalries within Europe'? (Welsh, 1981)
6 Explain and illustrate the increasing interest of European powers during the late nineteenth century in either (a) Africa or (b) the Far East. (Welsh, 1982)

7　What do you consider to be the most convincing explanation for the policies of imperial expansion pursued by many continental countries down to 1914? (Welsh, 1983)

8　In what ways did the 'scramble for Africa' affect the relations between the European powers during the period 1870–1914? (Welsh, 1983)

9　Should European imperial expansion be explained in economic terms? (You may, if you wish, confine your answers to one country excluding Great Britain.) (Oxford and Cambridge, 1982)

10　What prompted continental powers to engage in 'the Scramble for Africa'? (Oxford and Cambridge, 1983)

11　Did colonial rivalries in the late nineteenth century increase or diminish tension in Europe? (AEB, 1982)

12　How far is it possible to explain in economic terms the imperialist ambitions of the European powers between 1880 and 1914? (AEB, 1983)

13　'The building of overseas empires in the late nineteenth century owed more to the desire of Europeans for national prestige than to any other reasons.' Examine the validity of this opinion. (London, 1981)

14　Why did the French acquire such a vast overseas empire during the century before 1914? Is it true that the acquisition of this empire involved remarkably little conflict with other European powers? (London, 1982)

15　Which countries on the continent of Europe possessed large overseas empires at the beginning of the twentieth century, and in what ways were these empires of any real benefit to Europeans? (London, 1983)

16　What part did economic considerations play in the European scramble for Africa? (JMB, 1981)

17　'Diplomatic and political, rather than economic, considerations explain European interest in Africa between 1870 and 1914.' Discuss this statement. (JMB, 1984)

C　*The causes of the new imperialism*

1　Examine again the section on pages 354–357 above. Then list briefly what you consider to have been the major factors leading to the new imperialism of the late nineteenth century. You may find it helpful to:
   (a) distinguish between the reasons for the initial interest in colonies in the 1870s as opposed to the factors influencing the major period of expansion in the 1880s and 1890s. You could make this distinction by drawing up two separate lists.
   (b) refer back to page 90 and utilize the ideas suggested there, i.e. consider geographical, religious, individual, political, economic and chance factors. (You may also like to reconsider the validity of this approach to the study of causation.)

2　Now undertake several aspects of comparative work:
   (a) Compare the reasons that the different European countries had for undertaking imperial adventures, and comment on the similarities and differences between countries.
   (b) Compare the reasons the Europeans had for expanding in Africa with their reasons for going into parts of the Far East. Again, draw your own conclusions.
   (c) Examine any other period of European expansion and compare the factors involved. If you are not familiar with another period, Unit 5 of the Schools Council History Project *What is History?* course (*Asking*

Questions) has a self-contained section on the expansion of Europe in the late fifteenth century. A comparison between this and the 'new imperialism' will give you a different perspective.

3 Utilizing the answers you have already written, produce a list of factors in what you consider to be their order of importance, and explain why you have put them in that order.

4 Having come to your own conclusions, read what others have written on this subject. Most books in the bibliography on page 2 have sections on this, but you might like in particular to note the views in the following: A. Wood—*Europe 1815–1945* pages 273–279, D. Thomson—*Europe since Napoleon* pages 491–498, J.M. Roberts—*Europe 1880–1945* pages 102–103, K. Perry—*Modern European History* pages 91–96. In reading these other works, you should become familiar with the major aspects of the debate on this subject, i.e. the extent to which the Marxist interpretation that stresses economic factors is still acceptable.

D *Essay Writing Skills 9: Introductions and Conclusions*
How best to begin and end their work is often an aspect of essay writing that students find most worrying. Different teachers frequently offer conflicting advice, and are all too ready to criticize poor introductions and conclusions. In this section, you will find a further set of guidelines to consider and discuss. Throughout it, for purposes of examples, questions 1 and 2 from section B above have been used.

(a) Introductions
Firstly, never use introductory paragraphs as 'warm-ups' to 'get into the subject'. Many students feel an extraordinary urge to get something (anything?) on paper and feel they have made a start. As a result, they put down almost random thoughts, such as this, in answer to 2.:
'In 1884–5 the Berlin Conference was held at Bismarck's bidding to avoid future conflict in Africa. Economic factors, as explained by Hobson and Lenin, were important in bringing about the partition of Africa. But they must not be exaggerated. The Fashoda crisis of 1898 perhaps illustrates best the motives of the great powers in Africa.'
Clearly, the writer of this knows something about the subject, but this introduction tells the reader little more than that, and is of very limited value.
Equally, introductions are not the place for a narrative of events. Students often seem to think that they are required to show their knowledge of *what* happened before explaining *why* it happened. They therefore launch into detailed accounts of the stages of colonization, full of names, dates and places, and often spilling on to two pages. If examiners wanted narratives of events, they would ask for them; to provide them unsolicited is to waste time and effort.
Avoid answering the question asked in your introduction. If, as in 1., you are asked to consider different points of view, do not give your own opinion immediately; the examiner is looking for a measured consideration of all the arguments, *followed by* a logical conclusion. He does not wish to be told 'I agree entirely that the motives for the partition of Africa were diplomatic, and in this essay I intend to prove it.'

Resist the temptation to use the introduction to outline your argument. Although this type of introduction is harmless, it does mean that your essay is bound to be repetitive, and if you have set your argument out clearly in the opening sentence of each paragraph, an introduction of this kind is unnecessary.

Given these points, it is fairly obvious that introductions are of limited value. As long as your essay is clearly structured and argued, and you make your points cogently, there is little need for one. If anything, an introduction can be a waste of valuable and vital time. Given the 40–50 minutes available to write an exam answer, few students will write more than four sides, or 7–8 paragraphs. If an introduction outlines what you are *going* to say, and a conclusion explains what you have just *said*, there cannot be a lot of jam in the middle of the sandwich.

However, introductions can be helpful in showing your understanding of the question. For example, if a question is based on an extensive quote, an introduction can be used to explain how you plan to break the question down. Similarly, if it points to an obvious area of debate—as in 1. or 12. here—an introduction can be used to show your awareness of this, with, perhaps, a mention of the major protaganists concerned. Finally, if you feel the wording of a question is deliberately open to various meanings, the introduction can be used to elucidate your interpretation of it.

In all other circumstances, beware the pitfalls of the introduction! Rather, have confidence in your ability to put your argument across clearly and forcefully in the essay itself.

(b) Conclusions

Paradoxically, conclusions are more often omitted than introductions, probably for reasons of time. In fact, they can be much more valuable.

Firstly, conclusions can be used to answer the question in the title. In discussion questions, the examiner is looking for your point of view, which is likely to be a guarded yes or no. The conclusion is the best place for this. Similarly, your opinion is sought in significance questions, while in list questions, you have the opportunity to express your viewpoint on the relative importance of different factors.

Equally, conclusions can be used to give your work a touch of class. For instance, if you have an original explanation or interpretation that is uncommon, it may be explained. You may use the conclusion to make comparisons with other events or other periods, or to show your knowledge of the most recent developments in an historical debate. While avoiding introducing an entirely *new* line of argument, the conclusion can be an appropriate place to make your essay different to the majority of others.

On the other hand, avoid using your conclusion as merely a repetition of all your previous arguments. To do so is to admit your failure to make them clear in the first place. Even worse, avoid using the conclusion to try to outline the arguments you have just failed to put forward: the giveaway opening for such conclusions is 'Thus it can be seen that . . .' This almost always suggests that 'it' cannot be 'seen' at all. . . .

Finally, in conclusion, it may be seen that there is little to be gained from opening your final paragraph with phrases such as these. Everybody else does.

With these ideas in mind, and having discussed them, write appropriate introductions (if you consider them necessary) and conclusions to numbers 1 and 2 from Section B. Having done so, exchange your efforts with others and discuss the results.

3 The Bismarckian Alliances

(a) The League of the Three Emperors (1873)

It can now be seen that the Franco-Prussian War was a turning-point in the history of nineteenth-century Europe. It completed the unification of Germany under Prussian leadership. It also, as a British diplomat observed, resulted 'in the rooting up, once and for all, of the pretension of France to a privileged and exceptional position in Europe.' It marked the end of two centuries of French predominance on the continent of Europe, and henceforward, as her relative economic strength and population declined, the balance of power went steadily against France in comparison with Germany. This, however, was not recognized by all contemporaries for some time. The strength of the German standing army during the 1870s and 1880s was hardly and sometimes not at all greater than that of France; and it was commonly believed that French desire for revenge constituted the chief threat to European peace and might bring about an early war.

The Franco-Prussian War changed Bismarck himself from a poacher to a gamekeeper. In less than a decade he had waged three wars for the aggrandisement of Prussia, but now he considered that the creation of the German Empire had brought his ambitions in Europe to an end. And, despite the changes he had brought about in the map of Europe, this suited his fundamentally conservative temperament. He now wanted no further change. He was, indeed, on the defensive. He feared that he had perhaps succeeded too quickly and too completely and thought that there might be a general reaction against Germany. He wished also to preserve peace in Europe because Germany could not gain anything from further wars. 'We have no further demands to make,' he was to say in 1890. 'Germany does not need the three million Dutchmen who have no desire to be absorbed by us, nor the Baltic countries, nor Poland, nor any other territory. We have enough annexed populations.' Germany, he declared, was 'a satiated power with no desire to advance beyond the frontiers he had gained for her, but he believed that France, deprived by Germany of Alsace-Lorraine, would 'regard revenge as her principal mission.'

Bismarck did not fear France on her own; he believed that she was too weak to challenge Germany independently, but he did fear the possibility of France entering into an alliance with other powers and so compelling Germany to fight on two fronts. He feared this because of what had happened to Prussia in 1760, when Frederick the Great had made her a strong European state, but was overwhelmed by a coalition between France, Russia and Austria. He wished, therefore, to keep France in diplomatic isolation and to prevent any international development that would give her an opportunity to make such an alliance.

The area in which he considered this most likely to happen was south-eastern Europe, the old troubled scene of the Eastern Question. The danger there was the possibility of war between Russia and Austria-Hungary. Panslavism in Russia was turning her attentions again to the Balkans, and Bismarck's own support for her abrogation of the Black Sea clauses of the Treaty of Paris in 1870 had assisted her in strengthening her position there. Austria-Hungary, now that he had excluded her from Germany and Italy, was bound to be concerned if Russia were able to extend her influence there by supporting Slav nationalism. A war between these two empires would provide France with the opportunity of gaining an ally and would inevitably involve Germany sooner or later.

Bismarck's attempt to meet this situation came about through Andrassy's desire for German friendship to prevent a possible understanding between Germany and Russia which would be unfavourable for Austria-Hungary. When he made an approach to Germany, the Russian government intervened to prevent such a development, which might be hostile to it. This resulted in several meetings between the sovereigns of these three empires in 1872 and 1873 in Berlin, Vienna and St. Petersburg and finally in the formation in the League of the Three Emperors (*Dreikaiserbund*) in October 1873. This was little more than an uncertain understanding by which the three rulers agreed to settle peaceably any differences they might have in the Near East in order to uphold monarchical solidarity in the face of subversive republicanism and socialism. Bismarck encouraged and supported this agreement, partly to promote the isolation of the French Republic, but still more to enable Germany to remain diplomatically apart from either of the two hostile empires. He did not want to have to make a choice between them which might have dangerous consequences for Germany.

(b) The Dual Alliance (1879)
In forming the League, neither Russia nor Austria-Hungary abandoned their conflicting aims in foreign policy. The League was like the earlier Holy Alliance. It was vague and made no attempt to settle the differences between the powers. This would have been impossible and produced disruption instead of concord. The League, therefore, was a superficial arrangement, which could exist only as long as there was peace and understanding in Europe; and it was strained by two successive crises in the 1870s.

The first, the so-called 'war-in-sight' crisis, came in 1875 and was a consequence of France's rapid payment of the indemnity imposed upon her after the Franco-Prussian War and the reorganization of her army (*see page 289*). Bismarck feared France might try to take advantage of the *Kulturkampf* to arouse Roman Catholic opinion in Europe against

Germany. He reacted sharply to a report that the French army was preparing to buy 10 000 saddle-horses from German dealers. He prohibited the export of the horses, which gave rise to a rumour the German mobilization was impending, and inspired a newspaper article headed 'Is War in Sight?' Bismarck did dislike the French recovery and military plans and did not want her to think of interfering in German internal affairs. He probably hoped that he could make France realize that she must accept a position of permanent inferiority in Europe; but both Britain and Russia became alarmed and warned Bismarck not to consider a preventive war; and Bismarck denied that he had any such intention and abandoned his press campaign. This artificially-raised crisis was no more than a minor diplomatic defeat for Bismarck, but it did show the fragility of the League of the Three Emperors and the possibility of co-operation by Britain, Russia and France against Germany with the implications that Bismarck feared (see page 370).

This first crisis was designedly brought about by Bismarck as an attempted war of nerves against France, but the second, the Bulgarian crisis of 1875–78, was real enough and not of his seeking. It did threaten to bring about the general war which he wished to prevent. He did not mind if Russia gained her aims in the Balkans, but he was bound to try to prevent this happening because it would arouse Austrian hostility. If he did not, Germany would lose Austria's friendship, particularly as the crisis was placing her on good terms with Britain. He could not, therefore, allow the Treaty of San Stefano to take effect. At the Congress of Berlin he sought to avoid having to support either side and claimed that he had acted as an 'honest broker', but the Russian government did not agree and blamed him for not being able to keep all the fruits of her victory over the Turks.

Russia's attitude alarmed Bismarck. He feared that if she continued to be inspired by Panslavonic ideas, she would provoke an alliance against her by the western powers and that this alliance would be joined by Austria-Hungary. Moreover, such a new alliance might take action which would further humiliate Russia and gain prestige for itself, and it would then be in a position to oppose Germany. In order to check any further Russian aggression and to detach Austria from Britain, so making unlikely the formation of such an alliance, he made with Austria the Dual Alliance of 1879. This was a formal military alliance, valid for three years and stipulating that 'if one of the two Empires shall be attacked by Russia, the High Contracting parties are bound to assist each other with the whole of the military power of their Empire and consequently only to conclude peace conjointly and by agreement.' If either were to be attacked by any power other than Russia, the other must give no help to the assailant and must observe at least a friendly neutrality towards the ally so attacked, but if the assailant were to be supported by Russia 'whether in the way of active co-operation or by military measures threatening the assailed power,' then the other power had to give immediate assistance to the ally.

The Dual Alliance, the terms of which remained secret until 1888, was described by Bismarck in his reminiscences as the completion of a grand design planned in 1866, but there is no evidence to suggest that he considered it before 1879. It was undoubtedly a temporary expedient to meet the situation after the Treaty of Berlin, and in fact it represented a change of policy by Bismarck, who had hitherto wished to prevent Germany being involved in the turmoil of the Eastern Question. As early as 1854 he had declared that he would be distressed 'if Prussia should seek protection from a possible storm by tying our trim and seaworthy frigate to the worm-eaten and old-fashioned Austrian man-of-war'; and in 1876 he had said in the Reichstag that the Balkans were not worth 'the healthy bones of a single Pomeranian grenadier'. He was careful to make it a defensive alliance: Austria-Hungary would only get help from Germany if she were attacked by Russia. But Andrassy did not view it in this limited way. To him it was the triumph of his career. It rescued Austria from the diplomatic isolation which she had endured since the Crimean War; and successive Austrian statesmen considered that it gave her German support for an active policy in the Balkans. Henceforward the Dual Alliance was regularly renewed until 1918 and became a fixed corner-stone of German foreign policy, but it continued to be marked by the differing German and Austrian interpretations of its implications, and it was bound to be full of danger unless Germany could keep a close control over Austrian foreign policy.

The Alliance was also a departure in European diplomacy. It was the first formal, permanent military alliance concluded in peacetime since the days before the French Revolution. Bismarck again had previously opposed the idea of such alliances. It was the first such alliance he signed, and he attached no particular significance to it. He regarded it, like all his other diplomatic moves, as only a temporary tactical expedient made necessary then by the need to deter Russia from aggression and maintain Austria-Hungary's friendship with Germany. He regarded it as an arrangement which could be abrogated or replaced whenever occasion arose in the future. He did not intend it to involve Germany more and more deeply in the recurrent troubles in the Near East. Nor did he envisage it as the beginning of the period of the system of alliances in Europe, which was to divide the great powers into opposing groups and counter-groups.

(c) The Triple Alliance (1882)

The Dual Alliance soon proved to be a precedent for other more formal diplomatic agreements. For the rest of his career, Bismarck had to give a great deal of attention to trying to prevent Austria-Hungary using the Alliance for aggressive moves in the Balkans. The best way of doing this seemed to be to bring about Austrian and Russian reconciliation. Russia was ready for this. She had turned eastwards instead of reacting to the Berlin settlement as Bismarck had feared. She now only wanted the Straits to be closed to British warships and the Balkan states to be free from foreign interference; and when Alexander III became Tsar in 1881 he favoured an understanding with Austria-Hungary. Bismarck found that Austria did not like the idea, but she was in no position to oppose him, and when Gladstone came into power in 1880 and abandoned Disraeli's policy towards the Eastern Question, her attempt at resistance collapsed.

In 1881, therefore, Bismarck was able to renew the League of the Three Emperors in a different form. Previously it had looked back uncertainly to the period of the Congress System and Metternich's wish to uphold the authority of the existing rulers of Europe. Now it became a formal (and secret) alliance of a military nature, which was to be valid for three years. By it the three empires agreed to prior consultation among themselves about any intervention in Turkish affairs and guaranteed that if any one of them was at war with a fourth power (except Turkey), the two others would remain neutral. This benefited Germany and Russia since it meant in practice that Russia would not support France against Germany, and Austria-Hungary would not support Britain against Russia. Russia also secured the recognition of 'the European and mutually obligatory character of the Straits,' which the Sultan must enforce, and an Austrian promise not to oppose the reunion of the two Bulgarias. In return Russia accepted Austria-Hungary's right to annex Bosnia and Herzegovina.

The renewal of the League in this form pleased Bismarck because it seemed again to free him from having to choose between Austria-Hungary and Russia. 'I knew that the Russians would come to us once we had pinned the Austrians down,' he said. Russia gained also from the renewal. In return for regaining her friendship with Germany, she got security for the Black Sea against a British attack through the Straits. Austria, however, renounced further co-operation with Britain merely in return for an overlapping confirmation of the alliance with Germany which she already had.

Austria-Hungary, indeed, felt that she had got nothing out of the new League. She disliked having to come to terms with Russia, her inevitable rival in the Balkans, whom she did not trust. Bismarck sought to placate her in a strange way. He turned to Italy. The Berlin settlement had brought Italy nothing. The Italian representative at the Congress said that he came back clean-handed, but other Italians said that he was also empty-handed. The French annexation of Tunisia in 1881 further angered Italian opinion, and the government was ready to negotiate with Bismarck. The outcome was the signing in 1882 of the Triple Alliance between Germany, Austria-Hungary and Italy. This was not an extension of the Dual Alliance, but a separate secret treaty which was valid for five years. Germany and Austria-Hungary were to assist Italy if she were attacked by France, and Italy would reciprocate if France attacked Germany; but the clause that was important in placating Austria was Italy's promise to stay neutral in a war between Russia and Austria-Hungary, which was, Bismarck claimed, 'worth four army corps' to Austria-Hungary since she would not have to maintain troops on her Italian frontier. Since France did not intend to attack either Italy or Germany, Bismarck was prepared to make these terms which pleased Austria because they drew her nearer to Germany and pleased Italy because they recognized her as a great power, but he was still determined not to support Austrian expansion in the Balkans (or Italian designs in the Mediterranean).

The League of the Three Emperors was renewed in 1884, but the next year it again broke down through the tension in the Balkans caused by the union of Eastern Roumelia with Bulgaria. Bismarck replaced it by negotiating the secret Reinsurance Treaty of 1887 with Russia by which Germany promised to support Russia's claims to the Straits and agreed that she should exercise the main influence in the Balkans. The two empires also promised to remain neutral if either were attacked by a third power, unless Russia attacked Austria-Hungary or Germany attacked France. The Reinsurance Treaty did not indicate any change in Bismarck's policy. It showed that he still hoped to retain Russian friendship by refusing to uphold Austrian aims in the Balkans. At the same time, the Treaty revealed that he had not achieved the objects of his policy. He had to recognize that Germany might have to fight a war in support of Austria-Hungary and that he had failed to prevent the idea of Russian approaches to France. He could not really persist in his wish to remain aloof from both powers. The Triple Alliance was renewed for another five years in 1887.

(d) The End of the Bismarckian Period (1890)

For twenty years Bismarck had followed a policy aimed at keeping France isolated and preserving German friendship with both Austria-Hungary and Russia. As those years passed, he seemed to have managed to overcome one by one the successive difficulties and crises, which threatened his purpose, and to have succeeded in achieving the essential objects of his policy. There has been a tendency among historians, therefore, to praise him for the successful results of his statesmanship and to compare it favourably with the course taken by German foreign policy during the period from 1890 when William II secured Bismarck's dismissal from his position as Imperial Chancellor.

The comparison, however, is too simple and slight to be true. Bismarck had not been able to overcome his difficulties by following a consistent, overall policy to meet the general situation. Rather as these difficulties had multiplied, so he had multiplied the solutions—the League of the Three Emperors, the Dual Alliance, the renewed League, the Triple Alliance and the Reinsurance Treaty. All these were short-term solutions, which did not eliminate the difficulties. They merely saved Germany from their possible immediate consequences and at the same time brought about fresh difficulties because the underlying motives of the other powers remained hostile to him. French resentment persisted; Russia was discontended with German diplomacy; Austria considered that Germany should support her openly in the Balkans; and Britain was potentially likely to be alarmed by German colonialism. The Bismarckian system was balanced upon an evermore difficult tightrope which was likely to have collapsed even if its author had remained in office after 1890.

Moreover, German opinion, which was shared by William II, was becoming increasingly opposed to the keystone of Bismarck's foreign policy—friendship with Russia. Many Germans regarded Russia as the inevitable enemy of their country. They saw her as the greatest threat to their security, the Continental power most likely to be willing and able to defeat the Empire. Particular sections had their own reasons for hostility to her, from the Junkers, who feared for their estates in East Prussia, to the Social Democrats and trade unionists, who regarded her as the epitome of tyranny and oppression of the working-classes.

William II believed that a lasting German understanding with Russia was impossible and a dangerous delusion. He thought that Germany must associate herself completely with Austria-Hungary and that the establishment of good relations with Britain would make this more likely. One of his first actions was to refuse to renew the Reinsurance Treaty. This marked the beginning of a period of fundamental change in the European situation during which Germany found herself opposed by the very combination of powers which Bismarck had tried to prevent.

Bibliography
W.E. Moose, *The European Powers and the German Question, 1848–1878* (CUP, 1958), I. Geiss, *German Foreign Policy, 1871–1914* (Routledge & Kegan Paul, 1976) and W.L. Langer, *European Alliances and Alignments, 1871–1890* (Knopf, 1950).

Exercises
A   *This section consists of questions that might be used for discussion (or written answers) as a way of expanding on the chapter and testing your understanding of it*:
1   Why is the Franco-Prussian War now regarded as such a turning point in the history of nineteenth-century Europe?
2   To whom was the Dreikaiserbund of 1873 most advantageous? Why did the other powers agree to it?
3   Why was 'war-in-sight' in 1875?
4   How did the Bulgarian crisis of 1875–8 differ from the crisis of 1875?
5   Why was Bismarck alarmed by Russia's Panslavonic ambitions?
6   Outline the terms of each of: the Dual Alliance, the Dreikaiserbund (1881), the Triple Alliance, the Reinsurance treaty. Comment on the differences between their terms.
7   In what way was the Dual Alliance a change of policy for Bismarck?
8   What was the difference between Germany's view of the Dual Alliance and Austria-Hungary's?
9   Why did Austria-Hungary get so little out of the renewal of the Dreikaiserbund in 1881?

10 Why have historians praised Bismarck's diplomatic skills? Do you consider this praise justified?

B *Essay questions*

1 To what extent were the lines of Bismarck's foreign policy between 1871 and 1890 determined by crises in the Balkans? (Cambridge, 1981)

2 Why did Bismarck attach so much importance to the Dreikaiserbund and how successful was he in countering the forces which threatened it after 1875? (Cambridge, 1983)

3 What difficulties did Bismarck encounter in his efforts to maintain the Dreikaiserbund? (Oxford, 1981)

4 Was Bismarck's foreign policy after 1870 a success? (Oxford and Cambridge, 1982)

5 'In 1871 he sought security for the German Empire; by 1890 he had achieved domination in Europe.' How valid is this comment on Bismarck's foreign policy between 1871 and 1890? (JMB, 1983)

C *The Bismarckian alliances: an evaluation*

By now, you will have realized that several major questions are generally asked of Bismarck's foreign policy. In this section, you are going to consider these, by devising arguments to either support or refute each of the statements below.

	Arguments to support the view expressed	*Arguments to refute the view expressed*
1) 'Bismarck's foreign policy after 1871 lacked real aims and purpose—it consisted of a series of short term expedients.'		
2) 'The only purpose of the Dreikaiserbund was to provide Germany with a bulwark against France.'		
3) 'Bismarck's foreign policy was too dependent on the diplomatic skills of its own architect.'		
4) 'By 1890, the cracks in Bismarck's foreign policy were increasingly apparent.'		

You will obviously find it helpful to refer to the books listed in the bibliography on pages 2 and 378 to do this exercise, and will find Lee, *Aspects of European History 1789–1980*, chapter 15, especially valuable.

Appendix 1: the Century's Ideas

(a) Liberalism

> We hold these truths to be self-evident: that all men are created equal: that they are endowed by their Creator, with certain unalienable rights; that among these are life, liberty and the pursuit of happiness. That, to secure these rights, governments are instituted among men, deriving their just powers from the consent of the governed; that, whenever any form of government becomes destructive of these ends, it is the right of the people to alter or abolish it, and to institute new government, laying its foundation on such principles, and organizing its powers in such form, as to them shall seem most likely to effect their safety and happiness.

These words from the Declaration of Independence, promulgated by the Congress of the United States of America in 1776, represent the principles of eighteenth-century political rationalism, and throughout the nineteenth century were regarded by progressive and reforming groups in every country as a classic expression of their beliefs.

These ideas were echoed in the Declaration of the Rights of Man and other statements made during the French Revolution, and they came to be the inspiration of the important European liberal movement. As a political term, the word 'liberal' was taken from Spain, where the French invasion of the country in 1808, the enforced abdication of the King and the consequent collapse of the traditional framework of society enabled reformers in the name of 'liberty' to attack the feudal powers still possessed by the Church and the nobility. The resulting Spanish constitution was widely regarded as the best in existence (*see page 26*).

Indeed, liberals in the nineteenth century were constitutionalists. Despite the varying circumstances of their countries, their general aim everywhere was to secure a national form of government which would enable their political ideals to be protected and put into effect. As Metternich said, 'There is . . . scarcely any epoch which does not offer a rallying cry to some particular faction. The cry since 1815 has been "Constitution".' The liberals shared the belief of the American and French revolutionaries that, since men are by nature good, a perfect society could be achieved by the establishment of a regime which preserved their liberties and empowered them to choose their rulers.

Such constitutionalism was, in fact, already powerful by 1815. Louis XVIII on his restoration to the French monarchy had been compelled to grant a constitution to his kingdom; Tsar Alexander I of Russia provided his Polish state with a constitution; and the statesmen at the Congress of Vienna drew up a constitution for the German Confederation they had established. All this was a recognition that the changes brought about by the French Revolution could not entirely be undone and a hope that these arrangements would prevent a return to the extremism and anarchy of the Revolution. In the years after 1815, however, there were countries that did not have constitutions; every Italian state was without one, and so were most of the German states. And the rulers of these countries where constitutions existed were often able to restrict or interpret them in ways which increased their own powers and diminished the liberties of their subjects. Hence liberalism during this period became identified with the determination to establish constitutions or amend unsatisfactory ones that were already in being.

Constitutionalism was the cause of the middle class, who had lost control of the French Revolution, but were now determined to fashion government according to their beliefs. They were usually professional men, as Metternich realized (*see page 44*) and students, who were being educated for such careers. In countries where trade and industry became important, they were also to be found among merchants, manufacturers, businessmen and financiers. Some landowners were liberals, but they were usually the newer, 'improving' landowners, rather than members of the great and noble families of Europe (*see page 122*).

These men wanted a state with a constitution which would give them a final say in its policies and also provide them with the opportunity to follow unhindered their profession or way of life. They wanted, therefore, to abolish the traditional sway of king, priest and aristocrat in Europe with their absolute power, personal privileges and restrictive limitations upon the law courts, universities and newspapers. They wanted a constitution wide enough to allow them political authority and freedom from such restraints as censorship or social inequalities.

At the same time, they were determined to maintain their own preeminence in the State. They believed that it should be governed by those who owned land and property or led it in the army, the law, education and national and local government. They were opposed, therefore, to any form of constitution which would give power to the lower classes. They considered that this would not only threaten their rightful position in the State, but also condemn it to violence, extremism and anarchy. This to them was the lesson of the course taken by the French Revolution in the time of the Reign of Terror and the mob violence which had led to reaction and military dictatorship; and they did not wish it to be repeated. When they had to ally themselves with these classes they made sure that the succeeding political settlement confined power to their own hands. Thus, the constitution adopted by

Belgium, after the revolt of 1830, was admired by liberals throughout Europe, but it only gave political power to a small minority in the new kingdom (*see pages 98, 105*).

The sort of constitution most liberals favoured was a limited monarchy on the British model. It should provide for a parliament with considerable powers, free to conduct its discussions without interference and able to compel the government of the country to carry out its wishes, but the right to elect this parliament must be restricted by a tax-paying or property-owning qualification. The constitution must provide also for equality before the law, religious toleration, freedom of the press and individual liberty.

Otherwise, however, the actions of the State must be carefully limited. Liberals insisted that liberty and equality would be threatened if the lives and activities of the people were subjected to unnecessary governmental interference. Beyond the protection of its frontiers and the preservation of law and order among its subjects, the State should do as little as possible. It should not infringe upon individual choice nor engage in unnecessary undertakings nor favour particular sections of the populations. Governments must stand aside to allow freedom to flourish and talent to achieve its success.

Liberals adopted the same attitude in economics as in politics. They held to the ideas expressed by the Scottish professor and economist, Adam Smith, in his *Wealth of Nations*, which was published in the same year as the American Declaration of Independence. He argued that artificial restrictions by way of taxation, regulation, restraint or monpoly upon the free and natural course of manufacture and commerce were harmful to the interest of all concerned. And in the nineteenth century liberals did not wish governments to involve themselves in economic matters. They wished it to leave the owners of businesses, factories and farms to do as they wished—hence the term '*laissez-faire*' often used to express this belief—because these people would know best how to manage their affairs and bring prosperity to everyone. So liberals were opposed both to the survival of medieval guild and apprenticeship restrictions and to the development of trade unions among workpeople.

Internationally, liberals also wanted governments to interfere as little as possible in matters of international trade. They were particularly critical of tariffs (or customs duties) because they held that under conditions of free trade each country would produce what it could do best and exchange these products with others to their mutual benefit. British liberals particularly favoured free trade because it suited Britain's economic circumstances in the nineteenth century. It would enable her to make the most of her industrial supremacy by selling her manufactured exports advantageously and importing cheap raw materials in return. She herself adopted free trade during the 1840s and 1850s. Other European countries were doubtful about following her example, but the commercial treaty signed between Britain and France in 1860 began a movement towards free trade among the countries of western Europe during the next decade (*see page 225, 314*).

Though liberalism was the most influential and advanced system of belief in the first half of the nineteenth century and offered the most powerful political challenge to the established order in Europe, it entered upon a period of decline from the 1850s. The risings of 1830 and 1848 showed its great weakness, which was that its adherents could only hope to gain power with the support of the working classes with whom they refused to share the fruits of victory. Their weakness was revealed with particular starkness in Germany, where Bismarck was able to outwit and oust them before and after the establishment of the German Empire. And free trade could not withstand the economic depression of the late 1870s and 1880s, when Germany, France and other countries abandoned it in favour of economic nationalism.

(b) Nationalism

The other powerful force influencing Europe during the nineteenth century was nationalism. It was to flourish while liberalism declined, though at first there seemed to be an inseparable connection between them. European nationalism in its modern sense was a product of the French Revolution, which had destroyed the conception of a French kingdom possessed and symbolized by the monarch and had replaced it by the complete identification of the French nation with the French state. The Declaration of the Rights of Man in 1789 stated, 'The principle of all sovereignty resides in the nation.' The revolutionaries claimed to speak on behalf of the French nation, the people of France who were bound together by ties of common traditions, language, race and aspirations. The French people had the duty to obey the government and defend the country, but they also had the right to a state of their own to protect them and uphold their common inheritance. And to do this the new regime gave the country a united system of law and administration and waged war against its enemies.

In 1792 the French republican government issued the Edict of Fraternity, proclaiming its war to be a revolutionary struggle to liberate the peoples of every state from their tyrannical rulers, and at first the invading armies were welcomed by the people they conquered. When, however, Napoleon's armies dominated much of Europe (*see page 7*), imposing upon some and threatening others with military rule, heavy taxation and increasing exploitation, this turned to fear, resentment and hatred. This stimulated the growth of nationalism in Europe. In those countries, such as Britain and Spain, which had long been independent, nationalism took the form of a determination to fight France as a single united 'nation' and to work together to preserve or restore what had existed before the wars. In other areas, which had previously consisted of a number of smaller states, such as Italy and Germany, or had been ruled over by another power, such as the Austrian Empire and Poland, nationalist ideas developed differently. Nationalists in these countries realized that Spain, France and Britain, which had been the three leading European powers since the sixteenth century, were each a 'nation state'—an independent country in which the people shared the same linguistic, cultural and national heritage. The nationalists, therefore, sought to establish such united, independent, self-ruling states for their own national group.

Since such nationalism was anti-French, the victorious allied armies in the last stages of the Napoleonic War represented themselves, therefore, as the true liberators of these peoples of Europe from an alien tyranny. At the Congress of Vienna in 1815, however, the statesmen suspected nationalism as a dangerous, unstable force (*see page 17*) and did not satisfy the aspirations of nationalists in these parts of Europe, particularly in Germany and Italy.

This had an important influence upon the nature of European nationalism after 1815. It was strongest among those peoples who were still divided into a number of small states and under foreign domination or influence. It became for them a desire to assert their unity and independence in opposition to the rulers, whether foreign or not, who were denying them this. It took several forms among them. It was partly cultural. Efforts were made to revive national language and customs, music and literature. In Germany, for instance, *Grimm's Fairy Tales* (1824) was part of a movement to recover the old folk stories and myths of the German past (*see page 118*), and in Italy nationalists wanted to establish an Italian language spoken by all the people (*see page 117*). It was also political, seeking to create a nation state that would preserve the national identity of the country. Thus, Leopold von Ranke wrote in 1830 that Germans should 'create the pure German state corresponding to the genius of the nation.' Finally, in countries where there was despotism and foreign control, nationalism had to be revolutionary. Mazzini hoped for a national, popular revolution by the Italian people which would bring them to independence and nationhood (*see page 114*).

Above all, nationalism became closely identified with liberal constitutionalism. Its aspirations were thwarted by despotic princes, and it wished to replace them by a parliamentary form of government. Moreover, it gained its leaders and supporters from the same middle class as liberalism because its objects too seemed likely to satisfy their aims and wishes. In those days to be a nationalist was to be a liberal also. Liberals everywhere supported the nationalists in these countries and saw them as fellow-upholders of a common cause. One of the main reasons that led Gladstone to join the Liberal Party at the end of the 1850s was that he came to believe in 'the overwhelming weight and interest of the Italian question and of our foreign policy in connection with it'.

Indeed, the most powerful exposition of the liberal nature of nationalism came from Italy in the person of Mazzini, the prophet of Italian unity. To him the winning of independence and unification by the oppressed nations would not only solve their own national problems, but the international problems of Europe as well. 'Every people has its special mission,' he wrote, 'which will co-operate towards the general mission of humanity. That mission is its nationality. Nationality is sacred.' He believed that the creation of a collection of independent and sovereign, democratic and republican states would work together for the preservation of peace and agreement everywhere. And in the first half of the nineteenth century, this was the assured hope of European liberal-nationalists. Their cause seemed inseparable and certain to gain its inevitable fulfilment (*see page 378*).

These expectations proved, however, to be empty and false. Nationalism and liberalism came into conflict with each other, and liberalism was to be the loser. This was foreshadowed in the events of the revolutions of 1848, when the revolutionaries revealed themselves unwilling to consider the rights of other peoples when they came into conflict with their own national aspirations. This was particularly true in the multi-racial Austrian Empire, where the insurgents in Vienna gave neither sympathy nor support to the Italians or Hungarians, and this lack of co-operation assisted the Habsburg recovery of power. A similar attitude was adopted by the German liberals in that year, and their failure was held to indicate that a national state would only be established by organized military force; and in the following years German nationalism parted company with liberalism and became anti-democratic and warlike. Nor did international events indicate that the fulfilment of nationalist aims would bring any improvement in diplomatic relations and lead to co-operation between the countries of Europe.

(c) Socialism and Marxism

Another reason for the declining influence of liberalism was the rise of socialism, which was hastened by the disenchantment felt by many political reformers and working-class leaders at the defection of liberals from the radical cause. Their middle-class aloofness from the common people and unwillingness to consider political and social changes which would benefit these classes inevitably narrowed their popular appeal. In the revolutions of 1848 in Europe and the Commune of 1871 in France, it was possible for liberals and socialists to believe that they could fight in a common cause, but the rift between them became increasingly wide as the century progressed.

In the realm of political ideas, the socialists wished to go beyond the aims of liberalism. They could not support its insistence upon the limitation of the powers and action of the State. For them, political liberty in itself was not attractive. It appeared to benefit the wealthy and do little for the poor. Nor did mere legal equality satisfy them. They wished to remedy the social evils brought about by the unequal distribution of material possessions, and they came to believe that the State should be prepared to assist the establishment of some form of communal ownership of property and of the means of distribution and production, so as to make possible a wider distribution of the wealth of the country among the people who took part in creating it. Socialists did share with liberals an idealistic approach to politics. They too held that human nature was fundamentally good, and that once people were relieved from the artificial distortions caused by social inequality and poverty, they would naturally act towards each other in a fraternal and tolerant manner. A socialist state would be a perfect state.

The need and the possibility of nineteenth-century socialism orginally arose through the creation of a large, propertyless working class by the Industrial Revolution. Since this occurred first in Britain, it was only to be expected that socialist ideas should make an early appearance there. This first British socialism was markedly idealistic and utopian, its best-known exponents being Robert Owen and his followers, some of whom adopted the name of 'socialist' for themselves. From 1800 Owen became a successful and prosperous cotton millowner and dissipated much of his fortune in social experiments. He set up a model housing estate for the workpeople of his mills at New Lanark and provided them with schools and other social services. Later he set up model villages organized co-operatively (nicknamed 'Owen's parallelograms') in Scotland and the United States of America, all of which were unsuccessful. Yet although Owen was a socialist in the sense that he believed that the workers should benefit from a greater share of the profits of industry in which they were employed, he was a paternalist and would-be educator, unwilling to accept the intervention of the people in politics and without faith in popular self-government. And, although Britain was the leading industrial country, factors such as the two-party system, the failure of Chartism in the 1840s and the economic aspirations of the trade unions meant that socialism played little part in British politics during the nineteenth century.

This was not so in the rest of Europe. Early in the nineteenth century, France was the most industrialized country on the Continent, and here Continental socialism began. It owed much in its origins to the French Revolution and especially to the ideas of Rousseau, who came from a lower social class than the other French philosophers. They belonged to the wealthy middle class, but he had known poverty and homelessness. He was more radical in thought than they were. The ideal of equality under the law for everyone, which the other philosophers upheld as the supreme good of political endeavour, did not satisfy him. He wanted social and political equality as well. He taught that in the original condition of nature all men were free and equal, having all things in common, each individual drawing on the general store according to his need, and that the fall of man from happiness and innocence had resulted from the institution of private property. He insisted, 'The first man who, having enclosed a piece of ground, could think of saying, "This is mine," and found people simple enough to believe him,' was the real founder of government. He wanted the State, instead of regarding itself as having a supreme duty to protect the possession of private property, to promote a condition of equality among its citizens. 'By equality,' he said, 'we should understand, not that the degree of power and riches are to be absolutely identical for everybody; but that power shall never be great enough for violence and shall always be exercised by virtue of rank and law; and that in respect of riches, no citizen shall ever be wealthy enough to buy another and none poor enough to be forced to sell himself.'

The early French socialists showed much the same idealistic outlook as Robert Owen. Both Charles Fourier's co-operative communities and Louis Blanc's socialist workshops looked to the development of a new society based upon the joint efforts of the workers themselves, the exchange of goods by a perfect division of labour and the distribution of the proceeds in a fair manner. Unlike Owen, however, the French socialists after 1815 came increasingly to believe that their ideals had to be put into practice in the sphere of politics. Louis Blanc in particular wanted the government to set up his socialist workshops in the most important branches of industry because he considered that all attempts to set up co-operative organizations in rivalry with the state were bound to fail ultimately; he wanted the state to act and drive private capitalists peaceably out of the field. Though this aim won him support from French industrial workers, especially those suffering from poverty and unemployment, and enabled him to take a leading part in the events of 1848, there was never any likely prospect of being able to persuade the ruling class to deprive themselves both of economic wealth and political power in favour of a collection of self-governing, profit-sharing communities (see page 143).

In the later part of the nineteenth century socialist thought was deeply and lastingly affected by the work of two men—Charles Darwin and Karl Marx—whose ideas became increasingly influential. These ideas were put forward in two books—Darwin's scientific treatise, *The Origin of Species by Means of Natural Selection* (1859), and Marx's political dissertation, *Capital* (1867). Both expounded theories which changed the climate of opinion in which socialism had so far developed and acted.

Darwin's theory of organic evolution most obviously and immediately had religious implications (see page 391); but it also influenced political thinking and particularly that of the socialists. His belief that living things have developed by long-term adaptations to their material environment seemed to give them scientific confirmation of their insistence that social progress could only come about through a more rational organization of communal life and economic activity. And, although Darwinism proclaimed the 'survival of the fittest' in the animal world, socialists could support themselves in their ideas by holding that man's mental development had made him dependent for existence upon the acquisition of an ability to co-operate rather than of physical characteristics for competitive struggle.

Karl Marx was born in 1818 at Trier and was the son of a Jewish lawyer, who had accepted Christianity. While studying at the universities of Bonn and Berlin, he was influenced by the ideas of the contemporary German philosopher, George Hegel, whose law of the dialectic asserted that progress comes about through the interacting of conflicting half-truths which produces a final completely true solution. In 1843 Marx had a short and troubled career as editor of the democratic *Rhineland Gazette* (*see page 49*). The next year he fled to Paris, where he associated with the French socialists. Expelled from France in 1845, he moved to Brussels, where he co-operated with another German socialist, Frederick Engels, in writing the *Communist Manifesto* of 1848 for a small group of exiled German revolutionaries. The term 'Communism' had been adopted in the early 1830s by some French socialists to indicate that they advocated a society in which there should be no private ownership, but that all property should be vested in the community and organized for the common benefit of all. Marx returned to Cologne in 1848, expecting the revolutionary movement to succeed, but on its failure he went to London and lived there with his family in obscurity and poverty until his death in 1883.

Marx claimed to have replaced the older, utopian socialism by a new 'scientific socialism'. He said that he had 'found Hegel upside down and put him the right way up.' Hegel had explained human progress as resulting from the conflict of ideas. Marx insisted that the evolution of mankind has been and is determined by economic factors and bodily necessities. This was his 'dialectic materialism' which was closely related to Darwin's theory of biological evolution. Though Darwin declined to have *Capital* dedicated to him, Engels declared, 'Just as Darwin had discovered the laws of evolution in organic nature, so Marx discovered the law of evolution in human history.' Marx claimed that he was able both to explain the past and to foretell the future course of history. This meant, he asserted, that he knew how men should act in accordance with the unfolding of events. 'The philosophers have only interpreted the world in varous ways', he insisted. 'The point, however, is to change it.'

Hegel, when considering the way in which successive stages of civilization had followed each other, had thought in terms of the rise and fall of states, but Marx spoke of social classes instead. He saw the history of society as dominated by class warfare, in which victory went to those who gained possession of the most effective means of wealth of the time. The French Revolution brought about the defeat of the old land-owning aristocracy by the capitalist middle class, whose power rested upon the new industry. They now exploited the workers, whose labour produced a greater value than the wages they received; but when the workers inevitably realized their wrongs and their strength, they would seize power and replace capitalism by the new communist society. Though claiming to be inevitable because it was based upon 'scientifically' ascertained 'laws' of history, Marxism was, in fact, as idealistic as the earlier liberalism and socialism. It looked to the State somehow withering away and being replaced by a novel classless utopia.

It was a theory which could appeal, not only to the working classes, but also to intellectuals, who might hope to organize and dominate the inevitable revolution and consequent new society. They would lead the 'dictatorship of the proletariat' by which it would be conducted, for Marx despised parliamentary democracy as government by bribery. Marx had originally written with the Germans in mind, but his ideas gained their greatest support from Russian intellectuals, who had always been attracted by western ideas and now believed that they were provided with an effective way of rallying popular support against the Tsarist regime (*see page 335*).

In 1846 Marx founded the First International Workingmen's Association to co-ordinate the efforts of socialists in all countries. By 1870 it claimed a total membership of 800 000, mostly in Belgium and Switzerland, but also in Italy, Spain and Germany; and between 1866 and 1869 it held four fiery Continental conferences at Geneva, Lausanne, Brussels and Basle, which were dominated by Marx. He was rashly optimistic about the date of the expected revolution and was soon disappointed. The Franco-Prussian War split socialists in all countries into violently antagonistic groups. The First International was gravely weakened and was dissolved in 1876.

The Marxist groups in the various countries did not, however, vanish. They survived, maintaining contact with Marx and Engels until their death and forming themselves into politically active Social Democratic parties. The German party was founded in 1875, the French in 1879, and others followed. Everywhere on the Continent, unless they were suppressed, these national parties gained growing working-class support, and in 1889 they founded in Paris the Second International Workingmen's Association, which held regular congresses attended by their representatives.

(d) Romanticism and Religion

Romanticism was a general eighteenth-century artistic movement in Europe which reached its culmination in the later 1830s. It was a rebellion against the classical tradition which had hitherto dominated the arts. This had established an absolute ideal of beauty only to be realized through following certain rules of balance and harmony, which restrained and disciplined the personal inspiration of the artist, and these rules were not suited to romantic ideas which aimed at the expression of individuality and originality. Romanticism sought to uphold emotional intensity in place of formal beauty; it emphasized imagination and intuition, enthusiasm, and emotion, above reason and intellect. The contrast between classicism and romanticism is between Claude and Turner in painting; Byron and Scott or Molière and Hugo or Kant and Heine in literature; and Handel and Chopin in music.

By its emphasis upon individualism, romanticism influenced the liberal and nationalist movements. Victor Hugo said, 'Romanticism is liberalism in literature,' and Lord Byron gave himself to the nationalist and liberal causes in Europe. It also assisted nationalism because it was attracted by the old folk music and legends of the past and encouraged a renewed interest in them which strengthened people's awareness of their traditional heritage. Romanticism particularly went back to the time before the fifteenth and sixteenth centuries when the Renaissance and the classical revival had begun. Sir Walter Scott fostered an interest in the Middle Ages through his Waverley novels; and there was a revival of Gothic architecture for many kinds of buildings (*see page 63*).

Another aspect of Romanticism was its association with the awakening of religious life and thought in Europe at this time. By 1815 there were evident signs of this. The numbers of the clergy and the religious orders increased, and congregations in the churches revived. The tradition, mystery and colour of the past, preserved in Christianity, appealed to the romantics, as it did also to those who reacted against the destructive rationalism and atheism of the French philosophers and revolutionaries. And in the countries occupied by French troops during the wars, religion had often been identified with resistance to the foreign invader, a feeling that remained after the dissolution of the Napoleonic empire.

As with nationalism and liberalism, the statesmen at the Congress of Vienna had to take account of the religious revival. The Papacy was restored to Rome and its territory in Italy; and subsequently the rulers who had lost their thrones and the classes who had suffered as a result of the Revolution naturally wanted now to restore the long accepted connection between Church and State, between altar and throne. The Bourbon monarchy did its best to restore the Church to its old position in the kingdom, and a number of concordats gave back much of its power to the Church in Spain, Sardinia, Bavaria and Naples. Everywhere, though religious toleration was generally accepted, ecclesiastical authority and influence seemed to have resumed its sway in a rapid and remarkable way.

Yet this restoration was in reality limited. The official support and recognition given to the Church and the laws passed to enforce its teaching aroused opposition from the beginning. In France particularly, the July Revolution of 1830 was as much a revolt against the Church as against the monarchy (*see page 64*). And liberals on the Continent generally became anti-clerical, disliking the Papacy's authoritarian control of the Church and wishing to restrict the part it took in public life, especially in education, believing that it acted as a conservative and reactionary force. Cavour's maxim, 'A free Church in a free State,' expressed their view that the Church should be transformed into a purely voluntary organization, deprived of any official position in society and leaving religion as entirely a private matter for individuals; and the idea, indeed, soon won general acceptance by the middle of the nineteenth century.

Behind this development lay the fact that in 1815 rationalism and anti-clericalism were firmly established, chiefly in intellectual and professional circles. In the first eight years of the peace, more than 2 200 000 copies of anti-Christian books were printed in Paris and sold throughout France. And as the century passed, the European climate became more difficult for traditional Christianity. The French Revolution was seen, in fact, to have destroyed beyond repair the traditional relationship between Church and State. Industrialization was remoulding the whole of society, and the Church was weaker in the new large towns than in the peasant-villages of the countryside. Socialism was hostile to Christianity, Marx saying in his well-known sentence, 'Religion is the opium of the people.' At the same time, Biblical and theological scholarship, largely under German Protestant leadership, was developing a critical outlook and producing acute dissensions among Christians.

Of the studies in the realms of biology, geology and anthropology, which bore upon the nature and antiquity of the world and of man and seemed to undermine the Bible and the dogmatic systems that had been established upon it, the most serious was Darwinism. It challenged the myth of divine creation in Genesis with the theory which held that, throughout millions of years, those minute variations displayed by every form of life enabled the creatures that inherited them to survive if they made it easier for them to face the conditions of their life, and that these better adapted creatures split off and became new species, culminating in man himself. Though the acceptance of this theory required faith because, for instance, the evidence of the fossils only shows settled and established species and not any intermediate, evolving creatures, it gained steady acceptance, particularly from advanced thinkers. Like Marxism, it seemed to replace religion by a simple, definite secular process of human development which agreed with contemporary ideas of progress.

On the whole, the less rigidly organized and doctrinally uniform Protestant Churches were best able to meet the impact of the new political, social and scientific movements. They were prepared to make efforts to reinterpret their beliefs and come to terms with the reforming parties. In England both Anglicans and Nonconformists could be Liberals, and in France Guizot was only the most prominent among the Huguenots who held this political outlook.

The Roman Catholic Church, however, responded to the situation as it had done to the Reformation of the sixteenth century. It embarked upon a fresh Counter-Reformation. The Society of Jesus was re-established in 1814 and extended its activities with papal support throughout Europe. The Jesuits organized societies of Roman Catholic laymen, particularly in France, Spain and Italy, and their members used their influence to strengthen the power of the Church in politics, administration and education. The Papacy re-established the Index, the list of books which Roman Catholics were forbidden to read, and even the Inquisition re-appeared in Rome and Spain. New devotions were encouraged among the people, particularly in connection with the Virgin Mary. In France, the most important Roman Catholic country in Europe and yet where the struggle against disbelief and anti-clericalism was most marked (*see pages 64, 75*), five visionary appearances of the Virgin Mary were reported to have taken place during the nineteenth century to children or country women in provincial places, two of which—Lourdes and Lisieux—became places of pilgrimage and miraculous healing.

There were those in the Roman Catholic Church who disliked these tendencies, but they received no support from the Papacy. Lamennais, who played an important part in the establishment of Belgian independence (*see page 97*), founded in 1830 a paper, *L'Avenir*, with the motto '*Dieu et Liberté*', advocating democratic principles, including freedom of worship and of the press, but his ideas were condemned by Pope Gregory XVI. Pope Pius IX completed the structure of nineteenth-century Roman Catholicism. In 1854 he proclaimed the dogma of the Immaculate Conception of the Virgin Mary, which held that she was conceived without any taint of original sin; this strengthened both Marian doctrine in the Church and the authority of the Papacy. Ten years later he issued the Syllabus of Errors, which censured 'the chief errors of our times' (*see page 271*) and contained the famous and all-inclusive condemnation of the idea that 'the Roman pontiff can and should reconcile himself with progress, with liberalism and with recent civilization.' Finally, he was able to secure the approval of the Vatican Council in 1870 for the doctrine of Papal Infallibility, which held that the Pope was protected by God from error when defining belief in matters of faith and morals on his own authority.

The policy of Pius IX had, therefore, three consequences. It carried further the move, begun at the Council of Trent (1545–63), designed to give the Papacy the final authority in the Roman Catholic Church; the acceptance of papal infallibility gave doctrinal sanction to this supremacy. It also sought to maintain a traditional, popular faith and a definite, unalterable system of belief that was uncompromisingly opposed to contemporary developments in science, politics and social reform. And, finally, it set the Church apart as a close corporation, determined to have nothing to do with other Christians and to maintain its historic rights. This was to bring it an impressive strength and unity, but also to involve it in conflict with the State in France, Germany, Italy and other countries.

Bibliography

Books on the subjects considered in the course of this section are I. Babbitt, *Rousseau and Romanticism* (New York, 1919), H.K. Girvetz, *From Wealth to Welfare: The Evolution of Liberalism* (Stamford UP, 1951), C. de Ruggiero (trans. R.G. Collingwood), *European Liberalism* (OUP, 1927), M. Lamb, *Nationalism* (Heinemann, 1974), M.

Sakvadori (ed.), *Modern Socialism* (Harper & Row, 1968), R.N. Carew Hunt, *The Theory and Practice of Communism* (5th. edn., Bles, 1956), I. Berlin, *Karl Marx* (2nd. edn., OUP, 1948), R.E.D. Clark, *Darwin: Before and After* (Paternoster Press, 1948), A.R. Vidler, *The Church in an Age of Revolution* (Penguin, 1961).

Exercises

A *This chapter should enable you to begin to take an overview of all that you have studied, and to draw on examples from throughout the period. The questions in this section are designed to help you do this, while at the same time checking your understanding of the concepts outlined.*

1 'The period 1815–1848 was the era of liberalism; 1848–1871 the era of nationalism.' Do you agree?
2 When and where did liberals succeed in getting the kind of constitutions that they favoured?
3 How influential was nationalism (a) at the Congress of Vienna? (b) in the 1848 Revolutions?
4 How did liberalism aid the rise of socialism?
5 In what instances and in what ways did European socialists succeed in the period 1815–1890?
6 How did Marx's 'scientific socialism' differ from 'utopian socialism'?
7 Explain the appeal of both Romanticism and religion to nineteenth-century Europeans.
8 'The nineteenth century saw an increase in anti-clericalism, especially in the field of education.' Do you agree?
9 Comment on the reaction of the Roman Catholic Church to the growing anti-clerical opinion.

B *Essay questions*
1 Explain the close association between liberalism and nationalism in the thirty years after the Vienna settlement. (Cambridge, 1981)
2 Have historians tended to exaggerate the strength of nationalist feeling in Europe in 1815? (Welsh, 1982)
3 How true is it that nationalist uprisings during the twenty years after 1815 succeeded only when they had outside support? (Welsh, 1983)
4 To which social classes did nationalism most appeal? (You may confine your answer to any one country if you wish.) (Oxford and Cambridge, 1981)
5 Which classes of society mainly supported liberal and national movements in the first half of the nineteenth century? (You may confine your discussion to any one country if you wish.) (Oxford and Cambridge, 1982)
6 How powerful a force was either ultramontanism or Marxism in the nineteenth century? (Oxford and Cambridge, 1983)
7 Assess the influence of Karl Marx in Europe before 1914. (Cambridge, 1983 et al.)
8 Examine the impact of Darwinism on European thought in the fifty years after 1859. (AEB, 1983)
9 Either (a) 'Religion was the major obstacle to the reform of school education in the nineteenth century.' Discuss with reference to any two or more countries.

or (b) To what extent had realism replaced romanticism in either (a) literature or (b) painting in Europe by 1890? (Oxford, 1981)

10 Examine the impact of any one of the following on nineteenth century social and political thought: romanticism, ultra-montanism, *laissez-faire*, the theory of evolution. (Oxford and Cambridge, 1981)

C *Identifications*

In this chapter, you have read about a series of movements and ideas. Below you will find seven passages from primary and secondary sources. Each is concerned with one of the 'century's ideas'; write a commentary on each, in which, with quoted extracts, you identify which idea it is describing and explain what it says about that idea. (For example, 'C describes the views of a classic nineteenth-century liberal. It refers to . . . in politics, and. . . .')

Source A.

'The modern bourgeois society that has sprouted from the ruins of feudal society, has not done away with class antagonisms. It has but established new classes, new conditions of oppression, new forms of struggle in place of the old ones. . . .

Our epoch, the epoch of the bourgeoisie, possesses, however, this distinctive feature: it has simplified the class antagonisms. Society as a whole is more and more splitting up into two great hostile camps, into two great classes directly facing each other. . . .

Modern industry has converted the little workshop of the patriarchal master into the great factory of the industrial capitalist. Masses of labourers crowded into the factory, are organised like soldiers. As privates of the industrial army, they are placed under the command of a positive hierarchy of officers and sergeants. Not only are they slaves of the bourgeois class, and of the bourgeois state; they are daily and hourly enslaved by the machine, by the overseer, and, above all, by the individual bourgeois manufacturer himself. The more openly this despotism proclaims gain to be its end and aim, the more petty, the more hateful and the more embittering it is. . . .

The essential condition for the existence and sway of the bourgeois class, is the formation and augmentation of capital; the condition for capital is wage labour. Wage labour rests exclusively on competition between the labourers. The advance of industry, whose involuntary promoter is the bourgeoisie, replaces the isolation of the labourers, due to competition, by their revolutionary competition, due to association. The development of modern industry, therefore cuts from under its feet the very foundation on which the bourgeoisie produces and appropriates products. What the bourgeoisie therefore produces, above all, are its own grave-diggers. Its fall and the victory of the proletariat are equally inevitable. . . .'

Source B.

'Patriots began to demand the preservation of their historic cultures. They collected folk tales and ballads; they studied the languages, composing grammars and dictionaries, often for the first time; and they took to writing books in their mother tongues. They urged their own educated classes to give up "foreign" ways. They wrote histories showing the exploits of their several peoples in the Middle Ages. A new nationalism stirred the Magyars; in 1837 a national Hungarian theatre was established at Budapest. In what was to become Rumania a former Transylvanian peasant youth named George Lazar began as early as 1816 to teach at Bucharest. He lectured in Rumanian (to the surprise of the upper classes, who preferred Greek), telling how Rumania had a distinguished history back to the Roman emperor Trajan.'

Source C.
'When he discharges the office of Pastor and Teacher of all Christians by defining . . . a doctrine regarding faith or morals . . . by that divine assistance promised to him in Blessed Peter possessed of that infallibility which the Divine Redeemer wished to bestow . . . such definitions by the Roman Pontiff are in their nature, apart from the consent of the Church, irreformable.'

Source D.
'All of them regarded the existing economic system as aimless, chaotic and outrageously unjust. All thought it improper for owners of wealth to have so much economic power—to give or deny work to the worker, to set wages and hours in their own interests, to guide all the labours of society in the interests of private profit. All therefore questioned the value of private enterprise, favoring some degree of communal ownership of productive assets—banks, factories, machines, land, and transportation. All disliked competition as a governing principle and set forth principles of harmony, co-ordination, organization or association instead. All flatly and absolutely rejected the *laissez faire* of the liberals and the political economists. Where the latter thought mainly of increasing production, without much concern over distribution, they thought mainly of a fairer or more equal distribution of income among all useful members of society.'

Source E.
'Public Rights of the French
1. Frenchmen are to be equal before the law, whatever may be their titles or rank.
2. They are to contribute in the proportion of their fortunes to the charges of the stage.
3. They are to be equally admissible to civil and military employments.
4. Their individual liberty is hereby equally guaranteed. No person can be either prosecuted or arrested except in cases prescribed by law.
5. Each one may profess his religion with equal liberty, and shall obtain for his religious worship the same protection.
6. However, the Catholic, Apostolic and Roman religion is the religion of the State.
7. The ministers of the Catholic, Apostolic and Roman religion, and those other Christian denominations, receive their stipends from the Royal Treasury.
8. The French are entitled to publish and print their opinions while conforming to the laws which will repress abuses of this liberty.'

Source F.

'Just as the British Parliament in 1833 passed Althorp's Act regulating conditions for employing young people in textile factories, so in 1841 the French Parliament passed a Factory Act restricting the use of child labour in undertakings employing more than 20 persons. But whereas the merit of the British Act was that it instituted factory inspectors to enforce the law, the French Act did not, and its provisions were consequently largely ineffectual. It was 1848 before an inspectorate was set us, and then the February Revolution of that year prevented the scheme from operating. Just as the English Whigs reformed municipal government, so the French Liberals in 1831 set up general and district councils on which elected members could sit beside others nominated by the government. Although such elected departmental councils remained henceforth a permanent feature of local administration in France, at this time they had little real power.'

Source G.

'Young Italy is a brotherhood of Italians who believe in a law of *Progress* and *Duty*, and are convinced that Italy is destined to become one nation—convinced also that she possesses sufficient strength within herself to become one, and that the ill success of her former efforts is to be attributed not to the weakness, but to the misdirection of the revolutionary elements within her—that the secret of force lies in constancy and unity of effort. They join this association in the firm intent of consecrating both thought and action to the great aim of re-constituting Italy as one independent sovereign nation of free men and equals.'

These passages are taken from

A History of the Modern World, by R.R. Palmer & Joel Colton (Knopf, 1950) p.431 & p.436

General Instructions for the Members of Young Italy 1831 by G. Mazzini, from *Life and Writings of G. Mazzini* (Smith-Elder, London, 1891) quoted in Kertesz, op. cit. p.173

The Constitutional Charter of France, 4 June 1814 (from the 'Annual Register', 1814, pp.420–2), quoted in G.A. Kertesz *Documents in the Political History of the European Continent 1815–1939* (OUP, 1968) pp.44–5

Europe since Napoleon, by D. Thomson (Pelican, 1966) pp.189–90

The Manifesto of the Communist Party by K. Marx & F. Engels, quoted in *Left & Right in Twentieth Century* by David Smith (Longman, 1970) pp.77–78

Extract from Papal Bill of Infallibility quoted in *Success in European History* by Jack Watson (John Murray, 1981) p.148

Appendix 2: Essay Planning Sheets

Essay planning sheet: list essay (see page 88)

Title:

(Introduction):

	Arguments *(1st sentences)*	Evidence
1		
2		
3		
4		
5		
6		
7		
	Conclusion:	

Essay planning sheet: discussion essay (see page 137)

Title:

(Introduction):

Yes arguments		No arguments	
Arguments (1sr sentences)	Evidence	Arguments (1st sentences)	Evidence
1		1	
2		2	
3		3	
4		4	

Conclusion:

Essay planning sheet: significance essay (see page 180)

Title:

(Introduction):

A) Ways in which 'x' was significant

	Arguments (1st sentences)	Evidence
1		
2		
3		
4		

B) Ways in which 'x' was not significant

	Arguments (1st sentences)	Evidence
1		
2		

C) What else was significant

	Arguments (1st sentences)	Evidence
1		
2		
3		

Conclusion:

Index